THE
CAMBRIDGE HISTORY OF
ENGLISH LITERATURE

EDITED
BY
SIR A. W. WARD
AND
A. R. WALLER

VOLUME V

THE DRAMA TO 1642

PART ONE

CAMBRIDGE
AT THE UNIVERSITY PRESS
1964

PUBLISHED BY
THE SYNDICS OF THE CAMBRIDGE UNIVERSITY PRESS
Bentley House, 200 Euston Road, London, N.W.1
American Branch: 32 East 57th Street, New York 22, N.Y.
West African Office: P.O. Box 33, Ibadan, Nigeria

First edition	**1910**
New impression	**1918**
Reprinted	**1929**
Cheap edition (*text only*)	**1932**
Reprinted	**1934**
	1943
	1949
	1950
	1961
	1964

Printed in Great Britain at the University Printing House, Cambridge
(*Brooke Crutchley, University Printer*)

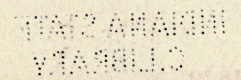

PREFATORY NOTE

The Cambridge History of English Literature was first published between the years 1907 and 1916. The General Index Volume was issued in 1927.

In the preface to Volume I the general editors explained their intentions. They proposed to give a connected account of the successive movements of English literature, to describe the work of writers both of primary and of secondary importance, and to discuss the interaction between English and foreign literatures. They included certain allied subjects such as oratory, scholarship, journalism and typography, and they did not neglect the literature of America and the British Dominions. The History was to unfold itself, "unfettered by any preconceived notions of artificial eras or controlling dates," and its judgments were not to be regarded as final.

This reprint of the text and general index of the *History* is issued in the hope that its low price may make it easily available to a wider circle of students and other readers who wish to have on their shelves the full story of English literature.

CAMBRIDGE
1932

THE CAMBRIDGE HISTORY OF
ENGLISH LITERATURE

VOLUME V

THE DRAMA TO 1642

PART ONE

CONTENTS

CHAPTER I

THE ORIGINS OF ENGLISH DRAMA

INTRODUCTORY

THE present volume and its successor will be devoted to the discussion of English drama—a growth which, in the meridian splendour of its maturity, is without an equal in the history of literature. Attic drama, in literary art, at all events, the choicest product of an age from which posterity has never ceased to derive its serenest conceptions of human culture, was restricted in its higher creativeness by the brief duration of that age itself. Spanish drama, nearest to English in the exuberance of its productivity, is, in its greatest period, associated with the decay of the nation's vigour. French classical drama, in a much larger measure than that in which the same assertion could be made of English, was bound by its relations to a royal court, and debarred from an intimate union with the national life. English drama, as, with marvellous rapidity, it rose to the full height of its literary glories, reflected and partook of the imaginative strength of an age in which England consciously, nor for a generation only, assumed her place in the van of nations.

In view of the twofold fact, that English drama was destined to rank not only among the most glorious but among the most characteristic of national achievements, and that an English nation and an English national literature were already in existence before the Norman conquest, it may seem strange that, with the exception of certain suggestive features in the church liturgy to which attention will be directed below, the beginnings of the growth which we are considering cannot be safely traced beyond that date. In other words, we are unable to assume the existence in these islands, before the Norman conquest, of anything recognisable by us as drama or dramatic literature. Our English ancestors, with whose advent the Roman empire in Britain had come to an abrupt end, can hardly, except in a few isolated instances, have been brought into contact with the broken and

scattered remnants of the Roman theatre—the strolling mimes
who, after their fashion, may have preserved some ignoble reminiscences of the Roman acting drama in the days of its decadence.
And when Christianity—that is to say, Roman Christianity—came
to England, and gradually, more especially through the efforts
of king Alfred, fostered the growth of English literature, the
last literary form which it was likely to introduce or sanction
was that of the drama, the feeder of the theatre. The strange
and shifting relations between the Christian church and the stage
had begun, in the fourth century, with loud anathemas launched
by the one against the other; in the fifth, the whole craft of
actors and entertainers was denounced by an ecclesiastical council;
and, as the empire of the west broke up under the inroads of
the barbarians, *histriones* and *nugatores* went forth as homeless
outlaws under the ban of both church and state. If any of these
found their way to England and, as they passed along the highways and byways, displayed their tricks for a crust of bread or a
cup of ale, they were, no doubt, despised and accounted infamous.
Far otherwise was it with the gleeman, who sat among the warriors,
telling in a solemn and religious strain of the great deeds of the
past, and the scop, whose songs had the king and his companions for
an audience, and who, on his travels, found himself everywhere an
honoured guest. Anything less dramatic could hardly be imagined
than the poems or recitations of the Old English singer, and even in
those dialogues which form an interesting part of English literature
before the Norman conquest a dramatic element is only occasionally perceptible—for there could be no greater mistake than to
suppose that a dialogue, be its progress never so vivacious, is,
of necessity, a drama in embryo. A certain species of English
dialogues, however, to which reference is made in the next
chapter, and of which examples are to be found both before and
after the Norman conquest, the *estrifs*, one of the forms of the Old
French *débats*, must be allowed to contain dramatic elements,
or the possibilities of dramatic development; and one of these,
The Harrowing of Hell, dealt with a theme afterwards treated
in religious drama (both in an isolated piece and in two of the
collective mysteries). In *The Pride of Life*, which, in its turn, has
been described as the earliest written text of an English morality,
a contention of this sort, as we learn from the prologue to the fragmentary play, was introduced in the shape of a disputation between
body and soul, held at the request of the Blessed Virgin, after the
devils had laid hands on the King of Life's soul, in the struggle

of the King with Death[1]. Other debates of the kind may, likewise, have incidentally influenced the early growth of English
drama; but no general connection between it and Old English
literature has been proved.

The Norman conquest brought into England a foreign baron-
age; the high places in church and state were now filled by foreign
occupants; at the altars of many of the churches of the land knelt
foreign priests; in the cloisters of most of its convents walked
foreign monks. But it also provided with an English 'establishment' many a French or Flemish adventurer of lowly origin or
doubtful past. Moreover, these very Normans, who had been the
hero-adventurers of the western world, who were the combatant
sons of the church, and some of whose most signal successes were
even now only in process of achievement, had begun to enter into
a phase of chivalry in which doughty deeds are done, and difficult
enterprises are carried on, with one eye to a crown of glory and
the other to material profit. Thus, the influence of the Norman
conquest upon English life, where it was something more than
the pressure exercised by overbearing masters, was by no means
altogether ennobling or elevating. The diversions, too, of what
was now the ruling class in England were so mixed in character
that the very names of their purveyors cannot be kept asunder
with precision. The *trouvères* of Normandy and northern France,
'inventors' of romances about deeds of prowess which they
sang to their own accompaniment on harp or lute or viol, were
frequently called *jongleurs* (*joculatores*)—a term so comprehensive that it may appropriately be translated by 'entertainers.'
The third designation, *ménestrels* or minstrels, which became the
usual term in England, is, of course, only another form of the
Latin *ministeriales,* servants of the house, implying the attachment of those who bore it to a particular household, whence,
however, they might set forth to exhibit their skill abroad. The
fourth term, gestours (singers of *chansons de geste*), whom Chaucer
couples with 'minestrales' as telling tales

> Of romaunces that ben reales
> Of popes and of cardinales,
> And eke of love-longing[2],

is, in its original significance, the exact equivalent of *trouvères*.
It will be shown in the next chapter how, with these 'singers'

[1] See the text in Brandl, A., *Quellen des weltlichen Dramas in England vor
Shakespeare.*
[2] *The Rime of Sire Thopas.*

and 'entertainers' came to be mixed up already in France and in
Normandy, and with them were by the Conquest transplanted to
England, those humbler strollers to whom reference has been
already made, and of whose survival from the days of the Roman
Caesars into those of the Carolings sufficient evidence remains.
There has at all times been a familiarity amounting to a kind of
freemasonry between all branches of the 'profession'; and *Activa
Vita's* contemptuous summary in *Piers Plowman* of the minstrel's
accepted accomplishments[1] includes the widest 'variety' possible
of resources open to those who 'live to please.'

Upon the whole, it may safely be asserted that the influence
of these minstrels (using the term in the widest sense permissible)
was not great upon the beginnings of English drama and was
very far from being one of its main sources. On the other hand,
some dramatic touches, reminiscences, traditions—call it what you
will, for of all crafts this is the most tenacious of what appertains
to its 'business'—must have lingered on in the performances
of that lower or more popular species of minstrels who cannot
but have retained some sort of contact with the higher and
more refined as well as more creative class. Thus, though invisible to the eye of the closest student, some slender thread of
continuity may connect the end of the ancient with the beginnings
of the modern, including the English, stage. It was the theatre
which, towards the close of the fifteenth century, in all but the
lowest spheres of their activity, cut the ground from under the feet
of the 'last minstrels'; yet this very theatre may owe them a debt
of the kind which it is never possible to recover. In England, the
performances of the minstrels cannot be shown to connect themselves with the beginnings of any particular dramatic species (as
the *jeux* of their French *confrères* connect themselves with the
beginnings of farce, and thus, indirectly, with those of comedy);
but the wandering minstrels with the tread of whose feet the
roads of England were familiar certainly sped the early efforts of
English drama if they did not contribute to them, and, what
is more, they helped to secure its vitality by making and keeping
it popular. In the nomad life of medieval England, of which
we owe an incomparable picture to the genius of Jusserand, the
minstrels were alike omnipresent and indispensable—as news-
bearers, as story-tellers, as makers of mirth; and the rewards
showered upon them, even if they were 'king's minstrels' by
no better right than that by which obscure 'provincial' playhouses

---

[1] *Piers Plowman*, Passus XIII.

call themselves 'Theatres Royal,' probably exhausted the kindly and charitable impulses of no small a proportion of the community. As Normans and Englishmen were more and more blended together, the diversions of the lords became more and more those of the people, although the latter might be less exacting as to the quality of the performances produced by the minstrels for their entertainment. Attempts at suppression as well as at restriction in the interests of the 'party of order' followed, and were met, in the Plantagenet period, by satire, by what might almost be called 'nationalist' ballads, and by 'merry tales' discreditable to the church—in all of which we shall not err in recognising the irrepressible voice of the minstrels. But neither their vitality nor their decay can occupy us in this place ; and all that the student will here be asked to concede is that the vigorous and long-lived growth of minstrelsy, which undoubtedly derived its origin in part from the remnants of the ancient theatre, in its turn effectively helped to prepare the soil for the advent of the modern drama, in England as elsewhere, and to foster the growth which gradually sprang up from the seed cast into it. The question still remains: whence did that seed come ?

Of that which was carried over from classical dramatic literature, very few grains, in this early period, impregnated the medieval ground, or even so much as fell by the wayside, now and then producing a stray flower. In insular England, more especially, little or no influence was exercised by the scant dramatic writings of the earlier Middle Ages which imitated Attic examples. Whatever may have been the contemporary knowledge of the tragedies and comedies said to have been modelled on Euripides and Menander by Apollinaris (who has been held identifiable with a Laodicean bishop of the later part of the fourth century) the *Suffering Christ* (Χριστὸς πάσχων), which, after being long attributed to St Gregory the Nazianzene in the fourth century, is now on sufficient grounds assigned to a Byzantine writer of the early part of the twelfth[1], and which may be described as a religious exercise in the garb of Euripidean diction, was composed for the closet, and probably remained unknown to western readers till the sixteenth century. For students of English literature, the chief interest of this much-mentioned play lies in the fact that, among many others, its subject commended itself, for dramatic treatment to the one English poet capable of addressing himself to it in a spirit corresponding, in some sense, to the sublimity of the theme. Milton at one time

---

[1] Theodore Prodromos, whose monastic name was Hilarion.

thought of a drama to be entitled *Christus Patiens*, on the scene of the Agony in the Garden. Other attempts seem, in the long course of the centuries, to have been made to clothe in a dramatic form borrowed from the ancients the Christian wisdom and morality which had become the norm of the spiritual life of the west; among these, the most notable were the Terentian comedies, written in the tenth century by Hrotsvitha, the Benedictine abbess of Gandersheim, in Eastphalian Saxony, for the edification of the inmates of her convent, where, very probably (though we have no evidence on the subject), they may have been performed. The moral and intellectual current of which these high-minded, if not very brilliant, efforts formed part and which is associated with the name and reign of Hrotsvitha's kinsman, Otto the Great, carried its influence beyond the Rhine into French territory. When, therefore, among the many strangers whom the Norman conquest brought into England, monks and nuns immigrated in large numbers and carried on in the new country their old avocation of trainers of youth, nothing could have been more natural than that there should have transplanted itself with them the practice of writing—and perhaps of performing—religious exercises in the regular dramatic form derived from classical examples, and recounting the miraculous acts of holy personages and the miraculous experiences of holy lives. At the same time, inasmuch as these compositions were virtually mere hybrids, and were primarily designed for the use of only a very limited class under very special direction and discipline, the dramatic element which they introduced might, at first sight, have seemed likely to prove so weak and transitory as to be almost negligible. Yet the literary monastic drama, whenever it first became an acting drama, was not a thing so entirely away from the world as might be supposed. In the period which comes into question, monasteries and nunneries were not so much retreats from, as centres of, social life and intellectual intercourse; and suggestions or influences imparted by them were not communicated by *habitantes in sicco*. From the church in general, and not the least from her monastic institutions, proceeded the main literary impulses felt in England for several centuries after the Norman conquest; Layamon was a priest, Ormin or Orm a monk, not to speak of the author or authors of *Piers Plowman*. When, half a century or so after the Conquest, pupils of convent schools in England represented religious plays in very much the same fashion as that in which the abbess Hrotsvitha's scholars may have performed her Terentian

comedies at Gandersheim, some knowledge of these performances
must have rapidly spread beyond the cloister, and, we may rest
assured, have been eagerly conveyed to the ears of all and sundry
by strolling minstrels, if by no other agents. Beginning with
the play in honour of St Catharine, acted (in what language is
not known) at Dunstable about the year 1110 by scholars of the
Norman Geoffroy, afterwards bishop of St Albans, and extending
through the series of 'miracles of saints and passions of holy
martyrs,' stated by William Fitzstephen to have been produced
between 1170 and 1182, these saints' plays, among which must be
reckoned one of the extant plays of Hilarius—very probably
a native of England—continued to appear and reappear in this
country, where, however, they cannot be said to have flourished
till the middle of the fifteenth century. Long before this, they
had begun to coalesce with a dramatic growth of very different
strength; and it is because of its separate origin, rather than
because it can be said to have run either a vigorous or a distinct
course of its own, that reference has been made in this introductory
section to what can only with hesitation be described as the
English monastic literary drama[1].

The roots of such a growth as the English drama lay, and must
have lain, deeper than in the imported remnants of more or less
alien civilisations which interwove their fibres with the national
life. Of that life itself, religious beliefs and conceptions were of
the very essence, though among these a considerable proportion
were survivals of earlier periods, into which Christianity had not
entered as a conquering, and, at times, a destructive, force. In the
earliest of the succeeding chapters it will be shown in what
directions the study of folk-lore has thrown light on the influence of
these survivals upon the growth of the drama in England. By
far the most important process in the present connection is the
gradual conversion of popular festivals, ancient or even primitive
in origin, with their traditional ritual of dance and song, into
plays; though it is their action, rather than its vocal accompaniment, which, in the case of these festivals, has exercised any
significant influence on English drama. Elements of the pagan
festivals in question are discoverable even in feasts whose origin
can be directly traced to the services of the Christian church,
but which grew into universally recognised occasions of fun and
licence, when no extravagance was accounted out of place or

[1] As to saints' plays, or 'miracles' (according to the French use of the term), see
chap. III below, and Schelling, F. E., *Elizabethan Drama*, vol. I, pp. 11, 12.

season by 'laughter, holding both his sides.' Such, above all, was
the feast of Fools, associated, in the first instance, with the ritual
of the feast of the Circumcision (New Year's eve and day), and
then developed into something very like the *Saturnalia*, or New
Year's festival of pagan Rome. It survived in England till
near the close of the fourteenth century, though, as early as the
thirteenth, it had attracted the censures of the spirit of reform
in the austere person of bishop Grosseteste. Still more pro-
tracted was the life in England of the kindred feast of Innocents,
which cannot be shown to have had any integral connection with
the ritual of Innocents' Day, but which was soon appended to it
as suiting the day on which the Boy bishop, elected by his fellow
choir-boys on the feast of St Nicholas, took office. The topsy-
turvydom of this celebration, to which there are other parallels
(as late as 1566 a 'Christmas Abbess' was elected by the nuns
at Carrow), was naturally of a more harmless kind and more
amenable to discipline, and, in consequence, less provocative of
prohibitions. Dramatic performances became a regular accompaniment of this festival, and, though the French or Anglo-Norman
St Nicholas plays which have been preserved (including one by
Hilarius) cannot be regarded as examples of the literary monastic
drama belonging to our literature, it may safely be concluded
that out of these performances grew those of the chapel boys and
schoolboys to which, as developed in the Elizabethan age, a special
chapter is devoted in the next volume. The general influence
of these festivals and their associations must have tended to
foster the element of humour and satire—the comic element—
which was to assert itself with enduring success in the course of
the growth of the religious, and, later, in that of the regular,
drama in England. Even at court, the authority of the Christmas
lord[1] or lord of Misrule survived the appointment of a permanent official with the title of master of the revels (1545),
and a conflict between the real and the mock authority naturally
ensued[2].

It is hardly necessary, before reaching the main root of the
growth which we are discussing, to point out that, by the side of,
or in connection with, the festival plays to which reference has

---

[1] See Schelling, *u. s.*, vol. I, p. 47; and cf. chaps. III and IV of Gayley's *Plays of
our Forefathers* for an admirable account of what he describes as 'the Invasion of the
Humorous.' The feast of Asses, which is there described with particular gusto on the
basis of Chambers's account of the Beauvais MS discovered by him, does not appear to
have been known in England.

[2] Schelling, vol. I, p. 76.

been made, the general favour bestowed in England as well as elsewhere, during the later Middle Ages, upon processional exhibitions
and moving shows of various kinds, devoid of either action or
dialogue, cannot be left out of account among the elements of
popular life which helped to facilitate the growth of the drama.
Notice will be taken below of the processional solemnities which
accompanied the celebration of the Corpus Christi festival, and
which certainly had their effect upon the pageants, as the particular religious plays afterwards collected into cycles were very
commonly called[1]. In later times, however, the term 'pageant'
came to be more generally employed in the sense which, at all
events till our own days, has usually attached to it—namely, a
show or exhibition in which costume, with its accessories, including,
sometimes, the suggestion of scenery, plays the principal part,
music lending its frequent aid, words being, at the most, used
in the way of illustration or introduction[2]. Pageants, in this
narrower sense of the term, were often called 'ridings'; and in
London, as is well known, this kind of exhibition secured a
popularity which has survived the lapse of many centuries. The
Norman conquest, supposed to have been largely responsible for
bringing horsemanship into permanent popular favour in England,
certainly introduced the refining influences of chivalry into these
occasions of contact between court and people; they continued
to be in favour throughout the whole of the Plantagenet, and
down into the Tudor, period; and it is needless to specify
examples of 'ridings in Chepe' or along the green Strand to
Westminster by kings, queens and other royalties, or by the lord
mayor, who, from 1457 onwards, substituted for his 'annual riding'
a procession still more characteristic of London and the true
source of her wealth, by water. At the same time, particular
note should be taken of the measure in which these ridings, by
the introduction of characters of national historical interest—such

---

[1] The term was applied to the plays even when regarded as literary productions:
thus, in the time of Henry VI, we hear of a 'Pageant of the Holy Trinity' painted with
gold—*i.e.* an illuminated MS of some dramatic piece in the nature of a mystery or
miracle-play.

[2] It is noteworthy that, in the pageants which have of late been exhibited in many
English towns, not only has the *admonitus loci* been emphasised as much as possible—
nowhere with such overpowering effect as at Bury St Edmunds, where the actual scene
of the performance was the Abbey gardens—but dialogue and even dramatic action
have formed an integral part of the presentment. In several instances, these modern
pageants have fully met their purpose, and, in any case, there is no reason for cavilling
at a perfectly legitimate development, except in so far as to point out that all moderni-
sations of an artistic species are apt to produce, for better or for worse, something
quite different from their supposed prototype in kind as well as in degree.

as St Edmund and king Arthur in the 'riding against Queen Margaret' at Coventry in 1445—fostered the patriotic sentiment to which the later chronicle histories made a direct appeal, cooperating with the influences of ballad literature and general popular tradition[1]. 'Disguisings' was a still more general term, applied to all processional and other shows of the kind dependent on costume and its appurtenances, without any approach to dramatic action, but, at least in Tudor times, accompanied by dancing. The old term 'mummings,' which, at one time, was applied to the unexpected appearance of masked and disguised revellers, who invited the company to dance, was also used more widely in much the same sense as 'disguisings,' though the account of the 'mummers' plays' and their origin which will be found in the next chapter lends colour to Collier's assertion that a 'mumming' was properly a dumb show as well as an assumption of disguise. The development of these amusements into a form of composition, the masque, a name first heard in the reign of Henry VIII—the Italian origin of the species did not prevent it from becoming one of the glories of English literature, although always standing apart from the main growth of the English drama —will be separately treated in a later chapter of this work. Meanwhile, 'disguisings' of one sort or another, besides serving to foster the love for the assumption of character—for 'being someone else'—had helped, as we shall see, to build a bridge by which players and plays passed into the sunshine of court favour, and, under the influence of the renascence and humanistic learning, encouraged the growth of a species of the religious drama in which the didactic element, clothed in a more or less conventional series of abstract conceptions, gradually asserted its predominance.

It was not, however, from half fortuitous, half barren survivals, or from exhibitions primarily designed to gratify the eye, that a drama could spring which was not only to mirror, but to form part of, the national life, and more and more so as that life advanced in vigour, in intensity and in self-consciousness. As will be shown in the chapter devoted to the discussion of this all-important aspect of the beginnings of English drama and of English dramatic literature, it was from the services of the Christian church of the Roman obedience that, in England as elsewhere in Europe, the medieval religious drama directly took its origin;

[1] On this head see chap. I ('Forerunners of the Chronicle Play') of Schelling, F. E., *The English Chronicle Play*, New York, 1902.

and it was thus that the growth with a survey of which down to the days of the puritan revolution these volumes are to be occupied actually began. How could it have been otherwise? On the one hand, those services, culminating in that of the mass, display their symbolical design by a variety of processes illustrating in turn all the dogmas which the church proclaims as possessed of commanding importance. On the other, the very circumstance that her worship was conducted according to one rule, in one ecclesiastical tongue accepted by all nations, shows how the main effect of that worship lay not in its words but in its symbols[1].

The history of the religious drama in England, if in it be included a survey of the adjuncts to the church liturgy in the form of alternating song and visible action, goes back to a period before the Norman conquest. Out of the mystical liturgy, the liturgical mystery grows by a process alike inevitable and un-forced, of which sufficient illustrations will be given—beginning with the *Quem quaeritis* of the Easter morning Mass. In England, however, we meet with no examples proper of *tropes*, by the inter-polation of which in the offices of the church the liturgical mystery had advanced beyond its earliest stage, or what might be called that of mere ornamentation—such as the Provençal production of *The Foolish Virgins*, and *The Raising of Lazarus*, written by Hilarius in Latin with occasional French refrains. These and other examples seem to show that, in the century succeeding that of the Norman conquest, the process of the emancipation of the dramatic mystery from the liturgy had already begun in France, where, in the eleventh century, we know that the former had been considered an integral part of the latter. To the twelfth century belongs the famous Norman-French—perhaps Anglo-Norman—play of *Adam*, which may very possibly have grown out of a processional representation of the prophets[2], but which seems (for the later portion of it is lost) to have aimed at dramatic representation of the entire Scriptural story, after the manner of the French and English collective mysteries of later date. We may safely conclude that the Norman conquest, or the period which followed immediately upon it, introduced into England as a virtually ready-made growth the religious performance or ex-hibition which could and did edify the devout, without actually

---

[1] Hagenbach, *Kirchengeschichte*, vol. II, p. 397.

[2] Gayley, C. M., *Plays of our Forefathers*, p. 27. Cf. Schofield, W. H., *English Literature from the Norman Conquest to Charles*, p. 136, where *Adam*, which consisted of three parts—the Fall, the Death of Abel, and the Prophecies of Christianity—is described as 'the earliest extant mystery in the vulgar tongue.'

forming part of the religious exercises incumbent upon them. At the same time, the English mystery-play did not fail to reveal its liturgical origin by such stage directions as *Tunc cantabit angelus* in the Chester *Ascensio*, or by the disquisitions of the Chester Expositor and the Coventry *Contemplacio*, recalling the priest's elucidatory comment[1]. These plays were acted either within the church walls, or on a scaffold immediately outside them, the performers being no doubt, in the first instance and ordinarily, ecclesiastics or the pupils of ecclesiastics. Gradually, the professional secular entertainers, who, as we saw, were unlikely to forego such a chance of attracting the public, sought to compete with the clerics and to interfere with their monopoly; in the middle of the thirteenth century, it was certainly no unheard-of thing for secular players to solicit the favour of audiences—surely by means of plays in the vernacular; in 1258, they were forbidden to give such performances in the monasteries of the land. Either this prohibition was effectual, or the practice never became quite common; for, a century and a half later, Lydgate, though in some of the verses he wrote to accompany the mummings of his age he showed a strong dramatic instinct[2], makes no mention of players in his poem *Danse Macabre*, while among the representatives of divers classes of men he introduces minstrels and 'tragitours' (*i.e.* jugglers).

Thus, then, it seems clear that what dramatic performances were to be seen in England during the latter part of the eleventh, the twelfth and the greater part of the thirteenth centuries, were mainly in the hands of the clergy. Attempts were not wanting, even in this early period, to free from exclusive clerical control a species of entertainment the popularity of which was continually on the increase; and there doubtless were from the first, as there certainly were later, voices in the church itself which reprobated loudly and authoritatively this method of attracting the public to the church door or its vicinity. But, as is shown in a subsequent chapter, it was not long before the strongest impulse ever given in a contrary direction by the church was imparted by pope Urban IV's institution of the great Roman Catholic festival of Corpus Christi. It does not appear that this pope, who, at the foundation of the feast, granted a 'pardon' for a certain number of days to all who attended certain parts of the divine service performed on it, took any note of the representation of religious

---

[1] Cf. Hohlfeld, A., 'Altenglische Kollektivmysterien,' etc., in *Anglia*, vol. xi.
[2] Schelling, F. E., *Elizabethan Drama*, vol. i, p. 74, and note.

plays; the 'pardon' mentioned in the proclamation for Whitsun plays at Chester, and attributed to 'Clement then bishop of Rome,' together with the concomitant excommunication of whosoever should interfere with the performance of the said plays, is supposed to have been issued by Clement VI, *i.e.* about a generation later than the confirmation of the institution of Corpus Christi. As is shown below, the Corpus Christi processions of trading-companies in England very soon developed into the performance by them of religious plays; but what in the present connection it is desired to establish is the fact that the *redintegratio amoris* between church and stage due to the popularity of Corpus Christi long endured, though exposed to many interruptions and rebuffs from high quarters. The friars, above all, as it would seem, the Minorites, were active in fostering an agency of religious excitement which the older and more aristocratic orders were probably less disposed to look upon with favour[1].

The further development of the relations between the church and the drama is examined at length elsewhere. No religious plays preserved to us from this early period are known with certainty to have been written by secular priests or monks for performance by themselves or their pupils. Possibly some of the extant isolated mysteries may have had clerical authors, but we lack any knowledge on the subject[2]. There is, however, no reason for supposing that these clerical or monastic plays for popular audiences differed very largely from the plays written for lay performers by which, to all intents and purposes, they were superseded, or into which they were absorbed—more especially as there seems every reason to believe that of these latter a large proportion were, at least in the earlier part of the period, written by monks. Nor can it be at all confidently asserted that the comic element was less freely cultivated in clerical than in lay plays, and that the friars were likely to exercise much self-restraint when desirous of tickling the palates of their audiences. In general, though an attentive study will prove capable of marking not a few distinctive characteristics in particular religious plays or in groups of

---

[1] The disclaimer of the friar minor in *Piers Plowman* is too well known to need quotation; but, as Collier, citing Drake's *History of York*, points out, another friar minor, in 1420, not long after the composition of that poem, is found exerting himself at York to procure the annual representation of holy Corpus Christi plays; and he was described as a 'professor of pageantry' (*History of Dramatic Poetry*, new ed., vol. I, p. 20).

[2] The late miracle-play of *Kynge Robert of Cicylye* was stated to be written by a priest (see chap. III below). Of the collective mysteries, the *Towneley* and the *Coventry Plays* at all events must be ascribed to monkish hands.

them, of which the variance is due to difference of time or place, it is by no means surprising that an essentially popular growth, not at all intended to satisfy more elevated or refined tastes, still less to secure to its products a place in literature, should have altered but little in the course of several centuries. In nothing are the illiterate more conservative than in their amusements; and in this instance it could not be in the interests of the purveyors, whether clerical or lay, to move far out of the beaten track.

It will be shown in our next chapter by what steps the religious drama in England had passed out of the hands of the church into those of lay performers in town or gild, who, in ever increasing numbers, were found desirous of gratifying their aspirations by the practice of an art in which few think themselves incapable of excelling. By the fifteenth century the process was complete, and a considerable literature of religious drama was in existence, although, from the nature of the case, every part of it was to be subjected to more or less continuous revision and extension.

Of English religious plays, under their threefold designation of *mysteries*—a name not in use in England, but convenient as designating plays mainly founded upon the biblical narrative —*miracles* or saints' plays, and *moralities*, a full account will be found in the third chapter of the present volume; the question of the relative antiquity of particular extant English plays (*The Harrowing of Hell*, dating from the middle of the thirteenth century, not being yet to be accounted a play proper) will be there discussed, and special attention will, of course, be given to those cycles of plays, following the chronological order of biblical events, which, though not absolutely peculiar to our literature, are by no other possessed in several complete examples. It will be shown what was the relation of these plays to others of the same species in foreign literatures, and in French more especially[1], and from what sources besides Holy Writ, apocryphal, apocalyptic, or legendary, they at times derive the incidents or the colouring of their action. Thus, the basis of most of the

---

[1] The paradox—for, considering that the *Chester Plays* are the youngest series of the four, it may almost be so described—according to which these plays were based on a French original, is discussed by Hohlfeld, A., in the notable essay on the collective mysteries already cited, and by Hemingway, S. B., *English Nativity Plays* (Yale Studies in English), New York, 1909. The conclusion seems to be that there is certainly evidence of the traces of a French original, but that this was not a collective series, and that it was not copied by the writer who elaborated the *Chester Plays* in their present form.

Christmas plays is not the Scriptural, but the apocryphal, narrative[1]. The most evident source of the episodes of *Joseph of Arimathea*, *The Harrowing of Hell*, and *The Coming of Antichrist*, is the Latin *Gospel of Nicodemus*[2]. The influence of *Cursor Mundi*, extant in a large number of MSS, is particularly strong in the *York Plays*, and to this source, and to the *Legenda Aurea* of Voragine and similar sources, are largely due the traditions which are reproduced in the English religious plays, and which have little or no basis in the Scriptural narrative. Such are the conception of the hierarchy of the angelic orders, the developed story of the fall of Lucifer, and the legends of the Oil of Mercy and the Holy Rood-Tree[3].

The Cornish miracle-plays, their language being the native Cymric dialect, stand apart from the English; but though the illusion of the still existing amphitheatres or 'rounds' may carry the imagination of the modern visitor back into the past to a time when York, the home of the earliest English cycle, was young; and, though it is not impossible that the Cornish cycle, in its original form, was earlier than any of the rest, there is not much in these plays to distinguish them from French and English dramatic mysteries, and, indeed, French words occasionally make their appearance in them. Their language is stated to carry back the date of their composition to a period earlier than the fourteenth century, though the earliest MS, apparently, dates from the fifteenth[4], and though we possess no notice of the actual performance of plays in Cornwall earlier than that in Richard Carew's *Survey*, first printed in 1602, where mention is made of the representation of the Guary miracles in amphitheatres constructed in open fields. The extant Cornish plays consist of a connected series of three sub-cycles: *Origo Mundi*, a selection of episodes from the creation to the building of the Temple; *Passio Domini*, the life of Christ from the temptation to the crucifixion; and the resurrection and the ascension; and the whole cycle ends with a chorus of angels, and an epilogue by the emperor. But to the first sub-cycle (or first day's performance) is added a saint's play on the constancy and martyrdom of Maximilla, and in the third is inserted an episodical play on the death

---

[1] Hemingway, *u.s.*

[2] See Gayley, C. M., *Plays of our Forefathers*, p. 260.

[3] See *ibid.* pp. 224 ff.; and cf. ten Brink, vol. I, p. 360.

[4] This assumption is supported by the fact, noted by Gayley, that in the opening scene of *Passio Domini* a verse-form is used which closely approximates to the nine-lined stanza used with great effect in *Secunda Pastorum* (*Towneley Plays*).

of Pilate, which stands quite apart from the rest[1]. In addition
to this cycle a further saint's play, *The Life of Saint Meriasek,
Bishop and Confessor*, was discovered in 1869, and edited with
a translation by Whitley Stokes (1872). Its language is by him
described as Middle-Cornish, and rather more modern than that
of *Passio*[2].

The English mysteries and miracle-plays in general—for the
moralities, in this respect, are to be judged from a somewhat
different point of view—and the plays of the former class combined in the four great cycles described below in particular,
possess certain artistic features and qualities which entitle them
to a place in our literature, not merely as interesting remains of
a relatively remote phase of our national civilisation. They were
written to please as well as to edify ; and, in some of them, which
were almost indisputably from the hands of ecclesiastics, the
literary sense or instinct may occasionally be said to overpower
what sense of propriety existed in the writers. For to speak, in
this connection, of lack of reverence would be to betray a mis-
apprehension of the general attitude of the church militant of the
Middle Ages towards sacred names, and things, and persons.
Above all, it behoved the revisers of these plays—for whatever
may have been the original form of each of the four cycles, not
one of them has come down to us from the hand of a single
author, or without repeated changes and cross-borrowings—to
remain true to that spirit of *naïveté* which had presided at their
origin and which (with the exception, perhaps, in some respects,
of the *Coventry Plays* in their present form) they, on the whole,
consistently maintained. In this spirit they should be read and

---

[1] See Norris, E., *The Ancient Cornish Drama*, 2 vols., Oxford, 1859, where these
plays are translated as well as edited.

[2] The scene of part I of this long drama is partly Britanny, where Meriasek, the
son of a duke of Britanny, is sent to school by his loving parents, returns home with
the best of characters, declines a splendid marriage, preferring to be 'consecrated a
knight of God,' and, after incurring much resistance, performs his first miracle, sails
for Cornwall, miraculously tames a wolf and builds himself a hermitage. He then
performs a miracle on a larger scale, which purges Britanny from outlawed robbers,
and beholds the defeat of his pagan foe. The rest of the action is at Rome, where
Constantine is healed by pope Silvester and converted. In part II, the double action
continues; but a sort of unity is given to it by the consecration of Meriasek as bishop,
in accordance with the pope's bull, before his last miracle and death. At the close of
each of the two parts, the audience is invited to drink and dance. The comic element,
which Stokes states to be *de rigueur* in all Cornish plays, is supplied by the torturers, a
quack doctor and one or two other characters; but its humour has evaporated, and,
with the exception of a pathetic passage or two, the play may be pronounced devoid of
literary merit. The metrification is varied and elaborate.

criticised by later generations—the quality of quaintness, or of unconscious humour, being left to take care of itself. This quality is most abundantly exhibited in the accounts, which we must of course suppose to have been made out by the officers of the gilds or crafts by whom, in the main, the plays were produced and represented, and who would be just the men to see nothing comic in 'a link to set the world on fire,' 'paid for making of 3 worlds, 3*d*.' '2 yards and a half of buckram for the Holy Ghost's coat, 2*s*. 1*d*.,' and the like; or in the matter-of-fact descriptions of 'properties' such as 'Hell-mouth, the head of a whale with jaws worked by 2 men, out of which devil boys ran.' Apart from other merits of composition, which, however, are of too frequent occurrence to be justly regarded as incidental only[1], it is by the conscious humour as well as by the conscious pathos perceptible in these plays that certain of them, and even particular groups definitively marked out by careful and ingenious criticism, must be held to rank as literary productions of no common order. The pathos was, of course, directly suggested by the materials out of which these plays were constructed; but it is quite distinct and often 'drawn out' (if the phrase is appropriate) with considerable effect. Such a passage is the dialogue between Abraham and Isaac, while preparing for the sacrifice, in the *Chester Play*, which comes home to a modern as it did to a medieval audience, though the *dénouement* is already lurking in the thicket[2]. Another passage of the kind is the wonderful burst of passionate grief, which can have left no eye dry, from the Mother of the Sufferer in *The Betraying of Christ* in the *Coventry Play*. Of a different sort is the pathos—a touch of that nature which comes home to the spectator in any and every kind of drama— in the salutation by the shepherd who, reverencing in the infant

---

[1] I have elsewhere (*History of English Dramatic Literature*, vol. i, pp. 73 ff.) directed attention to the evidence offered in these plays of other literary qualities— including ease and appropriateness of dialogue; a dramatic vigour quite distinct from the vehement raging (deliberately intended to terrify the populace) of the Herods and Pilates; conciseness and clearness of exposition; and adequacy—I can find no better word—of meditative passages such as the opening reflections in the *Prima Pastorum* on the uncertainty of human life: 'Lord, what thay ar weylle that hens ar past,' etc. Nor is a grand severity of tone wanting where it is most in place; Jusserand has pointed out that the discourses or 'sermons,' as they were called in the French *mystères*, spoken by the Father in the Old, and by the Son in the New, Testament plays, lack neither dignity nor power; see, for an English example, *The Emission of the Holy Ghost* in the *Chester Plays*.

[2] Unless I mistake, this was the *Abraham and Isaac* presented at the Charterhouse after the memorable first performance of *Every-man*, but then judiciously withdrawn, as an afterpiece unsuitable to the morality, which, moreover, needed none.

Saviour the victor over the powers of hell, is won by his smile
into simple human sympathy with the Babe on His Mother's
knee:

> Haylle comly and clean: haylle yong child!
> Haylle maker, as I mene, of a madyn so mylde.
> Thou has waryd, I weyne, the warlo[1] so wylde,
> The fals gyler of teyn[2], now goys he begylde.
>   Lo, he merys;
> Lo, he laghys, my swetyng,
> A welfare metyng,
> I have holden my hetyng[3],
>   Have a bob of cherys[4].

More notable, because imported of purpose prepense, is the
conscious humour introduced in these plays with the object of
gratifying the spectators. An audience must be amused, whatever may be offered to it, all the more so if that offering be a
periodical repetition of the same kind of spectacle, and if this
constitutes a strain upon the serious emotions[5]. The collective
mysteries, as they are preserved to us, are generally true in
intention to the principle of allowing no occasion of the kind to
slip; but in the *York*, and still more so in the *Towneley*, *Plays*,
this intention manifestly becomes a progressive tendency towards
the elaboration of opportunities for realistic humour. It may
seem going rather far to speak of the York schools of humour
and realism, and of the Wakefield master who exhibits the full
flower of the promise of his predecessors; but it is one of the
legitimate—it is, indeed, one of the highest—functions of criticism
to discover and to verify the presence and the influence of
personality. And there can be no reasonable doubt as to the
individuality of the work in the *Towneley Plays*, of which the
outward sign is the use, preferential rather than uniform, of the
nine-lined stanza, not less effective in its way than the Spenserian in
its own, of which the unknown contributor may have been the
inventor, and of which an example was cited above. 'If anyone,'
writes A. W. Pollard, 'will read the plays' which bear this mark
together, I think he cannot fail to feel that they are all the work of the same
writer, and that this writer deserves to be ranked—if only we knew his
name!—at least as high as Langland, and as an exponent of a rather
boisterous kind of humour had no equal in his own day[6].

---

[1] Wizard.   [2] Sorrow.   [3] Promise.

[4] *Secunda Pastorum* in *Towneley Plays*.

[5] Even at Oberammergau, where the strain was heavy, and where all humour had
been effaced from the composition, the escape of Barabbas with a single cut of the whip
was hailed with a modest burst of merriment (1871).

[6] Introduction to the *Towneley Plays*, p. xxii (cf.) cited by Gayley, C. M., in the two
very notable chapters in *Plays of our Forefathers* (xi and xii) in which the position
stated in the text is fully explained and illustrated.

In his hands, the time-honoured incident of what Chaucer[1] calls

> The sorwe of Noe with his felawship[2]
> Or that he might get his wif to ship

becomes a farcical play in a series of scenes, of which the interest centres in the tenacity of Noah's wife rather than in the preservation of the patriarch and the human race[3]. The curious *Processus Talentorum*, which treats of Pilate's decision as to the Saviour's garments, is, in its details, singularly original. But the height of independent treatment, with the comic element in the ascendant, is reached in an earlier play of the same series, the famous *Secunda Pastorum*, the merry tale of the sheep-stealing Mak— which is nothing short of a play within a play, and which, in freshness of conception and in gaiety of treatment, may be ranked alongside of the famous *Maître Pathelin*, and the *Schwänke* of Hans Sachs, though considerably earlier in date than either of them. In the *Chester Plays*, though altogether they are less popular in treatment, the popular demand which the *Play of the Shepherds* brought with it, is satisfied by the coarse fooling of Trowle; in the *Coventry Plays*, both humour and coarseness are further subdued, and literary endeavour directs itself rather to the preservation of regularity of form on the one hand and to the display of biblical learning on the other, while humour occasionally takes the form of satire[4]. Contrariwise, it was but natural that the danger of the degeneration of the comic element in religious plays should be ignored, especially where no care was taken for maintaining the time-honoured character of a celebrated cycle. The Digby *Conversion of St Paul* (of which the MS seems to belong to the close of the fifteenth century or a slightly later date) contains a scene of unsavoury fun; and in the *Mary Magdalene* of the same collection (which, generally, by its almost unprecedented accumulation of sensational effects betrays its late date) there is a burlesque scene between a priest and his boy, who, after being threatened with a flogging, proceeds to deserve it by intoning a mock service in nonsense Latin with

> snyguer snagoer werwolfforum
> standgardum lamba beffettorum.

What could be sillier or more modern[5]?

---

[1] *The Miller's Tale.*   [2] His other, in this instance not his better, half.

[3] In the *Chester Plays* she does not absolutely refuse to come, but, in the spirit of a true head of the family, she insists on taking all her relations with her.

[4] See, for example, the passage against extravagance in dress, in *The Council of the Jews* (*Coventry Mysteries*, xxv).

[5] It is only right to say, as to the serious side of this strange play, which has a

The great English collective mysteries are, of course, differen-
tiated by linguistic, as well as by literary, features; for, while both
the *York* and the *Towneley Plays* are written in the Northumbrian
dialect, which suits so many of their characteristics though it
makes them by no means easy reading, we seem in the *Chester*
and *Coventry Plays* to be moving on ground less remote from the
more common forms of fifteenth century English.   The so-called
Coventry Plays show east-midland peculiarities in their dialect,
which agrees with the conclusions as to their origin reached by
some of the best authorities, such as ten Brink and A. W. Pollard.
In the matter of metre, the most striking feature common to
English religious plays is the great variety exhibited by them.
(*The Harrowing of Hell*, which in form has hardly passed from
that of the dialogue into that of the drama, and in metre confines
itself to a very irregular octosyllabic couplet, can hardly be cited
as an exception.) This variety of metrification, contrasting very
strongly with the consistency with which the French miracle- and
mystery-plays adhere to the metre of the octosyllabic couplet,
though permitting themselves an occasional excursion into the
fashionable form of the triolet[1], is already very noticeable in the
York Plays: in the *Towneley*, notwithstanding their close connection with the *York Plays*, there seems a recognition of the
expediency of maintaining the octosyllabic metre as the staple
metre of the drama, though, as has already been noticed, the last
and most conspicuous writer of all who had a hand in these plays
enriched them by the introduction of a new and elaborate stanza
of his own. His ordinary stanza-form, which is to be found in
practically all the plays in this collection which reveal the comic
elaboration of his master hand, is the thirteen-lined stanza riming
ababababcdddc[2]. The *Coventry Plays* show a less striking
metrical variety, and a tendency towards that length of line,
which was to end in the fashion of the doggerel alexandrine,
and thus, as Saintsbury observes, to help, by reaction, to establish
blank verse as the metre of the English drama. In the *Chester
Plays*, there is again that marked variety of metre which speaks

romantic colouring almost removing it out of the general sphere of the religious
drama, that the figure of the much-erring and much-suffering heroine is not devoid of
true pathos, while Satan rejoicing over her fall reminds us of Mephistopheles gloating
over that of Margaret in *Faust*.

[1] Saintsbury, G., *A History of English Prosody*, vol. I, pp. 203 ff., where, in
book III, 'The Fifteenth Century,' chap. I, 'The Drama,' see a full discussion of the
metrification of the religious plays.

[2] Hohlfeld, *u.s.* pp. 287 ff.

for the early origin of these plays in their first form; and this conclusion is corroborated by the frequent use of alliteration. Altogether, the religious plays exhibit a combined looseness and ingenuity of metrification corresponding to what the historian of English prosody terms its 'break-up' in the fifteenth century, to which the bulk of the plays in their present form belong, and harmonising with the freedom of treatment which, notwithstanding the nature of its main source, and what may be termed the single-mindedness of its purpose, was characteristic of the English mystery- and miracle-drama.

In the chapter of this work dealing with the early religious drama, it will be shown how its third species, the 'moral plays' or 'moralities,' originated in the desire to bring into clear relief the great lesson of life—the struggle between good and evil to which every man is subjected, and the solution of which depends for every man upon his relation to the powers contending for his soul. The conception is familiar to religious literature long before it is put into dramatic shape, and theological moralities were produced some time before they found their way to the popular stage. The productions of the Anglo-Norman *trouvère* Guillaume Herman (1127—70) and of Étienne Langton, doctor of theology at Paris and afterwards, as everyone knows, archbishop of Canterbury (1207) and cardinal, in general conception and treatment resemble the moralities of later date ; though in each the strife of Mercy and Peace against Truth and Righteousness on behalf of sinful man, indirectly suggested by *Psalm* lxxxv, 10, 11, is solved by the personal intervention of the Saviour[1]. It is clearly erroneous to suppose that the English moralities, to which these remarks are confined, grew gradually out of the mysteries and miracles, under the cooperating influence of the pageantry which had become a public custom in the English towns in the latter part of the Middle Ages. The love of allegory from a very early period onwards domesticated itself in the English mind, to which there seems to be nothing intrinsically congenial in this species of composition, but which at all times has been singularly tenacious of tastes and tendencies to which it has once given admittance. This particular taste must have been implanted by Christianity by means of the Bible. Paraphrases of the Bible are the chief fruits of the earliest productive age of English poetical literature. The Old and the New Testament were alike

---

[1] The same four Virtues, *Veritas, Justitia, Misericordia* and *Pax*, appear in *The Salutation and Conception* in the *Coventry Plays* (xi).

composed in eastern tongues; the scenes of their narratives are eastern; certain books of the Bible have always been declared by the church to be allegorical in design; and there are few portions of the holy text that are not full of allegory, parable and symbolism. It is needless here to pursue further a theme which has been fully treated elsewhere, and which has not been left out of sight in earlier volumes of this *History*[1]. Before English literature, in which the love of allegory had continued to assert itself wherever that literature continued most popular in its forms as well as in its sympathies, had produced one of the masterpieces of the species in the *Vision concerning Piers the Plowman*, the taste of western literature in general, and of French in particular, had already set in the same direction, and the *Roman de la Rose* had established an ascendancy in the world of letters which was to reflect itself in our own allegorical literature, and which endured down to the time of the renascence and the reformation. To the French taste for allegorical poetry and satire, the drama, which, in the thirteenth century, had completely emancipated itself from the control of the church, no doubt in its turn contributed; by the end of the fourteenth, the *Confrérie de la Passion* found it difficult to maintain its religious plays against the moralities, full of polemical satire, of the *Confrérie de la Basoche*, or against the Aristophanic *soties* of the *Enfans sans souci*; while the *Basoche*, which had begun with moralising allegories, soon took a leaf out of their rivals' book, and interspersed their moralities with *farces* and *soties*, till the didactic species virtually passed away. If, then, the love of allegory which had been early implanted in the English people, and the impulse given to this predilection by French examples both in literature and on the stage in the period between Chaucer and the renascence be remembered, it will not be difficult to account for the growth, side by side with the biblical and saintly religious drama, of a species differing from it in origin, except as to their common final source, and varying from it in method, and, as time went on, more or less in character also. Nevertheless, the growth of this didactic species accompanies that of the plays following, with more or less of digression, the biblical narrative, or dealing with lives of saints or the after-effects of their martyrdoms in the form of miracles, and continues to affect these sister species in many instances, or actually in some cases to

[1] See vol. I, chap. IV *et al*; and cf. Courthope's *History of English Poetry*, vol. I, chap. IX, 'The Progress of Allegory.'

intermingle with them. Gradually, and under the influence of the general widening of the range of ideas and interests due to the renascence, the moralities begin to abandon the path of religious teaching for that of the inculcation of intellectual or philosophical, and even of political, principles and truths; and a further step is thus taken towards the complete secularisation of the drama.

The following pages will, it is believed, sufficiently illustrate the consummation of this change, and describe the process by which, after the biblical religious drama had begun to die out in England, where saints' plays had never enjoyed much popularity, the abstract figures of the moralities were associated with concrete personages of the national past, or types of actual contemporary life, and gradually gave way before them. The progress of the narrative will show how thus, with the aid of the transitional species of the chronicle history on the one hand, and of the interlude, in the narrower sense of the term, on the other, tragedy and comedy were found ready to be called into being, so soon as the light of classical example shone forth which had been lit by the enthusiasm of the renascence.

CHAPTER II

SECULAR INFLUENCES ON THE EARLY ENGLISH DRAMA

Minstrels. Village Festivals. Folk-Plays

Before the religious origins of the English drama are specially considered, certain secular influences should be noted. The first of these is that of the minstrels, a heterogeneous class of composers and performers, drawn from several sources.

The theatrical history of the Roman empire is the story of the degradation of tragedy into pantomime, of comedy into farce. The tragic actor became the *pantomimus* who danced, first the lyric portions and, finally, the whole 'book' of the play, to an accompaniment of music, for the pleasure of the more refined classes; while, in place of the comedy imported from Greece, the old Italian (Campanian) *Fabula Atellana*, united with the farcical μῖμος, imported from Magna Graecia, became the amusement of the vulgar. Both *pantomimus* and *mimus* (the names being equally those of performer and performance) degenerated into sensuous displays, and performers, though their rivalries led to public brawls and they were the spoiled darlings of their admirers, fell back, as a class, to the low social level from which the later republic and the earlier empire had done something to rescue them. The Christian church, naturally, was no friend to such exhibitions as the multilingual and degraded population had come to expect; but more important than the opposition of the church was the contempt of the barbarians of the later irruptions. The coming of the Lombards, in the sixth century, dealt the death-blow to the scotched art of public amusement.

Private amusement, however, in which these *scenici* had been as busily employed as on public stages, continued in all parts of the empire, and was the means of prolonging the existence of the class. Its members became confused and intermingled with the lower orders of entertainer, tumblers, rope-walkers, bear-leaders and so forth, and shared with them a precarious and a wandering existence. The evidence as to their dramatic *répertoire* in England is very slight; but the conclusion is reasonable that it decreased to the smallest dimensions and may, in time, have come to include little more than imitations of beasts and of drunken or half-witted men, combined with displays of such indecent buffoonery and ribald rimings as naturally delighted the medieval population in both castle and village. For several reasons, however, it is almost necessary to suppose that these tricks were linked together by some sort of dramatic interest, however rude. They are more amusing when so treated. Dialogue was certainly among the strollers' accomplishments; and so was the use of marionettes, which implies not only dialogue but plot. The literature of medieval Germany and France contains several works, such as *Le Roi d'Angleterre et le Jougleur d'Ely,* and *Le Garçon et l'Aveugle,* which seem to show the existence of a *répertoire* founded more or less on mere farce. And, by the fourteenth century, we find in England not only a mention in the *Tretise of miraclis pleyinge* of 'other japis' distinct from miracles[1], but a fragment of the text of the *Interludium de Clerico et Puella,* a humorous little play, founded on the popular medieval story of Dame Siriz[2]. There is, however, in England scarcely a trace of anything corresponding to the *Schembartlaufen* of the *Meistersingers* of Nürnberg, or such amateur organisations as the *Enfants sans souci* or the *Basoche* in Paris, which secured a healthy existence for farce. In the fourteenth century (1352), indeed, we find bishop Grandison of Exeter prohibiting a performance by the youths of the city *in contumeliam et opprobrium allutariorum,* a satirical attack on the cloth-dressers' guild, who had been charging too high for their wares. But, for the most part, the early history of the comic element in secular drama in England is dark. It appears to have remained in the hands of the descendant of the ribald *mimus,* and seldom, if ever, to have achieved the honour of association with his betters. Until its appearance in literature in the work of John Heywood, its existence in England can only be inferred. Nevertheless, merely for preserving its existence, however rudely, the *mimus* deserves our gratitude. When English drama became secularised, the interlude found at least some sort of criticism of social types and of the actual world on which to work.

Another stream of tradition, affecting mainly the serious, as distinct from the comic, side of his *répertoire,* contributed to the formation of the medieval entertainer. This flowed from the minstrels, who were in England some centuries before the spread

---

[1] Chambers, *Mediaeval Stage,* vol. I, p. 84.   [2] Cf. *ante,* vol. I, pp. 365—6.

of Latin civilisation opened the country to invasion by *mimi* as well as by ecclesiastics. When the bard emerged from the communal singing of pagan races it is impossible to say; but the state of war for which, in their migrations westward, they exchanged their pastoral life brought into existence a class of heroes, and the existence of heroes accounts for the singing of *cantilenae* to celebrate their exploits. By the fifth century, there is plenty of evidence of the existence of a class of professional singers attached to the courts of great leaders. Such a singer was not despised, like the *mimus* and the *joculator*, his successors, but honoured, an owner of land and gold, the professional representative of an art in which his master himself was not ashamed to be his rival. Such a scop or minstrel was Widsith[1], who was both attached to a leader's court and allowed to wander abroad. *The complaint of Deor* and the feast in Hrothgar's hall in *Beowulf* give other pictures of the Teutonic minstrel's life. The duty of such a minstrel was to sing to the harp the praises of his lord and the delights of war, and, under the names of scop and gleeman[2], he was a prominent figure in unconverted England. In converted England, the ecclesiastic, as a man, encouraged this minstrelsy; as an official, he discouraged it; and, from the eighth to the eleventh centuries, its history is obscure. During these centuries began the gradual assimilation of Teutonic and Latin entertainer, of scop and *mimus*. During the same centuries in France, there grew up the distinction between the Norman *trouvères*, or minstrels of war, and the Provençal *troubadours*, who sang in the south their songs of love. The Norman conquest opened up England still further, not only to the *trouvères* or *jongleurs*, the Taillefers and Raheres who brought honour and glory to the exploits of feudal lords, but to entertainers of all kinds, from respectable musicians and reciters to the juggling, tumbling rogues who haunted the highways of Europe. Under this invasion, the English minstrel sank yet lower. He was forced to appeal, not to the great ones of the land, whose language he did not speak, but to the down-trodden of his own race; and the assimilation with the vagabond mime must be supposed to have become more complete. In the eyes of the church, at any rate, the confusion between the higher and the lower class of minstrel was always an accomplished

---

[1] See vol. I of the present work, chaps. I and III, and Chambers, vol. I, pp. 28—30.

[2] Scop = maker; gleeman = the man of glee or mirth; but, originally at any rate, the two terms were interchangeable and do not imply the separation into a higher and lower class of minstrel which will be seen later.

fact ; but her indiscriminate condemnation of both kinds was not, on the whole, to the disadvantage of the lower class, inasmuch as, in conjunction with the common taste of both noble and peasant for something a little more amusing than the court minstrel could supply, it helped to break down a class distinction between the various kinds of entertainer. To some extent, the court minstrel learned to be a buffoon ; to some extent, the despised English minstrel learned the language and the stories of the conquerors, and began to translate the disputations, the *jeux-partis* and the *tençons*, which were popular in Norman castles, following them in time with the *estrifs*, among which *The Harrowing of Hell* formed an important link between the *répertoire* of the minstrels and the early drama, and may, indeed, be considered one of the sources of the morality. Aided, no doubt, by the *goliardi* or wandering scholars, vagabond disseminators of learning and wit, English minstrels formed at least part of the means of union between conquerors and conquered. In this, they may be contrasted with the Celtic minstrels, the harpers and the bards, who, though they sang their own heroes, as English minstrels had continued to sing of Hereward, did not, like the English minstrels, act, whether in intention or in fact, as peace-makers between the conquered, Wales, and the conqueror, England.

In France, where conditions were more favourable, a definite influence was exerted by professional minstrels on the religious drama. In England, it was not so. There is, indeed, some slight evidence that minstrels, to some extent, took up the composition and performance of religious plays[1]. For the most part, however, their share appears to have been limited to supplying the music and, occasionally, some comic relief, in the later days when town, parish or guild had taken over from the church the production of the miracle.

When, therefore, we look for the influence of the minstrel on the formation of the English drama, we find it to be, at any rate until the fifteenth century, of the very slightest. The superior class, whose art descended from that of scop and *trouvère*, may have prepared the ground for the morality by the composition, if not the recitation by two mouths, of *estrifs* in dialogue form. The lower class may have been of service in two ways : first, by their preservation of the art of the puppet-show[2] or 'motion,' though, even here, during the later period, when a dramatic

---

[1] Ward, vol. I, p. 50.
[2] On the subject of marionnettes see Magnin, Ch., *Histoire des Marionnettes* (2nd edition, 1862), especially Books II and VI.

literature for puppets can be distinctly traced and the nascent secular drama was ripe for its influence, that art appears to have been chiefly practised by new-comers from the continent; and, secondly, by their relation, noted above, to the art of farce. But, perhaps, the most genuine service performed by both classes up to the fifteenth century was nothing more than that of keeping alive the desire to be amused ; while, in the case of the lower class, we may add to this the fact that they did consistently carry on, no matter how poorly, the practice which lies at the root of dramatic art and of the pleasure to be gained from it—that of pretending to be someone or something else.

By the fifteenth century, religious drama had passed out of the hands of the church into those of the amateur performers of town or guild. Moreover, the stimulus given to the love of dramatic performances had resulted in the birth of the interlude— the short play, sometimes religious, but usually moral, in character, which could be played in the banqueting hall of the noble or in the market place or village green by a few players, and without the expensive and elaborate machinery of the miracle. The popularity and ease of preparation of the interlude soon induced its amateur performers to extend a practice not unknown in the case of miracles, and take it 'on tour,' as we should say now, from town to town and village to village. The minstrels had already suffered, not only from the invention of printing, which left them no longer the sole repositories of story and poem, but from the increasing command of literature by the amateur (knight or tradesman) which followed the development of the English language. The poaching on their preserves of the amateur interlude player spurred them to double action. In the first place, they consolidated their formation into guilds. A charter of Edward IV (1469)[1]—after reciting that certain 'rude rustics and artificers' were pretending to be minstrels and neglecting their business, to go about the country, levying heavy exactions on the lieges—orders all minstrels to join the guild on pain of suppression; and this guild still exists in the corporation of the Musicians of London. In the second place, they took the wind out of the sails of the amateurs by becoming interlude players themselves. They are found doing this probably so early as 1427[2]; and it was not long before the greater convenience of hiring professional players than of training amateurs began to make itself felt—not to mention the element of

---

[1] Analysed in Chambers, vol. II, Appendix F, pp. 260—1.
[2] Rymer, *Foedera*, vol. x, p. 387.

farce, which the minstrels had kept alive and were ready and able to contribute to the attractions of the show. While the great towns continued to produce miracle-plays by means of their craft-guilds, smaller places and private houses depended on the transformed minstrels. They are found attached to the establishments of nobles by the middle of the fifteenth century, and Henry VII and his successors kept their own companies. Under Elizabeth, they, in their turn, made way before, or were incorporated into, the professional actors of the new drama[1].

The history of the other influence on our early drama with which this chapter has to deal belongs in a large measure to the study of folk-lore[2]. The pagan festivals of summer and winter which had, or came to have, the object of securing by ritual observance plenteous crops and fruitful herds, had, also, a side which explains what influence they may have had on the drama—the holiday mood, the desire for the exercise of activity purely for the pleasure in it, to which we give the name of play. The churl who would not play on festival days was, from immemorial times, the object of the holiday-makers' dislike and rough treatment.

At the same time, the ritual itself came to include many elements—disguise, combat, procession, dance, song, action—which, arising from whatever symbolical and ritual origins, lent themselves easily to the spirit of play, and approximated to the acted drama. It is not possible, of course, to trace any such direct road from village festival to drama in England as in Greece; but a certain connection, besides the mere fostering of the spirit of play, is to be observed between the early drama and pagan observance, wholly or partly or not at all absorbed by Christianity.

On the literary side, the connection is very slight. The folk had their *cantilenae*, or songs celebrating mythological or historical heroes[3]; but epic poetry owes more to these than does the drama. The people had, also, their festival songs, sung in procession or during the dance round the sacred fire or tree, of which *Sumer is i-cumen in* is a sophisticated remnant[4]; and in these songs the growth of the amoebaean form shown in the existence of the burden[5] implies

---

[1] See vol. VI, chap. x below.

[2] For a fuller treatment of the subject of early village festivals and their development, from the point of view both of the student of folk-lore and the historian of the stage, see Chambers, vol. I, pp. 89 ff.

[3] Ten Brink, *History of English Literature*, vol. I, p. 148; Chambers, vol. I, p. 26.

[4] *Ante*, vol. I, pp. 360—1.

[5] Chambers and Sidgwick, *Early English Lyrics.*

the same seed of drama which grew in Greece to the pre-Aeschylean tragedy, with its protagonist and chorus, but had no corresponding development in England.

The influence, or the remnants, of *cantilenae* may, indeed, be traced in certain later growths, like the mummers' play and the Hock-Tuesday play, to which we shall return; but folk-song, either heroic or pastoral, may be held to have been practically without effect on the main stream of English drama. A more valid influence is to be traced from the dances, combats and ritual actions of village-festivals. Writers on folk-lore point out that such games as football and hockey descend from the struggles for the possession of the head of the sacrificial victim, and the tradition still survives in special varieties, such as the 'Haxey-hood' contest at Haxey in Lincolnshire. They point out, also, that disguise has its origin in the clothing of leaves and flowers or of the skin or head of the sacrificed animal, with which the worshipper made himself 'a garment of the god,' thus bringing himself into the closest possible contact with the spirit of fertilisation. The maypole, which was a common feature of every green in England till the Rebellion, and enjoyed a shadow of its former glory after the Restoration, stands for the sacred tree, and the dance round it for the ritual dance of the pagan worshipper, just as some children's games, like 'Oranges and Lemons,' enshrine the memory of the sacrifice and of the succeeding struggle for possession of the victim's head. In some instances, folk-observances have grown into something like plays, or have affected plays drawn from other sources; and of these a few words must now be said.

In the form in which its scanty remnants have reached us, the folk-play has mainly been affected by humanist learning through the hands of the local scholar. A play—at least a performance consisting of 'actionz and rymez'—which appears to have comparatively or entirely escaped that kind of improvement, was the 'olld storiall sheaw' of the Hock-Tuesday play at Coventry. Our knowledge of it is chiefly derived from the description in Robert Laneham's letter to his friend Humfrey Martin, mercer, of London, describing the festivities before Elizabeth at Kenilworth in 1575, during which the play was revived[1]. We there read that it was 'for pastime woont too bee plaid yeerely'; that it

had an auncient beginning, and a long continuauns: tyll noow of late laid dooun, they knu no cauz why, onless it wear by the zeal of certain theyr Preacherz.

---

[1] Reprinted by Furnivall for the Ballad Society in 1871. The reprint, with additional notes, is included in *The Shakespeare Library*, 1908. See pp. 26—28, 31, 32, of that edition.

Its argument, according to Laneham, was: how the English under Huna defeated the Danes and rid the realm of them in the reign of Ethelred on St Brice's night (13 November 1002—he gives the date in error as 1012). Rous[1] ascribed to it another origin, the sudden death of Hardicanute, and the suspicion of his having been poisoned at a wedding, together with the delivery of England from the Danes at the accession of Edward the Confessor in 1042. Both explanations are held by some to be later substitutes for the real origin, which, in their opinion, was the immemorial folk-custom of obtaining by force a victim for the sacrifice. Hocktide—the Monday and Tuesday after the second Sunday after Easter—has parallel customs in other parts of the country, in which the women 'hocked' the men (caught and bound them with ropes), or *vice versa*, or strangers or natives were whipped or 'heaved.' Women acted prominently on the offensive in these customs, and they did the same in the Hock-Tuesday Coventry play. First of all, the Danish 'launsknights' and the English, armed with alder poles, entered on horseback and fought together; then followed the foot and, after manoeuvring, engaged.

Twise the Danes had the better; but at the last conflict, beaten doun, overcom, and many led captive for triumph by our English wéemen.

It is possible that the combat for the victim's head referred to above may have had some influence on the game; and the evolutions of the footsoldiers in ranks, squadrons, triangles, 'from that intoo rings, and so winding oout again' may be connected with the sword-dance, mentioned below. It seems clear, however, that this was a genuine folk-play; and it is suggested[2] that 'the rymez' had been worked up from local *cantilenae* of the folk. The Hock-Tuesday play, as we have seen, was only a revival in the early days of Elizabeth, and it is not heard of afterwards.

Another folk-custom, out of which grew a play of more importance than the Hock-Tuesday play, was the sword-dance. This dance seems to have had its ritual origin in the primitive expulsion of Death or Winter, the death and resurrection of Summer, or in that conflict between Winter and Summer which, on the literary side, was also the origin of many *débats* and *estrifs.* It was, moreover, a natural mode of play for warlike peoples. Like all dancing, it became mimetic in character. Its chief personages are the fool, who wears the skin of a fox or some other animal, and the 'Bessy,' a man dressed in woman's clothes—figures

[1] *Historia Regum Angliae* (1716), pp. 105, 106.
[2] Chambers, vol. II, p. 155.

in which folk-lore finds the survival of the ritual of agricultural worship. One of its off-shoots in England is held to be the morris-dance, which, however, in Robin Hood (who sometimes appears) and in Maid Marian (who always does) has drawn to itself features of other celebrations to be mentioned later. The points of interest in the sword-dance, for our present purpose, are its use of rimed speeches to introduce the characters, and its development into the mummers' or St George play, still to be seen in many rural districts of the British Isles.

Some types of sword-dance still or recently extant, mainly in the north of England, have many more characters than the fool or 'Bessy[1].' In one case at least, that of the Shetland dance, they include the 'seven Champions of Christendom.' It is possible that their names only superseded those of earlier national heroes, and that the verses introducing the characters in the dance are, in fact, the remains of the folk *cantilenae* which have been mentioned before. In several of the extant sword-dances in Britain and on the continent, one of the dancers is, in different manners, attacked or killed, or, perhaps, merely symbolically surrounded or approached, with the swords; and this feature, which enshrines the memory of the sacrifice, becomes the principal point of action in the mummers' or St George plays which developed from the sword-dance. In these, the dance has developed into a play. Amid a bewildering variety of nomenclature and detail, the invariable incident of the death and restoration to life of one of the characters is the point upon which has been based the descent of this play from pagan festivals celebrating the death and resurrection of the year. The fact that this play is nowadays usually performed at Christmas-time is largely due to a well-known shifting of the seasons of festivals, due to the fixing of the Christian ecclesiastical feasts.

Analysis of the many varieties known would extend this chapter unduly[2], and it must be our task rather to point out what is common to all. A transition stage between the sword-dance and the play may be noticed in the performance of the 'plow boys or morris dancers' at Revesby in Lincolnshire, probably on Plough Monday (the Monday after Twelfth Night) in the last quarter of the eighteenth century[3], and several Plough Monday performances in the eastern midlands. These have retained their original season—that of the resumption of

---

[1] The motley crew are collected by Chambers, vol. II, pp. 193, 194.
[2] The reader is referred to Chambers, vol. II, pp. 208 ff. and to Ordish.
[3] Printed by Manly, *Specimens of the Pre-Shakespearean Drama*, vol. I, p. 296.

agricultural work after winter, and they are entirely unaffected by heroic influences. In both, the characters are the traditional grotesques of village festivals—the fool and the Hobby-horse, who represent worshippers disguised in skins of beasts, and the 'Bessy,' the woman or man dressed in woman's clothes. The latter custom is recorded as obtaining among the Germans by Tacitus. Some of the eastern midlands performances introduce farm-labourers. In both there is much dancing; at Revesby, the fool, and, in the eastern midlands the old woman, Dame Jane, are killed and brought to life again.

The mummers' plays show another stage of advance. In them, the central incident is still the killing and restoring to life of one of the characters, and there is still enough dancing to show their descent from the sword-dance. First, the characters are introduced in a speech; then comes the drama, in which each personage has his own introductory announcement; and the whole winds up with the entrance of subsidiary characters, more dancing and the inevitable collection—in itself a survival of hoary antiquity. The old grotesques of the village festival are mainly relegated to the third part of the performance; and the principal characters, presented under almost infinite variety of manner and style, are a hero, his chief opponent and the (usually comic) doctor. The hero sometimes kills and sometimes is killed by his opponent; in either case, the doctor comes to restore the dead man to life. The name of the hero is almost always saint, king, or prince George; the chief opponent is divisible into two types: the Turkish knight, who sometimes has a black face, and a kind of *capitano* or blustering Bobadill. There is also a large variety of subsidiary fighters. The grotesques of the sword-dance, now pushed away into the third part of the performance, include such figures as the fool, or the Beelzebub, who, perhaps, are the same person under different names, the 'Bessy' and the Hobby-horse. Sometimes, these figures are allowed a subordinate position in the drama itself.

The presence of St George (for king and prince George may be regarded as Hanoverian 'improvements') implies the influence of heroic legend and literature. It is very seldom that anything more than a passing reference to the exploits of the saint is found in the mummers' play; and, though the dragon appears here and there, the contest with him is never the main point of the action. How St George came into the story at all is a matter of some obscurity. He was, undoubtedly, the patron saint of England.

His day, 23 April, was a day on which processions or 'ridings' in his honour—in which the representations of his defeat of the dragon had replaced, perhaps, the earlier subject of the victory of summer over winter—were organised by the guilds of St George in many parts of England. These 'ridings,' which lasted even as late as the eighteenth century[1], were dumb shows or pageants rather than plays; but cases are known[2] of religious dramas on the subject. It is possible that the sword-dance, in its development into the mummers' play, was influenced by these 'ridings' and by the miracle-plays. On the other hand, the name of St George may have come into them by way of Richard Johnson's *History of the Seven Champions*, first published in 1596—7. In either case, the introduction of this character has modified the popular *cantilenae* which formed the basis of the rude dialogue accompanying the symbolical representation.

Another instance of folk-festivals turned into plays and modified by the introduction of principal characters of later date is the development of the May-game into the Robin Hood play. From the earliest times, dance and song had celebrated the coming of spring; and we have seen the elements of drama in the amoebaean form of the *reverdies* as well as in the use of the *cantilenae*. In France, a direct descent can be traced from the *chansons* of the folk to the plays of Adam de la Halle; the lack of English folk-song makes a corresponding deduction impossible with regard to English drama. But it is known that, both in spring or summer and in autumn, a 'king,' or 'queen,' or both, were appointed leaders of the revel; and the May-game—the 'Whitsun Pastorals' to which Perdita in *The Winter's Tale* (act IV, sc. 4) likens her play with the flowers—was protested against by the clergy as early as the thirteenth century.

The influence of the May-game on the drama may be traced in such plays as *The Winter's Tale*, Chapman's *May Day* and Jonson's *Sad Shepherd*; but it achieves its highest importance through an impetus towards the dramatic form derived from the minstrels. In France, Robin, as we see from de la Halle's plays, was the type-name of the shepherd lover, and Marion of his mistress. It is suggested[3] that these names were brought to England by French minstrels, and that here, by the sixteenth century, Robin became confused with the Robin Hood (or

---

[1] For a description of the 'riding' at Norwich see Chambers, vol. I, p. 222.
[2] At Lydd and Bassingbourne. See Chambers, Appendix W, vol. II, p. 383.
[3] By Chambers, vol. I, pp. 175, 176.

â-Wood) who first appears in *Piers the Plowman*, but who, perhaps, had, long before this time, been a popular hero of the ballads, his origin being purely fictitious, or, perhaps, nothing less than the personality of Woden himself. Robin becoming Robin Hood, Marion became Maid Marian, who does not appear at all in the earliest ballads; the May-game king and queen were now the central figures of a story, in which subsidiary characters—Friar Tuck, Little John, the sheriff of Nottingham and others—found their places; and the old May-game—probably consisting merely of dances, processional or circular, with the inevitable *quête* or collection, still maintained by small boys who go a-maying in the streets of London—was transformed into the Robin Hood play. The Paston letters[1] mention a servant who played Robin Hood and the sheriff of Nottingham. A fragment of such a play dating from the fifteenth century is extant[2]. And the Garrick collection in the British Museum includes a 'mery geste' of Robin Hood, 'wyth a newe playe for to be played in Maye games' printed about 1561[3]. In Scotland the play of *Robin Hood* survived, in spite of Puritan protest and of legal prohibition, at least till 1578[4]; and in England the new drama was not slow to avail itself of the story. Anthony Munday was writing for Henslowe in February 1598 a *Downfall and Death of Robert Earl of Huntingdon*, 'surnamed Roben hoode[5],' and introduced him again in his pageant, *Metropolis Coronata* (1615). He appeared, also, in Haughton's *Roben hood's penerthes*[6] and other lost plays, as well as in Peele's *Edward I*, Greene's *George a Greene—the Pinner of Wakefield* and the anonymous *Look About You*. After the Restoration, he is to be found in *Robin Hood and his Crew of Soldiers* (1661). At least four other Robin Hood plays or operas are noticed in *Biographia Dramatica*, and a recent production in London proves that the public is not yet tired of the old story. More important, however, than the actual subject is the fact that Robin Hood, whatever his origin, became a national hero, and, as such, was celebrated in the drama. The new national spirit awakened in the days of Elizabeth was destined to extend this narrow field into the spacious domain of the chronicle play.

---

[1] Gairdner's edition, vol. III, p. 89.   [2] Manly, vol. I, p. 279.
[3] Furnivall's *Laneham's Letter*, pp. li, liii, liv.
[4] See Chambers, vol. I, p. 181, vol. II, pp. 335, 336, and references.
[5] Greg's *Henslowe's Diary*, Part I, pp. 83, 84.   [6] *Ibid.* pp. 124, 125.

CHAPTER III

THE EARLY RELIGIOUS DRAMA
MIRACLE-PLAYS AND MORALITIES

THE growth of the medieval religious drama pursued the same course in England as in the other countries of Europe joined together in spiritual unity through the domination of the Roman Catholic church. Everywhere, we may follow the same process, and note how, from about the tenth century, the production in churches of a certain species of alternating songs is combined with a sort of theatrical staging; how, simultaneously with the progress of this staging, the texts of the songs were enlarged by free poetical additions, till, finally, a separation of these stage performances from their original connection with religious service took place, and they were shifted from the church into the open air.

Most of the literary monuments that enable us to reconstruct the gradual rise of the Christian drama are of German or French origin; but England, too, furnishes us with several such monuments representing the earliest stage of the growth in question. One of special importance is *Concordia Regularis*, which contains rules for divine service in English monasteries, and which was composed during the reign of Edgar (959—975). In this, we have the oldest extant example in European literature of the theatrical recital of an alternating song in church. These rules prescribe that, during service in the night before Easter, an alternating song between the three women approaching the grave, and the angel watching on it, shall be recited; the monk who sings the words of the angel is to take his seat, clad in an alb and with a palm-twig in his hand, in a place representing the tomb; three other monks, wearing hooded capes and with censers in their hands, are to approach the tomb at a slow pace, as if in quest of something. This alternating song was composed at St Gallen about the year 900 and was intended to be sung during mass on Easter morning[1]; the statement as to its theatrical

---

[1] The original is as follows:

Quem quaeritis in sepulchro, o Christicolae?
Jesum Nazarenum crucifixum, o caelicolae.
Non est hic, surrexit, sicut praedixerat. Ite, nuntiate, quia surrexit de sepulchro.

production can hardly be a fiction that originated at St Gallen, or Ekkehard, the historian of that monastery, who generally gives detailed reports of such matters, would surely not have failed to mention it. But the custom, undoubtedly, is of continental origin ; in the preface to *Concordia Regularis,* it is expressly stated that customs of outlandish monasteries, such as Fleury-sur-Loire and Ghent, served as models for the present composition; and, in the description of the ceremonies at the place which is to represent the tomb, reference is made to a commendable practice of priests in some monasteries who 'had introduced this custom, in order to fortify the unlearned people in their faith.' These words also reveal to us the original purpose of Christian drama: it was to be a sort of living picture-book ; the people, ignorant of Latin, were to perceive by sight what was inaccessible to the ear. For this reason, also, the tendency to place the whole action visibly before the eyes of the spectator, to leave nothing to be done behind the scenes or told by messengers, prevailed in medieval drama from the very beginning. Thus, the chief difference between ancient classical and modern romantic drama manifests itself in the first stage of medieval drama.

That the theatrical development of Easter celebrations in England did not stop short at this initial stage is proved by several MSS, more especially by one of the fourteenth century, and of Sarum origin, where the scene is enlarged by various additions, including a representation of the race to the tomb run by Peter and John (*St John* xx, 4). Nor can it be doubted that, in England as on the continent, a drama on Christ's birth and childhood gradually shaped itself out of the Christmas service, where the dramatic development likewise began with an alternating song ; thus, *e.g.,* the tin crowns, mentioned in an inventory of Salisbury cathedral, drawn up in 1222, were evidently for the use of the magi at the crib of Bethlehem.

Another species of Latin church drama consisted of the plays acted by pupils in monastery schools in honour of their patron saints. The younger pupils honoured as their patron St Nicholas, whose cult, after the transportation of his body from Asia Minor to Bari in 1087, spread over all Europe, and of whom legends told how, on one occasion, he restored to life three convent pupils put to death for the sake of their money. The patron of older pupils was St Catharine of Alexandria, who had been victorious in disputes against heathen philosophers. The best evidence of the existence of these plays is, again, furnished from England. About the year 1110, Godefroy of Le Mans, a Frenchman, headmaster of the monastery school at Dunstable, caused his pupils to perform a play on St Catharine; as costumes for the players, he borrowed church robes from the abbey of St Albans, to which the school belonged. As it chanced that, on the following night, these robes were burnt in his lodgings, Godefroy—so Matthew Paris tells us—offered himself in compensation and entered the monastery as a monk. But the most remarkable of all school dramas are those composed by Hilarius, a pupil of Abelard, about 1125. Hilarius, probably, was an Englishman, for a large proportion of his verses are addressed to English persons; at all events, he is the first definite personality in the way of a dramatic author who crosses the student's path. In the collection of his poems, worldly merriment and loose libertinism are apparent, together with all the enchanting melody characteristic of the songs of vagrant clerks. This collection contains three small religious dramas, two of which belong to the Christmas- and Easter-cycles, respectively; the third is a half-humorous play about St Nicholas, who helps a *barbarus* to recover a treasure stolen from him. In this play, the poet intersperses his Latin verses with French.

The often-quoted mention by William Fitzstephen of religious plays in London may also, possibly, relate to performances in Latin. Fitzstephen observes, in his *Life of Thomas Becket* (*c.* 1180), that London, instead of the *spectacula theatralia* acted in Rome, possesses other, holier, plays—representations of miracles wrought by holy confessors, or of the tribulations in which the constancy of martyrs splendidly manifested itself. It is, however, possible that performances in Anglo-Norman are here intended; for we see that in France, too, after the vernacular language had taken possession of the drama, subjects from legends of the saints were preferred to Scriptural themes. It is well worth note that here, for the first time, we hear of dramatised *martyria,* which take a prominent place in the religious *répertoire* of the later Middle Ages. By 'miracles,' it would seem that chiefly those are to be understood which saints wrought after their death, when invoked by their faithful worshippers. In any case, all the miracles produced in the Nicholas plays are of this sort; and, in France, the application of the word 'miracle,' as a theatrical term, continued to be restricted to plays treating of subjects of this kind only; whereas, in England, it assumed a more general meaning. Thus, in the statutes of Lichfield cathedral, *c.* 1190, mention is made of *repraesentatio miraculorum in nocte*

Paschae; and bishop Grosseteste, likewise, seems to use the word in a more general sense, when ordering, in 1244, the suppression of *miracula* in the diocese of Lincoln.

The use of the vernacular as the language of religious drama was not brought about in England by any process analogous to that observable in continental countries. For the normal development of the English language was interrupted by the Norman conquest, in consequence of which the chief offices in bishoprics and abbeys were occupied by men of foreign origin. Thus it happened that the oldest vernacular dramas written in England belong not to English, but to French, literary history : the play of *Adam* and the play of the *Resurrection*, the oldest two dramatic poems in the French language, were, according to general opinion, composed in England in the twelfth century. Only a very small number of dramatic works and accounts of performances have been preserved belonging to the long period which begins with the introduction of the vernacular into medieval drama and ends at the point at which it had reached its height—that is, from about 1200 to 1400—in England, as well as in Germany and France. The material is insufficient for reconstructing the process of growth, and the historian must needs limit his task to that of a mere recorder. Later monuments, however, suffice to indicate how, in this domain too, the native English element regained its superiority. A remarkable document has been discovered recently at Shrewsbury, which shows how, in English literature also, the vernacular drama was prepared by the insertion of vernacular verses in Latin songs. The MS, written in a northern dialect, is not a complete play, but consists of three parts written out in full in both English and Latin, with the respective cues : namely, the part of one of the three Maries at the tomb, the part of a shepherd at Christ's nativity and the part of a disciple on the way to Emmaus. The English words paraphrase the Latin by which they are preceded ; but they are not, like the Latin, provided with musical notes. As the vernacular found its way into Latin texts, declamation simultaneously took its place by the side of song, which, till then, had been the only form in use. Here, we observe a remarkable analogy to the Easter play of Treves, which represents the same transitional stage in the history of the German drama.

The earliest purely English drama known to us (if ten Brink's date be right) was a play on *Jacob and Esau*, now only preserved as part of one of the large collections of mysteries of the fifteenth century, the *Towneley Mysteries*, where it is distinguished from its surroundings by its short, detached manner of representing facts, as well as by the simplicity of its versification (short riming couplets). It is possible that this play, in its original connection, belonged to a series of prophetical plays: that is to say, plays in which some of the chief passages from Old Testament history are selected in chronological order, and which were produced in the Christmas season, with the intention of showing forth the birth of Christ as the fulfilment and conclusion of the whole process of historical evolution preceding it.

Hereupon, however, the tendency manifested itself to compose in English, too, legendary narratives of miracles, besides Bible stories. We met with early instances of this in the period immediately after the Norman conquest ; and the custom was specially fostered by the increasing cult of the Virgin Mary in the Roman Catholic church. Ever since the great religious movement of the eleventh century, we find in all European literatures a multitude of miraculous stories, which relate how those who devote themselves to the service of Mary are aided by her in seasons of oppression and peril, and how her protection is not denied even to wrongdoers and criminals, if they but show her the reverence which is her due. Dramatic handlings of the miracles of Mary are particularly frequent in French literature, where an example occurs so far back as the thirteenth century; and, in a MS dating from the beginning of the fifteenth century, no less than forty of these plays are preserved. Events which have, originally, nothing to do with the legend of Mary are here, also, represented in dramatic form : thus, for instance, the story of Bertha, mother of Charlemagne, is fitted into this cycle by the single link of the heroine's losing her way in a wood, where the Mother of God appears to her and consoles her. Such plays were probably known and popular in England also, though only one possible specimen of this group is now extant. In a parchment roll of the fourteenth century, a single part belonging to a drama in the east midland dialect has been preserved : that of a duke Moraud. It is still recognisable that this drama was based on a story widely spread in medieval literature : that of a daughter who lived in incest with her father and, to keep the crime secret, murdered her child and her mother ; whereupon, the father repenting of his sin, she murdered him also, but, shortly afterwards, fell herself into a state of deep contrition, confessed her crimes with tears and died a repentant sinner. This story was certainly quite suitable for dramatic treatment after the manner of the miracles of Mary; though this cannot be said to be satisfactorily proved by the one part preserved, that of the father. From the first words, addressed by the duke to the spectators, we learn that the play was produced for payment, within an enclosed space ('fold')—whether by the members of some brotherhood, as was usually the case with French miracles, is not evident.

A remarkable proof of the widespread popularity of religious plays at this period is furnished by the *Manuel des Pechiez* by William of Wadington, composed, probably, about the end of the thirteenth century, and translated into English out of the author's clumsy Anglo-Norman as early as 1303. William of Wadington finds no fault with the representation in churches of Christ's burial and resurrection, for this promotes piety; but he most energetically censures the foolish clergy who, dressed up in masks and provided with borrowed horses and armour, perform in the streets and churchyards plays of the sort generally called miracles. About the beginning of the thirteenth century we meet with an account of such a performance in St John's churchyard at Beverley, where the resurrection, 'according to traditional custom, was acted in word and gesture by people in disguise.' The performance, perhaps, took place in English; at least, we are told that boys climbed up into the triforium gallery of the church, in order better to see the action and hear the dialogue from the height of the windows; on which occasion, one boy fell down into the church and was saved by a miracle. A poem on Christ's descent to hell, from the middle of the thirteenth century (*The Harrowing of Hell*), which has often been called the oldest English drama, does not, in reality, belong to this species; it is, for the most part, in dialogue; but, in the beginning, the author says: 'A strif will I tellen on, Of Jesu and of Satan'; and, at the end, he likewise speaks in his own person. Evidently, the poem was intended to be delivered, with changes of voice, by a professional reciter—an art that had been brought to great perfection by the wandering *jongleurs*.

From the last period of the Middle Ages—otherwise than for the thirteenth and fourteenth centuries—we have an abundance of texts and documentary statements. We can perceive how, at this time, in England, just as in Germany and France, the great advance of town life caused religious drama likewise to progress with increasing vigour, the plays constantly assuming larger dimensions. Historians of literature, from Dodsley onwards, usually call these large dramas of the late Middle Ages by the name, given them in France, 'mysteries'; whereas, in England, the simple word 'play' was generally used. The treatment of facts from Bible story is much the same in England and in other countries; additions, intended either to adorn the argument poetically or to furnish the actions of the *dramatis personae* with a psychological foundation, are here, as elsewhere, not of the author's own invention, but are taken over from ecclesiastical literature, for the most part from the works of contemplative theologians absorbed in meditation on the work of salvation, the passion, the pains of the Blessed Virgin, or from the sermons of enthusiastic preachers, whose brilliant imagination, in its lofty flight, brought before their audience all the different stages of our Lord's life and passion.

Thus, in the *York Mysteries*, use is made of one of the most famous works of contemplative literature, the *Meditations of St Bonaventura*; from this source, for instance, are borrowed the following details: Joseph, at Christ's birth, observes how the ox and the ass press close to the crib in which the Child lies, in order to protect it by their warm breath from the cold; and Mary adores the new-born as Father and Son. Some decorative additions, too, can be traced back to the works of medieval Bible commentators—above all, to the most erudite and famous work of this sort, the *Postilla* of Nicholas of Lyra. The appearance of Mary Magdalene, for instance, in the mystery called by her name, surrounded by the seven deadly sins, is founded on Lyra's interpretation of the words in the *Gospel of St Mark* (xvi, 9) as to the seven devils driven out of her by Jesus. When the *Gospel of St John* tells us (viii, 7) how Christ, after the adulteress had been brought before Him, wrote something with His finger on the ground, but, during the writing, looked up and said to the scribes : 'He that is without sin among you, let him first cast a stone at her,' whereat the scribes went away one after another, Lyra explains that Christ had written the secret sins of the scribes in the sand ; and this explanation is followed by the authors of the mysteries. Some additions, again, are from the apocryphal Gospels. Thus, for instance, in the *York Mysteries*, the standards in Pilate's house bow of themselves at the entrance of Christ. In this way, many agreements between French and English plays can be accounted for, which used to be wrongly explained by the supposition that English poets had used French models ; as a matter of fact, these coincidences are either accidental or due to the identity of intellectual aliment and conformity of religious thought throughout the whole of society in the Middle Ages. Only in the case of several purely theatrical effects can it be supposed that they came over from France, where the art of stage management was more developed than anywhere else.

On the whole, however, in considering these mysteries, we cannot escape the impression that, neither in Germany nor in France and England, were the later Middle Ages a period of great poetical splendour. True, in England, authors of mysteries attach a great value to artistic metrical form ; so early as the miracle of duke Moraud, manifold and complicated forms of stanzas are used; but this is an artistic embellishment which is not necessarily advantageous to the vivid interchange of dramatic speech. It would, however, be unjust to judge these plays altogether from a literary standard. The authors, apparently, had scarcely any other intention than, by recasting traditional materials from their narrative form into a dramatic mould, to make concrete representation possible ; they had but little thought of their productions as procuring literary enjoyment by reading. Only once is any reference made in any English play to a reader : namely, in a play on the lowering of Christ from the cross, intended for performance on Good Friday and, therefore, preserving a more severe style. It was composed about the middle of the fifteenth century ; but, in the MS, which dates from the beginning of the sixteenth century, the play is preceded by a prologue, exhorting pious souls to read the tract ensuing. It is equally characteristic that, in England, during the whole of this period, no authors of religious dramas are known by name, and that not a single play appears to have been printed.

In England, as everywhere, it is in comic scenes that writers of mysteries are most original. Here, of course, they could not borrow anything from theological authors, and they moved in a domain much more appropriate to the spirit of the later Middle Ages than the tragical. If, in the fragmentary remains of the English religious drama of earlier times, the element of burlesque is entirely missing, this, assuredly, can be nothing else than mere accident ; the mingling of comic with tragic elements, which is characteristic of the romanticism of the medieval drama, must, beyond doubt, here as elsewhere, have been accomplished at a period when Latin was still the language, and the church the place, of these performances ; the protests of some rigorous moralists against religious drama, mentioned above, are, unmistakably, to be explained in the main, in England as well as in other countries, by this intrusion of the comic element. Some comic effects in English mysteries belong to the common and international stock of literary property : such, for instance, as the merry devil Tutivillus or Titinillus, whose special task it is to watch and denounce women who talk in church. Another comic *intermezzo*, a grotesque dance, performed by the Jews, with accompaniment of music, round the cross on which Christ hangs, is to be met with not only in the *Coventry Mysteries*, but, likewise, in some German mystery plays. Other comic devices, chiefly in the Mary Magdalene mysteries and some of those in the shepherds' scenes of the Christmas plays, seem to be borrowed from France. But, besides these, in England as well as in other countries, it is precisely in comic scenes that national traditions were developed. A scene especially characteristic of English mysteries is the quarrel between Noah and his shrewish wife, who obstinately opposes her husband's will when he is about to take the whole family into the newly built ark.

The performance of one of these mysteries was a serious undertaking, requiring long preparation and considerable expense. On the continent, the stage for performances was generally erected in a large open square, and on the stage were represented, one beside the other, the places of action—thus, in a passion play, the garden of Gethsemane, the praetorium of Pilate, the hill of Calvary, the entrance to hell. The personages moved from one place to the next before the eyes of the spectators ; if the performance, as was more frequently the case, lasted for several days together, change of scenery was possible. Such monster productions were known in London in the time of Richard II; thus, in 1384, the 'clerks' of London gave a *ludus valde sumptuosus* at Skinnerswell, which lasted five days ; in 1391, one, of four days, on the Old and New Testaments; then, again, in 1409, in the presence of Henry IV, one lasting four days, comprising events from the creation of the world to the last judgment. For such a stage arrangement, the play of *Mary Magdalene*, preserved in the Digby MS, was, likewise, intended, and, undoubtedly, many other English mysteries of whose existence only documentary evidence survives. But, in the majority of texts and accounts of performances handed down to us, we find a different sort of *mise-en-scène* adopted, in accordance with national custom and preference.

The usual method of treatment developed, not like that mentioned above, from liturgical scenes performed within churches, but from the procession on Corpus Christi day. In 1264, the feast of Corpus Christi was instituted ; this soon grew into a solemnity in the celebration of which the church displayed her highest splendour. The Corpus Christi procession was a sort of triumphal progress, by which the church, after centuries of struggle, solemnised her absolute and full victory over the minds of men, and by which, at the same time, she satisfied the perennial inclination of the people for disguisings and festal shows. Very soon it became customary for groups to walk in the Corpus Christi procession, which groups, in their succession, were to typify the whole ecclesiastical conception of universal history from the creation to the judgment day. It was a frequent practice to distribute the arrangement of these groups among the different crafts, which always made it a point of ambition to be represented in the procession as splendidly as possible. In some countries, these processions assumed a dramatic character, especially in England, where the processional drama was fully developed as early as the fourteenth century. Here, it was customary for each of the crafts presenting a certain group to explain its significance in a dramatic scene. The different scenes, whenever possible, were distributed in such a way as to bear some relation to the occupation of the craft that performed it: *e.g.*, the task of producing Noah's ark was entrusted to the boat-builders, the adoration of the magi to the goldsmiths. The actors stood on a stage ('pageant'), moving about on wheels. In the course of the procession, a certain number of stations was appointed, at which the several pageants stopped in passing, and on which the respective scenes were performed. For instance, the first craft at the first station acted the creation of the world; then it passed to the place where it stopped for the second time, and repeated the performance; at the same time, the second craft acted at the first station the sin of our first parents, and afterwards repeated the same at the second station. In the meantime, the first craft had proceeded to the third station, and the third craft began at the first station to act the play of Cain and Abel. If, in such a processional play, one character appeared in several scenes, it was, necessarily, represented by different persons : Christ on the Mount of Olives was a different individual from Christ before Pilate or on Golgotha. As early as 1377, Corpus Christi plays are mentioned at Beverley; and, in 1394, this system of plays is spoken of in an ordinance of the municipality of York, as of old tradition. The earliest documentary mention of them in this city dates from the year 1378.

By this stage arrangement, every drama was divided into

a series of little plays. The progress of the action was, necessarily, interrupted as one pageant rolled away and another approached; on each occasion, order had to be kept, and the attention of the multitude crowding the streets had to be attracted anew. The function of calling the people to order was, wherever feasible, entrusted to a tyrant, say Herod, the murderer of the Innocents, or Pilate, who, dressed up grotesquely and armed with a resounding sword, raged about among the audience and imposed silence on the disturbers of peace. Repetitions, also, frequently became necessary, in order to take up again the broken thread of action; on the other hand, authors could not give way so freely to an easy flow of speech as in 'standing plays' (plays performed in one fixed place, so called in contrast with processional plays).

Of such processional plays, three complete, or almost complete, cycles have been handed down to us—those of York, Wakefield and Chester. Besides these, we possess single plays from the cycles of Coventry, Newcastle-upon-Tyne and Norwich; two fifteenth century plays of Abraham and Isaac are also, probably, to be considered as originally forming part of a cycle. Of the collective mysteries, none is uniform in character; in all of them may be distinguished, besides older parts, sundry later additions, omissions and transpositions; and a comparison of the collections with each other reveals mutual agreements as to whole scenes as well as to single stanzas. Nevertheless, each cycle has distinguishing qualities and a pronounced character of its own. The York series, preserved in a fifteenth century MS and consisting of forty-nine single plays (inclusive of the Innholders' fragment), is notable for many original features in the representation of the passion. Tyrants, especially, and the enemies of our Lord, are depicted with powerful realism: Annas, for example, shows a grim joy at holding the defenceless victim in his power, but then falls into a violent passion at what he takes to be that victim's obduracy; he says, 'we myght as wele talke tille a tome tonne'; he even attempts to strike Jesus, but Caiaphas holds him back. When Herod addresses Jesus in a jumble of French and Latin, and Jesus gives no answer, the bystanders think He is afraid of the boisterous tyrant. But, above all, the figure of Judas is represented in a way more dramatic and more impressive than in any other medieval mystery, both in the scene where he offers his services as betrayer, and in another where, in an agony of remorse, he implores the high priest to take back the money and spare Jesus. He is coldly refused, and, when he grows more and

more violently importunate, Caiaphas bids him be off, or he will
be taught how to behave to his betters.

The so-called *Towneley Mysteries* are preserved in a MS of
the second half of the fifteenth century, and consist of thirty-two
plays. They were, probably, intended to be produced by the
crafts of Wakefield town, and it seems that, in this case, they were
not played on movable scenes but on fixed stages erected along
the route of the procession, so that the actors did not go to
the spectators, but *vice versa*. The characteristic feature of this
collection is a certain realistic buoyancy and, above all, the
abundant display of a very robust kind of humour. Thus, the
merry devil Tutivillus has found access into the last judgment
scene (which, otherwise, is in accordance with the corresponding
play in the York collection); the family quarrels in Noah's household are nowhere else depicted so realistically; and, in the shepherds'
Christmas Eve scenes, the adventures of Mak the sheep-stealer
take the foremost place. But the most grotesque figure of all
is certainly Cain, who appears as the very type of a coarse and
unmannerly rustic. According to medieval tradition, the reason
why the Lord did not look graciously upon Cain's offering was
that Cain offered it unwillingly; and thence grew the commonplace
of church literature, that Cain was the prototype of stingy
peasants who tried to evade the obligation of paying tithes to the
priests. Though moral teaching does not play a great part in
mysteries, clerical authors repeatedly made use of the occasion
to impress the payment of tithe upon peasants as an important
moral duty; and nowhere is this done with so palpable a directness
as here. Cain selects sixteen sheaves for his offering, and, in doing
so, he feels more and more heavy at heart, until, instead of sixteen,
he gives but two. And when, after the ungracious reception of
his offering, he swears and curses, the Lord Himself appears and
says that the recompense for the offering will be exactly according
as Cain delivers his tithes in a right or in a wrong proportion.
After this long-drawn-out scene, the murder of the brother is
treated quite shortly, almost *en bagatelle*. Joseph, who, in the
York Plays, was described with evident tenderness, here has a
few humorous features. After receiving the order for the flight
to Egypt, he complains of the troubles that marriage has brought
upon him, and warns the young people in his audience not to
marry. Again, the boisterous tone of the tyrants is in this drama
accentuated with particular zest.

Of the *Chester Plays* (twenty-five parts), five complete MSS from the period between 1591 and 1607 have been preserved. They were doubtless intended for representation on perambulating pageants. It might seem astonishing that the performance used to take place at Whitsuntide, not on Corpus Christi day; however, this is not unexampled; at Norwich, for instance, processional plays were acted on Whit Sunday, at Lincoln on St Anne's day (26 July). But, besides this, the stage arrangement here has several peculiarities of its own. Dramatic life is not so fully developed as in other processional plays; the *Chester Plays*, in fact, remind us of the medieval German processional plays of Zerbst and Künzelsau, from which we still may see how the procession gradually assumed a dramatic character. As in these, there appears in the *Chester Plays* an 'expositor,' who intervenes between actors and audience; instead, however, of his place being with the rest of the actors on the stage vehicle, he accompanies them on horseback. He declares expressly that he is about to explain to the unlearned among his audience the connection and the deeper meaning of the performances; he joins moral reflections to the actions represented; sometimes, he supplies a narrative of events passed over in the plays. The contents of several scenes are chiefly instructive or didactic, such as the offering of bread and wine by Melchizedek, or the prophecies of Ezekiel, Zechariah, Daniel and St John concerning the end of the world. The traditional humorous figures of Noah's wife, and of the shepherds on Christmas Eve, are still kept up; but, generally speaking, the original purpose of these processions, namely, a representation of the ecclesiastical history of the world in its chief passages, appears more plainly here than in the *York* and *Wakefield Plays*, which, for the sake of what was theatrically effective, almost entirely neglected the original instructive element. It may be further noted that, at Chester, processional plays were not all acted consecutively on a single day, the performance being spread over Whit Monday and the two following days of the week.

A collection of plays standing altogether apart is preserved in a MS of 1468, with the much later title *Ludus Coventriae*; whence they are generally known as *Coventry Plays*. Their Coventry origin is a matter of doubt on the ground of their language, and the collection has certainly nothing whatever to do with the Corpus Christi plays of the Coventry crafts (preserved in fragments), which were of high fame in the fifteenth century and were several times honoured by the presence of English kings. Where and how this text was performed is quite unknown. It is preceded by a prologue, in which the stanzas are recited alternately by three standard-bearers (*vexillatores*) and contain an invitation to witness the performance to be given on the following Sunday at some town unnamed. According to this prologue, the play is to consist of forty pageants; but, to this, the divisions of the text fail to correspond. Evidently, we have before us no processional, but a 'standing' play, made up of elements originally not forming a whole; nevertheless, this is the only text that does not show any verbal correspondences with other collected mysteries. By their didactic spirit, the *Coventry Plays* are allied to the *Chester Plays*; in the former, too, we have an intermediary between actors and public, who appears in a doctor's robes under the name *Contemplacio*. The text of the plays is overcharged with curiosities of medieval theology; when, for example, Mary, three years old, mounts the fifteen steps of the Temple, the priest allegorically explains these steps as the way from Babylon to the heavenly Jerusalem. But, even here, a realistic tendency is not altogether absent; as, for instance, when the author dramatises the events of the apocryphal *Gospel of pseudo-Matthew*, where Mary is brought into court for suspected infidelity; in the history of the adulteress, too, occur some very realistic additions. The soldiers at Christ's tomb are depicted with admirable humour.

Dramas from legends of the saints, performances of which are mentioned in English deeds and chronicles—for example, those of St Laurence, St Botolph, St George, St Christina—were, probably, of a character analogous to the numerous medieval dramas of this kind that have been preserved in other countries, especially in France. At least, the single English play preserved that is based on a saint's legend, that of *Mary Magdalene* (about 1500), as has been noticed before, decidedly exhibits reminiscences of the French manner. It consists of 2144 lines, about one-half of which are filled with events of the saint's life until the resurrection; then follows the legend of her stay in Provence, where she converts the heathen king of Marseilles by her sermons and miracles. The comic element is represented by a priest at the king's court and his impudent acolyte, who says a burlesque service before the priest bids all present pray to 'Mahownde.' A short play (of 927 lines), on the profanation of a consecrated host by the Jews, is to be classed with miracle-plays; in the end, the evil-doers are converted and baptised. In this class, we may also include a lost play on king Robert of Sicily. It is based on a story, from *Gesta Romanorum*, of a monarch who, for his over-proud consciousness of power, is punished by an angel assuming his shape and dignity, while he is in his bath. This play was acted at Lincoln in 1453; on the occasion of a performance of *Kynge Robert of Cicylye* at Chester, in 1529, we learn, from a letter addressed from that town to a gentleman in the royal court, that the piece was 'penned by a godly clerke' and had been previously acted, in the reign of Henry VII; evidently, under Henry VIII, a play was no longer thought quite unobjectionable in which a frank lesson was given to the great ones of this world.

Finally, three plays from the later Middle Ages must be mentioned which remind us of the simpler dramatic forms of past ages. Of one of these, the first part was designed for performance on Good Friday afternoon, the second for Easter morning; the first contains lengthy complaints of the Virgin Mary, such as also occur in other countries in the Good Friday service; here, the author could make the most ample use of the extant contemplative literature. In the second part, the complaints of the repentant Peter occupy much space. For performance on St Anne's day (26 July), a play was written which comprises the murder of the Innocents and the purification of Mary; the poet, who offers excuses himself for his 'sympyll cunning,' apprises us that, in the foregoing year, the adoration of the shepherds and the magi had been produced, and that the dispute in the temple was to be presented in the year following; and a comic personage, the messenger of Herod, mars with his stale jests the tragical scene of the murder of the Innocents. Similar in style is a play on the conversion of Paul the apostle.

That the production of mysteries was a pious and godly work, so long as humour did not enter into them too largely, seems, in the period during which this species of plays flourished, to have been as little doubted in England as in other countries. It was believed that men were effectually deterred from sin if the punishment of it by the devil was shown forth in a play; that, by the bodily representation of the sufferings of Christ and the saints, spectators could be moved to tears of pity, and, in this way, become possessed of the *gratia lacrimarum*, to which medieval ascetics attached a great value. And, besides, they thought that it was very useful for common folk to see the events of sacred history thus bodily and visually presented before them and that, since occasional relaxation was a common need, religious plays were indisputably better than many other diversions. A singular exception to this universal opinion occurs in an English tract, composed towards the end of the fourteenth century, and evidently connected with the Wyclifite movement[1]. The author of this tract points out that, by the mysteries, people are drawn away from more precious works of love and repentance, and allows no moral value to the tears of spectators of the passion, since Christ Himself blamed the women who wept for Him. In several points, the author's ideas already resemble the later puritan opposition to the stage.

The religious dramas hitherto discussed were chiefly designed to serve the purpose of visibly representing the facts of Scripture; but, in the later Middle Ages, there grew up another kind of dramatic poetry with a moralising, didactic tendency; the *dramatis personae* were now, altogether or for the most part, personified abstractions. This species is also international; in France, it was called *moralité*, and, accordingly, in England, literary historians generally use the name of 'morality' for a play of this class, whereas, anciently, they were called 'moral plays' or 'moral interludes.' The theme running through all these plays is the contention between the personified good and bad powers of the soul for the possession of man: a subject first dealt with in Christian literature about the year 400 by Prudentius in his allegorical epic *Psychomachia*, where the great battle between virtues and vices is, like a Homeric combat, broken up into a series of single fights between *Ira* and *Patientia*, *Superbia* and *Humilitas*, *Libido* and *Pudicitia*, and so forth. Prudentius was one of the authors most frequently read in schools during the Middle Ages, and the main subject of his poem was sundry times imitated; so, in the *Vision of Piers the Plowman*, where the combat is imagined as the siege of a castle in which man and Christianity are shut up. In all these imitations, man, as the object of battle, takes a more prominent place than with Prudentius.

But it was only at a comparatively late date that the contention between the good and the bad powers of the soul was put into dramatic form: no instances are to be found earlier than the last decades of the fourteenth century. About this time, a brotherhood existed at York, formed for the express purpose of producing the Pater Noster play. Wyclif[2] tells us, that this was 'a play setting forth the goodness of our Lord's Prayer, in which play all manner of vices and sins were held up to scorn, and the virtues were held up to praise.' It would seem that this

---

[1] Cf. vol. vi, chap. xiv.   [2] *De officio pastorali*, cap. 15.

play was founded on an idea in medieval moralising literature, according to which each of the seven supplications of the Pater Noster contained a means of protection against one of the seven deadly sins; and the correctness of this supposition is attested by the fact that one of the plays acted by the York brotherhood had the title *Ludus Accidiae* ('a play of sloth'). Most probably, this play belonged to the species of moralities; and we may form the same conclusion as to a play on the Creed, which, from 1446, was acted every ten years by the Corpus Christi brotherhood at York. But, from the fifteenth century, we possess English and French examples fully revealing to us the character of the new species.

Probably from about the middle of this century date three moralities, which are handed down together in one MS, all three of which represent the allegorical combat for the soul of man. In *The Castle of Perseverance, Humanum Genus,* the representative of mankind, is introduced first as a child, finally as an old man; in youthful age, he falls into the power of the mortal sin *Luxuria,* but is brought by *Poenitentia* to trust himself to *Confessio,* who leads him to the castle of perseverance, visible in the centre of the circular scene; the assault of the vices against the castle is victoriously foiled. But, in his old days, *Humanum Genus* succumbs to the temptations of *Avaritia*; so, after his death, the evil angel claims the right to drag him into hell, but he is set free by God at the prayers of Pity and Peace. In the morality *Mankynd,* there are numerous additions of a rough kind of humour. The chief representative of the evil principle is our old acquaintance, the merry devil Tutivillus, who begins the work of temptation by stealing from man his implement of work, a spade. In the morality to which modern editors give the title *Mind, Will and Understanding,* there reigns more of the subtle scholastic spirit; here, it is not a single representative of humanity who is courted by allegorical figures, but the three mental faculties which give the piece its title appear, each one by itself. Besides them, *Anima* appears as a distinct character, first in a white robe, then, after the three faculties of the soul have been tempted astray, 'in a most horrible guise, uglier than a devil.' Another fragment of a morality has been preserved, to which the title *The Pride of Life* has been given; the MS seems to belong to the first half of the fifteenth century; here, the typical representative of humanity is a king who, putting full trust in his knights, Strength and Health, will not think of death and things beyond the grave, although his queen and a pious bishop try to

move his conscience; he considers that he still has time to turn
pious, the church will not run away from him. As appears from
the prologue, the portion of the play which is lost was to show how
the king, in the fulness of his sin, is called away by death, and
how devils are about to take his soul; but, at this point, the
Mother of God was to intercede with her prayers and to point
out to the Judge of the world that the body, not the soul,
was the really guilty part. Thus, it was intended to weave into
the texture of the play one of those debates between body and
soul that had been a widely popular subject in medieval
literature.

The most famous, however, among all these moralities is
Every-man, whose date of composition cannot be defined precisely;
we only know that the earliest printed editions, both undated,
must belong to the period between 1509 and 1530; but so
early as 1495 a Dutch translation was printed[1]. *Every-man* treats,
in allegorical style, of the hour of death, and thus deals with a
sphere of ideas which, in the devotional literature of the later
Middle Ages, is one of the main subjects; the most famous
book of that sort, *Ars moriendi*, was published in an English
translation by Caxton in 1491. The poet endeavoured to give
dramatic animation to his subject by making use of a parable
which is told in the legend of *Barlaam and Josaphat*: how a man
had three friends, of whom one only declared himself ready to
accompany him before the throne of the judge before whom he is
summoned. This friend symbolises a man's good deeds, which
alone accompany him after death before the throne of God and
interpose their prayers for him. The series of scenes—how, first,
Death, as God's summoner, bids man come; how, then, Fellowship, Kindred and others, when asked to bear him company, by
empty phrases talk themselves out of the affair—exercises

---

[1] Some take this Dutch *Elckerlijk* for the original of the English morality; but
de Raaf, who inverts the relation, is, most probably, correct. The most convincing
instance pointed out by him is vv. 778 f., where it appears, beyond doubt, that the
Dutch text must have come from the English. Every-man, after receiving the last
sacraments, says to his fellows:

> Now set eche of you on this rodde your honde
> And shortly folwe me...,

where *Elckerlijk* has (vv. 749 f.):

> Slaet an dit roeyken alle u hant
> Ende volghet mi haestelic na desen.

Here, *roeyken=virga* has been written by a misunderstanding for *rodde=crux*: it is
evident that Every-man-Elckerlijk had in his hand one of those crosses for the dying
which play an important part in the *Ars moriendi* literature.

its impressive power even today, not only in the reading but also on the stage. Only Good-deeds, who lies on the ground fettered by Every-man's sins, declares herself ready to assist him. How Every-man is directed by Good-deeds to Knowledge and Confession, and, finally, leaves the world well prepared, is shown forth in the last part of the play, where the Catholic point of view is insisted on with much unction and force. The comic element disappears almost entirely.

Generally, however, the tendency to give a certain prominence to the comic element grows more and more distinct ; above all, allegorical representatives of the vices are more and more richly endowed with realistic features, especially with local jokes concerning London. This is shown, *e.g.*, in *Nature*, composed by Henry Medwall, chaplain of archbishop Morton of Canterbury (1486— 1500), who is also mentioned in the play. Here, we see how Sensuality drives away Reason from man's side ; how, after all, man is reconciled to Reason by Age ; but how Avarice comes in at the end, and gives the chaplain an opportunity for a bitter attack upon his own profession. In the morality *The World and the Child* (printed 1522), man, the object of strife between allegorical figures, appears, successively, as child, youth and man ; he is persuaded by Folly to lead a dissolute life in London ; nor is it until, reduced to a low state, he quits Newgate prison, that good spirits regain possession of him. Similar in character are the moralities *Hick Scorner* (printed before 1534) and *Youth* (printed 1555), which both seem to date back to the pre-reformation period. So, probably, does the morality *Magnyfycence*[1], the only play by Skelton that has been preserved ; it was not printed till after his death. Here, instead of the usual commonplaces from medieval devotional books, a warning frequently given by classical and humanistic moralists is allegorically represented, namely, that against excessive liberality and false friends. In the same manner, Medwall, if we may trust Collier's account, treated another humanistic commonplace, namely, the persecution of Truth by Ignorance and Hypocrisy, in an interlude acted before Henry VIII at Christmas 1514—15. Skelton and Medwall are the earliest writers of plays in English whose names have been preserved.

As Dodsley justly remarked, the importance of moralities in the development of the drama lies in the fact that here the course of action is not, as with mysteries, prescribed by

---

[1] See vol. III of the present work, chap. IV.

tradition; the individual author's own inventive power is of much greater importance. Besides, otherwise than in the case of mysteries, hearing is more important than seeing. In the stage arrangement of a morality, however, the costume of allegorical characters, the choice of symbolic colours for clothes, the providing of the different figures with emblems illustrating their moral essence, were all matters of first-rate importance. And the greater significance of the spoken word in moralities also accounts for the fact that several of these plays are extant in contemporary prints, which is not the case with any of the mysteries.

Besides the serious drama, in which an admixture of the comic element was seldom wanting, there existed, in the Middle Ages, a very popular kind of short farce, which was acted at festive and convivial meetings by professional minstrels or by young fellows who combined for the purpose[1]. But, of these, an account has been given in a previous chapter. From France and Germany, numerous farces of this kind have come down to us; not so from England, where they were also highly popular, but where, unfortunately, one only has been preserved, and this but in fragments. Besides the *Interludium de Clerico et Puella*[2], composed, to judge by the handwriting, toward the beginning of the fourteenth century, we possess an account of another play which proves that in England, just as in France, events and problems of the day were satirised in these farces. Bishop Grandison, in 1352, forbade the youth of Exeter, on pain of excommunication, to act a satirical play which they had prepared against the drapers' guild of the town; at the same time, drapers were called upon not to push their prices too high; thus, evidently, the guild was itself the cause of the hostile feeling.

The humanistic and reforming movement naturally exercised everywhere a powerful influence on the drama, which, up to that time, had been a faithful expression of the medieval view of life. In England, as in all other countries, the particular circumstances under which the movement took place left their traces on the drama. Here, performances of mysteries on the medieval

---

[1] The usual name for such a farce was interlude (*interludium*); but this word, as all other names of species in medieval theatrical terminology, has no precise and definite application: it is, likewise, used for all kinds of religious drama. Among the different etymologies which have been suggested for the word, that of Chambers (vol. II, p. 183) is the most plausible: '*Interludium* is not a *ludus* in the interval of something else, but a *ludus* carried on between (*inter*) two or more performers.'

[2] Cf. *Dame Siriz*, *ante*, vol. I, pp. 365—6, and chapter II of the present volume.

model continue far into the sixteenth century; for, in the first phase
of the reformation in England, when the domain of dogma proper
remained intact, the old religious plays could live on undisturbed.
Of course, in the reign of Henry VIII it could no longer be tolerated
that such a champion of papal supremacy as Thomas Becket
should, in his archiepiscopal see of Canterbury, be honoured every
year by a processional play.   However, performances of mystery-
plays lasted even through the six years' reign of the protestant
king Edward VI; though, in the famous performances at York,
the scenes relating to the Virgin's death, assumption and coronation were suppressed;   and   a   magnificent processional play,
instituted at Lincoln, in 1517, in honour of Mary's mother,
St Anne, a saint especially in fashion in the later Middle Ages,
came to an end in the very first year of the new reign, and the
apparel used for it was sold.   In the reign of queen Mary,
mysteries were, of course, produced with particular splendour,
and the suppressed plays on St Thomas and St Anne also
experienced a short revival.   But, even after the final victory
of protestantism under Elizabeth, people would not—especially in
the conservative north of England—miss their accustomed plays.
On this head, too, the citizens of York showed their 'great stiffness
to retain their wonted errors,' of which archbishop Grindal complained.   And, in Shakespeare's native county, during the poet's
boyhood and youth, the performance of religious plays was still in
full flower.   Only towards the end of the century did mysteries
gradually cease; in Kendal, Corpus Christi plays were kept up
as late as the reign of James I; the inventory of the cap-
makers of Coventry for 1597 shows that, as in preceding years,
the guild still preserved faithfully the jaws of hell, a spade for
Adam, a distaff for Eve and other properties, probably hoping for a
revival of the old plays; but this hope proved illusory.   Mysteries
came to an end, under the double influence of puritan enmity to
the stage and of the vigorous growth of Elizabethan drama.

Moralities proved more tenacious of life; in them, among the
representatives of the evil principle, a new realistic and comic
personage now appears with increasing distinctness.   He probably
descended from the merry devil Tutivillus, who, as we have seen,
was taken over from the mysteries into the moralities.   For this
combination of clown and devil, in the course of the sixteenth
century, the name 'Vice' came more and more into use.   His
chief pleasure is to make mischief, and to set men against their
neighbours; his constant attribute is a dagger of lath; and it is

a stock effect to make him, after having acted his part, return to hell, riding on the back of his friend Lucifer.

For the rest, moralities continued to deal with the old subject—man, as an object of contention between the good and the bad qualities of the soul. Such was the theme of *Like will to Like*, by the schoolmaster Ulpian Fulwell (printed 1568), and of the lost play, *The Cradle of Security*, where, as we have seen in the case of *The Pride of Life*, the typical representative of humanity appears as a king; he is subdued by Luxury and other female personifications, who lay him in a cradle and put on him a mask with a pig's snout.

But, besides these, there are other moralities extant, where, as in Skelton's *Magnyfycence*, the old form is animated by new matter. The most remarkable among these plays is the *Interlude of the Nature of the Four Elements* by John Rastell (d. 1536), printer in London and brother-in-law of Sir Thomas More. Here, man is diverted, by the allegorical figures of Sensual Appetite and Ignorance, from the study of geography, into which *Natura naturata* and Studious Desire are about to initiate him; the latter shows him, in a map, the new countries discovered twenty years ago, and expresses his regret that the English cannot claim the glory of having been the discoverers. In the prologue, the author shows himself a prudent and far-seeing man; he says it is not good to study invisible things only and not to care for this visible world. An educational and scientific tendency is also proper to three plays in which the marriage of Wit and Science is represented; in his allegorical quest of a bride, Wit appears like the hero of a romance of chivalry: he slays the monster Tediousness and, thereby, wins the hand of his beloved. The oldest of these plays dates from the reign of Henry VIII, and was composed by a schoolmaster named Redford; the repeated variation of this theme shows how familiar pedagogues were with the conception of a regular course of study as a conflict sustained against hostile powers. Similarly, in the morality *All for Money*, by Thomas Lupton (printed 1578), the value of a scientific education is dwelt upon, and, as has happened very often since the secularisation of the learned professions, the insufficient appreciation of scholarly labours, and the inadequate reward meted out to them, are lamented. These ideas Lupton symbolises by new allegorical impersonations, some of the strangest creations in this kind of literature, *e.g.*, Learning-with-Money, Learning-without-Money, Money-without-Learning, Neither-Money-nor-Learning.

Of particular interest, in England as in France, is the treatment of political and religious problems by authors of moralities. Of political moralities, but few have been preserved. From Hall, the chronicler, we learn that, at Christmas 1527—8, a play entitled *Lord Governaunce* was acted at Gray's inn, which cardinal Wolsey, who was present, took for a satire directed against himself; but he was appeased by the assurance that the piece was twenty years old. Of a remarkable drama, *Albion Knight*, printed, probably, in 1566, we unfortunately possess but a fragment; here, instead of the usual symbolical representative of humanity at large, a personified England is the object of contest between the allegorical representatives of good and evil powers.

Above all, however, the morality furnished an easy opportunity for bringing the great ecclesiastical controversies on the stage, where, as everywhere else, innovators showed far more skill and activity than their conservative adversaries. The first drama relating to the reformation of which we have knowledge is, however, directed against Luther; it was acted in Latin, in 1528, by the pupils of St Paul's school, before Henry VIII, and seems, besides some mockery about Luther's marriage, to have contained gross flatteries addressed to the all-powerful cardinal Wolsey. And, even after the king had broken with Rome, it was quite in accordance with the despotic character of the English reformation that the spirit of the new movement was not advocated and upheld to the same extent as elsewhere by dramatic satire. Only when Thomas Cromwell endeavoured, jointly with Cranmer, to advance the English reformation movement on the lines of the German, and more resolutely than had originally lain in the king's design, several favourites of the influential chancellor are found seeking to work upon public feeling in favour of his church policy. Foremost of all was the zealous, militant theologian John Bale, in whose dramas an ardent hate of popery is strangely combined with ponderous pedantry. The tendency of most of the twenty-two 'comedies' enumerated by himself in his *Catalogus* of 1548 is recognisable from the very titles, which are extremely outspoken as to the 'adulterators of God's Word,' the 'knaveries of Thomas Becket,' and so forth. Of the five that are preserved, one, *The Three Laws*, belongs to the domain of the moralities; it shows how the three laws which God successively revealed to mankind—the law of nature, the law of Moses, and the law of Christ—are corrupted by hostile powers; one of these powers, Sodomy, appears as a monk; and, in this part, of course, the most monstrous things from the anti-clerical *chronique scandaleuse* are brought out. In the beginning, the First Person of the Trinity, with delightful *naïveté*, introduces Himself to the public: 'I am God Father, a substance indivisible.'

A far more lively picture is unrolled by the Scottish statesman and author, David Lyndsay, in his *Pleasant Satyre of the Thrie Estaitis*, which was probably acted for the first time on Epiphany, 1540, before James V of Scotland. But of this, by far the longest morality in the English language, designed for a great number of actors and a large scene of action, an account has been given in an earlier volume[1]. Cromwell must surely have been well satisfied when an account (which has been preserved) of the great success of this play reached him.

But, just about this time, a change came over England. Henry VIII proved more and more decidedly averse to any alteration of ecclesiastical doctrine in the sense of the continental reformation movement; in 1540, Cromwell fell; and, in 1543, it was expressly forbidden to publish in songs, plays and interludes any explanations of Holy Writ opposed to church teaching, as fixed now or in the future by his majesty the king. Bale, who was compelled to flee from England, complained that dissolute plays were allowed, but such as taught Divine truth persecuted. But when, with the accession of Edward VI, the protestant party regained the superiority, it was again shown how English drama took part in all the fluctuations of English church policy. Now, plays were produced such as Wever's *Lusty Juventus*, where the traditional scheme of the morality is made subservient to party interests, good abstractions assiduously quoting the apostle Paul, while the devil and his fellows continually swear 'by the Mass' and 'by the Virgin.' And when, after Edward's early death, the Catholic reaction set in, 'in the first year of the happy reign of queen Mary' (1553), 'a merry interlude entitled *Respublica*' was acted at the Christmas festival by boys, probably in the presence of the queen. In this production, however, dogmatic controversies remain, for the most part, unnoticed, the anonymous author inveighing chiefly against those who, during the preceding reigns, under cover of religion, had enriched themselves by church property. Evil allegorical figures, who appropriate stolen goods, assume well-sounding names, as is often the case in this class of literature, ever since the example set by Prudentius, in whose *Psychomachia*, for instance,

---

[1] See vol. III of the present work, chap. VI, pp. 122 ff.

Avaritia, calls herself *Parsimonia.* So, here, Oppression assumes the name of Reformation, Insolence that of Authority and so forth. In one excellent scene, 'People' (the common man) complains, in blunt popular language, of the new government. Of course, this extremely interesting contribution towards a clear perception of public feeling in the beginning of Mary's reign likewise ends with the triumph of the good cause.

Elizabeth did not favour the traditional usage of clothing political and church agitation in dramatic form; for, so early as 1559, she issued directions to magistrates not to tolerate any 'common interludes in the English tongue' in which questions of religion or state government were touched upon. It seems, also, that the traditional form had had its day. William Wager, in his morality *The longer thou livest, the more fool thou art,* published, probably, in the first years of Elizabeth's reign, conducts the hero of the play, after a fashion with which we have now become sufficiently acquainted, through the various stages of his life, and, in the course of it, enters into theological controversy on the protestant side, wherever an opportunity offers itself. So does the anonymous author of *The Trial of Treasure,* where, in opposition to the usual practice, two courses of life, a good and a bad, are produced in contrast. George Wapull, again, in his morality *The Tide tarries no man* (printed in 1576), shows himself as a partisan of reformation. Another morality, *Impatient Poverty,* has recently been discovered, which was published in 1560 and which exhibits a slight resemblance to Skelton's *Magnyfycence.* Of yet another, *Wealth and Health,* the year of publication is unknown; it was entered in the Stationers' register as early as 1557, but the extant copy of the play certainly belongs to the reign of Elizabeth. A morality of even less importance is the likewise recently discovered *Johan the Evangelist,* which derives its title from the speaker of the moralising prologue and epilogue. The morality *New Custom* (printed 1573) illustrates in a remarkable way the occasional use, even by a rigorous puritan, of the dramatic form, comic effects, of course, being entirely renounced.

CHAPTER IV

EARLY ENGLISH TRAGEDY

The history of renascence tragedy may be divided into three stages, not definitely limited, and not following in strict chronological succession, but distinct in the main: the study, imitation and production of Senecan tragedy; translation; the imitation of Greek and Latin tragedy in the vernacular. This last stage, again, falls into three sub-divisions: the treatment of secular subjects after the fashion of sacred plays long familiar to medieval Europe; the imitation of classical tragedy in its more regular form and with its higher standards of art; the combination of these two types in a form of tragedy at once popular and artistic.

It was, perhaps, only in England that the movement thus outlined attained its final development. For it may be questioned whether French classical tragedy was ever truly popular, and it is beyond doubt that renascence tragedy in Italy was not; but the earlier phases of development may be most easily observed in the history of Italian tragedy, in which other nations found not only a spur to emulation, but models to imitate and a body of critical principles laid down for their guidance.

All three nations had a share in the edition of Seneca which Nicholas Treveth, an English Dominican who seems to have been educated at Paris, prepared, early in the fourteenth century, at the instance of cardinal Niccolò Albertini di Prato, one of the leading figures of the papal court at Avignon. But Italy very soon took the lead in Senecan scholarship, and long maintained it. Lovato de' Lovati (d. 1309) discussed Seneca's metres; Coluccio Salutati, as early as 1371, questioned the tragedian's identity with the philosopher and the Senecan authorship of *Octavia*; before the end of the century, the tragedies were the subject of rival lecture courses at Florence, and the long list of translations into modern European languages had begun. But, above all, it was in Italy that the important step was taken of imitating Seneca in an original tragedy on a subject derived from medieval history.

Albertino's *Eccerinis* won for its author the laurel wreath, with which, in 1315, he was solemnly crowned in the presence of the university and citizens of Padua, and the cognomen of Mussatus, *quasi musis aptus*. Other Latin tragedies by Italian authors followed; but two centuries elapsed before a similar achievement was accomplished in France and England. Italy also led the way in printing editions of Seneca's text, and in the performance of his tragedies in Latin.

The composition of an Italian tragedy in the vernacular after the classical model was preceded by a number of plays called by literary historians *mescidati*, in which a secular subject was developed in rimed measures, on a multiple stage, with a hesitating division into acts and scenes[1]. The connection of these with the *sacre rappresentazioni* is obvious; but they show traces of classical influence. For instance, Antonio Cammelli's *Filostrato e Panfila* (1499), founded upon the first novel of the fourth day of the *Decameron*, is opened by a prologue or argument spoken by Seneca, and divided into five acts by choruses. In these, Love (end of act I), the four Sirens (act II), the three Fates (act III), and Atropos individually (act IV) appear, besides the chorus proper — prototypes of later *intermedii* and English dumb-shows. The stricter classical form was established by Trissino's *Sofonisba* (1515), which followed Greek, rather than Latin, models, and is divided into episodes, not into Seneca's five acts. It is noteworthy for its adoption of blank verse, and, undoubtedly, had considerable influence, being twice printed in 1524 and often later in the century; but there is no proof that it was acted before the celebrated production by the Olympic academy at Vicenza in 1562, though a French version by Mellin de Saint-Gelais was performed and published by 1559. The predominant influence in Italian tragedy was, unquestionably, that of Giambattista Giraldi Cinthio, whose *Orbecche* (acted at Ferrara in 1541) is the first known regular tragedy in the vernacular produced on a modern European stage. Its adoption of the Senecan form, and of the Senecan rhetoric and sensational horrors, decided the fate of Italian tragedy, and greatly influenced that of other nations. Luigi Groto, a generation later, speaks of it as the model of all subsequent tragedies, and Giraldi himself writes of it in his *Discorso sulle Comedie e sulle Tragedie*:

The judicious not only have not found fault with it, but have deemed it worthy of so great praise that in many parts of Italy it has been solemnly presented. Indeed, it was so much the more pleasing that it speaks in all

---

[1] Neri, F., *La tragedia italiana del cinquecento*, Florence, 1904.

the tongues which have knowledge of our own, and the most Christian king did not disdain the command that it should be solemnly performed in his tongue before his majesty.

It is difficult to establish any direct connection between Giraldi and Elizabethan tragedy except through his novels, which furnished plots to Whetstone, Greene and Shakespeare; but the influence of his disciple Dolce is clearly proved. Early French tragedy developed features of the Senecan model which were alien to English taste and tradition—restriction of the action to a single incident and expansion of the choral lyrics [1]—and this is probably the reason why its influence on the other side of the Channel was slight. Jodelle's *Cléopatre Captive* (acted 1552, and printed 1574) was, doubtless, known in England; and, at a later date, the countess of Pembroke, with the assistance of Thomas Kyd and Samuel Daniel, supported the classical theories of her brother's *Apologie* by translations and imitations of Garnier [2]; but Elizabethan tragedy was not to be turned aside from the way marked out for it by stage tradition and popular taste.

The first stage of evolution, as stated above, represented in Italy by the *drammi mescidati*, has its counterpart in England in tragicomedies such as Richard Edwards's *Damon and Pithias* (printed 1571, licensed 1566, and probably acted at Christmas, 1564), John Pickeryng's *Horestes* (printed 1567), R. B.'s *Apius and Virginia* (printed 1575) and Thomas Preston's *Cambises* (licensed 1569—70). The first makes a rude attempt to copy Seneca's *stichomythia* and borrows a passage from *Octavia*; the last mentions Seneca's name in the prologue, but all alike have nothing classical about them beyond the subject. *Damon and Pithias* and *Apius and Virginia* are described on the title-pages of the early editions as 'tragical comedies,' *Cambises* as 'a lamentable tragedy'; but none of them has any real tragic interest—not even *Horestes*, which is, perhaps, the dullest of the series. *Damon and Pithias* shows a certain advance in its lack of abstract characters; but the work of Edwards, if we may judge of it by what is extant,

---

[1] In Jodelle's *Cléopatre*, the chorus takes up more than one third of the play— 607 lines out of 1554. Karl Boehm, in the six tragedies that he has examined in *Beiträge zur Kenntnis des Einflusses Seneca's auf die in der Zeit von 1552 bis 1562 erschienenen Französischen Tragödien* (*Münchener Beiträge*, 1902), notes a considerable increase in the lyric, and a decrease in the dramatic, elements as compared with Seneca; and a table prepared by John Ashby Lester shows that in five of Garnier's tragedies the chorus takes up from one sixth to one fourth of the play. Lester's thesis, *Connections between the Drama of France and Great Britain, particularly in the Elizabethan Period*, is in manuscript in the Harvard library.

[2] See *post*, chap. XIII.

was overrated by his contemporaries. The other three plays
are closely connected with moralities. In *Apius and Virginia*,
if we include Haphazard the Vice, half the characters are abstractions. About the same proportion holds in *Cambises*, where the
Vice Ambidexter enters 'with an old capcase on his head, an old
pail about his hips for harness, a scummer and a potlid by his
side, and a rake on his shoulder'; he is seconded in the usual
stage business of singing, jesting and fighting by three ruffians,
Huff, Ruff and Snuff. In *Horestes*, too, the abstract characters
are numerous; the play opens with the conventional 'flouting'
and 'thwacking' of Rusticus and Hodge by the Vice, and closes
with the conventional moralising by Truth and Duty. Though the
literary value of these plays is slight, their obvious appeal to popular
favour gives them a certain interest. *Horestes* and *Cambises*
were evidently intended for performance by small companies,
the 'players names' (31 in number) of the former being 'devided
for VI to playe,' and the 38 parts of the latter for eight; *Damon
and Pithias* has been convincingly identified by W. Y. Durand[1]
with the 'tragedy'[2] performed before the queen at Whitehall
by the Children of the Chapel at Christmas, 1564, and the edition
of 1571 is provided with a prologue 'somewhat altered for the
proper use of them that hereafter shall have occasion to plaie it,
either in Private, or open Audience'; the stage direction in *Apius
and Virginia*, 'Here let Virginius go about the scaffold,' shows
that the author had the public presentation of his play in mind.
The stage directions are of importance, as illustrating the way
in which these early dramas were produced. In *Horestes*, the
action oscillates at first between Mycene and Crete, shifts to
Athens and ends at Mycene; but, throughout, the back of the
stage is, apparently, occupied by something representing the wall
of Mycene. After much marching about the stage, the Herald
approaches this object, and, in answer to his challenge, Clytemnestra speaks 'over the wal,' refusing to surrender. Then we have
the direction:

Go and make your lively battel and let it be longe, eare you can win the
Citie, and when you have won it, let Horestes bringe out his mother by the
armes, and let the droum sease playing and the trumpet also, when she is
taken; let her knele downe and speake.

[1] 'Some Errors concerning Richard Edwards' in *Modern Language Notes*, vol. xxiii,
p. 131. 'When and Where *Damon and Pythias* was acted,' in *The Journal of Germanic
Philology*, vol. iv, pp. 348—355.

[2] So Cecil calls it in a note on the revels accounts. See Feuillerat, *Documents
relating to the Office of the Revels in the Time of Queen Elizabeth* (Bang's *Materialien*,
vol. xxi, p. 116, and notes on pp. 447—8).

After more fighting, Egistus is taken and hanged, apparently from the same wall. 'Fling him of the lader and then let on bringe in his mother Clytemnestra; but let her loke wher Egistus hangeth.... Take downe Egistus and bear him out.' The same realistic method of presentation is to be noted in *Apius and Virginia*: 'Here tye a handcarcher aboute hir eyes, and then strike of hir heade.' In *Cambises*, when execution is done on Sisamnes, the stage direction reads: 'Smite him in the neck with a sword to signify his death,' and the dialogue continues:

> PRAXASPES.   Behold (O king), how he doth bleed,
>   Being of life bereft.
> KING.   In this wise he shall not yet be left.
>   Pull his skin over his ears,

... 'Flays him with a false skin.' The deaths of Smirdis ('A little bladder of vinegar pricked' to represent his blood) and of Cambises, who enters 'without a gown, a sword thrust up into his side bleeding,' further illustrate this point. Our early playwrights were troubled by no scruples as to the interpretation of the precepts about deaths on the stage, elaborated by the Italian critics from Aristotle and Horace, which Giraldi discusses with much learning and ingenuity in his *Discorso*. They accepted the tradition of the miracle-plays, and handed on to the early theatres a custom which was evidently in accord with popular taste.

The title of *Horestes*, 'A Newe Enterlude of Vice, Conteyning the Historye of Horestes, &c.' indicates its combination of historical and moral interests, or, rather, the attempt—not very successful—to subject what was regarded as history to a moral aim. The Vice prompts Horestes to revenge his father by the murder of his mother, for whom Nature pleads in vain; but, instead of suffering retribution, as in Greek tragedy, he marries Hermione and is crowned king of Mycene by Truth and Duty. The moralising at the end of the play has no vital or logical connection with the story, and is almost as conventional as the final prayer for Elizabeth, her council, the nobility and spirituality, the judges, the lord mayor and all his brethren, with the commonalty. In Bale's *Kynge Johan*, historical facts and characters are adapted to religious, or, rather, controversial, ends with elaborate ingenuity; but the spirit and method of the drama remain those of the moral play. The character of the king alone maintains, throughout, a well defined personality. It is not until nearly the end of the first of the two acts that Sedition assumes the name of Stephen Langton, Usurped Power becomes the pope, Private Wealth becomes Pandulphus and

Dissimulation Raymundus. Later, Dissimulation gives his name as 'Simon of Swynsett,' and, obviously, is Raymundus no longer. After the king's death, the action—if, indeed, there can be said to be any—is carried on entirely by abstractions. In spite of some interesting features, *Kynge Johan* belongs substantially to an earlier type than the group of plays just considered, and is, indeed, probably of earlier date.

No student of our drama, from Sir Philip Sidney onwards, has failed to recognise the enormous step in advance made by Thomas Norton and Thomas Sackville in *Gorboduc*, first acted, before Queen Elizabeth, in January 1562. Its imitation of Seneca's form and style is obvious; yet it shows independence, not only in the choice of a native theme, but in the spirit in which it is treated. Sidney praised it not only as 'full of stately speeches, and well sounding phrases, clyming to the height of Seneca his stile,' but also as 'full of notable moralitie, which it doth most delightfully teach, and so obtayne the very end of Poesie.' It is significant that the publisher of the third edition in 1590 printed *Gorboduc* as an annex to Lydgate's politico-moral tract, *The Serpent of Dissension*. A modern critic[1] says that 'the play is rather a political argument than a simple tragedy.' This overstates the case; but the didactic intention of the dramatists is obvious enough. The 'argument,' after recounting the tragic fate of the principal characters, continues :

The nobilitie assembled and most terribly destroyed the rebels. And afterwardes for want of issue of the prince, whereby the succession of the crowne became uncertaine, they fell to civill warre, in which both they and many of their issues were slaine, and the land for a long time almost desolate and miserably wasted.

To these consequences for the realm at large, the whole of the last act is given up ; and, from the very beginning of the tragedy, its political significance is insisted on. The first dumb-show is directed particularly to this end.

Hereby was signified, that a state knit in unitie doth continue strong against all force. But being divided, is easely destroyed. As befell upon Duke Gorboduc dividing his land to his two sonnes which he before held in Monarchie.

Nearly all the dialogue of the play—for the incidents occur off the stage—is delivered in the council chamber. The opening scene, it is true, consists of a private conversation between Ferrex and his mother ; but the longest passage in it is an elaborate political commonplace. After this short introductory scene,

[1] Courtney, L. H., in *Notes and Queries*, Ser. II, vol. x, pp. 261—3.

containing less than seventy lines in all, we have, in the first act, nothing but discussions in the king's council, his decision to divide the realm between his two sons being all that can properly be described as action. Ferrex and Porrex, each with his good and his evil counsellor, occupy the whole of act II. In act III, we are back in Gorboduc's council chamber, and the only incident is recounted by a messenger. With act IV, according to the printer of the first edition, Sackville's part begins; and this division is borne out by the fact that the remaining acts show greater power of thought and vigour of versification, more variety of tone and richness of character and incident. The speech of Porrex in his own defence has more dramatic significance than anything the English stage had yet known; the incident of the attempted poisoning, introduced by the dramatist into the story for the first time[1], and not mentioned in acts I—III, and the young prince's remorse at his brother's death, engage the sympathy of the audience for his own untimely end, which is recounted with many natural and moving touches by Marcella, an eye-witness of the assassination, and, therefore, able to communicate more passion than the conventional messenger. But, with act V, we are once more in the dull round of political disquisition, broken only by the soliloquy in which Fergus reveals his ambitious designs. The tragedy ends with obvious allusions to the political situation of the day:

> Such one (my lordes) let be your chosen king,
> Such one so borne within your native land,
> Such one preferre, and in no wise admitte
> The heavie yoke of forreine governaunce:
> Let forreine titles yelde to publike wealth.

One wonders how the queen took this, and, still more, how she received the advice directed to her in the concluding speech:

> This, this ensues, when noble men do faile
> In loyall trouth, and subjectes will be kinges.
> And this doth growe when loe unto the prince,
> Whom death or sodeine happe of life bereaves,
> No certaine heire remaines, such certaine heire,
> As not all onely is the rightfull heire
> But to the realme is so made knowen to be,
> And trouth therby vested in subjectes hartes,
> To owe fayth there where right is knowen to rest.

---

[1] Sackville perhaps got a hint from Geoffrey of Monmouth, *Historia Regum Britanniae*, Bk. II, chap. XVI: '*At Porrex majori cupiditate subductus, paratis insidiis Ferrecem fratrem interficere parat*' (ed. San-Marte, p. 30). The treachery here is attributed to the younger brother, who afterwards kills Ferrex in battle, so that the incident has not, in the *History*, the dramatic significance given to it by Sackville.

Alas, in Parliament what hope can be,
When is of Parliament no hope at all?
Which, though it be assembled by consent,
Yet is not likely with consent to end,
While eche one for him selfe, or for his frend,
Against his foe, shall travaile what he may.
While now the state left open to the man,
That shall with greatest force invade the same,
Shall fill ambicious mindes with gaping hope;
When will they once with yelding hartes agree?
Or in the while, how shall the realme be used?
No, no: then Parliament should have bene holden,
And certeine heirs appointed to the crowne,
To stay the title of established right,
And in the people plant obedience
While yet the prince did live, whose name and power
By lawfull sommons and authoritie
Might make a Parliament to be of force,
And might have set the state in quiet stay.

At the beginning of her reign, Elizabeth had given orders that 'common Interludes in the Englishe tongue' should refrain from handling 'either matters of religion or of the governaunce of the estate of the common weale,' 'beyng no meete matters to be wrytten or treated upon, but by menne of aucthoritie, learning, and wisedome, nor to be handled before any audience but of grave and discrete persons[1].' Presumably, the queen thought that these conditions were fulfilled at the Christmas revels of the Inner Temple in 1561—2; for, a few days later, the tragedy was repeated before her in her own hall; and, in 1563, Norton presented the same arguments as those of the passage cited above on behalf of a committee of the House of Commons in a petition for the limitation of the succession to the crown[2].

It is clear that our first tragedy is very far from being a servile imitation of Seneca. Its authors took over his general scheme of five acts divided by choruses, his counsellors and messengers, his rhetorical style and grave sententious precepts; in the reflective passages, one often detects an echo of the Roman original, though there is little direct imitation of phraseology, such as came to be the fashion later. The plot bears a general resemblance to that of Seneca's fragmentary *Thebais*; but the story is taken from Geoffrey of Monmouth, and, as we have seen, it is developed on independent lines[3]. The direct stimulus to production probably

[1] Collier, vol. I, p. 167.
[2] See Courtney, L. H., *u.s.* p. 261; *Commons Journal*, vol. I, pp. 62—64.
[3] For the relation of *Gorboduc* to its sources, see a doctor's dissertation now in course of publication at the university of Wisconsin by Watt, H. A., *Gorboduc; or Ferrex and Porrex* (1909).

came from Italian example; but the authors modified the custom of the Italian stage to suit their own ideas. It had long been the practice in Italy to enliven dramatic performances with spectacular entertainments between the acts, called *intermedii*. We have noted such representations above in connection with *Filostrato e Panfila*, and they were the invariable accompaniments of the early productions of comedy, both in Latin and in the vernacular. In tragedy, they were of rarer occurrence, choruses usually taking their place; they were almost always allegorical in character; sometimes they had relation to the subject of the play, sometimes not; and they were presented both with and without words. Though they figure largely in contemporary accounts of dramatic entertainments, they were not always included in printed editions of the plays; but Dolce published those used to adorn the performance of his *Troiane* (1566), and these may serve as an example of the type. After the first act of the tragedy, there was a discourse between the chorus and Trojan citizens on the misfortunes of their country; after the second, Pluto appeared with the ghosts of the Trojan slain; after the third, Neptune and the council of the gods; after the fourth, other deities, especially Venus and Juno. The spectators often paid more attention to these *intermedii* than to the drama, to the disgust of dramatists, who were loud in their complaints[1]; and a contemporary critic remarks that they were of special interest to foreign visitors, who did not understand Italian[2]. It can hardly be doubted that this Italian practice gave the authors of *Gorboduc* a hint for the establishment of a similar custom on the Elizabethan stage. But, here again, they showed a certain originality. They connected their allegorical dumb-shows with the subject of the tragedy, and, by making them precede each act, instead of following, as was the rule in Italy, gave them new weight and significance. They were no longer mere shows, distracting the spectator from the main theme of the drama, but helps to the understanding of it. Norton and Sackville, doubtless, were familiar with such allegorical representations at London, Coventry and elsewhere, as independent tableaux in honour of the festival of a patron saint or a royal visit, and they followed Italian example only in using them for the purposes of tragedy. In the fourth dumb-show, the three furies come 'from under the stage, as though out of hell'; and this, as well

---

[1] Cf. Isabella d'Este's letters to her husband during her visit to Ferrara in 1502, and Grazzini's prologue to *La Strega* (1582).
[2] See preface to d'Ambra's *Cofanaria*, acted at Florence in 1565.

as the phrase in Machyn's diary[1] with reference to the second performance, 'ther was a grett skaffold in the hall,' seems to indicate that the stage of *Gorboduc* was, substantially, that of the miracle-plays. In the observance of stage proprieties, the authors follow strict classical usage, for all the events are reported, and the realism of the native drama is carefully eschewed. But, in other respects, they are more lax, or inclined to compromise. The play begins, in the conventional Senecan fashion, with an allusion to the dawn; but the practice of Italian tragedy and the precepts of the Italian interpreters of Aristotle's *Poetics* are disregarded, as Sidney lamented in his *Apologie*:

> For it is faulty both in place, and time, the two necessary companions of all corporall actions. For where the stage should alwaies represent but one place, and the uttermost time presupposed in it should be, both by Aristotle's precept and common reason, but one day; there is both many dayes and many places inartificially imagined.

Whether this were accident or design, it secured to English tragedy from the beginning a liberty which all the efforts of Sidney's group of stricter classicists could not do away with.

Gorboduc seems to have found no imitators immediately: it was not published till 1565, and then surreptitiously. At King's college, Cambridge, in 1564, the queen saw 'a Tragedie named *Dido*, in hexametre verse, without anie chorus,' and 'an English play called *Ezechias*, made by Mr Udall.' At Christmas, 1564, as we have seen, *Damon and Pithias* by Richard Edwards was acted at Whitehall; and, in 1566, his *Palamon and Arcyte* was presented before the queen in the hall of Christ Church, Oxford, as well as a Latin play, called *Marcus Geminus*. But, of these, only *Damon and Pithias* has come down to us, and its freedom from classical influence has been already noted. When, however, the members of Gray's inn presented a comedy and a tragedy in 1566, they obviously took as their model for the latter the drama which had been acted with much applause by the gentlemen of the Inner Temple, and which had just been published. *Jocasta* is written in blank verse, which *Gorboduc* had introduced on the English stage: its authorship is divided according to acts, the first and fourth being 'done' by Francis Kinwelmersh, the second, third and fifth by George Gascoigne, while a third member of the society, Christopher Yelverton, contributed the epilogue. Gascoigne wrote the 'argument,' and, apparently, supervised the whole undertaking; for he afterwards

---

[1] Camden Society edition (1848), p. 275.

included the tragedy in his collected works, and Ariosto's *Supposes*, presented at the same time, was translated by him alone. As in *Gorboduc*, each act is preceded by a dumb-show with musical accompaniment, and the rimed choruses, which in the earlier tragedy were recited by 'foure auncient and sage men of Brittaine,' were given in *Jocasta* by 'foure Thebane dames.' The full title reads: '*Jocasta: A Tragedie written in Greeke by* Euripides, *translated and digested into Acte by George Gascoygne and Francis Kinwelmershe of Grayes Inne, and there by them presented,* 1566.' The claim of translation from the original Greek, apparently, passed without remark till 1879, when J. P. Mahaffy[1] first pointed out that Gascoigne and Kinwelmersh had not gone to *Phoenissae,* but to an adaptation of it by Lodovico Dolce, bearing the title *Giocasta* (1549). This was not Dolce's only contribution, as we shall see[2], in aid of Elizabethan tragedy, and some of his sonnets were translated by Thomas Lodge. He was a Venetian (1508—68), and much of his literary activity consisted of hack work for the well known publishing house of Gioliti. He translated Seneca's tragedies and other Latin classics. He professed to translate the *Odyssey,* but was somewhat hampered by his ignorance of Greek, the result being a story taken from Homer rather than a translation. He treated *Phoenissae* in the same fashion, relying upon a Latin translation published at Basel by R. Winter, in 1541, the misprints of which he reproduced. He dealt freely with his original, recasting choruses, omitting some scenes and adding others, generally from his favourite author Seneca. Both the 'original ode,' which Warton ascribes to Gascoigne and praises as 'by no means destitute of pathos or imagination,' and the ode to Concord by Kinwelmersh, in which the same critic discovers 'great elegance of expression and versification,' are loose translations of Dolce. In the dialogue, the translators followed the Italian text with greater fidelity, though there are some amusing blunders. Gascoigne, as a rule, is more successful in reproducing the sense of his original, but Dolce sometimes leads him astray. Thus, in *Phoenissae* (v. 1675), where Antigone threatens to follow the example of the Danaides (Νὺξ ἆρ' ἐκείνη Δαναΐδων μ' ἕξει μίαν), Dolce translates flatly: *Io seguirò lo stil d'alcune accorte*; and Gascoigne still more flatly: 'I will ensue some worthie womans steppes.' The same gradual depravation of a great original is to

---

[1] *Euripides* (*Classical Writers*), pp. 134—5.
[2] See *infra*, p. 74. Cf. also Symonds, J. A., *Shakspere's Predecessors*, pp. 221—2.

be seen in **v.** 1680, which descends, by clearly marked steps, to
bathos. When Antigone declares her determination to accompany
her father into exile, Creon says: Γενναιότης σοι, μωρία δ᾽ ἔνεστί τις.
The Latin version reproduces this prosaically but correctly:
Generositas tibi inest, sed tamen stultitia quaedam inest. Dolce
mistranslates: *Quel ch'in altri è grandezza è in te pazzia*; and
Gascoigne blindly follows his blind guide: 'What others might
beseeme, beseemes not thee.'

Jocasta did not advance English tragedy on its destined way;
indeed, on the whole, the movement is backwards, for its authors
not only showed less originality than their predecessors by adopting
the method of translation, but, in other respects, their efforts are
more imitative than independent. Neither tragedy had employed
the resource of romantic passion, and it seemed, therefore, as if
there were a real opportunity for development when *Gismond
of Salerne* was presented in 1567—8 by 'the worshipful company
of the Inner-Temple Gentlemen.'

> The tragedy was by them most pithily framed, and no less curiously acted
> in view of her Majesty, by whom it was then as princely accepted, as of the
> whole honourable audience notably applauded: yea, and of all men generally
> desired, as a work, either in stateliness of show, depth of conceit, or true
> ornaments of poetical art, inferior to none of the best in that kind: no, were
> the Roman Seneca the censurer.

So pronounces William Webbe, author of *A Discourse of English
Poetrie*, in the letter prefixed to the revised (1591) edition of
the play, and addressed to the editor, Robert Wilmot. From the
initials appended to each act in this edition, it appears that act II
was written by Henry Noel, act IV by Christopher Hatton and
act V by Wilmot himself; the authors of act I (Rod. Staf.) and
act III (G. Al.) have not yet been identified. The plot is taken
from Boccaccio's first novel of the fourth day, which had already
been used by Italian dramatists, though our authors were indebted
to none of these. They went directly to the Italian text of the
Decameron, and not, as has been generally supposed, to the
translation of the tale just published in *The Palace of Pleasure*,
for their version is closer to the original, and in some important
particulars more accurate, than Painter's. For instance, Ghismonda,
in her lament over her dead lover, says: *Ahi dolcissimo albergo
di tutti i miei piaceri, maladetta sia la crudeltà di colui, che
con gli occhi della fronte or mi ti fa vedere. Assai m'era con
quegli della mente riguardarti a ciascuna ora.* This is translated
by Painter:

Oh sweete harboroughe of my pleasures, cursed be the crueltye of him that hath caused mee at this time to loke uppon thee with the eyes of my face: it was pleasure ynoughe, to see thee every hower, amonges people of knowledge and understanding;

a grotesque misconception of the phrase, *con quegli della mente*. Wilmot reproduced the meaning of the original[1], and passages might be quoted to show that his collaborators also had Boccaccio's text before them, and were not content to rely on Painter's translation, which, indeed, is often inadequate. The story is one of the most tragic in the *Decameron*, and offers an excellent subject for dramatic treatment. Boccaccio's passion-wrought and desperate heroine, with her fearless assertion of the claims of nature and love against those of social convention, is a magnificent centre of interest for the tragic stage; but all this advantage, ready to their hand in the original story, the English dramatists laid aside. Gismond's lover is no longer *un giovane valletto*, but 'the Counté Palurine,' and she herself is not so much a victim of love as a terrible example of disordered passion. Moral considerations prevented the Inner Temple gentlemen from making Gismond their heroine. 'Herein they all agree,' Wilmot writes, 'commending virtue, detesting vice, and lively deciphering their overthrow that suppress not their unruly affections.' It was necessary, therefore, to make a complete change from Boccaccio's point of view and method of treatment. Part of the original material was transferred to other speakers or different occasions. Thus, Ghismonda's reflection that the spirit of her dead lover still lingers near, awaiting hers, is applied by the English dramatists to her dead husband; and her plea to her father that the flesh is weak is made more respectable—and much less effective—by putting it into the mouth of the aunt, Lucrece, and placing it before, instead of after, the event. Moreover, the chorus hold up 'worthy dames,' such as Penelope and Lucrece, as 'a mirrour and a glasse to womankinde,' and exhort their hearers to resist Cupid's assaults and be content with a moderate and virtuous affection (choruses II, III, IV). An epilogue (of the kind which, no

Ah pleasant harborrow of my hartës thought.
Ah swete delight, joy, comfort of my life.
Ah cursed be his crueltie that wrought
thee this despite, and unto me such grefe,
to make me to behold thus with these eyes
thy woefull hart, and force me here to see
this dolefull sight. Alas, did not suffise
that with my hartes eyen continually
I did behold the same?   (Act v, sc. 2, 25—33.)

doubt, would have been recited by 'sweet bully Bottom') assures the ladies in the audience that such inordinate passions are unknown 'in Britain land':

> Nor Pluto heareth English ghostes complaine
> our dames disteined lyves. Therfore ye may
> be free from fere. Suffiseth to mainteine
> the vertues which we honor in yow all:
> so as our Britain ghostes, when life is past,
> may praise in heven, not plaine in Plutoes hall
> our dames, but hold them vertuous and chast,
> worthy to live where furie never came,
> where Love can see, and beares no deadly bowe.

In this way, the interests of morality and the authors' reputations were saved, but at the sacrifice of much that was valuable in the original story, which the dramatists supplemented from other sources. Their thoughts, naturally, would be directed to classical examples of unhappy passion—Phaedra and Dido. The latter had been made the subject of a tragedy by Dolce (1547), and to this, undoubtedly, our authors had recourse. At the opening of their play, Cupid comes down from heaven and speaks the following lines:

> Loe I, in shape that seme unto your sight
> a naked boy, not clothed but with wing,
> am that great god of love that with my might
> do rule the world, and everie living thing.
> This one hand beares vain hope, short joyfull state,
> with faire semblance the lover to allure:
> this other holdes repentance all to late,
> warr, fiër, blood, and paines without recure.
> On swete ambrosia is not my foode,
> nor nectar is my drink, as to the rest
> of all the Goddes. I drink the lovers blood,
> and eate the living hart within his brest.

Cupid, likewise, opens Dolce's *Didone*, and the lines quoted above are merely a translation and re-arrangement of the Italian original:

> *Io, che dimostro in viso,*
> *A la statura, e à i panni,*
> *D'esser picciol fanciullo,*
> *Si come voi mortale:*
> *Son quel gran Dio, che'l mondo chiama Amore.*
> *Quel, che pò in cielo, e in terra,*
> *Et nel bollente Averno;*
> *Contra di cui non vale*
> *Forza, ne human consiglio:*
> *Ne d'ambrosia mi pasco,*
> *Si come gli altri Dei,*

Ma di sangue, e di pianto.
Ne l'una mano io porto
Dubbia speme, fallace, e breve gioia;
Ne l'altra affanno, e noia,
Pene, sospiri, e morti.

There are other parallels of less importance, but, as the play proceeded, the divergence in the development of the plot of *Didone* made it less suitable to the purpose of our authors, and they supplied their lack of invention with commonplaces taken direct from Seneca. As Dolce had done the same, it is hard to say whether a great deal of act I is taken from the Italian's borrowings or from the Latin original, but there are Senecan reminiscences, at first or second hand, from *Phaedra, Medea, Thyestes, Oedipus, Agamemnon, Hercules Furens, Hercules Oetaeus* and *Octavia.* The chorus of act II was, no doubt, suggested by *Octavia* 298—312 and 689—695. Act III lays *Octavia* and *Phaedra* under extensive contribution. The opening of act IV, by Megaera, is taken direct from *Thyestes*, and the invocation of Jove's thunder at the beginning of scene 2 may have been suggested by the same play or by *Phaedra,* 679—690. This stock device (which may be traced back to Sophocles: *Electra,* 823—6) had already been used in *Gorboduc* (end of act III, sc. 1); and the original passage in *Phaedra* is misquoted in *Titus Andronicus,* act IV, sc. 1, 81—82. But it is in act V of *Gismond of Salerne* that Seneca is most openly plundered. Lines 1—2, 21—38, 40—42, 45—68, 149—167, 182—188 and 207—208 are merely translations of Seneca, chiefly from *Thyestes.*

When due deductions are made for what the authors borrowed from Boccaccio, Dolce and Seneca, not much remains to be credited to their own originality. Of the characters neither found nor implied in Boccaccio's novel, Cupid is taken from Dolce; Renuchio, Megaera and the chorus from Seneca; Lucrece and Claudia are the conventional confidantes of classical tragedy. The order of events, in the main, is that of the novel, though a noteworthy change is made in that, after the discovery, Tancred sends for his daughter before he meets her lover—with this disadvantage, that, at the time of the interview, Gismond is not made aware of Guiscard's imprisonment and impending fate. The one important addition made by the English dramatists to Boccaccio's story is the death of Tancred, and this is only announced as an intention in the action, though we are informed parenthetically in the epilogue that he 'now himself hath slayen.'

In the later version of the tragedy which Wilmot prepared for
publication, Tancred plucks out his eyes after the example of
Oedipus and kills himself on the stage. The same elaboration
of the horrible is to be noted in the dumb-show introducing the
fifth act in the edition of 1591.

> Before this act was a dead march played, during which entered on the
> stage Renuchio, Captain of the Guard, attended upon by the guard. They
> took up Guiscard from under the stage; then after Guiscard had kindly
> taken leave of them all, a strangling-cord was fastened about his neck, and
> he haled forth by them. Renuchio bewaileth it; and then, entering in,
> bringeth forth a standing cup of gold, with a bloody heart reeking hot in it,
> and then saith, *ut sequitur.*

These dumb-shows are realistic rather than allegorical in
character, and set forth the action of the drama without words,
as in the play within the play in *Hamlet*. In the earlier version,
there are no dumb-shows, properly so called. Cupid opens the
first and third acts, but this device of a prologue was taken, as we
have seen, from Dolce, who also introduces Cupid and the shade
of Sichaeus at the beginning of act II of *Didone*, in obvious
imitation of the fury Megaera and the shade of Tantalus at the
opening of Seneca's *Thyestes*. The English dramatists' Megaera
(act IV) might be suggested by this passage in *Didone*, in which
she is mentioned by name, but, more probably, was taken from
Seneca direct. The choruses are recited by four gentlemen of
Salerne; and the versification turns back from the blank verse
of *Gorboduc* and *Jocasta* to the older rimed measures—a re-
trogression which Wilmot, in the later version, was at some pains
to correct. Cupid comes down from heaven, and Megaera up
from hell, marking a slight advance in stage machinery; and it
appears from the last line of the revised edition that curtains
were used. The scene is restricted to the court of Tancred's
palace and the chamber of Gismond lying immediately behind
it—the chamber 'within,' which was afterwards to become a
habitual resource of the popular stage—but there is no attempt
to observe the unity of time. The treatment of the plot, though
poorly contrived, is episodical, and this is an important point,
for it is characteristic of English tragedy that it aims at presenting
the whole course of the action, in its inception, development and
consequences, rather than a particular situation or crisis, as was
the custom in Senecan tragedy, and its Italian and French
imitations. The one merit of *Gismond of Salerne* is that it
endeavours to present a romantic subject with something of the

gravity and dignity of classical tragedy. From the latter point of
view, its superiority to its immediate predecessors, *Damon and
Pithias* and *Horestes*, is abundantly manifest; and, in both
interest of theme and manner of treatment, it surpasses the
earlier and more academic models. *Gorboduc* is overweighted
with political reflections, and the plot loses itself in abstractions. *Jocasta* has the double disadvantage of a time-worn
theme and frigid manner of presentation. *Gismond of Salerne*
struck out a new path, in which later dramatists followed with
infinitely greater art. It seems a far cry from Gismond and
Guiscard to the 'pair of star-cross'd lovers' of Shakespeare's first
Italian tragedy; but the Gentlemen of the Inner Temple at least
attempted what he achieved—to present the problem of human
passion *sub specie eternitatis*.

The most elaborate effort of its kind that has come down to
us was the Gray's inn entertainment presented to the queen in
1588, of which *The Misfortunes of Arthur*, by Thomas Hughes,
was the principal feature. The dumb-shows were more complex
in their apparatus and allegorical significance than ever before,
and, evidently, were regarded as of primary importance, for the
title of the pamphlet contemporaneously published reads: *Certaine
devises and shewes presented to her Majestie by the Gentlemen of
Grayes-Inne at her Highnesse Court in Greenewich, the twenty
eighth day of Februarie in the thirtieth yeare of her Majesties
most happy Raigne*, making no mention of the tragedy. 'The
dumbe showes,' we are finally informed,

> were partly devised by Maister Christopher Yelverton, Maister Frauncis
> Bacon, Maister John Lancaster and others, partly by the saide Maister
> Flower, who with Maister Penroodocke and the said Maister Lancaster
> directed these proceedings at Court.

Alternative introductory and final speeches for Gorlois, and two
alternative choruses, were provided by Flower, and the whole
entertainment was prefaced by an elaborate introduction penned
by Nicholas Trotte; in this, five gentlemen students were
presented to her majesty as captives by one of the muses, who
assured the queen that

> since your sacred Majestie
> In gratious hands the regall Scepter held
> All Tragedies are fled from State, to stadge.

As this was in the interval between the execution of Mary queen
of Scots and the coming of the Armada, the compliment was
extravagant enough to satisfy even Elizabeth's inordinate appetite

for flattery; and, all things considered, it is no wonder that, a few years later[1], the queen said that Gray's inn was 'an House she was much beholden unto, for that it did always study for some sports to present unto her.' The study undertaken by Thomas Hughes and his collaborators in 1587—8 was no light one. Following the example of Sackville and Norton, Hughes found a subject in ancient British legend and chose the same main authority—Geoffrey of Monmouth's *Historia Regum Britanniae*. This is proved[2] by the adoption of the main outlines of the story as they are found in Geoffrey and of his forms of proper names—Gorlois, Igerna, Anne (Arthur's sister), Cador, Gillamor, Cheldrich, Aschillus, Hoel, Angharad, Conan. But Hughes had recourse to other versions of the story as well—probably Malory's *Morte d'Arthur*—for we have also such forms as Guenevora, Mordred, Gawin, not found in Geoffrey. The incestuous birth of Mordred, and the slaughter of Arthur and Mordred by each other's hands, are in Malory and not in Geoffrey, who describes Mordred as Arthur's nephew. These additional horrors, doubtless, were selected by Hughes in order to bring his theme up to the level of Senecan sensationalism. In this, he was following the classical tradition of the time, and, no doubt, pleasing the queen, whose blank verse translation from the *Hercules Oetaeus* is still preserved in the Bodleian library, though, according to Warton, it has 'no other recommendation but its royalty.' Hughes chose as his first model the most horrible of Seneca's tragedies, *Thyestes*. The ghost of Gorlois, who comes up from hell to recite the first scene, is merely the *Tantali umbra* of *Thyestes* in another guise, and lines 22—28 are translated literally from this source. In the next scene, between Guenevora and Fronia, *Thyestes* proved inadequate to the demands made upon it, and the words of the injured or erring wives of *Agamemnon*, *Hercules Oetaeus* and *Medea* are reproduced; how extensive the borrowing is may be judged from the fact that in Guenevora's longest speech (19—47) there is only one original line (20), and that is a commonplace, quite in Seneca's manner. In the third scene, the general relation of Guenevora to Angharad is that of Phaedra to her nurse, but *Hercules Furens*, *Medea*, *Thebais* and *Oedipus* are also put under contribution, Guenevora's longest speech (43—54) being again taken entirely from Seneca. The conversation between Mordred and Guenevora in scene 4 is modelled on that of

---

[1] At the Gesta Grayorum, 1594. Nichols's *Progresses*, vol. III, p. 319.
[2] In the edition of the play by Grumbine, H. C.

Aegisthus and Clytemnestra in *Agamemnon*; Conan, in the latter part of the scene, introduces some of the sententious precepts put into the mouth of Seneca in *Octavia*. Then the chorus, four in number according to established tradition, recite, each in turn, a six lined stanza: this division of the chorus, which occurs again in the dialogue of the fifth act, is the one innovation Hughes has introduced.

It is hardly worth while to follow the dramatist in his borrowings through act II (where they are almost as extensive) and through the rest of the play to the last lines of the epilogue, which still echo Seneca; but one feature which affected Elizabethan tragedy throughout its history may be noted. The earlier dramatists had attempted, without much success, to imitate Seneca's *stichomythia*. Hughes copied this staccato style of antithetical and epigrammatic dialogue very closely. The following lines, of which only the first is taken from *Thyestes*, may serve as an example:

> CADOR. To rule is much.   ARTHUR. Small if we covet naught.
> CA. Who covets not a Crowne?   AR. He that discernes
> The swoord aloft.   CA. That hangeth fast.   AR. But by
> A haire.   CA. Right holdes it up.   AR. Wrong puls it downe.
> CA. The Commons helpe the King.   AR. They sometimes hurt.

This device is of frequent occurrence in later tragedy, and is sometimes very effectively used by Shakespeare, *e.g.* in the opening scenes of *Richard III* and of *Hamlet*.

The characters of *The Misfortunes of Arthur* not only indulge freely in Senecan aphorisms, but are cast in the regular Senecan moulds. Mordred is the typical usurper, Guenevora the faithless wife, and the messengers, counsellors and confidants show few gleams of personality; but an exception must be made in the case of Arthur, who, perhaps, is the first well-conceived character of English academic tragedy. Of course, he utters many Senecan commonplaces, but he is not a merely conventional type. His inclination to deal gently with his son is finely contrasted with his vigorous address to his troops when he is roused to action by Mordred's insolent message; and his lament over his son's body has been justly admired, in spite of a touch here and there of Senecan rhetoric. His last words breathe a dignity and mystery not unworthy of the situation:

> Yea: though I Conquerour die, and full of *Fame*:
> Yet let my death and parture rest obscure.
> No grave I neede (O *Fates*) nor buriall rights,
> Nor stately hearce, nor tombe with haughty toppe:

> But let my Carkasse lurk: yea, let my death
> Be ay unknowen, so that in every Coast
> I still be feard, and lookt for every houre.

The blank verse of Hughes, though it is still monotonous, has more power and life than that of his predecessors; and it seems reasonable to regret that he did not rely more on his own efforts. If he had left himself free to develop his theme according to his own ideas, he would probably have filled a larger place in the history of English tragedy, though, no doubt, the Senecan patchwork he produced was more in accordance with the expectations of his audience.

It seems unnecessary to pursue the fortunes of the academic drama further here; it had given to the stage standards of regularity and dignity of which that stage was sorely in need, and it had bestowed upon tragedy the blank verse which was to become its recognised means of expression. We must now turn our attention to those players of 'common Interludes in the Englishe tongue' who were continually harried by the London civic authorities, and alternately repressed and encouraged by the queen. The organisation of strolling players and noblemen's servants into regular companies, and the building of the first theatres, gave the drama the standing of a profession, and attracted to it university wits, who were soon to raise it to the dignity of an art. Whatever might be the amount of their Latin, popular dramatists were not without respect, according to their lights, for the authority of Seneca; they probably studied the tragedies at school, and were, perhaps, taught as Hoole, one of the masters at Rotherham, recommended, 'how and wherein they may imitate them, and borrow something out of them.' The translation of *Tenne Tragedies* published in 1581 gave even those devoid of classical lore the chance of making themselves acquainted with some, at least, of Seneca's characteristics. *Troas* had appeared as early as 1559, and all the other plays except *Thebais* by 1566. Some, at any rate, of the versions were intended, as Nevyle says of *Oedipus*, for 'tragicall and pompous showe upon stage,' but it is not known whether they were ever acted. In any case, their influence upon writers for the popular stage is beyond doubt. It was not against the dramatists of the inns of court (they were university men and went to the original Latin, as their versions show) that Thomas Nashe, in the prefatory epistle to Greene's *Menaphon* (1589), directed his jibe, '*Seneca* let bloud line by line and page by page, at length must needes die to our stage': it was against 'a sort of

shifting companions...that could scarcelie latinize their necke-
verse if they should have neede.' To these

English *Seneca* read by candle light yeeldes manie good sentences, as *Bloud
is a begger*, and so foorth: and if you intreate him faire in a frostie morning,
he will affoord you whole *Hamlets*, I should say handfulls of tragical
speaches.

It is not easy to give chapter and verse in support of Nashe's
accusation—he was too reckless a controversialist to be able
always to prove his statements by detailed evidence—but the
general inference to be made from his attack upon contemporary
dramatists is beyond question. Kyd, Marlowe and Marston saved
their credit as scholars by quoting Seneca in the original, but the
first-named—and he is probably the particular object of Nashe's
invective—also copied from Seneca without acknowledgment[1].
All three were indebted to him for the type of sensational and
rhetorical tragedy which they made popular, and smaller men, whose
work has now perished, would be no less affected. Elizabethan
tragedy adopted not only Seneca's five acts, and occasionally his
choruses, his stock characters—especially the prologuising ghost[2]
—and his philosophical commonplaces, but his exaggerated
passions, his crude horrors and his exuberant rhetoric. In the
induction to *A warning for Faire Women* (1599)—a play which,
itself, is an example of the faults it condemns—the typical
Elizabethan tragedy is described as telling

> How some damn'd tyrant to obtain a crown
> Stabs, hangs, impoisons, smothers, cutteth throats:
> And then a Chorus, too, comes howling in
> And tells us of the worrying of a cat:
> Then, too, a filthy whining ghost,
> Lapt in some foul sheet, or a leather pilch,
> Comes screaming like a pig half stick'd,
> And cries, *Vindicta*!—Revenge, Revenge!

Fortunately, more wholesome influences were brought to bear
on the popular stage by the renewed interest in English history
which followed the national triumph over the Armada, and which
the publication of chronicles enabled dramatists to gratify.
Thomas Legge's *Richardus Tertius*, acted at St John's college,
Cambridge, in 1573, 1579 and 1582 (if all the dates in the MSS are

---

[1] See Boas, F. S., *The Works of Thomas Kyd*, introduction, pp. xvii, xxiv, xxxii,
xxxiv—xxxv, xlv; Otto, M., *Der Stil in Thomas Kyds Originaldramen* (Berlin, 1905);
MacCallum, M. W., 'The Authorship of the Early Hamlet,' *An English Miscellany
presented to Dr Furnivall* (1901).
[2] See Moorman, F. W., 'The Pre-Shaksperean Ghost,' *The Modern Language
Review*, vol. I, p. 85 (Jan. 1906).

correct), is a remarkable early example of the treatment, after the Senecan manner, of a subject taken from comparatively recent national history. This, in itself, distinguishes it from earlier Latin plays, such as Buchanan's *Jephthes* and *Johannes Baptistes* and Grimoald's *Archipropheta*, which treated scriptural subjects after the classical model, and from later tragedies, such as Gager's, which were classical both in matter and form[1]. But, in spite of the numerous manuscripts in which *Richardus Tertius* has come down to us, and the references to it by Harington, Nashe and Meres, Churchill, in his excellent treatise on the subject[2], seems to imply too much when he says that 'to Legge was due the turning of the drama in England in an entirely new direction.' The character of the earliest surviving history plays in the vernacular suggests that the impulse to their composition was not academic but popular, and their models not classical tragedy, at first or second hand, but miracle-plays, the methods of which they apply to national history, as had been done in France more than a century before. *The Famous Victories of Henry the fifth* (printed 1598 and acted before 1588), by common consent the earliest example, though, doubtless, it is later in date than *Richardus Tertius*, departs as widely as possible from classical standards in its utter formlessness, its lack not only of choruses but of acts, its combination of comic and serious interests, its mixture of prose with indifferent verse. *The Troublesome Raigne of King John* (printed 1591), considered by A. W. Ward 'the best example of the chronicle history pure and simple,' has nothing classical about it, except a few scraps of Latin, mainly introduced for comic effect. It appeals, with a good deal more art than the preceding play, though there is still much to seek on this score, to the national spirit, which had hitherto found dramatic expression only in the folk-play. In the address 'To the gentlemen readers' (given in the edition of 1591, but omitted in that of 1611 reprinted by Nichols), the dramatist frankly makes this patriotic interest his first claim for attention :

> You that with friendly grace of smoothed brow
> Have entertained the Scythian Tamburlaine,
> And given applause unto an Infidel :
> Vouchsafe to welcome (with like curtesie)
> A warlike Christian and your Countreyman.

[1] See Churchill, G. B. and Keller, W., 'Die lateinischen Universitäts-Dramen Englands in der Zeit der Königin Elizabeth,' *Jahrbuch der Deutschen Shakespeare Gesellschaft*, vol. xxxiv (1898).

[2] 'Richard the Third up to Shakespeare,' *Palaestra*, vol. x (1900).

But the real hero of the play, as of that which Shakespeare founded on it, is the bastard Fawconbridge, who is given due prominence in the title, and whose character is developed with a good deal of spirit and skill[1]. On the whole, however, the artistic merits of the play have been exaggerated by recent critics ; blank verse, rime and prose are used with the same careless facility, and 'the scenes follow one another without any attempt at dramatic construction.' But in it, as in the earlier play, we catch the first tones of the voice of Elizabethan England to which Shakespeare gave fuller and nobler expression in the historical dramas founded on these first rude attempts[2]:

> Let England live but true within it selfe,
> And all the world can never wrong her State.
>
> *   *   *   *   *   *
>
> If Englands Peeres and people joyne in one,
> Nor Pope, nor Fraunce, nor Spaine can doo them wrong.

Apart from the use made of it by Shakespeare, *The True Chronicle History of King Leir, and his three daughters, Gonorill, Ragan, and Cordella* (printed 1605 and probably acted 1594[3]) has an interest of its own, though few will be found to subscribe to the opinion[4] that 'the whole of this old drama is incomparably and in every respect superior to Shakespeare's adaptation.' But it may be freely admitted that the old play is well contrived, and written in a light, easy style which is not unpleasing. In spite of its absurd disguises and coincidences, it is an organic whole, and not a mere succession of events taken haphazard from the chronicle, its main sources being, indeed, Warner, *Mirror for Magistrates* and *The Faerie Queene.* The contrast between the bearing of Cordella and her sisters is made more natural by the fact that they have an advantage over her in being informed beforehand that they will lose nothing by compliance with their father's test of affection ; and the characters

---

[1] The most striking episode, at the opening of the play, was apparently adapted by the dramatist, with additions of his own, from a story told by Hall and Stow of the bastard Dunois of Orleans. See Boswell-Stone, W. G., *Shakespeare's Holinshed*, pp. 48—50.

[2] The same comment might be made on the pre-Shakespearean *Richard II*, printed in *Shakespeare Jahrbuch*, 1899 (vol. xxxv), and commended by Boas in *Fortnightly Review*, vol. lxxviii (1902), pp. 391—404, for 'its breadth of canvass, its insight into popular feeling, and its abundant comic relief.'

[3] On this point see Perrett, W., 'The Story of King Lear,' *Palaestra*, vol. xxxv and Law, R. A., *Publications of the Modern Language Association of America*, vol. xxi, pp. 462—477 (1906).

[4] Leo Tolstoi, in *Fortnightly Review*, Jan. 1907, vol. lxxxvii, p. 66.

are clearly, though not deeply, conceived. There is a solitary
Senecan aphorism ('For fear of death is worse than death itself');
but the play is free, alike from the tedious commonplaces of
academic tragedy, and from the extravagant rhetoric which
Tamburlaine had brought into vogue. This is partly due to
the dramatist's vein of humour, not always duly restrained, but
seasoned with salt enough to withstand the changes of time.
Occasionally, he seems to criticise the absurdity of his own
dramatic expedients. There is more point than was, perhaps,
apparent to the author in Mumford's comment upon the disguised
king's extraordinary speed in the wooing of Cordella:

> Have Palmers weeds such power to win fayre Ladies?
> Fayth, then I hope the next that falles is myne:
> Upon condition I no worse might speed,
> I would for ever weare a Palmers weed.
> I like an honest and playne dealing wench,
> That sweares (without exceptions) I will have you.
> These soppets, that know not whether to love a man or no,
> except they first go aske their mothers leave, by this hand, I
> hate them ten tymes worse then poyson.

> KING.
> What resteth then our happinesse to procure?

> MUMFORD.
> Fayth, go to Church, to make the matter sure.

> KING.
> It shall be so, because the world shall say,
> King *Leirs* three daughters were wedded in one day:
> The celebration of this happy chaunce,
> We will deferre, untill we come to Fraunce.

> MUMFORD.
> I like the wooing, that's not long a doing.
> Well, for her sake, I know what I know:
> Ile never marry whilest I live,
> Except I have one of these Brittish Ladyes,
> My humour is alienated from the mayds of Fraunce.

The Lamentable Tragedie of Locrine (*Newly set foorth,
overseene and corrected. By W. S.* 1595) is a play of unusual
interest, not only because of the questions of authorship it raises,
but because of its combination of the diverse streams of influence
to which the drama was by this time subject. It adopts the dumb-
shows of academic tragedy, with Até as chorus; it has two ghosts
and a duplicated revenge motive; the opening scene is imitated

from *Gorboduc*; and there are numerous transcripts from Seneca[1]. But it has also a large and lively comic element and a good deal of stage fighting, and it borrows freely from Kyd, Marlowe, Greene, Peele and Lodge, and from Spenser's *Complaints* (entered in the Stationers' register 29 December 1590, and containing, in *The Ruines of Time*, a reference to the death of Sir Francis Walsingham, 6 April 1590). The dramatist has been accused of borrowing from another play, very similar in style, *The First part of the Tragicall raigne of Selimus* (printed 1594); but, in this case, the obligation seems to be the other way. The contributions to this interesting controversy have been numerous and varied. Tieck marked a number of parallels between *Locrine* and Spenser's *Complaints* in his copy of the fourth folio of Shakespeare; but these were first published, with a few additions by R. Brotanek, in 1900[2]. P. A. Daniel[3] had already drawn attention to the almost identical passages in *Locrine* and *Selimus*. Charles Crawford, who had undertaken the same investigation at the instigation of Grosart, charged the author of *Locrine* with wholesale 'cribbing' from *Selimus*, supporting the accusation with an elaborate array of parallel passages[4]. Emil Koeppel's attention was called to Crawford's articles by a summary of them published in the *Shakespeare Jahrbuch*; and, after an examination of the text, he arrived at an exactly opposite conclusion, viz. that *Selimus* borrowed from *Locrine*[5]. The same conclusion had been reached independently by F. G. Hubbard of the university of Wisconsin, and has since been supported by him with further evidence in a paper to which he kindly gave the present writer access before its publication. It is pointed out that the comic scene in *Locrine*[6], which is paralleled in *Selimus*, stands alone in the latter play, while, in *Locrine*, there is much other low humour of the same kind in connection with the same characters. Hubbard adds to this argument in favour of the priority of *Locrine* some important considerations with reference to the lines

---

[1] Cf. the passage in the second scene beginning (ll. 68—9)

> But what so ere the fates determind have,
> It lieth not in us to disannull,

with *Oedipus* 1001—16 : *Fatis agimur : cedite fatis.*

[2] *Beiblatt zur Anglia*, vol. xi, pp. 202—7.

[3] In a letter to *The Athenæum* of 16 April 1898, p. 512.

[4] In a series of papers contributed to *Notes and Queries* in 1901 (Ser. ix, vol. vii).

[5] Koeppel's paper was published in *Jahrbuch* for 1905 (vol. xli, pp. 193—200). See, also, Churton Collins, J., *The Plays and Poems of Robert Greene*, vol. i, pp. 61—67; Tucker Brooke, C. F., *The Shakespeare Apocrypha*, pp. xvi—xx; *Malone Society Collections* (1908), part ii, pp. 108—110. As to *Locrine*, cf. *post*, chap. x, and as to *Selimus*, chap. vi.

[6] Act iv, sc. 2.

in both plays taken from Spenser's *Complaints*. *Locrine* has
many such lines not found in *Selimus,* but (with the possible
exception of a single line) *Selimus* has nothing from the *Complaints* not found in *Locrine.* Moreover, one of these borrowed
lines in *Selimus* is followed by five other lines not found in
the *Complaints,* but found in *Locrine.* A consideration of the
whole passage in *Locrine* and its relation to the parallel lines
in *Selimus* and the *Complaints* bears out the contention that the
borrowings from the *Complaints* in *Selimus* were made through
Locrine[1]. The following parallels in the two plays show that the

---

[1] *The Ruines of Rome,* 149—160 :

> Then gan that Nation, th' earths new giant brood,
> *To dart abroad the thunder bolts of warre,
> *And, beating downe these walls with furious mood
> Into her mothers bosome, all did marre ;
> 　To th' end that none, all were it Jove his sire,
> 　Should boast himselfe of the Romane Empire.

XII

> Like as whilome the children of the earth
> *Heapt hils on hils to scale the starrie skie,
> And fight against the gods of heavenly berth,
> Whiles Jove at them his thunderbolts let flie;
> All suddenly with lightning overthrowne,
> *The furious squadrons downe to ground did fall.

(The lines copied are marked with an asterisk.)

Locrine, 800—811 :

> How bravely this yoong Brittain *Albanact*
> †Darteth abroad the thunderbolts of warre,
> Beating downe millions with his furious moode ;
> And in his glorie triumphs over all,
> †Mo[w]ing the massie squadrants of the ground ;
> †Heape hills on hills, to scale the starrie skie,
> †When *Briareus* armed with an hundreth hands
> †Floong forth an hundreth mountains at great *Jove,*
> †And when the monstrous giant *Monichus*
> †Hurld mount *Olimpus* at great *Mars* his targe,
> †And shot huge cædars at *Minervas* shield.

(The lines copied in *Selimus* are marked with a dagger.)

Selimus, 415, 416 :

> Ide dart abroad the thunderbolts of warre,
> And mow their hartlesse squadrons to the ground.

Selimus, 2423—9 :

> As those old earth-bred brethren, which once
> Heape hill on hill to scale the starrie skie,
> When *Briareus* arm'd with a hundreth hands,
> Flung forth a hundred mountaines at great *Jove,*
> And when the monstrous giant *Monichus*
> Hurld mount *Olimpus* at great *Mars* his targe,
> And darted cedars at *Minervas* shield.

author of the later drama outheroded Herod in the current practice of plagiarism:

Locrine, 1303—6:

> Where I may damne, condemne and ban my fill,
> The heavens, the hell, the earth, the aire, the fire,
> And utter curses to the concave skie,
> Which may infect the aiery regions.

Selimus, 1803—5:

> Now *Bajazet* will ban another while,
> And utter curses to the concave skie,
> Which may infect the regions of the ayre.

Locrine, 793—6:

> And but thou better use thy bragging blade,
> Then thou doest rule thy overflowing toong,
> Superbious Brittaine, thou shalt know too soone
> The force of *Humber* and his Scithians.

Selimus, 2457—60:

> But thou canst better use thy bragging blade,
> Then thou canst rule thy overflowing tongue,
> Soone shalt thou know that *Selims* mightie arme
> Is able to overthrow poore *Tonombey*.

All this does not help us much as to the authorship of the two plays, except negatively. It seems fairly certain that they were not written by the same man, for it is unlikely that even an Elizabethan dramatist would repeat himself to the extent indicated above, and, as Crawford pointed out, *Selimus* has numerous borrowings from *The Faerie Queene*, while *Locrine* has none. The light thrown on the respective dates of the two plays is more significant. *Locrine*, in its present shape, cannot have been completed before 1591, when Spenser's *Complaints* was published. Subsidiary proof of this is found by Hubbard in the line near the end of act v, 'One mischief follows on another's neck,' apparently copied from *Tancred and Gismund* (pub. 1591, with prefatory letter dated 8 August 1591)—'One mischief brings another on his neck'—a line not given in the earlier MS version of the play. *Selimus* was later than *Locrine*, from which it copied, and, as Greene died on 3 September 1592, this brings the issue of his authorship of the play within narrow limits. The dates also disprove Crawford's theory that *Selimus* was Marlowe's first play.

It is remarkable that, at this late date, when new and potent influences had begun to work upon English tragedy, a writer for the popular stage should retain characteristic features of the type of tragedy which the dramatists of the inns of court had founded upon the model of Seneca and his Italian imitators. Some of these features—the ghost and the revenge motive, sensational horrors and rhetorical exaggerations, philosophical reflections and highly polished lyrical or descriptive passages—became permanent characteristics, for good or ill, of Elizabethan tragedy. Other elements were taken from other sources; and, no doubt, it is well to keep in mind that, after the establishment of public theatres, writers of tragedies and historical plays gave their main attention to popular taste and national tradition, not to the classical authorities held in esteem in the universities and the inns of court, from which English tragedy had received its first bent. But, in theory, at any rate, the playwrights still honoured classical precepts and example; and their practice, though it departed widely from classical models, was not so lawless as it would have been without this restraining force. The valuable part of the Elizabethan inheritance from the classics in tragedy was, indeed, not that which lies on the surface—such mechanical devices as the use of the chorus and the division into five acts, the ghost and other exaggerated horrors; it was something more subtle and difficult to trace—the conception of a real, though not a formal, unity of interest, dignity of persons and decorum of style.

CHAPTER V

EARLY ENGLISH COMEDY

ONE of the leading notes of medieval literature in all its forms is its impersonality. Its most characteristic products of romance or saga or song bear the impress, not of an individual writer's art, but of the collective genius of a nation or an epoch. This is equally true of medieval drama, both of those scriptural and allegorical plays by which the church sought at once to entertain and edify all classes, and of the farces which, in continental countries, were a still more spontaneous product of the popular instinct for the theatre. Thus, it is a sign of the passing of the old order, when the historian of the English stage is for the first time confronted, not by the shadowy and elusive forms of the writers to whom we owe the miracles and earlier morality plays, but by the authentic figure of a dramatist the record of whose career is still in part extant in letters, legal documents and state archives.

John Heywood was born towards the close of the fifteenth century, in 1497 or 1498. In a letter to Burghley from Malines (18 April 1575), he speaks of himself as seventy-eight years of age. E. P. Droeshout, a Jesuit father, in a manuscript *Histoire de la Compagnie de Jésus à Anvers*[1], speaks of him in April 1578 as a '*vieillard octogénaire.*' J. Pitseus says that he was born in London ; and, as Pitseus was well acquainted with Heywood's younger son, Jasper, the statement may be accepted as correct. At an early age[2], Heywood entered the royal service, probably as a chorister. On 6 January 1514—15, he is set down in the *Book of Payments* of Henry VIII as receiving 'wages 8d. per day,' and, in 1519, he appears as a 'singer.' In 1526, he received, as a 'player

---

[1] See Bang, W., 'Acta Anglo-Lovaniensia : John Heywood und sein Kreis,' *Englische Studien*, vol. xxxviii, pp. 234—250. From manuscript and documentary sources Bang has thrown valuable new light upon Heywood's relationships, and upon his later years in the Netherlands.

[2] [See addenda.]

of the virginals,' the quarterly wage of £6. 13s. 4d., and, between
1538 and 1542, he is mentioned frequently in the same capacity at
a much lower salary. But, evidently, he was also engaged in other
ways. In January 1536/7, his servant was paid 20d. for bringing
princess Mary's 'regalles' (hand-organ) from London to Greenwich; and, in March of the following year, 40s. were paid him for
playing an interlude with his 'children' before the princess. These
'children' probably belonged to the song-school of St Paul's
cathedral.

Heywood is said to have been introduced to the princess by
Sir Thomas More. He belonged to More's circle by virtue of
his marriage with Eliza Rastell, though the details of the relationship are often incorrectly given. More's sister, Elizabeth, married
John Rastell, lawyer and printer. Their daughter Eliza became
Heywood's wife, and their elder son, William, was the printer of
two or more of his comedies[1]. In his combination of orthodoxy
with love of letters and with zeal for practical reform, and of exuberant gaiety of spirit with the constancy of martyrdom to his faith,
Heywood was a true kinsman, in spirit as well as in fact, of the
author of *Utopia*. His religious convictions brought him into
serious danger more than once in the later years of Henry VIII and
under Edward VI; but with the accession of Mary his fortunes rose
to their highest point. At her coronation, he sat in a pageant
under a vine against the school in St Paul's churchyard. In 1553,
he presented a play of children at court. In 1558, Mary granted
him a lease of the manor of Bolmer and other lands in Yorkshire;
but her death, later in the year, drove him and others of his circle
to the continent, where he settled at Malines. The state papers
of the ensuing period contain a number of references to him in
his exile; his letter to Burghley of April 1575, in which he thanks
him for ordering the arrears from his land at Romney to be paid
him, has already been mentioned. In the following year, as has
recently been shown from manuscript sources[2], he was brought by
his eldest son, Elizaeus, to the Jesuit college at Antwerp, where
he remained till May 1578. At Whitsuntide, the college was
attacked by a mob. Its members, including the two Heywoods,
were expelled and, after perilous experiences, found refuge at
Louvain. Here, presumably, he remained till his death; but there
is no further record till 1587, when he is spoken of by Thomas
Newton as 'dead and gone.'

---

[1] See *post*, p. 92.
[2] See *Englische Studien*, vol. xxxviii, pp. 236, 237.

Thus, in actual span of years, Heywood's diversified career lasted to the eve of, and may possibly have extended into, the decade when Shakespeare's chief predecessors were in full dramatic activity. But his extant plays all belong to the reign of Henry VIII, and four of these (including two assigned to him on general internal evidence) were printed in 1533. Thus, they date from a period when the morality was still a popular dramatic form, though often with a theological, political, or educational trend. It is Heywood's distinctive achievement that in his plays he dispenses with allegorical machinery and didactic aim, and gives a realistic representation of contemporary citizen types. His 'new and very mery enterludes,' as they are designated on the title-pages, therefore bring us far on the road towards fully developed comedy, though action and individual characterisation are still, for the most part, lacking; and it becomes a problem of firstrate interest for the historian of the drama whether Heywood's decisive innovation in theatrical methods was or was not due to foreign influences. The traditional view has been that he was the lineal successor of the writers of moralities; that, whereas some of them had introduced low life scenes under a transparent disguise of allegory, Heywood had taken the further step of dispensing with disguise entirely. According to this theory, the native English drama developed by an inner organic impulse from the Biblical to the allegorical phase, and thence to the 'human comedy' of Heywood.

But recent investigations indicate that Heywood's novel type of play was influenced by foreign models ; that his stimulus came, not mainly from the realistic elements in the moralities, but from the *soties* or *farces* which had long been popular in France[1]. If similar productions existed to any wide extent in medieval England, of which there is no proof, they have left only one survival, the fragmentary *Interludium de Clerico et Puella*[2]. In any case, he could not have had any difficulty in familiarising himself with part of the repertory of the contemporary French stage. During the earlier Tudor reigns, there was active intercourse between the courts on both sides of the Channel. There is official record of visits of 'Frenche Pleyers' in 1494 and 1495, and of '6 Mynstrells of France' about fourteen years later. No documentary evidence of similar visits in Henry VIII's reign has

---

[1] See, especially, Young, K., 'Influence of French Farce upon John Heywood,' *Modern Philology*, vol. II, pp. 97—124.

[2] Cf. *ante*, chaps. II and III.

yet been found, but they probably took place, and the story of
Maistre Pierre Patelin had found its way into English at least as
early as 1535. And between three plays traditionally assigned to
Heywood and three French works, as is shown more fully below,
the parallelism in design and treatment cannot be accidental.

While the fact of the relationship between Heywood's interludes and Gallic *farce* may, therefore, be taken as generally proved,
definite statements on details are hazardous, partly because of the
uncertainty of dates, and partly because the canon of Heywood's
plays cannot be fixed beyond dispute. Two interludes, *The Play
of the wether* and *A play of love*, were first printed by William
Rastell in 1533 and 1534[1] respectively, and have Heywood's name
on the title-page. *The Play called the foure P.P.*, is assigned to
him in the three editions issued by W. Myddleton, W. Copland
and J. Allde, of which only the last (1569) is dated. *A Dialogue
concerning Witty and Witless* is preserved in a British Museum
manuscript ending 'Amen q[d] John Heywood.' In addition to
these four unquestionably authentic plays, two others were printed
by William Rastell: *A mery Play betwene the pardoner and the
frere, the curate and neybour Pratte*, in 1533, and *A mery play
betwene Johan the husbande Johan Tyb his wyfe & syr Jhān the
preest* in 1533/4. A. W. Pollard was the first to lay stress on
the fact that these pieces, though always attributed to Heywood,
do not bear his name[2]. They may, however, be assigned to him
with reasonable certainty, as it is highly improbable that there
were two dramatists at work, closely akin in style and technique,
and both issuing plays simultaneously through Rastell's press[3].

Of the undisputed plays, three, *Witty and Witless, Love* and
Wether, form an allied group. They are dialogues or *débats*
discussing a set theme. Their method is forensic rather than
dramatic, in the strict sense; it is the method which, in the next
century, was to be glorified in the verbal fence between Comus and
the Lady, and in the dialectics of the fallen angels in Milton's Pande-
monium. *Witty and Witless* is the most primitive of the group.
James and John dispute whether it is better 'to be a fool or a
wise man.' James, who is far the more fluent in argumentation,
wins a paradoxical victory on behalf of the fool by proving that

---

[1] See bibliography to this chapter.   [2] Gayley, *R. E. C.*, pp. 6 and 10.
[3] Pollard points out (*loc. cit.* p. 6) that the omission of Heywood's name in the two
anonymously printed comedies 'is fairly well accounted for by the fact that in *The
Play of Love*, and *Play of the wether* Rastell printed the title and *dramatis personae*
on a separate leaf, whereas in *The pardoner and the frere* and *Johan the husbande*, etc.,
there is only a head title.'

he has not to toil for his living, that he is free from mental pain and that he is secure of the greatest of all pleasures—salvation. But, just as John confesses defeat, Jerome enters the lists; he retrieves the day for 'wytty' by driving James to admit that a reasonable man is better than a beast, while the 'wyttles' and the beast are one and the same. Many of the arguments of James have their counterpart in Erasmus's *Encomium Moriae*; but there is a still closer parallel to his debate with John in the French *Dyalogue du fol et du sage*. This *Dyalogue* was probably represented at the court of Louis XII, and may well have been Heywood's model, though the Socratic conclusion in which Jerome demonstrates the superiority of 'wytty' is the English writer's own addition.

No source has as yet been traced for *Love*. Like *Witty and Witless*, it is a debate on an abstract theme. The Lover not Loved and the Woman Loved not Loving contend as to who suffers the greater pain, while a parallel argument on pleasure takes place between the Lover Loved and Neither Lover nor Loved. Each pair ask the other to adjudicate upon their claims, with the banal result that the first couple are declared to have equal pain and the second to have equal pleasure. The argumentation is spun out to an insufferable length; but *Love* is not merely a formal disputation like *Witty and Witless*. There is the crucial difference that the four characters, for all their uncouthly abstract nomenclature, give voice to their own experiences and emotions. Lover not Loved, in especial, speaks at times with a genuinely personal accent of pain. Neither Loved nor Loving tells with humorous gusto the tale of how he was beaten at the game of *moccum moccabitur* by an artful 'sweeting.' Later, he contributes the one dramatic episode in the interlude. He 'cometh in running suddenly about the place among the audience with a high copper tank on his head full of squibs fired, crying water! water! fire! fire! fire!' and sends the Lover Loved into a swoon with a false alarm that his mistress has been burnt to death. It is noticeable that, while the central part of the play is written in couplets, the earlier sections are in rime royal, and that Heywood reverts to this in the closing speeches, in which the religious moralising was suitable to Christmastide, when *Love* was evidently performed.

The Play of the wether has similar metrical characteristics. Jupiter's opening and closing speeches are in rime royal, and the rest of the play is in couplets, save for occasional quatrains.

The interlude was written for an evening entertainment at court, or in some nobleman's hall[1], and introduces no less than ten personages—much the largest number that occurs in any of Heywood's works. He thus has an opportunity of sketching varied types, from the solemn and sententious Jupiter to his 'cryer,' the Vice, Mery-reporte, a bouncing self-confident rogue with an ungovernably free tongue. Mery-reporte's by-play, as the characters are successively introduced, furnishes an element of action lacking in the interludes discussed above. But, in spite of its wider range, *Wether* belongs to the same type as *Witty and Witless* and *Love*. It has no development of plot, but presents, in turn, representative exponents of divergent views on a debateable theme. Here it is the problem of the management of the weather, which a 'parlyament' of gods and goddesses, with the characteristic complaisance of a Tudor legislature, has 'holly surrendryd' to the autocrat Jupiter, who, also in accord with Tudor precedent, consults the opinion of 'all maner people' before taking action. The 'gentylman' wants dry and windless weather suitable for hunting; the merchant begs for variable, but not violent, winds; the ranger of woods is anxious for 'good rage of blustryng and blowynge.' The water-miller wants rain which will not fall while the wind blows; the wind-miller complains that there is 'such revell of rayne' that it destroys the wind. These two brethren of the craft are not content, like the other petitioners, with making their appeal to the god. They have an altercation on the merits of wind and water, to which trade rivalry gives a pungency and realism not often found in a *débat*. There are high words, too, between the 'gentylwoman,' who would banish the sun, lest it should ruin her complexion, and the 'launder,' who wants it to shine always, in order to dry clothes for him. Last, there runs in 'the Boy, the lest that can play,' with his delightful plea:

> All my pleasure is in catchynge of byrdes,
> And makynge of snow-ballys and throwyng the same;
> For the whyche purpose to have set in frame,
> Wyth my godfather god I wolde fayne have spoken,
> Desyrynge hym to have sent me by some token
> Where I myghte have had great frost for my pytfallys,
> And plente of snow to make my snow-ballys.

---

[1] Cf. ll. 1026—8, where the boy says that he has heard that 'god almighty,' *i.e.* Jupiter

> Was com from heven, by his owne accorde,
> This nyght to suppe here wyth my lorde.

This onys had, boyes lyvis be such as no man leddys.
O, to se my snow ballys light on my felowes heddys,
And to here the byrdes how they flycker theyr wynges
In the pytfale! I say yt passeth all thynges.

Jupiter, finally, declares that all the petitioners shall have in turn
the weather that they have asked for.   And, in the didactic vein
of a lecturer on economics, he points the moral of the mutual
dependence of all classes:

There is no one craft can preserve man so,
But by other craftes, of necessyte,
He must have myche parte of his commodyte.

The first edition of *The Play called the foure P.P.* was not
published till more than ten years after Rastell's edition of *Wether*.
The presumption, therefore, is that, of the two plays, *The foure
P. P.* is the later though the internal evidence is inconclusive.   It
contains a smaller and less diversified range of characters—the
'palmer, pardoner, potycary and pedler,' from whom it takes its
title; the structure is less compact, and the versification, which
consists almost throughout of couplets with four stresses in each
line, has not so much variety.   On the other hand, the verve and
pungent humour of the most notable passages are unequalled by
Wether or any other of Heywood's undoubted interludes, and the
climax to the triangular duel which forms the main episode of *The
foure P. P.* is an effective piece of dramatic technique.

The opening wrangle between the palmer, the pardoner and
the 'potycary on the merits of their respective vocations is in
Heywood's characteristic manner.   The entry of the light-hearted
pedler—a true fore-runner of Autolycus—with his well filled pack,
turns the talk into a more broadly humorous vein, ending in a
song.   The newcomer is then asked to decide between the claims
of the three rivals, but he modestly declines to judge 'in maters
of weyght.'   As, however, he has some skill in lying, and, as lying
is their 'comen usage,' he offers to pronounce upon their relative merits in this respect.   After some preliminary skirmishing,
in which the pardoner vaunts the virtues of his remarkable assort-
ment of relics, and the 'potycary those of his equally wonderful
collection of medicines, the pedler proposes that each shall tell a
tale as a test of his powers of falsification.   Though these tales
are not organically related to the preceding dialogue, they give
Heywood an opportunity for the display of his remarkable narrative faculty at its best.   The 'potycary's tale is coarse; but, regarded
from the point of view of a Munchausen romance, it is a capital

piece of writing. It is far outdone, however, by the pardoner's story of his visit to hell to rescue the soul of his friend, Margery Coorson, who had died during his absence. No such masterpiece of humorous narrative had appeared in England since Chaucer ceased to write, though the grimly grotesque vein of the recital is entirely Heywood's own. The description of the anniversary festival of Lucifer's fall, when all the devils appeared in gala dress:

> Theyr hornes well-gylt, theyr clowes full clene,
> Theyr taylles wellkempt, and, as I wene,
> With sothery butter theyr bodyes anoynted;

the account of Lucifer's audience to the pardoner, with the interchange of courtesies, and the formal compact that Margery may go free if the pardoner will undertake that 'there come no mo' women to hell—all these are combined in a chiaroscuro treatment unequalled of its kind till, in Byron's *Vision of Judgment,* it was applied to a similar theme, with added touches of sublimity and *saeva indignatio.* The pardoner's tale gives the palmer his chance. He cannot understand

> That women in hell such shrewes can be,
> And here so gentyll, as farre as I se.

He has known five hundred thousand women;

> Yet in all places where I have ben
> Of all the women that I have sene,
> I never sawe nor knewe in my consyens
> Any one woman out of paciens.

Such an unheard-of statement startles rivals and judge alike into involuntary exclamations:

> 'Pot. By the masse, there is a great lye.
> Pard. I never harde a greater, by our lady.
> Ped. A greater! nay, knowe ye any so great?

The palmer, manifestly, is the victor, and the situation should have been rounded off in a few lines. But the pedler spins it out by the prolix manner of his adjudication, and by his final homily on matters of conduct and faith.

Were Heywood's place in dramatic history to be determined purely by his indisputable works, it would be matter of doubt whether he had not chosen the wrong channel for his great gifts. His narrative powers might have made him the last and most brilliant of Chaucer's successors, while his services to the stage, great as they were, would be limited by his inability to portray action. But, if *The pardoner and the frere* and *Johan Johan* are placed to his credit, the range of his achievement is materially widened.

It must be allowed that both plays differ largely from Heywood's acknowledged pieces in one respect. The latter all end, as has been seen, upon an edifying note; but in *The pardoner and the frere* and *Johan Johan*, scoundrels and sinners go off triumphant. This, however, may be due to the influence of French farce; while, in general conception of character, in handling of metre and in peculiarities of vocabulary and nomenclature[1] there is close affinity between the two plays and Heywood's dialogues and interludes, especially *The foure P. P.* The balance of evidence is in favour of his authorship of the anonymous pieces.

The opening of *The pardoner and the frere, the curate and neybour Pratte,* where the two worthies set forth their claims and credentials, is strikingly parallel to that of *The foure P. P.* But here, the pardoner, in opposition to the evangelical pretensions of the frere, emphasises his papal commission to the utmost. And the dialogue method reaches its culminating point of humorous effectiveness in an amusing scene where, after each line of the frere's charity sermon, his rival interjects an appeal to the congregation to contribute to the restoration of the chapel of 'swete saynte Leonarde,' and to earn the remission of sins promised by the papal bull. This indirect process of recrimination is varied by bouts of direct personal abuse, till the quarrel reaches its height in a vigorous use of fists, not to speak of nails and teeth. At this point, the parson of the parish enters with an imprecation on the wranglers who are polluting his church, and who have only been restrained from bloodshed by the lack of staves or edged tools. While he deals with the frere, he calls in the help of the lay arm, in the shape of 'neybour Prat,' to manage the pardoner, who is also a layman. Prat promises his man a taste of the stocks, while the parson seeks to hale the frere off to prison. It looks as

---

[1] Some of these points have not been sufficiently noted. Thus, Heywood is fond of alluding to unfamiliar saints and shrines. The *locus classicus* is in the palmer's opening speech in *The foure P. P.* Among the shrines mentioned is the obscure one of ' our Lady at Crome,' by whom Johan is found swearing in his opening speech. Afterwards, Johan appeals to ' swete Saynt Dyryk,' and the priest mentions the shrine of ' Saynt Modwin,' which seems to have been at Burton-on-Trent. Two of the sham relics exhibited by the pardoner in *The foure P. P.*, 'the great toe of the Trinite' and ' of all Hallows the bless'd jaw bone' reappear (as Swoboda has noted) among the stock-in-trade of his colleague in *The pardoner and the frere.* But, possibly, more indicative of a single hand is the parallelism in the respective lists of the 'buttocke bone of Pentecoste' and the ' arm of sweet Saint Sunday,' and of the eye-tooth of the Great Turk, which prevents blindness, and the 'brayn pan' of 'Saynt Myghell,' a preservative against headache. It is worth noting, too, that the rare word 'nyfuls,' used in *Wether*, reappears in *Johan Johan*, and that the phrase 'vii yeare,' for an indefinite period of time, occurs in *Wether, Johan Johan,* and *The pardoner and the frere.*

if the two knaves were going to get their deserts, when, by an unexpected rally, they get the better of their captors, and go off with all the honours of war, and an ominous hint of a return visit!

Chaucer had supplied some of the materials for the characters of the pardoner and the frere, and there are also resemblances between the play and the *Farce nouvelle d'un Pardonneur, d'un triacleur et d'une tavernière.* In *Johan Johan,* the resemblances to episodes in the *Farce de Pernet qui va au vin* are so detailed that borrowing on the one side or the other is self-evident[1]. Apart from a number of verbal coincidences, the singular situation of a husband being set to chafe wax while his wife and her lover are making merry together can hardly have occurred independently to two playwrights. The only extant edition of *Pernet qui va au vin* dates from 1548, but it was then *nouvellement imprimé,* and it is probable that an earlier issue was available for Heywood's use. If not, the French play must have been indebted to the English, which is unlikely at this period.

The duped husband, Johan Johan, the central figure of the piece, is admirably sketched. During his wife's absence, he boasts loudly about the beating that he will give her; but, on her return, he protests that he has been merely talking of beating 'stokfysshe in Temmes Street' for a Lenten dish. He suspects, with only too good reason, that Tyb's frequent visits to Sir Jhan, the priest, have other than spiritual motives, but he unburdens himself only in 'asides,' and he dare not refuse to carry an invitation to Sir Jhan to come and share a 'pye.' As he starts on his ungrateful errand, he is repeatedly called back by his domineering partner to do various domestic offices. And, when he returns with the wily priest, who has accepted the invitation after well feigned reluctance, Tyb has further orders for him. He has to fetch a pail of water, but the pail has a 'clyfte, both large and wyde,' which is not likely to have come by mere accident. So, while the wife and the guest enjoy themselves, the master of the house has to sit at the fire and melt wax to mend the hole. As he ruefully mutters:

> I chafe the wax—
> And I chafe it so hard that my fyngers krakks;
> And eke the smoke puttyth out my eyes two:
> I burne my face, and ray my clothys also,
> And yet I dare not say one word,
> And they syt laughyng yender at the bord.

---

[1] See Young, K., 'Influence of French Farce,' etc., pp. 102—9, and Pollard, A. W., in Gayley, C. M., *R. E. C.* p. 15.

But, when the meal has been ended, and the two feasters, after the 'recreacion' of some spicy stories by Sir Jhan, turn to making mock of the wretched Johan, it is too much even for him. In a sudden outburst of valour, born of despair, he rounds upon his tormentors, gives them a drubbing and turns them out of doors—though he hurries after them for fear of further misdoing in Sir Jhan's chamber.

Assuming that *Johan Johan* and *Witty and Witless* are by the same author, we have thus seen Heywood's advance from the composition of abstract and prolix dialogue to that of tersely written and realistic farce. In any case, with *Johan Johan* English drama had come close to the confines of true comedy.

A still nearer approach, in more than one aspect, was made by *A new cōmodye in englysh in maner of an enterlude*, generally known, from its hero and heroine, as *Calisto and Melebea*. This work was published by John Rastell, probably about 1530. It was an adaptation of the earlier part of the Spanish dramatic novel *Celestina*, issued, probably, first at Burgos in 1499, of which Fernando de Rojas was the chief, if not the sole, author. *Celestina* originally contained sixteen acts; but these were increased in 1502 to twenty-one. A work of these proportions, and containing long narrative and descriptive passages, was evidently not intended for the stage, though written in dialogue form. But, in spite of its hybrid character, it took Spain and Europe by storm, through its union of a romantic love-story with realistic and intensely vivid pictures of the lowest social types[1]. The first four acts, which alone are adapted in the English version, tell of Calisto's passion for Melebea, who will not listen to his suit; his appeal, at the suggestion of his servant, Sempronio, to the noted bawd, Celestina, to use her arts to soften the heroine's heart; the misgivings of Parmeno, fellow-servant of Sempronio, as to Celestina's aims; and her success, when she has been sufficiently bribed, in wiling out of Melebea her girdle, to be carried as a token of goodwill to Calisto, whose fictitious toothache it is to cure. The author of *Calisto and Melebea* shows masterly skill in his transformation of the earlier part of the Spanish work into an interlude. With unerring instinct, he selects from the prolix original the salient points of character and action, and condenses into narrative form, as in Celestina's opening tale of Elicea and her two lovers, episodes of minor significance. He manages the

[1] For an account of Celestina, see Ticknor, G., *History of Spanish Literature* (ed. 1863), per. I, ch. XIII, pp. 235 ff.

rime royal, which is used throughout, with such dexterity that, even in broken passages of dialogue, it is sufficiently supple and flexible for his purposes. His power of turning the prose of Rojas into verse, with the minimum of verbal change, as in Calisto's rhapsody on his mistress's charms, anticipates, in humbler fashion, Shakespeare's marvellous transmutation of the prose of Holinshed and North in the English and Roman history plays. Had he but carried out his work to its natural close, he would have enriched English drama with its first romantic love-tragedy. The later pages of his original offered him splendid material in the clandestine meetings of the enamoured couple, the accidental death of Calisto after one of these meetings, the suicide of Melebea and the murder of Celestina by her accomplices. Here, a truly tragic nemesis overtakes passion and crime; but the English playwright could not be satisfied without a more obviously edifying ending. So he substituted a glaringly incongruous and abrupt finale to the interlude. After Celestina's interview with Melebea, the father of the heroine appears with an account of a dream, in which he has seen her lured by a 'foule roughe bych' to the brink of a foul pit. Thereupon, Melebea interprets the dream, and repents aloud of her sins, while her father points the moral in a long discourse upon the efficacy of prayer, the importance of youthful training and the remedial function of wise laws. There is no Tudor play in which the romantic and the didactic tendencies meet in such violent collision as in *Calisto and Melebea*. At the very moment when the interlude seems developing into a full-grown comedy or tragicomedy, it is strangled by a hostile reactionary force.

Whether there was the same collision of tendencies in *The Play of Lucrece*, issued, probably, like *Calisto and Melebea*, from the press of John Rastell, it is not possible to say. Only a fragment, apparently, survives[1]; but, from this, it is evident that the interlude includes a romantic love-story between a Publius Cornelius and a lady Lucrece otherwise unknown to history or to the stage. The portions of two scenes which have been preserved are written in lively manner, in short lines with, as a rule, three stresses.

Both *Calisto and Melebea* and *Lucrece*, though designed in interlude form, show the influences of the classical revival. It was from this revival and the neo-Latin drama which followed in its

---

[1] MSS Harl. 5919, fol. 20, No. 98. Facsimiled in Bang's *Materialien*, vol. XII, and printed in *The Malone Society's Publications*, part II, pp. 139—142.

wake that English comedy, in the full sense, finally sprang. The influence of the Roman stage never became entirely extinct throughout the medieval period, as Hrotsvitha's religious adaptations of Terence in the tenth century help to testify. Among his services to dawning humanism, Petrarch, about 1331, wrote a Terentian comedy, *Philologia*, and later products of a kindred type in Italy were Aretino's *Poliscene* (c. 1390) and Ugolino's *Philogena*, before 1437. The recovery of the twelve lost plays of Plautus in 1427 was a powerful stimulus to the study of Roman dramatists in Italy and to the representation of their works and of neo-Latin imitations of them. This movement soon spread beyond the Alps. A representation of Terence's *Andria* in the original took place at Metz in 1502, though the first attempt to perform it had to be abandoned owing to the riotous conduct of the spectators who did not understand Latin. Ravisius Textor, professor of rhetoric in the college of Navarre, at Paris, and, afterwards, rector of the university of Paris, wrote a number of Latin *Dialogi* for performance by his pupils. They were published, after his death, in 1530, and, though more akin to the interlude than to Roman comedy, they exercised, as will be seen, considerable influence. In Teutonic countries, neo-Latin drama had a still more vigorous growth. The German humanist, Reuchlin, in his *Henno* (1498) put the rogueries of Patelin into Terentian dress. Holland, early in the sixteenth century, produced a school of dramatists who, touched by the moral fervour of the reformation movement, gave the setting of Roman comedy to Biblical themes. A notable group of these plays, written for performance by young scholars, were variations on the story of the Prodigal Son. The most brilliant and popular plays of this type were the *Asotus* and the *Rebelles* of George Macropedius, the *Acolastus* of William Gnaphaeus, and the *Studentes* of Christopher Stymmelius. Another group of Biblical comedies, including those by Xystus Betuleius of Basel, centred round such figures as Ruth, Susanna and Judith. Scriptural personages of a different type, such as Haman, furnished protestant controversialists with materials for polemical plays directed against the Roman pontiff. This anti-papal drama culminated in the *Pammachius* (1538) of Thomas Kirchmayer (Naogeorgos) in which the Roman anti-Christ was overwhelmed in an unparalleled prodigality of saturnine humour.

The classical revival on the continent, and the consequent development of the new humanist drama, began to influence the

English stage early in the sixteenth century. In 1520, Henry VIII
provided 'a goodly comedy of Plautus' for the entertainment of
some French hostages. The boys of St Paul's school, under their
master, John Ritwise, performed *Menaechmi* before Wolsey in
1527 and *Phormio* in 1528. Ritwise, also, at some date between
1522 and 1531, 'made the Tragedy of Dido out of Virgil,' and acted
the same with the scholars of his school 'before the Cardinal';
and he was also responsible for an anti-Lutheran play acted in
1527 before Henry VIII. Thus, within a few years, the St Paul's
boys, under his direction, performed classical comedy, neo-Latin
tragedy and a controversial interlude. Plays at Eton can be traced
back to the same decade, as there is a record of the expenditure of 10 shillings '*circa ornamenta ad duos lusus*' at Christmas,
1525. Eton boys acted in 1538, under Udall, before Thomas
Cromwell, and, from Malim's *Consuetudinary*, it is evident that, by
1560, the custom of performing both Latin and English plays was
well established in the school. On Twelfth Night 1573, Eton
scholars, under William Elderton, their headmaster, acted before
Elizabeth at Hampton court. The boys of 'the Gramarskolle of
Westminster,' where the custom of performing Latin comedies was
to take permanent root, appeared before Elizabeth in *Heautontimoroumenos* and *Miles Gloriosus* in January 1567; in one of the
five English plays performed during the court Christmas festivities
of 1567—8[1]; and in *Truth, ffaythfulnesse, & Mercye*, apparently a
belated morality, on New Year's day, 1574. On Shrove Tuesday,
of the previous year, the Merchant Taylors' boys, under Richard
Mulcaster, had made their first appearance in a play at court; in
1574, they acted *Timoclia at the sege of Thebes by Alexander* at
Candlemas, and, on Shrove Tuesday, *Percius and Anthomiris*
(*i.e.*, probably, *Perseus and Andromeda*). So late as Shrove
Tuesday 1583, they performed *Ariodante and Genevora*, based
on an episode in *Orlando Furioso*.

Nor was it only schools in or near London, and within the
reach of court patronage, that produced plays. At King's school,
Canterbury, under the headmastership of Anthony Rushe, there
was keen dramatic activity, encouraged by the cathedral chapter.
In the treasurer's accounts 1562—3, there is an entry of £14. 6s. 8d.
'to Mr Ruesshe for rewards geven him at settynge out of his plays
at Christmas, *per capitulum.*' In *Acta Capituli*, vol. I, f. 20,
relating to the period between 1560 and 1563, a payment of

---

[1] See Chambers, E. K., 'Court Performances before Queen Elizabeth,' *The Modern
Languages Review*, vol. II, no. 1.

56*s.* 8*d.* is recorded 'to the scholemaster and scholars towards such expensys as they shall be at in settynge furthe of Tragedies, Comedyes, and interludes this next Christmas.' This practice of acting plays at the Canterbury school, which has only recently been made known[1], is, of course, specially interesting inasmuch as Marlowe was a pupil there.

At the opposite corner of the kingdom, in Shrewsbury, the boys of the town school gave performances under their master, Thomas Ashton, in the quarry outside the walls. In the northeast, there are records of school performances at Beverley. At Hitchin, a private schoolmaster, Ralph Radcliff, who was a friend of bishop Bale, wrote plays—*jocunda & honesta spectacula*—which were acted by his pupils. They included Scriptural subjects such as Lazarus, Judith and Job, as well as themes—Griseldis, Melibaeus, Titus and Gisippus—taken directly or indirectly from Chaucer and Boccaccio. Though produced, according to Bale, before the *plebs*, some of them, if not all, were written in Latin. Like most sixteenth century school plays, they have disappeared. But it was at Oxford and Cambridge, not at the grammar schools, that the English humanist drama attained its chief development. The products of the universities were so important and varied that they receive separate treatment[2]. But, as evidence of the importance attached by academic authorities to the acting of plays, at first mainly in Latin, reference may be made here to regulations in the statutes of two Cambridge colleges. At Queens' college, it was ordained (1546) that any student refusing to act in a comedy or tragedy, or absenting himself from the performance, should be expelled. At Trinity (1560), the nine *domestici lectores* were directed on pain of fine to exhibit at Christmastide in pairs a comedy or tragedy, while the chief *lector* had to produce one on his own account.

The earliest completely extant memorial in the vernacular of the revived study of Roman comedy is the translation of *Andria*, entitled *Terens in English*, printed by John Rastell before 1530. The further step of writing an English comedy on classical lines was taken by Nicholas Udall. Born in Hampshire in 1505, Udall was educated at Winchester and at Corpus Christi college, Oxford, where he became an exponent of Lutheran views. In May 1533, he combined with John Leland in composing some verses for a pageant at the coronation of Anne Boleyn. From 1533 to 1537, he

---

[1] See *History of the King's School, Canterbury*, by Woodruff and Cape (1908), p. 80.
[2] See *post*, vol. VI, chap. XII.

was vicar of Braintree, and may have written the play *Placidas* or *St Eustace*, performed there in 1534[1]. In February 1534/5, he issued from the Augustinian monastery in London his *Floures for Latine spekynge selected and gathered oute of Terence*. The 'floures' picked by Udall from the Roman playwright's *hortus fragrantissimus* are phrases from *Andria, Eunuchus*, and *Heautontimoroumenos*, followed by their equivalents in the vernacular. The compilation of such a handbook for his pupils, to whom it is dedicated, was an admirable training for Udall's more important labours in adapting Roman comedy to the English school stage.

In the latter part of 1534, he had become headmaster of Eton, where he remained till 1541, when he lost his office through misconduct which involved a short term of imprisonment. On his release, he devoted himself to theological work, including a share in the English translation of Erasmus's *Paraphrase of the New Testament*. His protestant attitude secured him ecclesiastical preferment from Edward VI, and, even after the accession of Mary he retained the royal favour through his gifts as a playwright. In December 1554, a letter of the queen states that he has at 'soondrie seasons' shown 'dilligence' in exhibiting 'Dialogues and Enterludes' before her, and directs the revels office to provide him with such 'apparel' as he may need for the Christmas entertainments. Before this date, he had resumed the scholastic career. In 1553 or 1554, he had been appointed to the headmastership of Westminster, which he retained till his death in 1556.

Udall was evidently a man of very versatile gifts and energies, and it is unfortunate that we have not the materials for a comprehensive survey of his work as a dramatist. The Braintree play (if it was his) is lost; the play performed before Cromwell in 1538 cannot be identified; the revels accounts for 1554 do not enable us to distinguish between 'certen plaies' provided by him and the other Christmas shows: Bale's reference (1557) to *comoediae plures* by him is tantalisingly vague, and the statement that he translated *tragoediam de papatu* is puzzling, and, perhaps, erroneous, as a version of Ochino's drama by Ponet, bishop of Winchester, was issued in 1549[2]; the Scriptural play *Ezechias*, produced posthumously before Elizabeth at Cambridge in 1564, is known to us only through the accounts of eye-witnesses[3].

Thus, *Ralph Roister Doister* is the sole work which remains to

---

[1] See Chambers, E. K., vol. II, pp. 342, 451.
[2] See Herford, C. H., *Literary Relations of England and Germany*, p. 110 n.
[3] Cf. *post*, vol. VI, chap. XII.

illustrate Udall's dramatic powers. The single extant copy of the play is undated, but it probably belongs to the edition entered to Thomas Hacket in the Stationers' register in 1566/7. The evidence in favour of its having been written in 1553—4 is very strong[1]. Thomas Wilson, who had been at Eton under Udall, published in 1550/1 *The Rule of Reason*; a second edition appeared in 1552, and a third in 1553 or, possibly, 1554. In the third edition only, Wilson uses as an illustration Roister Doister's mispunctuated love-letter in act III, sc. 4. The inference is that the play had been performed for the first time between 1552 and 1553/4, probably by the Westminster boys. That it is in any case later than 1546, and, therefore, cannot have been written when Udall was headmaster of Eton, is suggested by his frequent use of phrases which appear in John Heywood's *Proverbs*, published in the above year. Apart from its evidential value, this is an interesting link between the two dramatists. But, though Udall could borrow proverbial phrases from his predecessor, he has scarcely a trace, as far as *Roister Doister* shows, of Heywood's genius for incisive and pregnant expression or of his mordant wit. Nor is any figure in his play drawn with the vitalising art which, in a few scenes, makes of Johan Johan a being of flesh and blood. But, far inferior to Heywood in spontaneous literary gifts, Udall, partly through his scholastic occupations, and partly through a happy instinct, was led to direct English comedy into the path on which, in the main, it was to advance to its later triumphs. In imitation of Plautus and Terence, he substituted for the loosely knit structure of the English morality or dialogue or of French *farce*, an organic plot divided into acts and scenes. Within this framework, he adjusted figures borrowed from Roman comedy but transformed to suit English conditions, and mingled with others of purely native origin[2]. *Miles Gloriosus*, supplemented, especially in later scenes, from *Eunuchus*, suggested the theme of a love-sick braggart's wooing of a dame whose heart is given to another suitor. But Udall condensed into a single plot episodes connected with the two frail beauties in the Plautine play, and lifted the whole action into a less pagan atmosphere. Roister Doister is as vain-glorious and credulous as Pyrgopolinices, and he covets dame Custance's 'thousande pounde' rather than herself. So confident

---

[1] See Hales, J. W., 'The Date of the First English Comedy,' *Englische Studien*, vol. XVIII, pp. 408—421.

[2] Cf. Maullby, D. L., 'The Relation between Udall's *Roister Doister* and the Comedies of Plautus and Terence,' *Englische Studien*, vol. XXXVIII, pp. 251—277.

is he that the lady will yield at once, that he woos her at first by
deputy, sending, in turn, her old nurse with his love-letter, his
servant with a ring and his companion, Mathewe Merygreeke, to
bring back her instant assent 'to be wedded on Sunday next.'
Her refusal so overcomes him that he declares he must die; but,
after a mock requiem has been said over him, he revives at Merygreeke's suggestion to try the effect of a personal interview with
Custance. It does not even need Merygreeke's perverse mis-
reading of the love-letter in Roister Doister's presence to make the
widow 'fume and frette and rage.' The braggart is again over
come by his second repulse, and begins to 'blubber,' till his
companion prompts him to seek revenge. After much mock-
heroic preparation, he makes a grand assault upon Custance's
house, only to be put to shameful rout by her Amazonian legion of
maids. Throughout the play, these maids, with their high spirits,
their gay loquacity and their love of song, form one of its most
attractive and original features. They are closer studies from
life than are the semi-Plautine leading figures. Yet, in the
person of Merygreeke, Udall succeeded, to some degree, in
anglicising a classical type or combination of types. The first
suggestion for the character comes, of course, from Artotrogos, the
parasite in *Miles Gloriosus*. But the parasite appears only in the
opening scene, and takes no part in the action of the play. It
is Palaestrio, the captain's servant, who cajoles and tricks him,
as Merygreeke does Roister Doister. Yet, though Merygreeke
makes of Roister Doister his 'chiefe banker both for meate and
money,' he follows and serves him less for gain than for fun. He
is a light-hearted and whimsical mischiefmaker, after the fashion
of the Vice of the later moralities, who plays, in turn, upon every
weakness of his patron, but who, unlike the Plautine plotter, bears
his victim no real illwill. It is a touch of true dramatic irony that
the person whom his foolery brings, for the moment, into serious
trouble is not Roister Doister, but the virtuous Custance, whose
loyalty to her betrothed comes under unjust suspicion. When she
lifts a prayer to the same Lord, who helped 'Susanna' and 'Hester'
in their need, to vindicate her innocence, Udall, in the true spirit
of romantic drama, lets a graver strain mingle with the sprightly
tones of the comedy. But, on his return, Goodluck is soon convinced that she is still 'the pearle of perfect honestie,' and, in bluff
seafaring fashion, brings about a general reconciliation between
the former combatants—a suitably edifying close to a play written
for schoolboys.

Another adaptation from Plautus for performance by boys is *Jacke Jugeler*, entered for printing in 1562/3, but written, very probably, during the reign of Mary. The author states in the prologue that the plot is based upon *Amphitruo*, and it is true that the chief characters in the Roman play have English citizen equivalents. But the central theme of Jupiter's amour, in her husband's shape, with Alcmena, disappears, and nothing is retained but the successful trick of Jacke Jugeler—the Vice who replaces Mercury—upon Jenkin Careaway, who corresponds to Sosia, servant of Amphitryon. Disguising himself like Jenkin, Jacke, by arguments and blows, forces the hapless lackey to believe that he, and not himself, is the genuine Careaway. When Jenkin tells the tale of his loss of identity to his mistress dame Coy, and her husband Bongrace, he gets further drubbings for his nonsensical story

> That one man may have two bodies and two faces,
> And that one man at on time may be in too placis.

Regarded purely as a play, *Jacke Jugeler*, in spite of its classical origin, is little more than a briskly written farcical episode. But, beneath its apparently jocular exterior, it veils an extraordinarily dextrous attack upon the doctrine of transubstantiation and the persecution by which it was enforced. This is hinted at in the epilogue, where 'this trifling enterlude' is credited with 'some further meaning, if it be well searched.'

> Such is the fashyon of the world now a dayes,
> That the symple innosaintes ar deluded ...
> And by strength, force, and violence oft tymes compelled
> To belive and saye the moune is made of a grene chese
> Or ells have great harme, and parcace their life lese.

It has been the fate of many dramatic forms and conventions to go through a remarkable 'sea-change' in their transportation from one country or epoch to another. But seldom has any device of the comic muse been 'translated' more nearly out of recognition than the classical confusion of identity, when enlisted, as here, in the service of protestant theology.

But it was less in the classical than in the neo-classical drama that the earlier Tudor writers of comedy found their chief stimulus. Probably, the first of continental humanist playwrights (as recent research has shown[1]) to influence the English stage was Ravisius

---

[1] See, especially, Holthausen, F., 'Studien zum älteren englischen Drama,' in *Englische Studien*, vol. xxxi, pp. 77—103.

Textor. His dialogue *Thersites*, written in Latin hexameters, was adapted into English in a version which must have been acted (as a reference to the birth of prince Edward proves) in October 1537[1]. Thersites is an even more burlesque type of *miles gloriosus* than is Roister Doister. Arrayed by Vulcan in full armour, he boasts to the god and afterwards to his own mother of the mighty deeds that he will do. But at the sight of a snail[2] he is terror stricken, and calls upon his servants for help, though he plucks up courage enough, at last, to use club and sword, and to make the snail draw in his horns. While he is exulting over this feat, he is challenged by a soldier; whereupon, he first takes shelter behind his mother's back, and afterwards runs away dropping his club and sword. The author of the English version shows remarkable dramatic instinct in his handling of this grotesquely farcical plot. The medley of metres that he uses is more appropriate to the bizarre incidents of the story than are the stately hexameters of Textor. He considerably expands the original text, vivifying the dialogue by the addition of many details that would appeal to an English audience. Thus, Mulciber tells Thersites not to fear 'Bevis of Hampton, Colburne and Guy,' and the braggart challenges to combat 'King Arthur and the Knightes of the Rounde Table,' and afterwards 'Robin John and Little Hode'! These and similarly deft touches give a curious plausibility to the piece in its English guise. But there is loss rather than gain in the long irrelevant episode added towards the close, wherein Telemachus brings a letter from Ulysses, and is charmed 'from the worms wild' by Thersites's mother. Some of the relics that she invokes have a family likeness to those owned by Heywood's two Pardoners. Heywood, indeed, may plausibly be regarded as the author of the adaptation, which, in its verve, raciness and, it must be added, indecency, is akin to his own work. In any case, the adapter of *Thersites*, whoever he be, is almost certainly responsible for the version of another of Textor's dialogues, *Juvenis, Pater, Uxor*, of which a black letter fragment has recently been discovered and reprinted with the title *The Prodigal Son*[3]. The fragment con-

---

[1] G. C. Moore-Smith has recently shown (*Fasciculus Joanni Willis Clark dicatus*, p. 268) from an entry in the accounts of Queens' college, Cambridge, that a *dialogus* of Textor was acted at the college in 1543. A later entry, *pro picto clipeo quo miles generosus usus est in comoedia*, suggests that the dialogue was *Thersites*, probably performed in the original Latin.

[2] Called *testudo* by Textor, but apparently a snail (as in the English version), since it has horns.

[3] See *The Malone Society Collections*, part I, pp. 27—30, and part II, pp. 106—7.

tains the episode, greatly expanded from the original, in which the son, after his marriage against his father's wish, tries to support himself and his wife by selling wood. In its metrical and verbal characteristics, and in its introduction of English allusions, as to 'Oxynby' and 'Cambrydge,' it bears the same impress, mutilated though it be, as the spirited version of *Thersites*.

Another version of *Juvenis, Pater, Uxor*, which we possess in complete form, is *The Disobedient Child*, by Thomas Ingelend, 'late student of Cambridge.' Printed about 1560, it not improbably dates from the reign of Henry VIII or Edward VI, for, though it ends with a prayer for queen Elizabeth, the audience, a few lines previously, are bidden 'truly serve the King.' In this adaptation of Textor's dialogue, Ingelend shows rhetorical and inventive gifts; but, on the whole, compared with the original, *The Disobedient Child* is a heavy-handed production. The didactic element is spun out at wearisome length, and most of the new characters introduced, the priest, the devil and the perorator, who speaks the epilogue, deliver themselves of superfluous monologues. But the scene between the man-cook, Long-tongue, and the maid-cook, Blanche blab-it-out, who prepare the marriage feast, is a lively piece of below-stairs humour, which is supplemented by the racy account of the guests' uproarious behaviour given by the bridegroom's servant. And Ingelend shows a true lyric vein in the song wherein the lover declares to his 'sweet rose' his eternal fidelity :

> Wherefore let my father spite and spurn,
> My fantasy will never turn.

Though Textor's plays are neo-classic, in so far as they are written in Latin and under humanist influences, they and the English versions of them belong in form to the interlude type. It was from the Dutch school of dramatists that Tudor playwrights learnt to combine the 'prodigal son' theme with the general framework and conventions of Roman comedy. The most popular work produced by this school, the *Acolastus* of Gnaphaeus, was issued in England with a translation by John Palsgrave in 1540. It was intended primarily to serve as a schoolbook, each scene being immediately followed by the English rendering. But Palsgrave also desired 'to move into the hearts' of his countrymen 'some little grain of honest and virtuous envy' of the foreign author's achievement. It was, not improbably, in emulation of *Acolastus* that a writer who cannot be identified with certainty[1] wrote, probably about 1560, a play, *Misogonus*, which enables us to claim for England the credit of having produced one of the most elaborate and original comedies on the prodigal son. In its general structure and development of plot, *Misogonus* shows the influence of its Latin prototype. A distracted father, Philogonus, laments to his friend and counsellor, Eupelas, over the riotous living of his son Misogonus. The young prodigal is introduced by Orgalus and Oenophilus, nominally his servants but, in effect, his boon companions, to the courtesan, Melissa, with whom he drinks and dices and plays the wanton. When his fortunes fail, he is deserted by the 'vipers' whom he has cherished. Overcome with remorse and shame, he returns trembling into his father's presence to find immediate welcome and pardon. All these episodes have their counterpart in Gnaphaeus's comedy. But the author of *Misogonus* was a creative dramatist, not merely an imitator. He individualised the somewhat shadowy neo-classic types into English figures of his own period, though the scene is nominally laid in Italy. He added new personages of his own invention, and made the *dénouement* spring out of an ingenious secondary plot. His remarkable gifts in the way of dialogue and characterisation are displayed to the full in the realistic gaming scene, where the revellers are joined by the parish priest, Sir John, who is of the same kin as Heywood's clerics—drunken and dissolute, ready, even while bell and clerk summon him to his waiting congregation, to bandy oaths over the dicebox, and to dance himself into a share of Melissa's favours. But it is not merely this 'rabblement' of 'rakehells' that brings the prodigal to ruin. He has an elder twin brother, Eugonus, who,

[1] In the single mutilated manuscript of the play which survives, in the duke of Devonshire's library, the prologue is signed 'Thomas Richardes,' and the modest terms in which he begs the muses to ' guide your clients silly style,' suggest that he is the author of the play. Under the list of *dramatis personae*, there is a signature 'Laurentius Bariωna, Ketteringe. Die 20 Novembris, Anno 1577.' The signature is evidently a disguised form of Laurence Johnson, the name of the author of a Latin treatise, *Cometographia*, printed in London in 1578, and dated, with the same disguised signature, from Kettering, 20 January 1578. Johnson, possibly, was the author, but, more probably, was the transcriber of the play. See Brandl, *Quellen*, LXXV—LXXVII, and Kittredge, G. L., in *Journ. of Germ. Philology*, vol. III, pp. 335—341. It is, perhaps, worth noting that another 'prodigal son' play, *Nice Wanton*, printed 1560, has at the end 'Finis. T. R.' Can the initials be those of Thomas Richardes? *Nice Wanton* may, as Brandl states too confidently, have been suggested by *Rebelles*. But it develops on different lines, and introduces, by the side of the human figures, such allegorical personages as Iniquity and Worldly Shame. It is a slight and crude production compared with *Misogonus*, but its most powerful episode, the dicing scene between the prodigal son and daughter and Iniquity, is akin to the similar scene in the greater play.

immediately after their birth, has been sent to his uncle in 'Polona-land.' Owing to the mother's death, the secret is known only to a group of rustics, Alison a midwife, her husband, Codrus, and two of her gossips. Codrus, threatened with ruin by the death of his 'bulchin' and the loss of his sow, hints at the truth to Philogonus in the hope of reward, and then fetches Alison to tell the full tale. The exasperating circumlocution with which she spins it out in a half incomprehensible jargon; the foolish interruptions by her husband which lead to a violent quarrel and to further delay in her disclosures; the suspense, amazement and joy of Philogonus—these are all portrayed in masterly fashion. Equally effective in purely farcical vein is the scene that follows after a messenger has been despatched to bring home the missing heir. Cacurgus, the house-hold fool, remains faithful to Misogonus, and tries to frighten Isabel and Madge out of supporting Alison's story. He pretends that he is a physician, who can cure Madge of a toothache that makes her stammer with pain, and that he is also a soothsayer, who foresees damnation for them if they bear witness that Philogonus had two sons. But the return of the long-lost Eugonus resolves all doubts, and the prodigal has to confess his sins and beg for forgive-ness. The play lacks a fifth act in the manuscript, but the action seems virtually complete. Even in its mutilated state, it claims recognition as the finest extant comedy that had yet appeared in England. To the pungent satire of *Johan Johan* it adds the structural breadth of *Roister Doister*, and the insight into rustic types of the Cambridge farce, *Gammer Gurtons Nedle*. The last-named piece, which was 'played on stage' at Christ's college, probably not long after 1550, will be treated in another chapter, among university plays[1]. But it may be pointed out here that the triviality of its main incident—the loss of the gammer's needle—and the coarseness of much of the dialogue should not be allowed to obscure the fact that its author, like Udall and the writer of *Misogonus*, had an eye for characterisation and had learned plot construction from classical or other humanist models.

The Historie of Jacob and Esau, licensed for printing in 1557, but extant only in an edition of 1568, may be grouped with the 'prodigal son' plays, though it is a variant from the standard type. The Biblical story is handled in humanist fashion, and, with the addition of subsidiary characters, is skilfully worked up into a five act comedy of orthodox pattern. Esau is the central figure, and, in an early scene, two of Isaac's neighbours, Hanan and Zethar,

[1] See *post*, vol. vi, chap. xii.

Scriptural by name but classical by origin, lament that the
patriarch's elder son 'hath been naught ever since he was born,'
and predict that he will 'come to an ill end.' They contrast his
'loose and lewd living' with the exemplary conduct of Jacob, who
'keepeth here in the tents like a quiet man.' But Esau does not
follow the ordinary evil courses of an Acolastus or a Misogonus. In
his insatiable passion for hunting, he rises while yet it is dark,
robbing his voluble servant Ragau of his sleep, and waking the
tent-dwellers with the blowing of his horn. We are given a vivid
picture of the eager follower of the chase talking to his favourite
hounds by name, and ranging the forest from morn to night
without thought of food. Thus, the way is cleverly prepared for
the scene in which Esau, on his return from the hunt, is so
faint with hunger that he is ready to eat a 'cat' or 'a shoulder
of a dog,' and catches at Jacob's offer of a mess of pottage even at
the price of his birthright. And, when his hunger has been appeased, and his servant reproaches him with having bought the
meal 'so dere,' his speech of self-justification shows the dramatist's
insight into character and his analytical power.

> If I die to morow, what good would it do me?
> If he die to morow, what benefite hath he?
> And for a thing hanging on such casualtie:
> Better a mease of pottage than nothing pardy.

Jacob and Esau do not afford much scope for the author's inventive
power, but Rebecca is drawn with considerable subtlety. She seeks,
in an ingenious way, to justify her schemes on behalf of her younger
son by proclaiming that she is an agent of the Divine Will, and
also by pleading that she scarcely knows whether Esau is her son
or not:

> He goeth abroad so early before day light,
> And returneth home again so late in the night,
> And uneth I sette eye on hym in the whole weeke:
> No sometime not in twaine, though I doe for hym seeke.

Well may Mido, Isaac's 'boy,' speak of her 'quick answers' to his
master. Mido, himself possessed of a ready tongue, is one of a group
of servants whom the dramatist has introduced, and who are a very
attractive feature of the play. He prides himself upon his strength,
as Abra, the little handmaid of Rebecca, does upon her cleanliness
and her culinary powers:

> I trust to make such broth that, when all things are in,
> God almighty selfe may wet his finger therein.

They are both eager partisans of Jacob, as is also Deborah, 'the
nurse of Isaacs tent,' while Esau's only adherent is Ragau, whose

fidelity differentiates him from the Vice, a type to which, otherwise, he is related. The prominence given to servants, the frequent introduction of songs and the general reconciliation (without Biblical warrant) at the close, are features which *Jacob and Esau* shares with *Ralph Roister Doister*. There can be little doubt that it was a school play, and that 'the Poet,' who speaks an epilogue enforcing the protestant doctrine of 'election,' was the headmaster who had written the work for performance by his pupils.

With Gascoigne's *The Glasse of Governement* (1575), we return to the more orthodox type of prodigal son play. It cannot be merely a coincidence that Gascoigne had spent the two years (or there-abouts) preceding the date of its publication as a soldier in the Low Countries, the principal home of this dramatic type. He lays his scene in Antwerp, and his plot shows the influence of several of the masterpieces of the Dutch humanist cycle[1]. The contrast between the prodigal and the virtuous son which is exemplified in *Misogonus* and *Jacob and Esau* appears in Gascoigne's work in duplicate form. Two fathers are introduced, each with a pair of sons— the younger a model of virtue and the elder a scapegrace. The four youths are confided to the care of a schoolmaster, Gnomaticus, who forthwith proceeds to expound to them at in-sufferable length 'the summe of' their 'dutyes in foure Chapters.' The unregenerate couple Philautus and Philosarchus soon grow restive under this discipline, and find more congenial occupation in the company of the courtesan Lamia and her associates, Eccho and Dicke Droom. The revolt of the pupils against their pre-ceptor was suggested, probably, by the *Rebelles* of Macropedius; but the scenes in which Lamia and the parasites figure seem inspired by similar episodes in *Acolastus*. The arrest of Lamia by the markgrave and the sudden despatch of the scholars to the university of 'Doway' are incidents of Gascoigne's own invention. At 'Doway,' the virtuous younger pair grow still more exemplary, and have their fitting reward. Philomusus finally becomes secretary to the palsgrave; and Philotimus a preacher of 'singular commendation' in Geneva. Meanwhile, the elder couple tread the broad way to destruction, till Philautus is executed for a robbery in the palsgrave's court, 'even in sight of his brother,' and Philo-sarchus, for his evil courses, is whipped at Geneva 'openly three severall dayes in the market' and 'banished the Towne with great infamie.' In *Rebelles*, the two scapegraces are put on their trial for

---

[1] See the detailed comparison in Herford, *Literary Relations*, pp. 162—3.

theft, but are spared at the instance of the master whose authority they had flouted ; the harshly Calvinistic spirit that permeates Gascoigne's play could not tolerate such a solution as this. *The Glasse of Governement,* in fact, is a puritan tract disguised in the vesture of a humanist school play. It pictures an unreal world of saints and sinners, ranged in symmetrical groups, with no room for struggle and compromise, penitence and forgiveness. Hence, though Eccho and Dicke Droom are drawn with considerable spirit, the true merits of the play lie not in characterisation but in structure and in style. Great technical skill is shown in the last act, where the scene continues to be laid in Antwerp, though the chief incidents take place elsewhere. And the use, for the first time, of vernacular prose throughout a 'prodigal son' drama gives a note of realism to the dialogue, which goes far to counterbalance the artificial moral scheme of the play[1].

It is not a little singular that Gascoigne, who perverted a type of drama imported from northern Europe by exaggerating its didactic element, should, nine years before, have been the first to present in English dress a characteristic Italian comedy of intrigue. His *Supposes,* acted at Gray's inn in 1566 (and at Trinity college, Oxford, in 1582), is a version of Ariosto's *Gli Suppositi,* written first in prose, and performed at Ferrara in 1509, and afterwards re-written in verse. Ariosto's play is a masterly adaptation of the form and types of Roman drama to the conditions of sixteenth century Italy, and it is one of the earliest regular comedies in a European vernacular. Gascoigne appears to have utilised both the prose and the verse editions; but his translation is throughout in prose. His use of this medium for dramatic purposes makes *Supposes,* translation though it be, a landmark in the history of English comedy. And, though his version, judged by Elizabethan canons, is, in the main, an exceptionally close one, he does not hesitate to substitute a familiar native phrase or allusion, where a literal rendering would be obscure, or to add a pithy proverb or quip to round off a speech. *Supposes* has thus a curiously deceptive air of being an original work, and its dialogue has a polish and lucidity which anticipate the kindred qualities of Lyly's dramatic prose. Its enduring reputation is attested not only by

[1] In 'Euphues and The Prodigal Son,' *The Library,* October, 1909, Wilson, J. D., suggests that Lyly's novel was largely 'compiled' from a 'play belonging to the prodigal son school which has now, probably, been lost. . . . Lyly, or the forgotten dramatist from whom he took his material, has . . . *intellectualized* the prodigal son story.'

the revival at Oxford in 1582, but by its adaptation about 1590, with considerable changes and in verse form, as the underplot of the anonymous *Taming of a Shrew*[1]. When Shakespeare re-modelled the anonymous play, he gave the underplot a closer resemblance to its earlier shape in *Supposes*, though he clung to verse instead of reverting to prose.

Another English version of a typical Italian comedy is *The Bugbears*, an adaptation, first published in 1561, of *La Spiritata* by the Florentine A. F. Grazzini. *The Bugbears*, which is not yet conveniently accessible[2], was, probably, more or less contemporary with *Supposes*, but, unlike Gascoigne's play, it turned the prose of its original into verse. It also departed much more widely from the Italian text, adding scenes and characters based upon the *Andria* of Terence and *Gl' Ingannati*, and only mentioning some of the personages whom Grazzini brings upon the stage. But, though the action in the English piece is complicated by the introduction of an underplot, the unities of time and place are skilfully preserved. The main plot deals with the trick of Formosus to obtain 3000 crowns from his miserly father Amadeus, which he needs for the latter's consent to his marriage with Rosimunda. Formosus has already secretly wedded her; but Amadeus will not accept any daughter-in-law who does not bring the above dowry. With the aid of a friend, Formosus makes such a disturbance at night in his father's house that Amadeus is convinced that his home is haunted by spirits, the 'bugbears' of the title. On consulting an astrologer, Nostrodamus, who, in reality, is a disguised servant, named Trappola, in league with the conspirators, he is told that the spirits are angry with him for opposing his son's marriage, and that they have carried off as a punishment 3000 crowns from his cherished hoard. The money, of course, has been abstracted by Formosus, who is thus enabled to provide for Rosimunda's dowry. The mock-astrologer also predicts danger to Cantalupo, an elderly wooer of Rosimunda, and the chief figure in the underplot, unless he abandons his suit. To further it, Cantalupo has pressed for the marriage of his daughter, Iphigenia, furnished with the requisite dowry, to Formosus. But the girl has resisted because she loves Manutius, whom now, at last, she is set

---

[1] See Warwick Bond's *The Taming of the Shrew* in the Arden edition, pp. xliii—xliv, and the present writer's edition of *The Taming of a Shrew*, pp. xxi—xxii.

[2] It has been printed from the only MS (Lansdowne 807, ff. 55—77) by Grabau, C., in *Archiv für das Studium der Neueren Sprachen und Litt.* vols. xcviii and xcix, with notes on sources, etc.

free to wed. There are other lesser threads in the piece, including the humours of the servants of the chief personages; and it contains a number of songs, both solos and choruses. The style is racy and vigorous, and the play is in all respects a notable example of Italianate comedy in English.

The influence of the southern stage, and the southern novel (new and old), upon the English theatre, is attested by the statement of Stephen Gosson in *Playes Confuted in Five Actions* (1582):

> I may boldely say it because I have seene it, that *the Palace of pleasure, the Golden Asse, the Aethiopian historie, Amadis of France,* the Rounde table, baudie Comedies, in Latine, French, Italian and Spanish, have been thoroughly ransackt to furnish the Playe houses in London.

Gosson further mentions that, in his unregenerate days, he had himself been the author of 'a cast of Italian devises, called, *the Comedie of Captain Mario.*'

In the list of plays mentioned in the revels' accounts[1] occur several that are inspired by Italian themes, *The three Systers of Mantua* (1578) and *The Duke of Millayn and the Marques of Mantua* (1579) were acted by professional players, and *Ariodante and Genevora* (1583), as already mentioned, was performed by the Merchant Taylors' boys. Italian players, it is noticeable, had, in 1574, followed the queen's progress, 'and made pastyme fyrst at Wynsor and afterwardes at Reading.' From the list of properties supplied for the performance at Reading, it is evident that the foreigners acted a pastoral.

Probably, except for some school plays, the pieces performed before the queen, even when they were on Italian, or, as was more frequently the case, on classical and mythological, subjects, were not cast in the mould of Ariosto or of Terence. Written, for the most part, to be acted by professional companies before popular audiences, they did not follow the classic or neo-classic conventions the influence of which has been traced in the preceding pages. They adhered instinctively to the freer lines of native English drama, inherited from miracle and morality plays[2]. A few of them, in fact, as may be inferred from their titles,

---

[1] See *Documents relating to the Office of the Revels in the time of Queen Elizabeth,* ed. Feuillerat, A. (vol. XXI of Bang's *Materialien*).

[2] One play of this type, not mentioned, however, in the revels' accounts, has recently been brought to light. It is *The Plaie of Pacient Grissell,* written by John Phillip and printed by T. Colwell, to whom, in all probability, it was licensed for publication in 1565/6 and 1568/9. A unique copy found in lord Mostyn's library was sold in 1907, and from this the play has been reprinted by the Malone Society (1909). The plot is taken from the closing tale of the *Decameron,* probably through an intermediate source, though some of the episodes and the form of the proper names make it

were belated moralities; a large number treated fabulous and romantic themes[1]; at least two, *The Creweltie of a Stepmother* and *Murderous mychaell*, seem to be early specimens of the drama of domestic life[2].

With few exceptions, these plays have perished; but, doubtless, they were typical of the theatrical productions of the first twenty years of Elizabeth's reign. Together with other popular pieces no longer known even by name, they came under the lash of purist critics, such as Whetstone in his preface to *Promos and Cassandra* (1578) and Sidney in his *Apologie for Poetrie* (printed in 1595), who ridiculed their extravagances of plot and style, and their defiance of the unities. Sidney deplored the mingling in the same piece of grave and humorous elements, 'hornpipes and funerals,' and proclaimed that the salvation of the English drama could only be found in strict adherence to classical rules. But it was in vain for him to strive against the stream. Even in the plays adapted from Roman, neo-Latin, or Italian models, *Roister Doister*, *Misogonus* and *The Bugbears*, the native dramatic instinct for breadth of design, vigour of characterisation and a realism that often becomes coarseness, had largely transmuted, as has been shown, the borrowed alien materials.

On the other hand, the popular drama, increasingly produced by men with something of the culture of the universities or the capital, tended towards a higher level of construction and of diction. An example of early native farcical comedy is extant in the anonymous *Tom Tyler and his Wife*, acted by 'pretty boys,' which from its language and versification cannot have been written later than the beginning of Elizabeth's reign, and probably goes back further. Though allegorical figures, Destiny, Desire and Patience, are introduced, the play is in effect a domestic drama

---

unlikely that this source was Chaucer's *Clerk's Tale.* The comedy covers the whole lengthy history of Grissell's marriage, her sufferings, her abasement, and her restoration to her husband and her dignities. The author shows some skill in grouping his materials, but the characterisation is weak, and the 'fourteeners,' in which the serious passages are mainly written, are monotonous, though the piece contains some pretty lyrics. The most interesting feature of *Pacient Grissell* is that it mingles with the personages of the Italian story a number of allegorical figures, of which the chief is 'Politicke perswasion,' the nimble-tongued Vice, who acts as the evil genius of the marquis. Thus, more than thirty years before Chettle, Dekker and Haughton's similarly named comedy (as to which cf. vol. VI, chap. II) was written, the story of 'pacient Grissell,' always a favourite with playwrights (cf. Ward, A. W., *Eng. Dram. Lit.* vol. I, pp. 428—430 and *ante*, p. 15), had appeared in vernacular dramatic form.

[1] Similar plays, not performed before the queen, but still extant, are *Common Conditions* (imperfect) and *The Rare Triumphs of Love and Fortune.*

[2] Cf. *post*, chap. XIII.

of low life, showing how Tom suffers tribulation at the hands of
his shrewish wife, and how, even when a friend has tamed her by
drastic methods, he weakly surrenders the fruits of the victory
which has been won for him. The piece has a lusty swing and
vigour in its action and dialogue, and in its racy songs. It has
also a certain underlying unity in the idea that a man cannot
escape his fate, however unpleasant it may be. As Tom Tyler
ruefully exclaims :

> If Fortune will it, I must fulfil it;
> If Destiny say it, I cannot denay it.

But, if *Tom Tyler* be compared with *The Taming of a Shrew*
(to instance a play on a somewhat kindred theme, though it lies
slightly beyond the period dealt with in this chapter), it will be
evident how much native comedy had gained from contact with
foreign models in careful articulation of plot and in refinement
of diction and portraiture.

The fusion of classical with native elements appears very
clearly in Richard Edwards's *Damon and Pithias*, a 'tragical
comedy,' as he calls it, which was almost certainly acted before
the queen in 1564[1]. The plot is drawn from the annals of Syracuse,
and such figures as Carisophus, the parasite, Eubulus, the good
counsellor, Stephano, the slave-servant, and Dionysius, the tyrant,
are borrowed from the Roman stage. Many classical quotations
are introduced into the dialogue, which in the frequent use of
στιχομυθία and of rhetorical moral commonplaces shows the
influence of Seneca. Yet in spite of its debt to Latin drama
Damon and Pithias is not an academic product, but is, in form
and spirit, predominantly of native English type. It is not divided
into acts after the classical manner; and in its deliberate mixture
of pathos and farcical humour, and in its violation of the unity
of time, it runs counter not exactly to the precedents of the
classical stage, but to the current renascence perversion of them.
The Syracusan court at which the action is laid is modelled upon
the Elizabethan, and the rivalries of Aristippus and Carisophus
had their counterpart in the intrigues among the virgin queen's

---

[1] The play was not licensed till 1567, and the earliest known edition dates from
1571. But 'Edwardes' Tragedy' is mentioned in the Revels' accounts as having been
performed by the children of the chapel at Christmas, 1564. *Damon and Pithias* in
the loose terminology of the day might well be called a tragedy in contrast with his
earlier 'toying plays,' to which Edwards refers in his prologue. The play was
already familiar to the courtiers who saw his *Palamon and Arcite* at Oxford in
September 1566 (cf. *post*, vol. VI, chap. XII). *Damon and Pithias* was revived at
Oxford in January 1568 (cf. *loc. cit.*).

train, though the author protests against any topical interpretation of his 'courtly toyes':

We doo protest this flat,
Wee talke of Dionisius Courte, wee meane no Court but that.

Even more unmistakably English is the character of Grim the collier, who hails from Croydon, though he never mentions his birthplace, and shows remarkable familiarity with Syracusan affairs. There is genuine, if coarse, vernacular humour in the episode of the shaving of him by the saucy lackeys, Will and Jack, who pick his pockets on the sly, while they chant the refrain 'Too nidden and toodle toodle too nidden.' And the episode, though in itself grotesquely irrelevant, is due to the playwright's true instinct that comic relief is needed to temper the tragic suspense while the life of Pithias, who has become hostage for Damon during his two months' respite from the block, trembles in the balance. The high-souled mutual loyalty of the two friends and the chivalrous eagerness with which each courts death for the other's sake are painted with genuine emotional intensity. Though lacking in metrical charm or verbal felicity, *Damon and Pithias* has merits which go some way towards accounting for the acclaim with which, as contemporary allusions show, it was received; and the play possesses an importance of its own in the development of romantic drama from a combination of forces and materials new and old. As *Roister Doister* and *Misogonus*, based on Latin or neo-Latin plays, had by the incorporation of English elements gravitated towards a type of comedy hitherto unknown, so *Damon and Pithias*, an original work by a native playwright, showed the strong influence of classical types and methods. Starting from opposite quarters, the forces that produced romantic comedy are thus seen to converge.

George Whetstone's *Promos and Cassandra*, printed in 1578, is another tragicomedy in direct line of succession to *Damon and Pithias*. It is based on one of the tales in Giraldi Cinthio's *Hecatommithi*, though the names of the leading figures are changed, as they were to be changed yet again by Shakespeare when in his *Measure for Measure*, founded on Whetstone's play, he gave to the story its final and immortal form. Whetstone's sense of the importance of design and structure is seen in his prefatory statement, that he had divided 'the whole history into two commedies, for that, *Decorum* used, it would not be convayed in one.' Thus the story of the self-righteous deputy, Promos, who seduces Cassandra by a promise of pardon to her condemned brother,

Andrugio, is dramatised in two parts, each, after the orthodox classical pattern, divided into five acts. Yet the necessity for so complex and formal a scheme arises largely from the fact, not mentioned by the playwright, that with the overmastering English instinct for elaboration and realism, he adds a comic underplot, in which the courtesan Lamia is the chief figure. This underplot is much more closely linked to the main theme than is the humorous interlude in *Damon and Pithias*, for it heightens the impression of general social demoralisation and of hypocrisy in officials of every grade. With its far from ineffective portrayal of several characters new to English drama, and with its sustained level of workmanlike though uninspired alexandrines and decasyllabic lines, including some passages of blank verse, *Promos and Cassandra* is the most typical example of an original romantic play before the period of Shakespeare's immediate predecessors.

Edwards and Whetstone both prefaced their dramas with a statement of their theory of the function of comedy.

> In commedies the greatest skyll is this lightly to touch
> All thynges to the quicke; and eke to frame eche person so,
> That by his common talke, you may his nature rightly know.
> The olde man is sober, the yonge man rashe, the lover triumphyng in joyes,
> The matron grave, the harlat wilde, and full of wanton toyes.
> Whiche all in one course they no wise doo agree;
> So correspondent to their kinde their speeches ought to bee.

Thus wrote Edwards, and Whetstone, though without referring to him, paraphrases his words :

> To write a Comedie kindly, grave olde men should instruct, yonge men should showe the imperfections of youth, Strumpets should be lascivious, Boyes unhappy, and Clownes should speake disorderlye; entermingling all these actions in such sorte as the grave matter may instruct and the pleasant delight.

The playwrights who wrote thus realised the principle, which underlies romantic art, of fidelity to Nature in all her various forms. But they and their fellows, except Gascoigne in his derivative productions, had not the intuition to see that the principle could never be fully applied till comedy adopted as her chief instrument the infinitely flexible medium of daily intercourse between man and man—prose. It was Lyly who grasped the secret, and taught comedy to speak in new tones. It remained for a greater than Lyly to initiate her into the final mystery of the imaginative transfiguration of Nature, and thus inspire her to create

> Forms more real than living man,
> Nurslings of immortality.

CHAPTER VI

THE PLAYS OF THE UNIVERSITY WITS

Come foorth you witts, that vaunt the pompe of speach,
  And strive to thunder from a Stage-man's throate:
View Menaphon a note beyond your reach;
  Whose sight will make your drumming descant doate;
Players avant, you know not to delight;
  Welcome sweete Shepheard; worth a Scholler's sight.

THESE lines of Thomas Brabine, prefixed to Greene's *Menaphon* (1589), follow hard upon Nashe's involved and, today, obscure preface, 'To the Gentlemen Students.' This preface is one long gibe at the poets and the writers who, either without university education had risen from the ranks, or, though thus educated, had chosen ways of expression not in accordance with the standards of the university wits. John Lyly, Thomas Lodge, George Peele, Robert Greene and Thomas Nashe, however they may have differed among themselves, stood shoulder to shoulder whenever they were facing the 'alcumists of eloquence' whose standards were not their own. Though, in the period from 1570 to 1580, the curriculum at Oxford and at Cambridge was still medieval, yet, as an addition to it, or in place of it, groups of students, from year to year, received with enthusiasm whatever returning scholars and travellers from Italy and France had to offer them of the new renascence spirit and its widening reflection in continental literary endeavour. A pride in university training which amounted to arrogance, and a curious belief, not unknown even today, that only the university-bred man can possibly have the equipment and the sources of information fitting him to be a proper exponent of new, and, at the same time, of really valuable, ideas and literary methods—these were sentiments shared by all the members of the group of 'university wits.'

John Lyly, born in 1553 or 1554, was an Oxford man. He graduated B.A. in 1573, and M.A. in 1575, and, in 1579, was incorporated M.A. at Cambridge. By precedence in work and, probably, in actual historical importance, he is the leader of the group. Indeed, Lyly is typical of the university-bred man whose native commonsense and humour just save him from the pedantry which conceives that the *summum bonum* for man lies in books, and in books only. His remarkably receptive and retentive mind had been open at the university to all influences for culture, both permanent and ephemeral. Like a true son of the time, also, he could rarely distinguish between the two kinds.

Blount, the compiler of the first collected edition of Lyly's plays (1632), declared:

> Our nation are in his debt, for a new English which hee taught them. Euphues and His England began first that language: All our Ladies were then his Schollers; And that Beautie in Court which could not Parley Euphueisme, was as little regarded as shee which now there speakes not French. These his playes Crown'd him with applause, and the Spectators with pleasure. Thou canst not repent the Reading of them over; when Old John Lilly is merry with thee in thy Chamber, Thou shalt say, Few (or None) of our Poets now are such witty companions.

But Blount wrote after the fashion of a publisher turned biographer, not as a man thoroughly informed. In regard to both *Euphues* and the plays, Gabriel Harvey's malicious statement that 'young Euphues hatched the egges, that his elder freends laide' comes much nearer the truth. In the plays which Lyly wrote between his first appearance as an author, in 1579, with his novel *Euphues and his Anatomie of Wit*[1], and his death in 1606, he was rather one who mingled literary and social fashions, a populariser and a perfecter, than a creator. The composite product bears the imprint of his personality, but he borrows more than he creates. A brief review of material, methods and style in his comedy will prove this true.

What, in the first place, is the material? Usually, the slight theme is suggested by some legend of the gods and goddesses; sometimes, as in *Love's Metamorphosis*, the source is treated simply for its dramatic value—as Lyly understood drama, of course; sometimes for a fugitive allegory bearing on incidents in the career of the virgin queen, or in national affairs; sometimes, as in *Endimion, Sapho and Phao* and *Midas*, for what has been interpreted as complicated allegory; and, rarely, as in *Mother Bombie*, for mere adaptive fooling. Such material for tenuous plots is not new. Turning the pages of the *Accounts of the Revels at Court*, one finds titles of plays given by the children's companies—the choirboys of St Paul's, of the Chapel Royal, or the schoolboys of Westminster or of Merchant Taylors' under

---

[1] See, as to *Euphues* and its influence, vol. III, chap. XVI, pp. 392 ff.

Mulcaster—very similar to the names of Lyly's plays. There are, for instance, *Iphigenia, Narcissus, Alcmaeon, Quintus Fabius* and *Scipio Africanus.* We do not know precisely what was the treatment applied to such subjects—in themselves suggesting histories, possibly allegories, or even pastorals—but we do know that, from the hand of Richard Edwards, master of the children of the chapel in 1561, we find plays which, in structure, general method and even some details, provided models for Lyly[1]. For instance, the *Damon and Pithias* of Edwards, probably produced at court in 1564, deals with a subject of which Lyly was fond— contrasted ideas of friendship, here exemplified in two parasites and the famous friends. The piece is loosely constructed, especially as to the cohering of the main plot and the comic subplot. It derives its fun, also, from pages and their foolery. We possess too little dramatic work, especially work produced at court, of the period of 1560—80, to speak with assurance; yet it seems highly probable that Edwards was no isolated figure, but, rather, typifies methods current in plays of that date.

Moreover, as has now been clearly demonstrated, the style of Lyly, even with all his additions and modifications, is but a stage of the evolution, in Spain, Italy, France and England, of a pompous, complicated, highly artificial style, derived from the Latin periods of Cicero, to which each decade of the renascence and each experimental copyist had added some new details of self-conscious complexity. Lyly had two models: one, partly for style but mainly for material, and the other almost wholly for style. The first was *The Dial of Princes* of Don Antonio de Guevara (1529, with English translations by Berners in 1534 and by North in 1557[2]) ; the second was George Pettie's *The Petite Pallace of Pettie his Pleasure* (1576). What Lyly specially develops for himself is the elaborate and irritatingly frequent punning and the constant citation of the 'unnatural natural history' of Pliny. Nevertheless, Lyly was one of those—perhaps the chief among the prose writers of his day—who had a genuine feeling for style. He felt, as Bond has said,

the need of and consistently aimed at what has been well denominated the quality of mind in style—the treatment of the sentence not as a haphazard agglomeration of clauses, phrases and words, but as a piece of literary architecture whose end is foreseen in the beginning and whose parts are calculated to minister to the total effect.

[1] See, as to the plays performed by the children of the chapel, *post*, vol. VI, chap. XI.
[2] Cf. vol. II, p. 340, and vol. III, p. 345.

Yet his style is his own, rather because of the surpassing skill with which he handles its details and imprints the stamp of his personality on it, than because the details are original.

Moreover, in his attitude toward love—his gallant trifling; his idealisation of women, which, with him, goes even to the point of making them mere wraiths; above all, in the curious effect produced by his figures as rather in love with being in love than moved by real human passion—he is Italianate and of the renascence. Moreover, his interest in 'manners maketh man' shows the influence of *Il Cortegiano* and numberless other renascence discussions of courtly conduct.

Again, in his suspected allegorical treatment of incidents in the politics of the time, he, probably, does little more than develop the methods of political allegory current in the days of Henry VIII. Though the presumably large group of moralities which, in that reign, scourged conditions of the time, has, with the exception of *Respublica* and part of *Albion Knight,* disappeared, it is not difficult to believe that the allegory which we suspect in *Endimion,* *Sapho and Phao* and *Midas* glances at Lyly's own time, even as political moralities had represented people and conditions in the reign of Elizabeth's father. Here, again, Lyly is not a creator, but one who, in a new time and for a new audience, applies an old method to modified literary conditions. Trace Lyly back as you will, then, to his sources, he is, in material and style, in his attitude toward men, women, manners and love, thoroughly of the renascence; for, looking back to the classics, and stimulated by modern Italian thought, he expresses himself in a way that reproduces an intellectual mood of his day.

Nor, of course, is Lyly at all an innovator in his free use of the lyric. From the miracle-plays downward, the value of music both as an accompaniment for strongly emotionalised speech, and as a pleasure in itself, had been well understood: the direction in the Chester series 'then shall God speak, the minstrels playing' proves the first statement, and the gossips' song in the Chester Noah play proves the second. The presence, later, of choirboys in the miracle-plays and their performances at court, tended to maintain the lyric in the drama; for their clear boyish voices were particularly suited to the music of the time. Often, too, young actors were probably even better as singers, for singing was their vocation, acting only an avocation. Lyly, as the chief of those who, at one time or another, wrote for choirboys, merely maintains the custom of his predecessors as to lyrics. Perhaps, however, he uses them rather more freely[1].

That these charming songs in Lyly's plays are really his has lately been doubted more than once. Certainly, we do not find them in the quartos: they appear first in Blount's collected edition of 1632, nearly thirty years after Lyly's death. Yet Elizabethan dramatists in general seem never to have evaded any metrical task set them; and, usually, they came out of their efforts successfully. It proves nothing, too, that we find the song 'What bird so sings yet so dos wayl?' of *Campaspe* in Ford and Dekker's *The Sun's Darling* (1632—4), or another, 'O for a bowl of fat canary,' in the 1640 quarto of Middleton's *A Mad World, My Masters*. With the Elizabethan and Jacobean latitude of view toward originality of material, with the wise principle cherished in this age that 'we call a thing his in the long run who utters it clearest and best,' there was no reason why a dramatist should not omit quotation marks when using the work of a previous songster. On the other hand, when we recall the collaboration in the masques of Ben Jonson, not long afterwards, of Giles as master of song, Inigo Jones as architect, and Ferrabosco as dancing-master, there is no reason why Lyly should not have called in the aid of any of the more skilled composers about the court or the city. Words and music may have been composed by the music-master of the boys of Paul's. Though we have no verse certainly Lyly's which would lead us to expect such delicacy as he shows in 'Cupid and my Campaspe played at cards for kisses,' or juvenile bacchanalia like 'O for a bowl of fat canary,' yet, in the material from Diogenes Laertius which is the source of the scene in *Alexander and Campaspe* where the song of the bird notes occurs, there is certainly a hint for it. Therefore, as Bond has pointed out, though this song may have been written at Lyly's order, it may equally well have been a part of his usual skilful creative use of material thoroughly grasped by him. When all is said, however, it is not wise, in the light of present evidence, to rest any large part of Lyly's claim to the attention of posterity on his authorship of the songs in his plays. In all these respects, then—of material, method and attitude—Lyly, while genuinely of the renascence, is far more the populariser and perfecter than the creator.

What, then, justifies the increasing attention given to Lyly's

[1] As to the opportunities afforded to lyric poetry by the drama, cf. *ante*, vol. IV, chap. VI, p. 115.

work by historians of English drama? Wherein consists his real
contribution? It is a time-honoured statement that he definitively
established prose as the expression for comedy, that his success
with it swept from the boards the vogue of the 'jigging vein' of
men who, like Edwards, had written such halting lines as these :

> Yet have I played with his beard in knitting this knot;
> I promised friendship, but—you love few words—I spake it but I meant
>   it not.
> Who markes this friendship between us two
> Shall judge of the worldly friendship without more ado.
> It may be a right pattern thereof; but true friendship indeed
> Of nought but of virtue doth truly proceed.

For such cumbrous expression, Lyly substituted a prose which,
though it could be ornate to pompousness at his will, could, also,
be gracefully accurate and have a certain rhythm of its own. But
his real significance is that he was the first to bring together on
the English stage the elements of high comedy, thereby preparing
the way for Shakespeare's *Much Ado About Nothing* and *As You
Like It*. Whoever knows his Shakespeare and his Lyly well can
hardly miss the many evidences that Shakespeare had read
Lyly's plays almost as closely as Lyly had read Pliny's *Natural
History*. It is not merely that certain words of the song of
the birds' notes in *Campaspe* gave Shakespeare, subconsciously,
probably, his hint for 'Hark, hark, the lark'; or that, in the talk
of Viola and the duke[1] he was thinking of Phillida and Galathea[2];
but that we could hardly imagine *Love's Labour's Lost* as existent
in the period from 1590 to 1600, had not Lyly's work just preceded
it. Setting aside the element of interesting story skilfully developed,
which Shakespeare, after years of careful observation of his audiences, knew was his surest appeal, do we not find *Much Ado About
Nothing* and *As You Like It*, in their essentials, only developments, through the intermediate experiments in *Love's Labour's
Lost* and *Two Gentlemen of Verona*, from Lyly's comedies?
   What, historically, are the essentials of high comedy? It deals
with cultivated people in whom education, and refining environ-
ment, have bred subtler feelings. These gods and goddesses of
Lyly, who have little, if anything, of a classic past, but everything, in thought, attitude towards life and even speech itself, of
the courtiers of Lyly's day, are surely subjects for high comedy.
So close, indeed, are these figures of mythology to the evanescent
life of Lyly's moment, that we are constantly tempted to see, in

---

[1] *Twelfth Night*, act II, sc. 1.   [2] *Galathea*, act III, sc. 3.

this or that figure, some well known person of the court, to hear in this or that speech, some sentiments according with well known opinions of this or that notability. And what is love in these comedies? Not the intense passion that burns itself out in slaughter—the love of the Italian *novelle* and the plays of Kyd, Greene and others influenced by them. Nor is it at all mere physical appetite, as it often becomes, in the lesser Elizabethans and, generally, among the Jacobeans. Instead, as in *As You Like It* and *Much Ado About Nothing*, it is the motive force behind events and scenes, but not the one absorbing interest for author or reader: it is refined, sublimated, etherealised. Contrasts, delicately brought out, between the real underlying feelings of the characters and what they wish to feel or wish to be thought to feel, all of this phrased as perfectly as possible according to standards of the moment, are what interests Lyly and what he teaches his audience to care for particularly. Certainly, then, we are in the realm of high comedy ; for, surely, there can be no laughter from such sources which is not thoughtful laughter, the essential, as George Meredith has pointed out, of this form of drama. From start to finish, Lyly's comedy is based on thought, and cannot properly be appreciated without thought. At every point, it is planned, constructed, modelled, to suit the critical standards of its author and of an exacting group of courtier critics, both eagerly interested in all that Italy and the continent had to offer them as literary models of the past and present. Lyly especially rested, for his prospective success, on his skill in phrase. It is not merely that he is an artist in the complications of the euphuistic style to which his own *Euphues* had given vogue, but that he is a student of skilled phrase for dramatic and characterising purposes. And this is of great significance for two reasons: first, because high comedy demands, as a further essential, a nice sense of phrase—witness Congreve and Sheridan among our later masters of it ; and, secondly, because this careful phrasing of Lyly emphasises, for the first time in our English drama, the third essential of a perfect play. Story, the first essential, had been, crudely, understood so early as the trope in liturgical mysteries. By accretion of episode, constructive story, which is plot, developed. The need of characterisation soon came to be understood in miracle-plays, in moralities and in the interlude of the better kind. Yet phrase, not as a mere means of characterisation, but so treated, from start to finish, that it shall do more than expound plot and characterise, that it shall give pleasure for its own sake by its form or its content, is Lyly's great contribution to the drama. As he himself said, 'It is wit that allureth, when every word shal have his weight, when nothing shal proceed, but it shal either savour of a sharpe conceipt, or a secret conclusion.' More than anyone else before 1587, he raises our English drama to the level of literature; more than anyone else, he creates a popular drama—for the great public liked it—which was also enthusiastically received by audiences at the court as the embodiment of prevailing literary tastes. He bridges from the uncritical to the critical public more successfully than any one of the dramatists, till Shakespeare's depicting of character, as exhibited universally, revealed to all classes of men their community of experience and emotion. This raising of the intellectual level of the drama Lyly accomplishes, too, by the addition of the feminine qualities of literature—delicacy, grace, charm, subtlety. The English drama was masculine already to the point of swaggering. It was Lyly's pleasant duty to refine it, to make it more intellectual, and thus to win the plaudits of a court presided over by a queen who, if virile in her grasp on affairs of state, was certainly feminine in her attitude towards the arts.

If, then, Lyly looks back to an English, a continental and, even, a classical, past, for inspiration and models, he yet rises above his sources in an accomplishment which is individual and of not merely ephemeral significance, but of great importance to those who immediately follow him in the drama. He intellectualises the drama; he brings, not adaptation, but original work, into closest touch with the most cultivated men and women of the time; he unites the feminine to the already existent masculine elements in our drama; he attains, even if somewhat hazily, that great dramatic form, high comedy, and, attaining it, breaks the way for a large part of Shakespeare's work.

George Peele (born 1558) graduated B.A. at Christ Church, Oxford, in 1577, and M.A. in 1579. Either he must have made rapid advance as a dramatist during his first years in London, 1580—2, or, during his long career at the university, some nine years, he must have developed genuine dramatic ability. This is evident, because, in July 1583, he was summoned from London to Oxford to assist William Gager, author of *Rivales,* in an entertainment which the latter was arranging for the reception at Christ Church of Albertus Alasco, Polish prince palatine. Certainly, *The Araygnement of Paris,* Peele's 'first encrease,' as

Thomas Nashe called it, shows a writer who would seem to have passed the tiro stage. This play, entered for publication in April 1584, is evidently influenced by the dramatic methods of John Lyly, owing to the fact that, like Lyly's plays, it was acted before the queen by children. When we consider that Peele's activity covered sixteen or eighteen years (he was dead by 1598), at a time when dramatic composition was rapid, his dramatic work remaining to us seems not large in quantity. Nor was he himself a slow workman. *Syr Clyomon and Clamydes*, tentatively assigned to him by Dyce, is no longer believed to be his. It is clearly of an earlier date, and, very possibly, was written by Thomas Preston. Of *Wily Beguiled*, sometimes attributed to Peele, Schelling rightly says: 'There is nothing in this comedy to raise a question of Peele's authorship except the simple obviousness with which the plot is developed.' Nor does it seem possible at present to go beyond Miss Jane Lee's conclusions as to Peele's probable share in *The First* and *Second Parts of Henry VI*. The best proof as yet advanced for Peele's authorship of *Locrine* is, even cumulatively[1], inconclusive. Besides *The Arraygnement of Paris*, we have, as extant plays assigned to Peele, *The Old Wives Tale*, *Edward I*, *The Love of King David and Fair Bethsabe* and *The Battell of Alcazar*. The last of these plays is attributed to Peele only because a quotation from it in *England's Parnassus* (1600) is assigned to him and because of certain similarities of phrase; but the play is usually accepted as his. *The Hunting of Cupid*, a masque extant only in a slight fragment, and *The Turkish Mahomet*, which we know only by its title and some references, complete the list of Peele's plays.

Even this brief list, however, shows the variety in his work: the masque, in *The Hunting of Cupid*, and something very closely related to it, in *The Arraygnement of Paris*; the chronicle history, in *Edward I*, and, very probably, in *The Turkish Mahomet*, an even more marked mingling of romance and so-called history; something like an attempt to revive the miracle-play, in *King David and Fair Bethsabe*; and genuine literary satire on romantic plays of the day, in *The Old Wives Tale*. Whether this variety means that he merely turned his attention hither and thither as chance called him, or that he was restlessly trying to find his own easiest and best expression amid the many inchoate forms of the drama of the moment, it is perfectly clear that his inborn dramatic gift was slight. Neither dramatic situation nor characterisation

---

[1] Cf. as to *Locrine*, *ante*, chap. IV and *post*, chap. X.

interests him strongly. After years of practice, he is not good
in plotting. Even where he is at his best in characterisation, in
such little touches as the following, he cannot sustain himself at
the pitch reached:

> (Queen Elinor presents her babe to its uncle, Lancaster.)
>
> Q. Elinor. Brother Edmund, here's a kinsman of yours:
> You must needs be acquainted.
> Lancaster. A goodly boy; God bless him!—
> Give me your hand, sir:
> You are welcome into Wales.
> Q. Elinor. Brother, there's a fist, I warrant you, will hold a mace as
> fast as ever did father or grandfather before him.

Uneven in characterisation, loose in construction to the point of
recklessness, so extravagant in diction that, at moments, one
even suspects burlesque, Peele leaves a critical reader wondering
whether he was merely over-hurried and impatient of the work
he was doing, or genuinely held it in contempt. Certainly, the
chief merit of the fantastic *Old Wives Tale* is its clever satire on
such romantic plays as *Common Conditions*. Peele, in his play,
makes fun of just those qualities in the current drama which
Sidney criticised in his *Defence of Poesie*—the myriad happenings
left untraced to any sufficient cause, the confusion caused by this
multiplicity of incident, and the lavish use of surprise. *The Old
Wives Tale* confuses the reader as much as any one of the plays
which it ridicules; but, when seen, it becomes amusing and, in
respect of its satire, a fit predecessor of *The Knight of the
Burning Pestle*. As the first English play of dramatic criticism,
it deserves high praise.

This play shows, too, as Gummere has pointed out, the
peculiar subjective humour of Peele, which rests on 'something
more than a literal understanding of what is said and done, a
new appeal to a deeper sense of humour.' He does not get his
fun solely from time-honoured comic business, or clownery, but
from dramatic irony in the contrast of romantic plot and realistic
diction—indeed, by contrasts in material, in method, in characterisation and, even, in phrase. This is Peele's contribution to that
subtler sense of humour which we have noted in Lyly. In Lyly,
it leads to high comedy: in Peele it finds expression in dramatic
criticism.

Though Peele's life may have had its unseemly sides, he had
a real vision of literature as an art: *primus verborum artifex*,
Thomas Nashe called him; nor, for the phrasing of the time, were

the words exaggerated. Reading his songs, such as that of Paris
and Oenone in *The Araygnement of Paris*, or the lines at the opening of *King David and Fair Bethsabe*, one must recognise that
he had an exquisite feeling for the musical value of words ; that
he had the power to attain a perfect accord between words and
musical accompaniment. One can hear the tinkling lute in
certain lines in which the single word counts for little; but the
total collocation produces something exquisitely delicate. Yet
Peele is far more than a mere manipulator of words for musical
effect. He shows a real love of nature, which, breaking free from
much purely conventional reference to the nature gods of
mythology, is phrased as the real poet phrases. The seven lines
of the little song in *The Old Wives Tale* beginning, 'Whenas the
rye reach to the chin,' are gracefully pictorial; but the following
lines from *The Araygnement of Paris* show Peele at his best, as he
breaks through the fetters of conventionalism into finely poetic
expression of his own sensitive observation :

> Not Iris, in her pride and bravery,
> Adorns her arch with such variety;
> Nor doth the milk-white way, in frosty night,
> Appear so fair and beautiful in sight,
> As done these fields, and groves, and sweetest bowers,
> Bestrew'd and deck'd with parti-colour'd flowers.
> Along the bubbling brooks and silver glide,
> *That at the bottom do in silence slide;*
> The water-flowers and lilies on the banks,
> Like blazing comets, burgeen all in ranks;
> Under the hawthorn and the poplar-tree,
> Where sacred Phoebe may delight to be,
> The primrose, and the purple hyacinth,
> The dainty violet, and the wholesome minth,
> The double daisy, and the cowslip, queen
> Of summer flowers, do overpeer the green;
> *And round about the valley as ye pass,*
> *Ye may ne see for peeping flowers the grass: ...*

Is there not in the italicised lines something of that peculiar
ability which reached its full development in the mature
Shakespeare—the power of flashing before us in a line or two
something definitive both as a picture and in beauty of phrase?

One suspects that Peele, in the later years of his life, gave
his time more to pageants than to writing plays, and not unwillingly. He certainly wrote lord mayors' pageants—in 1585,
for Woolstone Dixie, and, in 1591, his *Discursus Astraeae* for
William Webbe. Moreover, all his plays except *The Old Wives
Tale* were in print by 1594, and even that in 1595. One of the

Merrie Conceited Jests of George Peele, those rather dubious bits
of biography, tells us 'George was of a poetical disposition never
to write so long as his money lasted.' Whether the *Jests* be
authentic or not, those words probably state the whole case for
Peele[1]. He was primarily a poet, with no real inborn gift for the
drama, and he never developed any great skill as a playwright.
This may have been because he could not; the reason may,
probably, be sought in the mood which finds expression in *The Old
Wives Tale*—a mood partly amused by the popular crude forms of
art, partly contemptuous towards them. Consequently, as he went
on with his work without artistic conscience, without deep interest
in the form, he could not lift it; he could merely try to give an
imperfectly educated public what he deemed it wanted. But even
this compromise with circumstance could not keep the poet from
breaking through occasionally. And in his feeling for pure beauty
—both as seen in nature and as felt in words—he is genuinely of
the renascence.

Robert Greene, born at Norwich in July 1558, took his B.A. at
St John's, Cambridge, in 1578, and his M.A. at Clare hall in 1583.
He was incorporated M.A. at Oxford in 1588. Apparently,
between the times of taking his B.A. and his M.A. degrees, he
travelled, at least in Spain and Italy. Certainly, then or later,
he came to know other parts of the continent, for he says in his
Notable Discovery of Coosnage, 'I have smiled with the Italian...
eaten Spanish mirabolanes...France, Germany, Poland, Denmark,
I know them all.' That is, by the time he was twenty-five, he had
had his chance to know at first hand the writings of Castiglione,
Ariosto and Machiavelli—the Italian authors to whom his work is
most indebted. He had had, too, his chance of contrasting the
newer learning of Italy with the traditional English teaching of his
time. A man of letters curiously mingling artistic and Bohemian
sympathies and impulses with puritanic ideals and tendencies, who
had been trained in the formal learning of an English university,
he was greatly stimulated by the varied renascence influences,
and, by them, in many cases, was led, not to greater liberty, but to
greater licence of expression. As novelist, pamphleteer and playwright, he is always mercurial, but always, no matter how large his
borrowings, individual and contributive[2].

---

[1] As to the *Merrie Conceited Jests*, cf. *ante*, vol. IV, chap. XVI, p. 360.
[2] See, as to Greene's literary activity other than dramatic, vol. III, chap. XVI,
pp. 353 ff. and vol. IV, chap. XVI, pp. 318 ff.

Greene seems to have begun his varied literary career while still at Cambridge, for, in October 1580, the first part of his novel, *Mamillia*, was licensed, though it did not appear before 1583. In the latter year, the second part was licensed, though the first edition we have bears date 1593. We are not clear as to what exactly Greene was doing between the time of taking the two degrees; but, in some way, it meant a preparation which made it possible for him to pour out, between 1583 and 1590, a rapid succession of some dozen love stories and ephemeral pamphlets— *Morando, Planetomachia, Menaphon, Perimedes, Pandosto, The Spanish Masquerado*, etc., etc. That, during this time or later, Greene was either a clergyman or an actor has not been proved. About 1590, some unusually strong impulsion, resulting either from a long sickness or, less probably, from some such contrition as his *Repentance* says the eloquence of John More at one time produced in him, gave him a distaste for his former courses, in literary work as well as in general conduct. Certainly, as Churton Collins has pointed out, Greene's *Mourning Garment*, his *Farewell to Folly*, 1590 and 1591, and his *Vision*—which, though published after his death (1592) as written when he was moribund, was evidently, for the most part, composed about 1590—show this changed mood. Indeed, the mood was sufficiently lasting for him to write, in 1592, when he published his *Philomela*,

I promised, Gentlemen, both in my Mourning Garment and Farewell to Folly, never to busy myself about any wanton pamphlets again . . . but yet am I come, contrary to vow and promise, once again to the press with a labour of love, which I hatched long ago, though now brought forth to light.

In any case, it cannot be denied that his non-dramatic production in the two years of life remaining before 1592 was, for the main part, very different from that which had preceded. Whether his series of coney-catching exposures formed part of a genuine repentance, it is quite impossible to tell[1]. The three or four pamphlets of this sort by Greene were not wholly the result of an observation which moved him irresistibly, either through indignation or repentance, to frank speaking.

Even more puzzling, however, than his change of attitude, about 1590, or than his real feeling in his so-called exposures, is the question raised with much ingenious argument by Churton Collins, whether Greene began his dramatic work earlier than 1590. Greene himself says in his *Repentance*: 'but after I had by

[1] As to this, see *ante*, vol. IV, pp. 319 ff.

degrees proceeded Master of Arts (1583) I left the University and away to London, where... after a short time... I became an author of plays and love-pamphlets.' That, certainly, does not sound as if Greene did not write any plays for some seven years after he left Cambridge. Moreover, another passage in *Perimedes* (1588)— 'Two mad men of Rome [that is London] had it in derision for that I could not make my verses jet upon the stage in tragical buskins'—is open to two interpretations : namely, that he was derided for not attempting to write blank verse plays, or for failure in the attempt[1]. Churton Collins skilfully emphasises what is true, that neither Nashe, in the preface to *Menaphon*, nor any of the writers of commendatory verse accompanying Greene's publications before 1590, mention his drama. But it is to be noted that two of the four passages cited by Churton Collins are dated as early as 1588. Now, most recent opinion does not favour the conclusion that, before this date, Greene had produced any surviving work besides *Alphonsus* and, in collaboration with Lodge, *A Looking Glasse for London and England*. Even in 1589, Nashe, in his preface to *Menaphon*, was looking for evidence to elevate Greene above the writers of blank verse plays, and, therefore, would hardly have counted the two plays mentioned, or even *Orlando*, against such overwhelming successes as *The Spanish Tragedie*, *Tamburlaine* and *Faustus*. For *A Looking Glasse* was written in collaboration ; one or both of the others may have been merely burlesque of the new high-flown style ; and there is more than a suspicion that *Alphonsus* was a failure. As will be seen when the probable dates of the plays remaining to us are considered, the safer statement, probably, is that, although Greene had been writing plays before 1589, he had not accomplished anything which could be compared on approximately equal terms with the original achievements of Marlowe or of Kyd, and that his best dramatic work was produced in 1590 or after this date.

The dramatic work remaining to us which is certainly his is small. A lost play of *Job* is entered in the Stationers' register in 1594 as his. The attribution to him of *Selimus* on the authority of the title-page of the first edition, 1594, and of two quotations assigned to him by Allot in *England's Parnassus*, 1600, which are found in this particular play, is not accepted by either A. W. Ward or C. M. Gayley ; and Churton Collins says that his authorship is

---

[1] Churton Collins, unfortunately for his argument, seems to favour both opinions. See p. 75, vol. I, of his *Plays and Poems of Robert Greene*, where he holds the former opinion ; and p. 40 of his introduction, where, apparently, he holds the second.

'too doubtful to justify any editor including [it] in Greene's works.'
It is now generally admitted that he was not the author of
Mucedorus, or of *The Troublesome Raigne of John, King of
England*, which have sometimes been assigned to him.   It seems
all but impossible to determine Greene's share in the *First Part
of the Contention betwixt the Houses of Yorke and Lancaster* and
The True Tragedie of Richard, Duke of Yorke.   Critical opinion,
following the lead of Miss Lee, is, on the whole, disposed to favour
the view that Greene had some share in the work, but where, and
to what extent, are mere matters of conjecture[1].   On the other
hand, the attribution to him of *George a Greene, the Pinner of
Wakefield* is not to be waived.   This attribution arises from
two manuscript statements in sixteenth century handwriting on
the title-page of the 1590 edition in the duke of Devonshire's
library, 'Written by...a minister, who ac[ted] the piner's pt in
it himselfe.   *Teste* W. Shakespea[re],' and 'Ed. Juby saith that ye
Play was made by Ro. Gree[ne].'   It is certainly curious that the
play is not known to have been acted until after Greene's death, in
1593, though Henslowe does not mark it as new at that time.   The
Sussex men, too, who appeared in it, though they had given two
performances of *Frier Bacon*, with Greene's former company, seem
never to have owned any of the unquestioned plays of Greene.
On the other hand, there certainly are resemblances between the
play and the dramatist's other work, and though, when taken
together, these are not sufficiently strong to warrant acceptance
of the play as certainly Greene's, no recent student of his work
has been altogether willing to deny that he may have written it.
If it be Greene's, it is a late play, of the period of *James IV*.

The two most recent students of Greene, C. M. Gayley in his
Representative Comedies and Churton Collins in his *Plays and
Poems of Robert Greene*, working independently, agree that the
order of Greene's plays remaining to us should be, *Alphonsus*,
*A Looking Glasse for London and England, Orlando Furioso,
Frier Bacon and Frier Bongay* and *James IV*.   *A Looking
Glasse* may best be considered in treating Lodge's dramatic work.
Alphonsus bears on the title of its one edition, 1599, the words,
'Made by R. G.'   Neither its exact sources nor the original
date of performance is known.   It is evidently modelled on
Tamburlaine, aiming to catch some of its success either by direct,
if ineffectual, imitation, or by burlesque.   Its unprepared events,
its sudden changes in character and its general extravagance

[1] Cf. *post*, chap. VII.

of tone, favour the recent suggestion that it is burlesque rather than mere imitation. Here is no attempt to visualise and explain a somewhat complex central figure, in itself a great contrast with *Tamburlaine*. Rather, with the slenderest thread of fact, Greene embroiders wilfully, extravagantly. The characters are neither real nor clearly distinguished. Whatever may be the date of the play in the career of Greene, it is, from its verse and its lack of technical skill, evidently early dramatic work. Churton Collins, resting on resemblances he saw between *Alphonsus* and Spenser's *Complaints*, wished to date the beginning of Greene's dramatic work in 1591. That this theory separates *Alphonsus* widely from the success of *Tamburlaine* in 1587 seems almost fatal to it ; for the significance of *Alphonsus*, either as imitation or as burlesque, is lost if there was so wide a gap as this between it and its model. It seems better, on the metrical and other grounds stated by C. M. Gayley, to accept *circa* 1587 as its date. Moreover, it should be noted that so early a date as this for Greene as playwright fits the words already quoted from his *Repentance* in regard to his having begun as a dramatist shortly after he left the university.

In 1592, Greene was accused of having sold *Orlando Furioso* to the Admiral's men, when the Queen's men, to whom he had already sold it, were in the country. This serves to identify the author, who is not named on the title-page of either the 1594 or the 1599 edition. Its references to the Spanish Armada, and the common use by it and *Perimedes*, 1588, of five names approximately the same, favour *circa* 1588 for its date. The earliest record of *Frier Bacon and Frier Bongay* is under 19 February 1591/2 in Henslowe's diary, when it is not marked as new. It was published in 1594. Were we sure whether it follows or precedes *Faire Em*, with which it has analogies, it would be easier to date. If it preceded, it belongs to about July or August 1589; if it followed, then 1591 is the better date. In either case, it is, perhaps, striking that there occurs in the play the name Vandermast, which appears, also, in Greene's *Vision*, written, as Churton Collins shows, so early as 1590, although not published till later. Though the name appears in the chapbook which, seemingly, was the source of the play, no such conjurer is known to history. This tendency to use common names in pamphlet and in play has already been remarked in *Perimedes* and *Orlando Furioso*. Greene may have borrowed it from his own play. This would favour the 1589 date for *Frier Bacon and Frier Bongay*. Or, the play may have borrowed from the *Vision*, in which case the evidence points to 1591. *The Scottish History of James IV, slaine at Flodden* is not at all, as its title suggests, a chronicle play, but a dramatisation of the first novel of the third decade of Giraldi Cinthio's *Hecatommithi*. It clearly shows some interpolation; nor is it indubitable that the interludes of Oberon, king of the fairies, were an original part of the play or by Greene. Certain resemblances between this play and *Greenes Mourning Garment*, 1590, besides references by Dorothea to the Irish wars and complications with France, point to 1590—1 as a probable date for this play.

If Nashe's statement be true, that Greene produced more than four other writers for his company, and a play each quarter, surely we must have but a small portion of his work. Yet what we have is marked by no such range of experiment as we noted in Peele's few plays. His sources, so far as known, are romantic—Ariosto's *Orlando Furioso*, a novel of Giraldi Cinthio and a series of fantastic tales about two conjurers. He handled his sources, too, in the freest possible way, sometimes using them as little more than frames on which to hang his own devices. In *Alphonsus*, for instance, it is nearly impossible to tell whether he had in mind either of two historical figures—Alphonso V, king of Aragon, Sicily and Naples, who died in 1454, and Alphonso I, king of Aragon and Navarre, who died in 1134. Probably, here, as in *Orlando*, where he follows Ariosto closely only in a few details, and in *James IV*, where he deliberately foists upon a seemingly historical figure incidents of pure fiction, he rather uses well known names because he may thus interest the prospective auditor than because either these figures or the historical material itself really interest him.

Nashe called Greene 'a master of his craft' in the art of plotting. This merit in him has not been enough recognised ; but any careful comparison of sources and play in the case of *Frier Bacon* or *James IV* will show that he was alive to the essentials of good play-writing and sensitive to the elements of inherent or potential interest in his material. In *Frier Bacon*, he develops the mere hint of the old romance[1] that a maid Mellisant had two suitors, and that she preferred the gentleman to the knight, into the somewhat idyllic incidents of Margaret of Fressingfield, Lacy and the king. He shifts the order of the stories at will and binds together rather skilfully those he selects. He adds several characters ; and he vividly develops others only barely suggested. In the opening act, he cleverly creates interest and suspense. In

---

[1] Chap. xv (1630). See Churton Collins's *Greene*, vol. II, p. 12.

James IV, he shows right feeling for dramatic condensation by representing the king as in love with Ida even at the time of his marriage with Dorothea, thus getting rid of the opening details of Cinthio's story. By making Ateukin witness the collapse of his plans rather than hear of it, as in the story, he meets the eternal demand of an audience to see for itself what is important in the motives of a central figure. The letter incident he changes for the sake of greater simplicity and verisimilitude. In other words, he is no haphazard dramatic story teller ; for his own time, he certainly is a master in the craft of plotting.

Moreover, as he matures, he grows to care as much for character as for incident, as his development of Nano, Margaret and Dorothea proves. Nashe, thinking of Greene's novels, called him the 'Homer of women'; and it would not be wholly unfitting to give him that designation among pre-Shakespearean dramatists. With him, as with Kyd, the love story becomes, instead of a by-product, central in the drama—not merely the cause of ensuing situation, but an interest in itself. To see clearly what he accomplished for romantic comedy, one should compare his *James IV* with *Common Conditions*. Greene took over the mad romanticism of the latter production, of which Peele was already making fun—all this material of disguised women seeking their lords or lovers, of adventure by flood and field—but, by infusing into it sympathetic and imaginative characterisation, he transmuted it into the realistic romance that reaches its full development in Shakespeare's *Twelfth Night, Cymbeline* and *The Winter's Tale.* As Lyly had broken the way for high comedy by his dialogue, the group of people treated and his feeling for pure beauty, so Greene broke the way for it on the side of story—an element which was to play an important part in Shakespeare's romantic work. He supplies just what Lyly lacked, complicated story and verisimilitude, and, above all, simple human feeling. Thomas Kyd, in his *Spanish Tragedie*, had raised such material as that of *Tancred and Gismunda* to the level of reality, making the love story central. Thus, Kyd opened the way to real tragedy. On the level, perhaps somewhat lower, of romantic comedy, Greene's verisimilitude is equal. The more we study these men, the more true in many cases we find contemporary judgment. As Chettle said, Greene, in 1590—2, was 'the only commedian of a vulgar writer in this country.'

Thomas Lodge, born 1558, was educated at Trinity college

Oxford; the exact dates of his degrees are not known. He was a man of manifold activities. As pamphleteer, he wrote against Stephen Gosson in defence of the stage[1]. He began his play writing as early as 1582, and his novel writing as early as 1584 with *The Delectable Historie of Forbonius and Prisceria*. He took part in the expedition to Tercer and the Canaries in that year, and whiled away the tiresome hours of the voyage by writing the source of *As You Like It*, namely *Rosalynde. Euphues' golden legacie.* On his return home, he published a book of verse, *Scillaes Metamorphosis.* Just before setting out on a voyage with Cavendish in 1592, he had published an historical romance, *The History of Robert, second Duke of Normandy, surnamed Robin the Divell* ; during his absence, Greene published for him his *Euphues Shadow,* and so facile was Lodge that, immediately on his return, he printed another historical romance, *The Life and Death of William Longbeard,* and his book of sonnets called *Phillis.* There followed on these the publication of his two plays, *The Wounds of Civill War* and *A Looking Glasse for London and England,* 1594, though the latter play was undoubtedly written much earlier ; his book of verse, *A Fig for Momus,* 1595 ; and his romantic story, *A Margarite of America,* 1596. The cessation of imaginative work by him after this date, though he lived on till 1625, is curious. He had become a convert to the church of Rome : for this, the influence of his second wife, herself a Roman Catholic, may have been responsible. After all his roving, he settled down to the life of a physician in London, though, for a time, before 1619, he was forced to live and practise in the Netherlands, because of complications in his London life.

Evidently, the activities of the man were varied. Of his plays, only two survive. Inasmuch as no two critics agree with regard to the exact parts to be assigned to Greene and Lodge in *A Looking Glasse for London and England,* and since the only other play by Lodge deals with wholly different material, it is nearly impossible to judge his characteristics on the basis of *A Looking Glasse*— one of the last survivals, in modified form, of the disappearing morality. *The Wounds of Civill War* is a *Titus Andronicus,* with all the thrills and horrors left out. Monotonous in style and in treatment, it is evidently the work of a man neither by instinct nor by training a dramatist. It shows, however, the jumbling of grave and gay usual at the time, without any of the

[1] See *post*, vol. vi, chap. xiv. As to Lodge's romances see vol. iii, chap. xvi, pp. 350, 358 f.

saving humour which kept Shakespeare, after his salad days, from
disastrous juxtapositions of this nature.

Lodge added nothing to the development of the English drama.
With 'his oare in every paper boat,' he, of course, tried his hand
at the popular form.   Starting with a university man's suspicion
of it as essentially unliterary, his feeling probably turned to
contempt when he made no real success.   At any rate, in 1589,
in his *Scillaes Metamorphosis*, he gave over the stage, deciding

> **To write no more of that whence shame doth grow:**
> **Or tie my pen to penny knaves' delight,**
> **But live with fame and so for fame to write.**

Lodge, at best but a wayfarer in the hostel of the drama, made
way for a throng of inpouring enthusiasts—and made way
contemptuously.

Thomas Nashe, though younger than Lodge, turned aside, like
Peele, from his real bent into drama, but not, like Peele, to
remain in it and to do a large amount of work.   He left St
John's, Cambridge, in the third year after taking his B.A., because
of some offence given to the authorities, and visited France and
Italy.   Returning to London, he not only published his *Anatomie of Absurditie* and his preface to Greene's *Menaphon*, both
of 1589, but entered with enthusiasm into the virulent Martin
Marprelate controversy[1].   Nor was his interest decreased when the
quarrel became a personal one between him and Gabriel Harvey.
The long series of politico-religious and maliciously personal
pamphlets poured out by him for some seven years made him
so noteworthy that it is not surprising he should have taken
advantage of his reputation by writing for the stage.   Whether
he worked with Marlowe on *Dido Queene of Carthage*, published
1594, or finished a manuscript left incomplete by the former, is not
clear.   Nor is it safe to base judgment of his dramatic ability on
this play because of the contradiction by critics in the apportion-
ing of authorship.   Of the lost *Isle of Dogs*, he says himself that
he wrote only the induction and the first act.   When the play bred
trouble, and Nashe, as author, was lodged in the Fleet for a time,
he maintained that he was not really responsible for the contents
of the play.   But any reader of his pamphlets will need no proof
that even an induction and a first act, if by Nashe, might contain
much venom.   *Summer's Last Will and Testament*, acted at or

---

[1] See vol. III, chap. XVII, pp. 392 ff. As to Nashe's other pamphlets and prose
fiction, see *ibid.* chap. XVI, pp. 362 ff.

near Croydon in 1592, gives little opportunity to judge Nashe's real dramatic quality. It suggests both a morality and a play written for a special occasion. Nashe here shows himself ingenious, at times amusing, satirical as always. But to know Nashe at his best in what is really individual to him, one must read his pamphlets, or, better still, his *Unfortunate Traveller*, of 1594, the first of English picaresque novels. The dramatic work of Nashe suggests that he has stepped aside into a popular form rather than turned to it irresistibly. He cannot, like Lyly, adapt renascence ideas to the taste and the ideals of the most educated public of the time ; nor is he even so successful as Peele, who, like him, stepped aside, but who succeeded well enough to be kept steadily away from what he could do best. Nashe is far enough from Greene, who, whatever his ideas gained from the university and from foreign travel, could so mould and adjust them as to be one of the most successful of popular dramatists.

As a group, then, these contemporaries illustrate well the possible attitudes of an educated man of their time toward the drama. Midway between Lyly and his successful practice of the drama, which, for the most cultivated men and women of his day, maintained and developed standards supplied to him, at least in part, by his university, and Thomas Lodge, who put the drama aside as beneath a cultivated man of manifold activities, stand Nashe, Peele and Greene. Nashe, feeling the attraction of a popular and financially alluring form, shows no special fitness for it, is never really at home in it and gives it relatively little attention. Peele, properly endowed for his best expression in another field, spends his strength in the drama because, at the time, it is the easiest source of revenue, and turns from the drama of the cultivated to the drama of the less cultivated or the un-cultivated. Greene, from the first, is the facile, adaptive purveyor of wares to which he is helped by his university experience, but to which he gives a highly popular presentation. Through Nashe and Lodge, the drama gains nothing. Passing through the hands of Lyly, Greene and even Peele, it comes to Shakespeare something quite different from what it was before they wrote.

University-bred one and all, these five men were proud of their breeding. However severe from time to time might be their censures of their intellectual mother, they were always ready to take arms against the unwarranted assumption, as it seemed to them, of certain dramatists who lacked this university training, and to confuse them by the sallies of their wit. One and all, they demonstrated their right to the title bestowed upon them—'university wits.'

CHAPTER VII

MARLOWE AND KYD

Chronicle Histories

Whether, in strict chronology, we should say Kyd and Marlowe rather than Marlowe and Kyd is but a minor problem of precedence. Even if it be found, as some suspect to be the case, that *The Spanish Tragedie* is earlier than *Tamburlaine*, we need not disturb the traditional order; for Marlowe, more truly than his contemporary, is the protagonist of the tragic drama in England, and, in a more intimate sense, the forerunner of Shakespeare and his fellows. After all, the main consideration is that the two poets may be grouped together, because, in ways complementary to each other, they show the first purpose of the higher and more serious type of English tragedy, the first hints of the romantic quality which is the literary token and honour of their successors, and, if Lyly be joined with them, the training and technical circumstance of Shakespeare himself.

Of the life of Christopher Marlowe[1], son of a Canterbury shoemaker and a clergyman's daughter, there is little on record. To some of his contemporaries, and, unfortunately, to later biographers, interest in his personality has been confined to an exaggerated tale of blasphemy and evil living; above all, to his death at the early age of twenty-nine, in a tavern brawl at Deptford, by the hand of a 'bawdy serving-man,' named Archer, or Fraser, or Ingram. The recent elucidation of the facts of the poet's career at Cambridge has happily diverted attention from the sordid ending and adjusted the balance of the scanty biography. In this short career there must, of necessity be little available to the antiquary; and yet we know as much of the man Marlowe as of the man Shakespeare, or, indeed, of any of the greater Elizabethans, Jonson excepted.

Marlowe proceeded from the King's school at Canterbury to Bene't (now Corpus Christi) College, Cambridge, about Christmas

---

This is the baptismal form, but the poet's father is referred to as 'Marley' or 'Marlyn,' and, in the Cambridge records, the name is spelt 'Marlin,' 'Marlyn,' 'Marlen,' 'Malyn.' In 1588, he is described as 'Christopher Marley of London,' and Peele speaks of 'Marley, the Muses' darling.'

1580. He was in residence, with occasional breaks, till 1587, when he took his master's degree, following on his bachelor's in 1583—4. There is evidence that, soon after 1587, he had fallen into disfavour at the university, and was already settled in London. He had probably been there for some time before the production of *Tamburlaine* in that year or the next. The interval between graduation and the appearance of this play is ingeniously filled in for us by Collier. We must, however, treat the ballad of *The Atheist's Tragedie*, which describes Marlowe's actor's life and riot in London, as one of Collier's mystifications, and, together with it, the interpolation in Henslowe's diary (fol. 19 v.) about 'addicions' to *Dr Faustus* and a 'prolog to Marloes tambelan.' Cunningham's suggestion that the young poet sought adventure as a soldier in the Low Countries, as Jonson did later, may be correct; but it must be proved on other grounds than his 'familiarity with military terms.' It is useless to speculate on the causes of the Cambridge quarrel and his alleged restlessness. Malone's view that Marlowe had become heretical under the influence of Francis Kett, fellow of Bene't, was based on a misconception of Kett's doctrine. If Kett resigned his fellowship in 1580[1], it would be hard to prove any association between him and Marlowe. The only extant piece which, with some show of reason, may be ascribed to this early period is the translation of Ovid's *Amores* (*Certaine of Ovid's Elegies*), which was printed posthumously, *c.* 1597. As an interpretation of the text, it does not reach even the indifferent level of Elizabethan scholarship, but it conveys the sensuous quality of the original. Marlowe's early choice of this subject and of another in the same vein (said by Warton to have been *The Rape of Helen* by Coluthus, non-extant) has many parallels in contemporary literature; but it has greater value as a commentary on the later work of the poet who, unlike Shakespeare, was not allowed time to outlive his youthful passion. We might find in the eighteenth elegy (*Ad Macrum*) of the second book of his *Ovid* a motto for his coming endeavour, when, sitting 'in Venus' slothful shade,' he says :

> Yet tragedies and sceptres fill'd my lines,
> But, though I apt were for such high designs,
> Love laughëd at my cloak.

If, later, he forsook the shade for the 'stately tent of war,' it was because his passion had been transformed, not because he had grown old.

[1] See *Dictionary of National Biography*, art. 'Marlowe.'

Marlowe's first original work was the two parts of *Tamburlaine the Great*, played in 1587 or 1588, and printed in 1590. The grandeur of the style, the gorgeous strutting of Alleyn in the title rôle, the contrast of the piece with the plays which had held the popular stage, gave *Tamburlaine* a long lease of popularity ; so that the Water Poet could truly say that the hero was not so famous in his own Tartary as in England. How strongly it impressed the public mind may be gauged by the number of attacks, some reasonably satirical, others merely spiteful, which came from literary rivals. From this onslaught, directed against what appeared, to classicists (like Jonson) and to 'rhyming mother wits,' to be an intolerable breach of all the laws of 'decorum,' has sprung the tradition of 'bombast' and 'brag' which has clung to Marlowe's literary name—a tradition which is at fault, not because it has no measure of truth, but because it neglects much that is not less true.

This sudden success confirmed Marlowe in his dramatic ambition. Hard words like Nashe's about 'idiote art-masters... who... think to outbrave better pens' could not deter this young Tamburlaine of the stage. On the heels of his first triumph came *The tragicall History of Dr Faustus*, probably produced in 1588, though its entry in the Stationers' register is as late as January, 1601, and the earliest known edition is the posthumous quarto of 1604. Interest in this play—a boldly drawn study of the pride of intellect, as consuming as the Tartar's ambition—has been seriously warped by speculation on the crude insets of clownage. Many readers have felt that the comic scenes are disturbing factors in the progress of the drama, and that Marlowe's text has suffered from playhouse editing. The presumption is supported by the evidence of the printer Jones, who tells us apologetically, in his edition of *Tamburlaine*, that he 'purposely omitted... some fond and frivolous gestures, digressing, and, in my poor opinion, far unmeet for the matter.' He saw the 'disgrace' of mixing these things in print 'with such matter of worth.' The bias for 'decorum' may, however, be too strong, and there may be reasons derived from consideration of the historical sentiment of the popular drama and of Marlowe's artistic mood to make us pause in saying that the original has been greatly, and sadly, altered. As bibliography cannot help us, the position of these alleged 'addicions' of tomfoolery and squibs in the Marlowe canon becomes a purely critical matter.

The same problem, but in a more difficult form, is presented in

the next play, *The Jew of Malta*. The first record of this piece is in
Henslowe's diary, February 1592, and two years later it is named
in the Stationers' register; but, as there is no evidence that it was
printed before 1633, when it received the editorial care of Thomas
Heywood, we have a ready excuse for disclaiming the poorer
passages as the result of the playhouse practice of 'writing-up'
for managerial ends. Yet, here again, caution is necessary, before
we say that only in the earlier acts, in which Barabas is presented
with little less than the felicity and dramatic mastery of Shakespeare's Jew, do we have the genuine Marlowe.

Tamburlaine, Dr Faustus and *The Jew of Malta* constitute
the first dramatic group. In his next play *The Troublesome
Raigne and Lamentable Death of Edward the Second*[1], Marlowe
turned from romantic tragedy to history. It is the first English
'history' of the type which Shakespeare has given in *Richard
II*; a drama of more sustained power, and showing some of
Marlowe's best work. It is this sustained power which has won for
it, since Charles Lamb's time, the honour of comparison on equal
terms with the later masterpiece; and, on the other hand, has
stimulated the suspicion of Marlowe's responsibility for the inequalities of the earlier plays. The most convincing proof of the
dramatist's genius is conveyed in the transformation of the existing
'chronicle' habit of the popular stage into a new genre. A fifth and
a sixth play—*The Massacre at Paris* and *The Tragedie of Dido
Queene of Carthage*—complete the list of the accredited dramas.
The first known edition of the former has been dated between
1596 and the close of the century[2]; the earliest text of the latter
belongs to the year 1594. In these, it must be admitted, the
suspicion of patchwork is reasonably strong, especially in *Dido*,
where Nashe is openly named on the title-page as a sharer in the
work. The literary interest of *The Massacre* is very small, except,
perhaps, in the second scene, where Guise's speech has the ring of
Tamburlaine:

> Give me a look, that, when I bend the brows,
> Pale death may walk in furrows of my face;
> A hand, that with a grasp may gripe the worlde.

An ingenious suggestion has been made that, in the more extravagant passages in *Dido*, such as the description of the death
of Priam[3], which Shakespeare parodied in *Hamlet*, Nashe was

---

[1] Perhaps acted in 1592; and printed in 1593, before the appearance of the earliest
extant text by William Jones.
[2] This play may have been composed before 1593.   [3] Act II, sc. 1.

'laughing in his sleeve,' and showing that he had learnt the trick of 'bragging blank verse' and could swagger in 'drumming decasyllabons.' It is better to take such passages at their poor face value, and to say that they cannot well be Marlowe's, even at his worst. Such blatant lines as fall to Dido when she addresses the 'cursed tree' which bears away the Trojan[1]—

> And yet I blame thee not: thou art but wood.
> The water, which our poets term a nymph,
> Why did it suffer thee to touch her breast,
> And shrunk not back, knowing my love was there?

cannot be by Marlowe; or even by Nashe, whether in prankish or in serious mood.

In these six plays we have all the dramatic work directly planned, and, with minor reservations, written, by Marlowe. It would be foolish to claim that the texts are approximately pure; but till a more exact canon of criticism than that a young genius may not be astoundingly unequal in his handling be available, we prefer to hold him responsible for nearly all that goes to the making of the current texts. The terms of this vexing problem of collaboration are changed when we come to consider Marlowe's claims to a share in other men's work. Here, it is clear that the plea must be that certain passages are in the manner of Marlowe, and of Marlowe at his best. There are few, if any, tests left to us, save the risky evidence of style—all the more risky in the case of a writer who is severely judged as an extravagant. Thus, *Locrine* appears to Malone—and as a firm article of his critical faith—to resemble the style of Marlowe 'more than of any other known dramatick author of that age.' It would be as difficult to make this strange claim good as it has been to show the play to be Shakespeare's[2]. So, too, with *Edward III*—or an earlier draft of that pseudo-Shakespearean play—which Fleay described, without evidence and against probability, as Marlowe's gift to his successor. Not less peremptorily may be dismissed the miserable play *A Larum for London* which Collier tried to foist on the dramatist on the strength of some forged rigmarole on his copy of that piece[3]; and *Lusts Dominion; Or, The Lascivious Queen* (printed in 1657), which Collier, by way of amends, showed to contain allusions to events posterior to Marlowe's death; and, with these two, *The Maiden's Holiday* (now lost, through Warburton's cook), a comedy asso-

---

[1] Act iv, sc. 4.

[2] See *post*, chap. x, where some striking resemblances between *Locrine* and *The Spanish Tragedie* are pointed out.

[3] Bullen's *Marlowe*, vol. i, p. lxxiv.

ciated with the name of Day, who was not at work in Marlowe's lifetime.

There remains the question of Shakespearean association. Four points of contact have been assumed; in *King John*, in *The Taming of the Shrew*, in *Titus Andronicus*, and in the three parts of *Henry VI*. That Marlowe had any share in the old play *The Troublesome Raigne of John, King of England* cannot be admitted; the refutation lies in the appeal of the prologue for welcome to a 'warlike christian and your countryman' from those who had applauded the infidel Tamburlaine. That Marlowe is the author of the older shrew play, *The Taming of a Shrew*, is not more reasonable ; for the mosaic of quotations and reminiscences of *Tamburlaine* and *Dr Faustus* prove, if they prove anything, that the author could not be the writer of these plays. There is a spirit of burlesque throughout in which the most incorrigible self-critic would have hesitated to indulge, and which only a 'transformed' Marlowe would have essayed. In the case of the much debated *Titus Andronicus* and the three parts of *Henry VI* there is some show of argument for Marlowe's hand. The more full-bodied verse of *Titus*, the metaphorical reach and, above all, the dramatic presentment of Aaron—which have helped to give the play a place in the Shakespearean canon—might well be the work of the author of *Tamburlaine*. But similar arguments, not less plausible, have discovered the pen of Peele, and of Greene. More has been said for the view that Marlowe had a share in *Henry VI*; but it is difficult to come nearer an admission of his association than to say that he probably had a hand in *The Contention betwixt the two famous Houses of Yorke and Lancaster* (written before 1590) which serves as the basis of the *Second Part*. We may guess that he collaborated in the revision of the *Third Part* ; but it is hard to find any hint of his style in the *First Part*, of which there is no evidence of an earlier version. On the other hand, it is clear that the author of the *First Part* was familiar with *Tamburlaine*, and in a way not to be explained as reminiscence[1].

The chronology of Marlowe's non-dramatic work, other, and presumably later, than the translation of Ovid already named, has not been determined. Two poems *Hero and Leander* and *The First Book of Lucan* are entered in the Stationers' register on 28 September 1593, that is, nearly four months after the poet's death. The first, which had been left unfinished, was printed in 1598, and again in the same year, with the text completed by

---

[1] Cf. on this subject, *post*, chap. VIII.

Chapman. The earliest known edition of the second is dated 1600; in which year also appeared two short pieces, the song 'Come live with me and be my love,' in *England's Helicon* (in fuller form than the 1599 text in *The Passionate Pilgrim*), and the fragment 'I walked along a stream for pureness rare,' in *England's Parnassus*[1]. The nearly simultaneous publication of these pieces appears to indicate an effort by friends to leave little or nothing of the poet's work unprinted; and the fact supplies contemporary evidence of a kind hardly consistent with the popular view of the disrepute of Marlowe's last years. Personal testimony from Edward Blunt (in his remarkable preface), Chapman and Nashe, supplemented by the praises which *Hero and Leander* won, from Shakespeare and Jonson and from humbler artists like the Water Poet, should go far to reduce the popular hyperbole of Marlowe's social and spiritual outlawry.

Since Marlowe's day, when rivals burlesqued his style, opinion has been concerned chiefly with the extravagance of his art, with his bombast and transpontine habit and, incidentally, with the craft of his dramatic verse. The fault of this criticism is that it is inadequate, that it enlarges on the accidental at the expense of the essential, and obscures both Marlowe's individual merit as a poet and his historical place in our literature. On the one hand, we make too much of the youthfulness of his muse, of his restless longing and 'buccaneering'; and, on the other, of his transitional or preparatory character. He is treated as a forerunner, a predecessor, a document for the prosodist; rarely, and, as it were, by chance, is he held in our literary affection for his own sake. He does not stand out as Shakespeare or Jonson or Fletcher does from the rush of scholarly controversy: he is a 'link,' a 'signpost,' to the historian of the English drama.

What is fundamental and new in Marlowe and was indeed his true aid to his dramatic successors is his poetic quality—the gift of the 'brave translunary things' of Drayton's eulogy. If there be anything in the common statement that Shakespeare is indebted to him, it is less for his great pattern of dramatic verse or even for his transformation of the crude history play than for the example of a free imagination, compassing great things greatly. It is harder to think of Shakespeare's profiting by direct study of Marlowe's

---

[1] To these has been added an unimportant *Elegy on* [Sir Roger] *Manwood*, preserved in MS in a copy of the 1629 edition of *Hero and Leander*; but the ascription has small authority, if any.

'experiments' in caesura and run-on lines than of his finding encouragement in the wealth of metaphor and in the energy of the new drama. In this poetic habit rather than in technical ingenuities are we to seek in such predecessors as Marlowe and Lyly for points of touch with Shakespeare. Let us, however, not exaggerate the borrowing : the kinship is of the age rather than of blood, the expression and re-expression of that artistic sense which marks off the literature of this period from all that had gone before. The interest of Marlowe's work is that it is the first to show how the age had broken with tradition. If it unveil so much to us, it may have helped even Shakespeare to feel his own power and reach. This feeling or understanding, we may call, though too crudely, the 'borrowing' from Marlowe.

A careful comparison of Marlowe's style, whether in verse-translation or in tragedy, with what had preceded, will show the insufficiency of the judgment that it is 'youthful' or 'preliminary.' It is too full-bodied, too confirmed in its strength. It conveys the impression, even in those passages which have been tardily excused, of a vigour and richness of poetic experience far beyond what we find in the artist who is merely making his way or is toying with experiment. If Marlowe fail to achieve the highest, it is not because he is a little less than a true poet, or because he cannot temper the enthusiasm of adolescence, but because the self-imposed task of transforming the 'jigging veins' of the national literature to statelier purpose was one of the hardest which genius could attempt. The familiar epithet 'titanic,' in which criticism has sought to sum up the poet's unmeasured aspirations, or J. A. Symonds's hard-worn phrase '*l'Amour de l'Impossible*[1]' may help us to express something of this imaginative vigour which was used in the transmutation of the old dross. Marlowe has the self-possession of the strong man ; he is no imitator, no pupil of a theory, Senecan or other, which he would substitute for what he found. The inequalities in his art are the effect of this strength, rather than the signs of undeveloped power. To a genius richly endowed from the first, and placed in such circumstance, literary development of the kind familiar to us in the careers of more receptive artists was impossible. In his plays we pass suddenly from creditable verse to lines of astounding power, both of imagery and form ; and we do so again and again. It is not our uncertainty of the chronology of his plays which prevents our placing them in a series of accomplishment, or doubt of his genius which makes us

---

[1] *Alias* ' The Impossible Amour ' (Symonds, *Shakspere's Predecessors* (1884), p. 608.)

chary of joining in the wholesale condemnation of the interludes of clownage and extravagance preserved in the texts. There is no younger or more mature Marlowe as there is a younger or more mature Shakespeare; and this is so, not because Marlowe's years fall short of the time which brings the harvest to most men.

The characteristics of Marlowe's style which the traditional criticism has singled out and deplored—the persistent hyperbole, the weak construction of the plays and their one-man and no-woman limitations, the lack of humour—are not to be confounded with the faults which go by the same name in the work of weaker contemporaries. Nor is it enough to say, in partial excuse of the first, that all Elizabethans, including Shakespeare, are of necessity hyperbolic in habit, and that Marlowe's excess is but the vice of that all-pervading quality. So much is certain: that the excess is not a mere makeweight or loading-on, to satisfy the clamour of the pit, and that the dramatist does not find an artistic pleasure in the mere use of bombast. There is always the sense of intimacy, even in the most extravagant passages, between the word and the situation which it expresses. The suggestion is literary; seldom, if ever, theatrical.

Indeed, we are on safer ground for the appreciation of Marlowe if we approach him from the literary side. Though he served English drama surpassingly well by giving it body and momentum, he rarely supplies a model in the technicalities of that genre. This is made clear, not only by the lack of variety in the choice of character and in the setting and construction, but by the absence of *dramatic* development in the portrayal of his heroes. What development we find is the outcome of a purely literary process, showing eloquence rather than action, a stately epical movement rather than the playwright's surprises of situation and character. Even in the passage where Tamburlaine laments by the bed of his dying Zenocrate, the poet achieves great pathos not by the mere 'stir' of the scene, but by that Miltonic know-ledge of word values, by the conscious (and rarely overconscious) delight in anaphora and line echo ('To entertain divine Zeno-crate'), and by the climax of metaphor. We feel that by the sheer verbal music of the recurring name, as in the scene of the wooing[1], and, again, in the great speech in part I, act V, sc. 1, the poet attains a dramatic effect undramatically. When has the magic of the word been used to better purpose than in the passage in which Tamburlaine, after hearing the speeches of

---

[1] Part I, act I, sc. 2.

Cosroe and Meander, and catching at the parting lines of the latter,

> Your majesty shall shortly have your wish,
> And ride in triumph through Persepolis,

says,

> 'And ride in triumph through Persepolis!'
> Is it not brave to be a king, Techelles?
> Usumcasane and Theridamas,
> Is it not passing brave to be a king,
> 'And ride in triumph through Persepolis?'[1]

This is the word music which rings out of such lines as

> By knights of Logres, or of Lyones,
> Lancelot, or Pelleas, or Pellenore,

and gives Marlowe as well as Milton his place as an 'inventor of harmonies.'

Marlowe's high seriousness (bluntly called lack of humour) suggests a further Miltonic analogy, and lends support to the view that his cast of thought, unlike that of many of his great successors in the drama, found readier expression in the processional of the imagination than in episode and the conflict of character. His contemporary, Kyd, had a stricter conception of the purpose and method of the playwright; but Marlowe's gift of the secret of stateliness was the true capital and endowment of the Elizabethan drama.

Two illustrations may be offered of Marlowe's transforming power: one, his treatment of the chronicle play; another, his creation of blank verse as a dramatic instrument.

The first examples of the English chronicle play belong to the early eighties of the sixteenth century. Historical personages appear in the drama of the transition, but neither in their treatment nor in their setting do we find anything which approaches what we must understand by a chronicle play or 'history.' The use of historical material by the stage represents three artistic intentions, more or less distinct. The first is didactic or satirical, and offers the key to some of the leading changes in the later morality. It appears early in the treatment of Bible story; later, in the humanising of allegorical characters, as in the identification of Herod with 'Cruelty'; later still, in the introduction of historical characters such as cardinal Pandulfus and Stephen Langton. The second is patriotic in *motif*, the expression of a strong national consciousness stirred by the political fervours of Elizabethan England, and stimulated on the literary side by the appearance of

[1] Part I, act II, sc. 5.

a multitude of prose works on historical subjects. Here, we have the true beginnings of the dramatic 'history' ushered in by such plays as the old *Henry V* and *Jack Straw* ; defined later by Peele and Marlowe in their *Edwards* ; and, by the end of Elizabeth's reign, already exhausted, after the masterpieces of Shakespeare. The third, the romantic, showing an interest in history because it offers an artistic relief from contemporary conditions, hardly falls under consideration at this point. Something of its mood appears in the mythical tales crudely dramatised in the early Tudor period and utilised by the Elizabethans ; but it was its strangeness, the opportunity given to fancy and emotion, which attracted the playwrights. It is the 'unhistorical' sentiment of the romantic revival of a later century which turned to the Middle Ages for the sheer delight of treading forgotten paths and escaping from the present.

It is a reasonable question whether there is any such genre as the chronicle or history play, for the term, in its strictest sense, means no more than a play, presumably a tragedy, which draws its subject from the national annals. The 'history play,' like the historical novel, is, at its best, an effort to analyse, by dramatic means, the development and effect of character. Rarely has it set itself the task of the general interpretation to which the historian proper is committed. Being a study of character which is incidentally historical, it does not stand apart from the accepted dramatic categories. The Elizabethan habit, familiarised in the division of Shakespeare's plays into 'tragedies,' 'comedies' and 'histories,' has exaggerated the value of the distinction. The true interest of the matter is that, in the popular appeal to history during the stirring close of the sixteenth century, not a few of the greater playwrights found their opportunity for the delineation of character in less tragic circumstance : seldom, perhaps only in Shakespeare, and in him not often, is the historical interpretation, the 'truth' of the 'true' tragedies, of any concern. Marlowe's merit as the beginner of the history play so-called lies in his humanising of the puppets of the *Kynge Johan* type, not in the discovery for us of the true Edward.

Edward II is not the first of the patriotic plays which supplanted the didactic and satirical morality (the dramatic counterpart of *A Mirror for Magistrates*), or of the Senecan variants, from *Gorboduc* to *The Misfortunes of Arthur* and *Locrine*. Of the extant forerunners, the roughly drawn *Famous Victories of Henry the fifth* and *Jack Straw* (printed in 1593) may be the earliest. A third, *The Troublesome Raigne of John, King of England*, in two parts (printed in 1591), supplies a link between the older *King John* by Bale and the later by Shakespeare, not merely as showing a progression in the treatment of a historical theme, but —and this gives force to the progression—in the humanising of the chief personages. This breaking with the dull habit of the chronicle play becomes clearer in Peele's *Edward I* (even though much of the roughness of the earlier models remains), and in *The First Part of the Contention betwixt the two famous Houses of Yorke and Lancaster* and *The True Tragedie of Richard, Duke of Yorke* (represented in later form by *Parts II and III of Henry VI*). We find like evidence in *The True Tragedie of Richard III* (printed in 1594) and in the 'troublesome' text of *I Henry VI*, as it appears in the Shakespeare folio. In this historical laboratory, in which some ask us to believe that Marlowe gained experience in the earlier texts on which *Parts I and II of Henry VI* were founded, as well as in the Shakespearean revisions, and even in the Shakespearean *Part I*, we have the making of *Edward II*, and, as a further effect of the collaboration, of *Richard II*.

The praise of *Edward II* has probably been extravagant. Because it is the first historical play of the stricter type, and because there is more characterisation and episode in it than in his earlier plays, it is singled out as Marlowe's best dramatic effort. It is necessary to supplement this half-truth. Such improvement as it shows, in construction and in development of character, is less real than may seem. Every play based on intimate history has an advantage in these respects. The 'fine restraint' for which *Edward II* has been admired is partly due to the fact that, unlike *Richard II*, with which it is often compared, it chooses a more extended period of action, and is, therefore, compelled to congest or select the episodes. The condensation, which has induced some critics to speak of the simplicity of Marlowe's treatment, makes against the dramatic interest, and denies the dramatist, often at the most urgent moments, the opportunity of fuller characterisation. Even when we make allowance for the greater number of characters of the first order and for the part of Isabella, it is impossible to separate the play from the earlier Marlowe category: not only because it is a re-expression of the simple problem of the impassioned resolute man, but because it is fundamentally literary in its mood. Such difference as exists is the effect of the medium, and of that only. That the old literary bias is strong hardly requires illustration. The keynote is struck in Gaveston's opening speeches, especially in that beginning

> These are not men for me;
> I must have wanton poets, pleasant wits,
> Musicians,

in Edward's talk with his friends in flight, and in the debate on his abdication. We are disappointed of the stricter dramatic requirements, of (in Swinburne's words) 'the exact balance of mutual effect, the final note of scenic harmony between ideal conception and realistic execution.' The characters do not 'secure or even excite any finer sympathy or more serious interest than attends on the mere evolution of successive events or the mere display of emotions (except always in the great scene of the deposition), rather animal than spiritual in their expression of rage or tenderness or suffering[1].' We may go further and say that neither as a pure literary effort nor as a drama does *Edward II* overtop, at least in its finest single passages, what Marlowe has given us elsewhere. In the gruesome death scene, we hold breath no harder than we do at the critical moment of Faustus's career. In passion and word music, the play never surpasses the earlier pieces : the shackles of the chronicle keep it, on the one hand, from the imaginative range of *Tamburlaine* or *Faustus*, and, on the other, from the reach of great tragedy. Yet, as an effort to interpret history on the stage, it is the first of any account, and hardly inferior to what is reputed best in this genre. Independent of such merit as is individual to it as literature is the credit of having reformed the awkward manners of the 'true tragedies' to statelier bearing. Marlowe satisfied the popular craving for the realities, as he had sought to satisfy the vaguer spiritual longings of his ambitious age. In no single case is his achievement final or artistically complete; but the cumulative effect of his insistence on a great idea, his undiminished force of passion and his poetic fulness are his great gift to English tragedy.

To Marlowe's literary instinct rather than to his faculty as a playwright the Elizabethan drama was indebted for the further gift of blank verse. Though the development of the instrument in his hands is the outcome of an experience which, unlike Milton's, was exclusively dramatic, it is easy to note that the phases of change, the discoveries of new effects, do not arise, as might be expected, from dramatic necessity. The plasticity of

---

[1] *Age of Shakespeare*, 1908, p. 6.

Marlowe's line, which is its most remarkable characteristic, is the direct expression of his varying poetic mood, the ebb and flow of metaphor, the organ and pipe music of word and phrase. The differences are apparent when we pass from such lines as in the great apostrophe to Helen to these[1]:

> From Scythia to the oriental plage
> Of India, where raging Lantchidol
> Beats on the regions with his boisterous blows,
> . . . .
> To Amazonia under Capricorn;
> And thence as far as Archipelago,
> All Afric is in arms with Tamburlaine;

and to these, in the first scene of *The Jew of Malta*:

> The wealthy Moor, that in the eastern rocks
> Without control can pick his riches up,
> And in his house heap pearls like pebble-stones,
> Receive them free, and sell them by the weight;
> Bags of fiery opals, sapphires, amethysts,
> Jacinths, hard topaz, grass-green emeralds,
> Beauteous rubies, sparkling diamonds,
> And seld-seen costly stones of so great price,
> As one of them indifferently rated,
> And of a caret of this quantity,
> May serve in peril of calamity
> To ransom great kings from captivity.

and to these, from *Edward II*[2]:

> The griefs of private men are soon allay'd,
> But not of kings. The forest deer, being struck,
> Runs to an herb that closeth up the wounds;
> But when the imperial lion's flesh is gor'd,
> He rends and tears it with his wrathful paw,
> And, highly scorning that the lowly earth
> Should drink his blood, mounts up to the air.

Such prosodic transitions do not show the intimate textual relationship to be found in Shakespeare's plays. In Marlowe's verse, each and all sort with a variety of mood which, in origin and expression, is epical, at times lyrical, rarely dramatic.

It is scarcely possible, without giving much space to illustration, to measure the differences in technical accomplishment between Marlowe and the earlier practitioners in blank verse. It matters not whether we take Surrey's rendering of the second and fourth *Aeneid*, which has the historical interest of being the first example of the naturalisation of the 'straunge meter,' or *Gorboduc*, also historically interesting as the 'first document' of dramatic blank verse in English: in these, it is as hard to foresee the

[1] Part II, act I, sc. 1. [2] Act v, sc. 1.

finding of a new prosodic instrument as in the experiments of Drant and his circle. Indeed, in both, there is only a violation of English sentiment; and nothing is given by way of compensation. In the confusion of accent and quantity the life of the verse has gone out; the quantitative twitchings never suggest vitality; each line is cold and stiff, laid out with its neighbours, in the chance companionship of a poetic *morgue*. These conditions are not entirely wanting in Marlowe: we see them when we institute a close comparison with Shakespeare and Milton. Nevertheless, his blank verse is, for the first time in English, a living thing: often as full-veined and vigorous as anything in the later master-pieces. This verse (if it be described in general terms) discloses greater variety in the accentuation of the line, greater regularity in the use of equivalence in the foot, an occasional shaking of the caesura from its 'classical' pose, the frequent employment of feminine endings even in exaggerated form, as

And Faustus hath bequeathed his soul to Lucifer,

or in the lines from *The Jew of Malta*, quoted on the previous page; above all, the breaking away from the pause and sense close at the end of each line. We have, in a word, the suggestion of that fluidity and movement which we find in the Miltonic verse paragraph. Marlowe achieves his line by the sheer rush of imagination, like a swollen river sweeping down on its dried-up channel, filling its broad banks and moving on majestically. It is accomplished by neither stage eloquence nor stage passion: its voice has the epical *timbre*, the *os magna sonaturum*. If there be anything in the hackneyed opinion that the poet weighted his lines with what has been called 'bombast' and 'rant' to make good the lost ballast of rime, it tends to a further confirmation of the belief that his technique was the outcome of an experience which was literary in origin and process.

The dramatic career of Thomas Kyd covers a shorter period than Marlowe's; and, despite the great popularity and influence of *The Spanish Tragedie*, it lacks both the range and sustained interest of the work of his junior and associate. He was the son of one Francis Kyd, a city scrivener, and was educated at Merchant Taylors' school, in which, from 26 October 1565, he was a fellow pupil with Edmund Spenser. This date and an earlier fixing his baptism on 6 November 1558 are the sole biographical evidence available, with the exception of sundry references, at the close of his short life, in papers connected with the judicial enquiry into Marlowe's religious opinions. For the rest, we must rely on the interpretation of the well known passage in Nashe's preface to Greene's *Menaphon* (1589) and of certain cryptic entries in Henslowe's diary. The former, by the elaboration of its satirical anger, acquires the value of a biographical document. Even if we had not the punning reference to the 'Kidde in Aesop' (a reminiscence of the 'May' eclogue of *The Shepheards Calender*) we should recognise, with due allowance for the extravagance of the attack, that the series of allusions constitutes strong circumstantial evidence as to the victim's career down to 1589. From this passage, therefore, we assume that Kyd had early forsaken his apprenticeship to his father's 'trade of *Noverint*'; that, being weak in Latinity (and so charged unjustly), he had turned to play-making and had 'bled' Seneca through its 'English' veins; that, in this barber-surgeon enterprise, he had interested himself in the story of *Hamlet*; and that, later, he had fallen to the task of translating from Italian and French. The reference to the botching up of blank verse 'with ifs and ands' seems to be explained by a line in *The Spanish Tragedie*[1]; and the ridiculed phrase 'bloud is a beggar' may prove to have a textual interest when fortune gives us the pre-Shakespearean *Hamlet*.

The earliest known dated work ascribed to Kyd is *The Householders Philosophie*, a version of Tasso's *Padre di Famiglia*. This volume, by 'T. K.,' printed in 1588, probably represents the 'twopenny pamphlet' work from the Italian to which Nashe refers towards the close of his depreciation. The French enterprise, also amiably described by the same hand, may remain to us in *Pompey the Great, his faire Corneliaes Tragedie*, which appeared under Kyd's name in 1595[2] as a translation of Garnier's *Cornélie*, and in the record of his intention to follow with a rendering of that author's *Porcie*. This intimation of Kyd's interest in the French Senecan brings him into immediate touch with lady Pembroke and her coterie, and gives point to Nashe's double-sensed gibe that the translators 'for recreation after their candle-stuffe, having starched their beardes most curiously' made 'a peripateticall path into the inner parts of the Citie' and spent 'two or three howers in turning over French *Doudie*.' The translation of *Cornélie* and a pamphlet on *The Murthering*

---

[1] Act II, sc. 1, 79.

[2] An anonymous text appeared in 1594. See bibliography.

of John Brewen, Goldsmith (printed by his brother John Kyd in
1592) appear to be the latest efforts of Kyd's short career, which
came to an end about December 1594. In the short interval
anterior to this hackwork, between 1585 and the publication of
Nashe's attack in 1589, the public were probably in possession
of the works on which his reputation rests, his *Hamlet, The
Spanish Tragedie,* and *The Tragedie of Solimon and Perseda.*
These and the discredited *First Part of Jeronimo* still supply
some of the thorniest problems to Elizabethan scholarship. Here,
only a partial statement can be attempted.

We know that in 1592 *The Spanish Tragedie* was enjoying the
fullest popular favour. None of the earliest quartos—Allde's
undated print, Jeffes's in 1594, White's in 1599—give a clue to the
authorship. The entry of the licence for *The Spanishe tragedie of
Don Horatio and Bellmipeia* (Bellimperia) on 6 October 1592 is
silent ; so, too, the later editions, and the notes in Henslowe of
Ben Jonson's additions in 1601 and 1602. It is not till we come to
the casual reference by Thomas Heywood to 'M. Kid' as the
author[1] that what might have proved another bibliographical crux
is fully determined. We may assume, from the hints in the in-
ductions to *Cynthia's Revels* and *Bartholomew Fayre,* that the
play was written between 1585 and 1587. Not only are there no
direct references to the great events of 1588, such as could hardly
be absent from a 'Spanish' tragedy—but the deliberate allusion
to older conflicts with England[2] shows that the opportunity which
Kyd, as a popular writer, could not have missed had not yet come.

The theme of *The Spanish Tragedie* is the revenge of 'old
Hieronimo' for the undoing of his son Don Horatio and the
'pittiful death' of the former in accomplishing his purpose.
Though contemporary satire fixed upon the play, and made it out-
Seneca Seneca in passion for blood, the essence of the drama
lies in the slow carrying-out of the revenge. In this, rather than
in the mere inversion of the *rôles* of father and son, is there analogy
with the Shakespearean *Hamlet*; as there is, also, in certain details
of construction, such as the device of the play within the play, the
presence of the ghost (with all allowance for Senecan and early
Elizabethan habit), and, generally, the coordination of three stories
in one plot. Consideration of this analogy helps us to define Kyd's
position in regard to both the English Senecan tragedy and the
Shakespearean: the more immediate matter is that Kyd's interest

---

[1] *Apology for Actors*, 1612.   [2] *E.g. The Spanish Tragedie*, act i, sc. 5.

in this 'variant' of the Hamlet story supports, rather than condemns, the conjecture that he had already been engaged on the
tragedy of the son's revenge.   Such recasting by one hand of a
single and simple dramatic *motif* is credible ; and, in Kyd's case,
likely, when we recall the alleged relationship of *Solimon and
Perseda* with *The Spanish Tragedie.*   There are few authors of
Kyd's repute whose work suggests more clearly a development
from within, a re-elaboration of its own limited material.   For this
reason, it is hard to disbelieve that he wrote a 'first part' to his
Spanish Tragedie, even if we be persuaded that the extant text of
the *First Part of Jeronimo* is not from his pen.

Kyd's authorship of a *Hamlet* which served as the basis for the
Shakespearean *Hamlet* is more than a plausible inference.   As the
arguments in support of this are too lengthy for discussion in this
place, only a general statement may be made.   In regard to the
date, we conclude, from the passage in Nashe, that the Saxo-
Belleforest story had been dramatised before 1589.   As there is no
evidence that it had attracted attention in England before the
tour of English actors on the continent, and, as they returned
from Elsinore towards the close of 1587, we may very reasonably
fix the date of production in 1587 or 1588.   The assumption that
Kyd is the author rests on these main bases: that the first quarto
of the Shakespearean *Hamlet* (1603) carries over some sections of
an original play, and that there are many parallelisms between the
Shakespearean play and *The Spanish Tragedie,* in construction, in
phrase and even in metre, and between it and Kyd's other works,
in respect of sentiment.   The likenesses in construction already
hinted at make up, with the textual data, a body of circumstantial
evidence which the most cautious criticism, fully conscious of the
risks of interpreting the re-echoed expressions of the spirit of the
age as deliberate plagiarism, is not willing to throw aside.   Indeed,
the cumulative force of the evidence would appear to convert the
assumption into a certainty.   If, as no one will doubt, Shakespeare
worked over, and reworked over, some *Hamlet* which had already
secured popular favour, why should we, with Nashe and the comparative testimony before us, seek for another than Kyd as the
author of the lost, perhaps unprinted, play ?   We are left with the
regret that, having Shakespeare's revisions, we are denied the
details of the master's transformation of the original copy.   The
lesson of this sequence would have told us more of Shakespeare's
'mind and art' than we could learn from the unravelling of all his
collaborated plays.

That Kyd, following his 'serial' habit of production, wrote a 'first part' for his 'tragedy' is, as we have said, possible, but not a tittle of evidence is forthcoming: that he wrote *The First Part of Jeronimo. With the Warres of Portugall, and the life and death of Don Andrœa,* which we have in the quarto edition of 1605, is, despite the authority lent in support of the ascription to him, wholly untenable. The problem of Kyd's association with a first part may be resolved into two main questions. In the first place, did he write, or could he have written, the extant text of 1605 ? In the second place, is this piece to be identified with the play entitled 'Done oracio' *alias* 'The Comedy of Jeronymo,' *alias* 'Spanes Comodye donne oracoe,' which appears seven times in Henslowe's list of the performances, in 1592, of *The Spanish Tragedie*[1]? A rapid reading of the *First Part* will show that, far from there being 'adequate internal evidence' for assigning the play to Kyd, there is proof that it must be by another hand. To maintain the ascription to Kyd, we should have to adduce very solid testimony, external as well as internal, that Kyd was capable of burlesque, was a veritable 'sporting Kyd,' and was Puck enough to make havoc of his art and popular triumph. For, from beginning to end, the piece is nothing but a tissue of rhetorical mockery, a satire of 'tragical speeches' and of inter-meddling ghosts ; often, on closer inspection, a direct quizzing of *The Spanish Tragedie* itself. By no access of literary devilry could the author of old Jeronimo transform that hero to the speaker of such intentional fustian as

> Now I remember too (O sweet rememberance)
> This day my years strike fiftie, and in Rome
> They call the fifty year the year of Jubily,
> The merry yeare, the peacefull yeare, the jocond yeare,
> A yeare of joy, of pleasure, and delight.
> This shall be my yeare of Jubily, for 'tis my fifty.
> Age ushers honor; 'tis no shame; confesse,
> Beard, thou art fifty full, not a haire lesse[2].

And it would be hard to believe that Kyd had joined in the raillery of Nashe and the pamphleteers,

> O, for honor,
> Your countries reputation, your lives freedome,
> *Indeed your all that may be termed reveng,*
> Now let your blouds be liberall as the sea[3];

or could write the ludicrous dialogue between the ghost of Andrea and Revenge at the close. The inevitable conclusion is that this

---

[1] Called *Jeronymo* in Henslowe.   [2] Act I, sc. 1.   [3] Act III, sc. 1.

First Part cannot have been written by the author of *The Spanish Tragedie*; and further (and almost as certainly), that this burlesque by another hand is not the piece which was interpolated by lord Strange's men in their repertory of 1592. The opportunity for the burlesque came more naturally in the early years of the new century, when *The Spanish Tragedie* had been refurbished by Ben Jonson, and attention had been called to it by his characteristic criticism of the old play. Internal evidence, notably the allusions to the Roman jubilee of 1600 and the acting of the play by the children of the chapel, supports the general conclusion against Kyd's authorship. It should, however, be noted that the argument that the *First Part* does not answer Henslowe's label of 'comodey' is irrelevant, if we make allowance for the vague nomenclature of the time and consider that the play makes no pretence to more than the 'seriousness' of burlesque. Further, the shortness of the text may be responsible for the view that the play was a 'fore-piece,' presumably to *The Spanish Tragedie*. The Henslowe play (never acted on the same night as the serious *Jeronimo*) might as well be called an afterpiece; but it is hard, in any circumstances, to conjure up an audience of the early nineties, or even of 1605, taking kindly to the two Jeronimos at one sitting.

Though no solid reason has been advanced against the ascription of *Solimon and Perseda* to Kyd, it is only on the slenderest grounds that it has been claimed for him. The story on which it is based appears in Henry Wotton's *Courtlie Controversie of Cupids Cautels* (1578), which also supplies the original of the pseudo-Shakespearean *Faire Em*; the play is entered in the Stationers' register on 22 November 1592, and is extant in an undated quarto and two quartos of 1599. Its association with Kyd has been assumed from the fact that he uses the same plot in the interpolated play which Jeronimo and Bellimperia present in *The Spanish Tragedie*. If we assume that one author is responsible for both renderings, the question remains as to which play was the earlier. Decision on this point is more difficult because of the long popularity of Wotton's translation, and of Jacques Yver's original, *Le Printemps d'Iver*—as shown in the successive references, from Greene's *Mamillia* (1583), to Shakespeare's *King John* and *Henry IV*. Shakespeare's pointed allusions to Basilisco—the captain Bobadil of *Solimon and Perseda*—imply an immediate and current popularity of the play; and for this reason we incline to dispute Sarrazin's conclusion that it was an early effort, and antecedent to *The Spanish Tragedie*. It appears, on the whole,

reasonable to fix the date of composition between the appearance
of *The Spanish Tragedie* and the entry in the Stationers' register
in 1592, and to consider it, if it be given to Kyd, as a fuller
handling of the sketch for Jeronimo and Bellimperia. Certain
similarities in *motif*, construction and phrase[1] are tempting aids to
the finding of a single author for both plays. On the other hand,
the closer we find the likeness, the harder is it to reckon with the
difficulty of believing that an author would thus repeat himself.
If, as Kyd's most recent editor maintains, *Solimon* lacks the show
of genius of *The Spanish Tragedie*, and if, as is also admitted,
there is a close family likeness (on which, indeed, the argument of
one parentage is based), we are in danger of being forced, contrary
to this critic's view and our own (as already stated), to the conclusion that the inferior play must be the earlier. The problem
is further complicated by the presence of a strange element of
comedy in *Solimon*. This, and, especially, the transcript of the
miles gloriosus type in the braggart Basilisco, introduces us, if
not to a new author, to a new phase of Kyd's art. And so we
float, rudderless and anchorless, on the sea of speculation[2].

The difficulty of determining the authentic work of Kyd makes
any general estimate of his quality and historical place more or
less tentative; yet the least uncertain of these uncertainties and
the acknowledged work in translation give us some critical foothold.
Kyd, in the words of his Hieronimo, proclaims his artistic
fellowship with the author of *Tamburlaine*:

> Give me a stately written tragedie;
> *Tragedia cothurnata* fitting Kings,
> Containing matter, and not common things[3].

Even if we allow, on the most liberal interpretation of the claims
set up by his editors, that he shows a subtler sense of humour than
is to be found in Marlowe, we are never distracted from the sombre
purpose of his art. A closer student of Seneca than was his brother
dramatist, he transfers, with direct touch, the 'tragical' rhetoric,
the ghostly personages, the revel in stage massacre; yet never in
the intimate fashion of the *Tenne Tragedies* or of his own version

---

[1] *E.g.* the words 'tralucent' (translucent) 'breast' in *Solimon*, act II, sc. 1, 60, and
The Spanish Tragedie (act I, sc. 4, 97).

[2] The suggestions that Kyd had a share in *The Taming of a Shrew* (see *Fleay's
English Drama*, vol. II, pp. 31—33) and in *Titus Andronicus*, that he wrote *Arden of
Feversham* (see Crawford, C., *Collectanea*, 1st series), or even the indifferent *Rare
Triumphs of Love and Fortune* (printed in 1589) are not convincing. The fragments
transmitted by Allott in *England's Parnassus* (1600) may not have had a dramatic
context; and they are too slight for the building up of any theory.

[3] *The Spanish Tragedie*, act IV, sc. 1, 156—8.

of Garnier. We have probably exaggerated his love of 'blood.' Despite the sensationalism of Horatio's death, Kyd never reaches to the depths of horror satirised in the induction of *A warning for Faire Women*, or disclosed in *Titus Andronicus* (and for this reason we discredit his association with this experiment of youth); and though, like Webster, whose career as a dramatist began after Kyd's had ended, he deals rawly with the story of revenge, we observe that his zest for the terrible is losing force. Popular opinion neglects these hints of approximation to the gentler mood of Shakespearean tragedy, as it chooses, also, to forget the contributory usefulness of his and Marlowe's extravagance in the making of that tragedy.

The interest of Kyd's work is almost exclusively historical. Like Marlowe's, it takes its place in the development of English tragedy by revealing new possibilities and offering a model in technique; unlike Marlowe's, it does not make a second claim upon us as great literature. The historical interest lies in the advance which Kyd's plays show in construction, in the manipulation of plot, and in effective situation. Kyd is the first to discover the bearing of episode and of the 'movement' of the story on characterisation, and the first to give the audience and reader the hint of the development of character which follows from this interaction. In other words, he is the first English dramatist who writes dramatically. In this respect he was well served by his instinct for realism. The dialogue of his 'stately written tragedy' is more human and probable than anything which had gone before, or was being done by Marlowe. In the working out of his plot, he escapes from the dangers of rhetoric by ingenious turns in the situation. In such a scene as that where Pedringano bandies words with the hangman when the boy brings in the empty box[1], or in Bellimperia's dropping of her glove[2], we are parting company with the older tragedy, with the English Senecans, with *Tamburlaine* and *Faustus* and even *Edward II*, and we are nearer Shakespeare. When we add to this talent for dramatic surprise the talent for displaying character, as it were, rooted in the plot, and growing in it—not strewn on the path of a hero who is little more than the embodiment of a simple idea—we describe Kyd's gift to English tragedy, and, more particularly, to Shakespeare himself. Direct references in Shakespeare and his contemporaries, though they be many, count for little beyond proving the popularity of *The Spanish Tragedie*. The indebtedness must be sought in the

---

[1] *The Spanish Tragedie*, act III, sc. 6. [2] *Ibid.* act I, sc. 4.

persistent reminiscence of Kyd's stagecraft throughout the Shake-spearean plays, of devices which could not come from any earlier source, and, because of their frequency, could not come by chance. We reflect on the fact that he, who may have been the young author making trial of Kyd's manner in *Titus Andronicus*, found more than a theatre-hack's task in working and re-working upon the early *Hamlet*. From the straggling data we surmise, not only that Shakespeare knew and was associated with Kyd's work, but that the association was more to him than a chance meeting in the day's round. Jonson with his 'additions'—even with the Painter's Part[1] placed to his credit—supplies an instructive con-trast ; he intrudes as a censor, and will not be on terms. Yet the fact is worth record in the story of Kyd's influence, that his work is found in direct touch with that of Shakespeare and Jonson. We want to know more of this association, above all of the early *Hamlet* which Shakespeare used ; and, wishing thus, we are driven to vain speculation, till the Jonsonian Hieronimo stays us, as he may well do elsewhere in the 'quest of enquirie' into Eliza-bethan authorship :

> 'Tis neither as you think, nor as you thinke,
> Nor as you thinke ; you'r wide all :
> These slippers are not mine ; they were my sonne Horatio's.

[1] *The Spanish Tragedie*, act III, sc. 12 A.   There are six 'additions,' including the 'Painter's Part.'   See bibliography.

CHAPTER VIII

SHAKESPEARE: LIFE AND PLAYS

ALL writing which is not of the loosest kind about Shakespeare must, almost necessarily, be dominated by one of two distinct estimates of the positive information available on the subject. There is the view that all this information really comes, as a matter of fact, to very little; and there is the view that, as a matter of fact, it comes to a good deal. The former is the more common, and—though the other has been held by persons whose opinion deserves the utmost respect, and to whom our debt for the labour they have spent on the question is very great—it is probably the sounder. The more impartially, the more patiently and the more respectfully, so far as regards the laws of critical and legal evidence, we examine the results of Halliwell-Phillipps among dead, and of Sidney Lee among living, enquirers, the more convinced do we, in some cases, at least, become that almost the whole matter is 'a great Perhaps,' except in two points: that one William Shakespeare of Stratford-on-Avon was, as a man of letters, actually the author of at any rate the great mass of the work which now goes by his name, and that, as a man, he was liked and respected by nearly all who knew him. These things are proved, the first critically, the second legally and historically. To the critical certainties we can add considerably, and to the critical probabilities immensely. But, legally and historically, we are left, at least in the way of certainties, with a series of dates and facts mostly relating to matters of pure business and finance—a skeleton which is itself far from complete, and which, in most points, can only be clothed with the flesh of human and literary interest by the most perilous process of conjecture. We are not quite certain of the identity of Shakespeare's father; we are by no means certain of the identity of his wife; we do not know, save by inference, that Shakespeare and she ever went through the actual ceremony of marriage; we do not know when he began his dramatic career; we know the actual date of the first production of very few of his pieces, let alone that of their composition.

Almost all the commonly received stuff of his life story is shreds and patches of tradition, if not positive dream work. We do not know whether he ever went to school. The early journey to London is first heard of a hundred years after date. The deer stealing reason for it is probably twenty years later. The crystallisation of these and other traditions in Rowe's biography took place a hundred and forty-six years after the poet's supposed birth. To hark back: it is not absolutely certain, though it is in the highest degree probable, that the 'Shake-scene' in Greene's outburst is Shakespeare. 'Shake-scene' is not so very much more unlikely a term of abuse for an actor than 'cushion-' or 'tub-thumper' for a minister. And Chettle's supposed apology is absolutely, and, it would seem, studiously, anonymous. The one solid ground on which we can take our stand is supplied by Ben Jonson's famous, but mainly undated, references. They form the main external evidence for the two propositions which have been ventured above; to them, as to a magnetic centre, fly and cling all the contemporary, and shortly subsequent, scraps of evidence that are true metal; they supply the foundation piece on which a structure, built out of internal evidence, may be cautiously, but safely, constructed. Next to them, though in a different kind, comes Meres's *Palladis Tamia* passage in 1598. The publication dates of *Venus and Adonis*, of *Lucrece*, of the *Sonnets*, as well as the fact and date of the purchase of New Place, are tolerably fast-driven piles; the death date is another; the publication of the first folio yet another. We are not, therefore, in a mere whirl of drifting atoms, a wash of conflicting tides; but we may be more exposed to such a whirl or wash than men who like solid ground could desire.

No biography of Shakespeare, therefore, which deserves any confidence, has ever been constructed without a large infusion of the tell-tale words 'apparently,' 'probably,' 'there can be little doubt'; and no small infusion of the still more tell-tale 'perhaps,' 'it would be natural,' 'according to what was usual at the time' and so forth. The following summary will give the certain facts, with those which are generally accepted as the most probable, distinguishing the two classes, so far as is possible, without cumbrous saving clauses, but avoiding altogether mere guesswork, unless it has assumed such proportions in ordinary accounts that it cannot be passed by.

The name of Shakespeare appears to have been very common, especially in the west midlands; and there was a William Shakespeare hanged (cf. his namesake's 'Hang-hog is Latin for bacon') as early as 1248, not far from Stratford itself. In the sixteenth century, the name seems to have been particularly common; and there were at least two John Shakespeares who were citizens of the town about the time of the poet's birth. It has, however, been one of the accepted things that his father was a John Shakespeare (son of Richard), who, at one time, was a 'prosperous gentleman'— or, at any rate, a prosperous man of business as woolstapler, fell-monger and so forth, thinking himself gentleman enough to make repeated applications for coat armour, which, at last, were granted. This John Shakespeare married Mary Arden, an heiress of a good yeomanly family, but as to whose connection with a more distinguished one of the same name there remains much room for doubt. The uncertainty of the poet's birthday is one of the best known things about him. He was baptised on 26 April 1564; and probability, reinforced by sentiment, has decided on the 23rd, St George's day, for the earlier initiation. He would seem to have had three brothers and two sisters.

There was a free grammar school at Stratford, to which, as the son of his father, he would have been entitled to admission; and it has been supposed that he went there. Aubrey, who is almost entirely unsupported, even says that he was a schoolmaster himself. The point is only of importance, first in regard to Jonson's famous ascription to him of 'small Latin and less Greek'; secondly, and much more, in relation to the difficulty which has been raised as to a person of no, or little, education having written the plays. The first count matters little—many schoolboys and some school-masters have answered to Ben's description. The second matters much—for it seems to be the ground upon which some persons of wit have joined the many of none who are 'Baconians' or at least against 'the Stratforder,' as certain anti-Shakespearean Germans call him.

The difficulty comes from a surprising mixture of ignorance and innocence. A lawyer of moderate intelligence and no extra-ordinary education will get up, on his brief, at a few days' notice, more knowledge of an extremely technical kind than Shakespeare shows on any one point, and will repeat the process in regard to almost any subject. A journalist of no greater intelligence and education will, at a few hours' or minutes' notice, deceive the very elect in the same way. Omniscience, no doubt, is divine; but *multi*science—especially multiscience a little scratched and ad-mitting through the scratches a sea-coast to Bohemia and know-ledge of Aristotle in Ulysses—is quite human. What is wonderful is not what, in the book sense, Shakespeare knew, but what he did and was. And the man—whoever he was—who wrote what Shakespeare wrote would have had not the slightest difficulty in knowing what Shakespeare knew.

The stories of his apprenticeship (to a butcher or otherwise) are, again, late, very uncertain and, in part—such as his making speeches to the calves he was to kill—infinitely childish, even when quite possibly true. The story of his marriage, though starting from some positive and contemporary facts, is a very spider's web of unsubstantial evolution. On 28 November 1582, two husbandmen of Stratford, named Sandells and Richardson, became sureties for £40 in the consistory court of Worcester to free the bishop from liability in case of lawful impediment, by pre-contract or consanguinity, to the marriage of 'William Shagspeare and Anne Hathwey' which might proceed hereupon with only one publication of banns. On 26 May 1583, Shakespeare's eldest daughter, Susanna, was baptised at Stratford. Moreover (a much more surprising thing than this juxtaposition), on the very day before the signing of the bond, a regular licence was issued for the marriage of William Shakespeare and Anne *Whateley*—a coincidence extraordinary in any case, most extraordinary if we note the extreme closeness of the names *Hathwey* and *Whateley* and remember that *Anne* Hathaway is not otherwise traceable, though *Agnes* Hathaway (the two names are in practice confused) is. This mystery, however, has been less dwelt on than the irregular character of the 'bond' marriage and its still more irregular chronological adjustment to the birth of Susanna. On this, on the apparent fact that the wife was eight years older than the husband, who was only eighteen, on his long absences from Stratford and on the solitary bequest (and that an afterthought) of his second-best bed to his wife, have been founded romances, moralisings, censures, defences, hypotheses of formal antenuptial contract, every possible symptomatic extravagance of the *lues commentatoria*, every conceivable excursion and alarum of the hunt after mares' nests. The only rational course of conduct is to decline to solve a problem for which we have no sufficient data ; and which, very likely, is no problem at all. Only, as Shakespeare's works have been ransacked for references to disapproval of marriages in which the bride is older than the husband, and to anticipations of marriage privileges, let us once more appeal to the evidence of those works themselves. No writer of any time—and his own time was certainly not one of special respect for marriage—has represented it so constantly as not only 'good' but 'delightful,' to retort La Rochefou-cauld's injurious distinction. Except Goneril and Regan, who, designedly, are monsters, there is hardly a bad wife in Shakespeare —there are no unloving, few unloved, ones. It is not merely in his objects of courtship—Juliet, Viola, Rosalind, Portia, Miranda —that he is a woman-worshipper. Even Gertrude—a questionable widow—seems not to have been an unsatisfactory wife to Hamlet the elder as she certainly was not to his brother. One might hesitate a little as to Lady Macbeth as a hostess—certainly not as a wife. From the novice sketch of Adriana in the *Errors* to the unmatchable triumph of Imogen, from the buxom honesty of Mistress Ford to the wronged innocence and queenly grace of Hermione, Shakespeare has nothing but the *beau rôle* for wives. And if, in this invariable gynaecolatry, he was actuated by dis-appointment in his own wife or repentance for his own marriage, he must either have been the best good Christian, or the most pigeon-livered philosopher, or the most cryptic and incomprehensible ironist, that the world has ever seen. Indeed, he might be all these things, and feel nothing of the kind. For the next incident of the biographic legend—the deerstealing and consequent flight to London—there is, it has been said, no real evidence. It is not impossible, though the passage in *The Merry Wives of Windsor* which has been supposed to be a reference to the fact is at least equally likely to be the source of the fiction. That Shakespeare went to London somehow there can be no doubt ; how, and when, and for what reason, he went, there can be no certainty. If the Greene reference be accepted, he must have been there long enough to have made a reputation for himself in 1592 ; by next year, 1593, the year of *Venus and Adonis*, he had begun his unquestionable literary career, and made the acquaintance of lord Southampton ; and, by next year again (1594) (though at the end of it), we first find him a member of the famous company of which he became a leader, and which included Burbage, Heminge, Condell and other persons famous in connection with him.

How long the career—which emerges from obscurity, perhaps with the first, certainly with the second and third of these dates and facts—had been going on is, again, guesswork. Casting back, however, we get a reasonable *terminus ante quem non*, if not a certain *terminus a quo*, in the birth of twins (Hamnet, who died young and Judith, who lived) to him and his wife, before 2 February 1585, when they were baptised. Four years later, again, than 1594, the

Meres list of 1598 shows to Shakespeare's name, besides *Venus and Adonis* and *Lucrece* (1594), the goodly list of plays which will be seen presently, and the as yet unprinted *Sonnets*, while Shakespeare had also become at least a competent actor—a business not to be learnt in a day—and had acquired money enough to buy, in 1597, the famous New Place, the largest house in his native town.

The literary progress of these nine or thirteen years, according as we take the first theatrical record or the Meres list for goal, can be assigned, in some cases, with certainty: of the life, hardly anything whatever is known. Legends about horse-holding at theatres, in the first place; of the organisation of a brigade of horse-boys, in the second; of promotion to callboy and to actor— are legends. William Shakespeare's name seems to occur, in April 1587, in a deed relating to some property in which his family were interested. Otherwise, all positive statements in biographies of credit will be found qualified with the 'doubtless' or the 'probably,' the 'may have' and the 'would have,' until we find him taking part in the Christmas entertainments presented to the queen at Greenwich on St Stephen's day and Innocents' day 1594. Then, and then only, does the mist disappear; though it hardly leaves him in a very lively 'habit as he lived.' But we have mentions of houses in London and (before the New Place purchase) at Stratford; details of financial disaster to his father which seems to have been repaired, and of the subsequent application for arms, in his father's name, which was at last granted in 1599; suits about the property in dispute ten years earlier—a good many business details, in short, but little more that is satisfying.

But the nature of commentators abhors a vacuum: and this vacuum has been filled up (excluding for the present the various arrangements of the *Works*) from two different sides. In the first place, we have a series of conjectures dealing with the progress of Shakespeare's novitiate as actor and playwright, and his relations to his immediate predecessors in the latter capacity. In the second, we have the application of hypothetical hermeneutics to the *Sonnets*[1].

The first is guesswork pure and unadulterated; or, to speak with more correctness, adulteration without any purity, except in so far as concerns the *Works* themselves—which are reserved for the moment. From them, it derives whatever shadow of substance it possesses. We do not know that Shakespeare ever personally knew a single one of the 'university wits.' The Greene reference,

---

[1] For the poetical aspect of these, see the following chapter.

taken at its fullest possible, is, distinctly, against personal knowledge. The Chettle reference, from its obvious and definite disclaimer of personal knowledge, strengthens the counter-evidence. The (probably much later) passages in *The Returne from Pernassus* give no support to it. Parodies of phrasings universal in Elizabethan drama go for practically nothing. And the famous and beautiful appeal to the 'Dead Shepherd' in *As You Like It* contains as little to indicate that, wherever Shakespeare was and whatever he did, from 1585 to 1593, his circle and that of the 'wits' anywhere overlapped.

So, also, the present writer can see no valid evidence of any personal connection with Spenser. 'Our pleasant Willy' has, almost necessarily, been given up : the connection of 'Aetion' with Shakespeare appears to be wholly gratuitous. 'No doubt,' as is pointed out, Shakespeare's company, if he belonged to any before 1594, probably, and, after that, certainly, 'toured in the provinces'; but there is no evidence that he ever was, and no necessity that he ever should have been, in Germany or Scotland or Denmark ; nor any reason of either kind why he should have surveyed the battle-fields of Towton or of Shrewsbury or of Bosworth any more than those of Actium or Pharsalia. London and Stratford are the only places in which, from evidence, we can place him. Excepting his family, business folk in the two places mentioned, lord Southampton and Ben Jonson, there are hardly any persons with whom, on evidence, we can associate him.

This manner of handling the subject must, of course, be profoundly unsatisfactory to those who think that, in consequence of the long discussions of biographical facts and fictions by scholars, 'final judgments' should be possible on such points as Shakespeare's marriage, his religious views, his knowledge of law, his conduct in business relations and the like. It seems to be impossible to get a very large number of presumably educated and not unintelligent people to perceive the difference between proof and opinion. In all the instances just given, we have no basis for proof; and, as to all of them, opinion can never be final, because every person of fair intelligence and education has a right to his own. Of such argument as that Shakespeare's father could not have been a butcher because he was a glover and guild rules forbade the combination, there can be no end. Those who love it may follow it in its endless course ; it cannot be too peremptorily asserted that those who do not love it are entitled to reject it entirely and to say 'fight

Tradition : fight Presumption' to this shadowy dog and that unsubstantial bear.

The solid fact, however, of Meres's mention of the *Sonnets*, two of which (though the whole collection was not published till ten years later) appeared surreptitiously, it would seem, next year (1599), introduces another range of hypothetical exercise in biography, which has sometimes been followed in opposition to the former method, but has been more frequently combined with it so as to permit of even more luxuriant and wilder expatiation. This is the autobiographic reading of Shakespeare's work ; and, more particularly, of the *Sonnets* themselves. The extravagances of this 'method' are a by-word ; yet it may be questioned whether almost everybody—sometimes in the very act of protesting against them—has not been caught in the mazy meshes. Are we to say to John Shakespeare 'Thou art *this* man,' when we read about testy and platitudinous fathers like old Capulet and Egeus and Polonius ? Should we substitute the 'best silver bowl' argument for the 'second-best bed' argument and, calling in *The Tempest*, see Judith Quiney, to whom that bowl was left, in Miranda? Criticism, it is to be feared, shakes its head and observes that the 'colours' of different ages date from long before Aristotle ; and that, doubtless, there were charming girls even before Nausicaa.

It may, however, be fully admitted that the *Sonnets* stand in a very different category from that of the plays. Not only does the poet of this kind speak *ex professo* from his heart, while the dramatist speaks *ex professo* as an outside observer and 'representer,' but there is no poetry of this kind which approaches Shakespeare's *Sonnets* in apparent vehemence and intensity of feeling. There is even hardly any which mingles, with the expression of that feeling, so many concrete hints, suggesting so broadly a whole romance of personal experience, as they do. How are we to take all this?

One of the best known things in Shakespearean study—even to those who have hardly dabbled in it—is that one of the ways in which it has been taken is an endless series of earnest and almost frantic attempts to reconstruct this romance as a history. The personality of the Mr W. H. to whom the complete edition of 1609 is dedicated, though perhaps the chief, is but one, of the points of dispute. The reality and identity of the fair young man and the dark lady who are by turns or together concerned in the *Sonnets* themselves come next, and, with some enquirers, first ; while the incidents and sentiments, expressed, implied, commemorated, in them, have occupied a not small library of discussion, appreciation, attack, defence and so forth.

The extravagance of much of this has always been perceptible to impartial observers ; and, perhaps, the extravagance of most of it—except the particular theory to which they are themselves inclined—has been clear enough even to the theorists themselves. Sometimes—and of late with especial learning and elaboration by Sidney Lee—a sort of general *caveat* has been entered on the ground of the peculiarly traditional and conventional character of sonnet writing, especially at this particular time. Sometimes, all attempts to interpret have been shaken off, angrily, contemptuously or critically, according to temperament. And it may be suspected that some people who would confess it, and more who would not, have always inclined to Hallam's curious but courageous wish that Shakespeare 'had never written them.'

But he did write them—there is hardly a thing of his as to the authorship of which—what with Meres's early ascription, the publication with his name seven years before his death and the entire absence of denial, counter-claim, or challenge of any kind—we can be so certain. And, probably, there is no lover of poetry as poetry who would not wish that anything else 'had never been written,' so that these might be saved. But, undoubtedly, the mean is very hard to hit in the interpretation of these poems. Although it is quite certain that the sonnet tradition, starting from Petrarch and continued through generations of Italian, French and English practitioners, had resulted in a vast and complicated 'common form' of expression—a huge mass of *publica materies* of which the individual builder took his store, sometimes directly from other individuals, sometimes indirectly—it is possible to lay too much stress on this. After all, even if the sonnet thoughts and phrases were as stereotyped as the figures of a pack of cards—and they were not quite this—there is infinite shuffling possible with a pack of cards, infinite varieties of general game and still more of personal play, above all, infinite varieties of purpose and stake. You may play 'for love' in one sense or 'for love' in another and a very different one. You may play for trifles or for your last penny—to show your skill, or merely to win, or to pass the time, or from many other motives. That Shakespeare was the Deschapelles or Clay of sonnet whist is pretty certain. But that he did not play merely for pastime is almost more so to any one who takes the advice of Sidney's 'Look *in thy heart*' and applies it to reading, not writing.

The *Sonnets*, then, are great poetry, that is to say, in a certain sense, great fiction ; and they are intense expressions of feeling, that is to say, in another certain sense, great facts. But to what extent and degree are this fiction and this fact dosed and proportioned ? How are we to separate them? How do they colour and react upon one another ? Here, no doubt, is the rub—and it is a rub which it seems to the present writer impossible to remove or lubricate. Once more, to those who have accustomed themselves really to weigh evidence, it is impossible to accept it either as proved or disproved that 'Mr W. H.' was Pembroke, or Southampton, or any other friend-patron of Shakespeare, or merely somebody concerned with the publication, or, in fact, a 'personage' of any kind in this play. Nor is it possible to extricate, from the obscurity in which, to all appearance designedly, they were involved, either the other *dramatis personae* or even, save to the vaguest extent, the *scenario* itself. Friendship and love—*bene velle* and *amare*—exchange parts, combine, divorce, sublimate or materialise themselves and each other in too Protean a fashion to be caught and fixed in any form. The least unreasonable of all the extravagant exegeses would be that the whole is a phantasmagoria of love itself, of all its possible transformations, exaltations, agonies, degradations, victories, defeats. The most reasonable explanation, perhaps, and certainly not the least Shakespearean, is that it is partly this—but partly, also, in degree impossible to isolate, a record of actual experience. And it is not unimportant to observe that the *Sonnets*, a lock in themselves, become a key (Dryden would have recognised the catachresis) to the plays. How far they reveal Shakespeare's facts may be doubtful ; his method of treating fact, his own or others, is clear in them.

Before generalising on what this is, we may turn to the individual plays themselves, to which we have now come in well grounded chronological advance. The Meres list is well known ; it is as follows : *Gentlemen of Verona*, [*Comedy of*] *Errors*, *Love labors Lost*, *Love labours wonne*, *Midsummer night dreame*, *Merchant of Venice*, *Richard II*, *Richard III*, *Henry IV*, *King John*, *Titus Andronicus* and *Romeo and Juliet*. Of these, we know all—for the proposed rejection of *Titus Andronicus* will be dealt with presently—except *Love's Labour's Won*, which has been identified, as plausibly as mere conjecture can identify anything, with *All's Well that Ends Well*. It is, however, all-important to observe that Meres gives no order of sequence ; and that so large a bulk of work as this, greater than the whole theatre of some considerable dramatists, must have taken no short time to write, especially when we consider that the writer, during four years unquestionably and, beyond reasonable doubt, for a good deal longer, had been busily employed in acting. Twelve years possibly, since the baptism of Hamnet and Judith, six at least, if we accept the Greene reference, may be suggested as not conjectural items in the problem; eight or ten as a plausible splitting of the difference. To the fruits of this time we may add, fairly enough, if no certainty be insisted upon, Shakespeare's part, whatever it was, in *Henry VI* (see below and the chapter on the doubtful plays) as well as portions or first sketches of others and, perhaps, some whole plays. But the Meres list, from its solidity, affords such an invaluable basis for investigation and classification that it is wise, in the first place, not to travel outside of it in quest of either external or internal evidence of order, or characteristics of quality.

The external evidence is of the smallest. No one of the plays except *Titus* was published till the year before Meres wrote, and some not till the folio of 1623. A *Comedy of Errors* was acted near the close of 1594. The Greene reference quotes a line of *Henry VI*—not a Meres play. Several, *Romeo and Juliet*, *Richard II*, *Richard III*, were printed in 1597; *Love's Labour's Lost* (with alterations) in the next year. *Titus Andronicus* was acted in January 1593/4 and printed in the latter year, in which *The Merchant of Venice*, as *The Venetian Comedy*, may have appeared. This is all; and it will be observed, first, that much of it comes close up to the Meres date itself; secondly, that it concerns only a few of the plays. We have, therefore, to fall back on internal evidence, as it is called. But internal evidence is of very different kinds; and it is important to distinguish them from each other with the greatest possible care. One kind—or, rather, group of kinds—has figured very largely, indeed, in Shakespearean study. It is based on what may be broadly called 'allusions'—passages in the plays which seem to refer to contemporaneous and known events, coincidence of the general subject of them with such events, or, sometimes, references in other more or less certainly dated work to them. It cannot be too strongly asserted, from the point of view of the present survey, that this class of evidence is open to the gravest suspicion. It ought not, of course, to be judged from its caricatures, as in the case where the mention of 'pepper' is supposed to be connected with a known capture of a large cargo of that comforting spice. But, in almost all cases, it is exceedingly difficult to be sure that the coincidences are not

purely imaginary. Nor is this the worst part of the matter. Admit
that they are not purely imaginary—that the actual cited passages
may have had some connection with the actual known events.
How are we possibly to be certain that these passages were parts
of the play as originally acted, much more as originally written ?
'Those who live to please must please to live': the topical insertion
or 'gag' is one of the best known features of theatrical composition
and is probably as old as Thespis in ancient times or Boileau's
imaginary pilgrims in modern. Some of Shakespeare's plays, we
know, were not printed till nearly thirty years after they were
first acted ; it is not impossible that, in some cases, the interval
may have been even longer. Even if you can date the passage, it
will give you no right whatever to date the play accordingly. If,
therefore, this whole class of 'evidence' is not to be ruled out
bodily, it must be relegated to the utmost margin—kept strictly in
the court of the Gentiles.

The other kind of internal evidence is not itself quite homo-
geneous, except that it is, or should be, always and entirely
concerned with literary matters—with the quality, style, construction, form, character generally, of the work. Even here,
there are dangers—and quite as fantastic tricks have been played
in this way as in the other. By judging piecemeal, by adopting
arbitrary standards of judgment and, above all, by considering,
not what Shakespeare wrote but what we should like Shakespeare
to have written, or think he ought to have written, it is possible to
go as far wrong in this as in any way whatever. In no way, however, is it possible to reach so far and so safely, if due precaution
be observed and if there be brought to the enterprise, in the first
place, a sufficient study of the whole of Shakespeare's work, and,
in the second, a competent knowledge of preceding and contemporary English literature.

The invaluableness of the Meres statement is that it provides
us with a trustworthy and far reaching criterion between Shakespeare's earlier and his later work. It is, of course, possible that
Meres may not have known of some early pieces or may have
omitted them by accident ; but in a list already so considerable as
his and, as in the case of the *Sonnets,* showing knowledge of a more
than merely outside character, it is very improbable that he omitted
much that was completed, publicly performed and notoriously
Shakespeare's. On the other hand, we have this early body of
work 'coted' and named as early. If we can discover any characteristics of the kind least likely to deceive—the characteristics of

construction, style, prosody—which differ remarkably as wholes from those of the plays not named, or most of them, this will give us light of the most important and illuminative kind. If we can perceive that, in these same respects, the plays of the early list differ from each other singly or in groups—that there is evidence of the same progress and achievement inside the group as there is between it and plays like *Hamlet, As You Like It, Antony and Cleopatra, Othello*—we may almost know that we are in the right path. And we may branch from it, though with caution and almost with fear and trembling, into comparison of the same kind with immediately preceding or contemporary writers, to obtain additional illustration and illumination.

By the steady carrying out of all these processes—the comparison of the Meres list with the other plays; the comparison of the plays in that list with each other; and the comparison of the work of the Marlowe group, of Lyly and of a few other known or unknown writers—the least hasty or fanciful of critics will probably be induced to mark off from the Meres list of undoubtedly early plays a smaller group of almost undoubtedly earlier and, perhaps, a smaller still of probably earliest. From this last, he will probably be wise in refusing to select an 'earliest of all,' because the marks of earliness in them are not quite the same. They are all such as would characterise a genius in its novitiate; but it would be an exceedingly rash person who should undertake to say that, of the various kinds of literary measles which they show, one would be likely to attack the patient sooner than another. The group in question consists, as it seems to the present writer, of three plays, which, to mention them in the unquestion-begging order of the folio, are *The Comedy of Errors, Love's Labour's Lost* and *Titus Andronicus. The Two Gentlemen of Verona,* which, in the same notoriously haphazard order, comes before them all, is, in this order of criticism, very near them as a whole, but with perhaps later qualities; and so is Meres's probable *Love's Labour's Won (All's Well that Ends Well).* Let us take the five in order and the three, together and separately, first. That *The Comedy of Errors* is, in substance, a mere adaptation of the *Menaechmi* of Plautus would, in itself, have very little to do with probable earliness or lateness; for it is a point so well known as to require no discussion, explanation, apology or even frequent statement, that Shakespeare never gave himself the slightest trouble to be 'original.' Its earliness is shown by the comparative absence of character, by the mixed and rough-hewn quality of the prosody (a connected view of Shakespeare's versification will be given later) and, last and most of all, by the inordinate allowance of the poorest, the most irrelevant and, occasionally, the most uncomely wordplay and 'foolery.' This last characteristic has, of course, been charged against Shakespeare generally, and the charge will have to be dealt with in general. It need only be said now that in no play or passage from *The Tempest* to *Pericles* is there anything to which, as it seems to the present writer, the words above used can be applied as they can to passage after passage between the Dromios and their masters. He does not therefore think, as would some, that Shakespeare did not write these latter passages ; he does think that Shakespeare wrote them before he knew better. But that Shakespeare was certain to know better before long is proved in this very play by the fine, though stiff, tirades of the opening scene, by the extremely beautiful poetry of Adriana and her sister, as well as by touches of nascent power over character in both of them, and by numerous flashes here and there in which the spirit, not quite fullgrown as yet, hurries itself through the bonds of imperfect training in speech and metre. It is, however, on the whole, the crudest and most immature of all the plays, and may well have been the earliest. That position has more commonly been assigned to *Love's Labour's Lost,* and here, too, the assignment has justifications, though they are different. The play exhibits not so much (though there is something of this) the inability of youth to finish, as its prodigality and want of selection. The poet cannot make up his mind what metre to select : blank verse, couplets, stanzas, fourteeners more or less doggerel—he tries them all by turns and does them all with a delightful improvisation. He has a real plot—partly borrowed, of course—but he overloads it in every direction with incident and character. Of the latter, in hasty but astonishingly creative forms, he is the most prodigal of younkers. Nobody is a mere figure-head : Biron, Armado, Holofernes, Costard, Rosaline, even Sir Nathaniel, are of the true Shakespearean family ; and the exquisite Shakespearean lyric makes its appearance. There is almost every-thing in the piece but measure and polish ; and one is almost tempted to say : 'Measure and polish are most excellent things ; but they can wait or we can wait for them.'

Titus Andronicus, as we have it, has been denied to Shakespeare, but this denial really passes the bounds of all rational literary criticism. The play, we know, was acted and published in 1594 ; it is included with Shakespeare's by Meres in 1598 ; it is included in the folio by Shakespeare's intimates and dramatic associates in 1623. If we are to disregard a three-fold cord of evidence like this, the whole process of literary history becomes a mere absurdity—a game of All Fools, with the prize for the craziest topsyturvyfier, as Thackeray would say, of actual fact. It is, of course, possible—almost everything is possible—that the wrong play got into the folio, that Meres was mistaken, that the piece acted and printed in 1594 was not Shakespeare's; but it is also possible that all the world is mad, except the inhabitants of lunatic asylums. As it happens, too, there are reasons given for the denial; and these reasons are valueless. *Titus* is the one play of Shakespeare which is assuredly of the Marlowe school; the one play, too, which is almost wholly what is called 'repulsive' throughout; the one play in which (see below) the stiff 'single moulded' blank verse line hardly ever—but not never—ruffles itself and grows social. Granted: but this is exactly what we should expect as one very probable result of the novitiate in such a case as Shakespeare's. Considering the shreds and patches in the same style which are actually to be found in his work up to *Macbeth* and *King Lear*, not to say *Hamlet*; considering, further, the genuinely Shakespearean character of Aaron, and the genuinely Shakespearean poetry of more than one or two passages—the internal evidence would be strong. Joined to the external, it is simply irresistible. But the novitiate on another side is equally unmistakable here: though the novice, scholar, tiro, explorer (call him what you will) is in a different mood. He is playing a particular game—the game of the tragedy with horror as its main motive and a stately, but monotonous and verbally 'bombasted,' blank verse as its vehicle. In a certain sense, it is the complement of *The Comedy of Errors* and might be called *The Tragedy of Horrors*—outrage and bloodshed taking the place of horseplay and buffoonery for stuff, rhetorical and conceited diction that of wordplay and coarseness for language. And, as there, so here, the novice, though he cannot keep his identity and quality wholly invisible, cramps and curbs them in order to play somebody else's game. In the order of thought, perhaps, *Love's Labour's Lost* should come later—as a burst of relief, an incoherent but untrammelled exercise in the writer's own game or games for his own pleasure. But even a Shakespeare is unlikely to write two plays like *Love's Labour's Lost*; or, rather, a Shakespeare is least likely of all men to write them. He will do better or worse, accordingly as he pays more or less attention to parts of his composition, while improving that

composition itself. He will have more of the picture and less
of the panorama or kaleidoscope; but it does not follow that his
whole picture will, for a time at least, have as much charm.

And this is the state of things that we actually find in *The Two
Gentlemen of Verona* and *All's Well that Ends Well*. Julia, in the
former, as a serious character, and Parolles, in the latter, as a comic
personage, are much above anything that Shakespeare had hitherto
done in the way of live human figures. The plot, though 'romantic'
enough in both, is much closer knit and more thoroughly carried
out by the *dramatis personae* than the shuffle of stock characters
in the *Errors*, the sanguinary dream procession of *Titus*, or the
masque-like intricacies of *Love's Labour's Lost*. The verse, still
of the same general character, is settling down towards blank
verse only and that blank verse free. But the progress is not
like that of a faultless and hopeless schoolboy, who proceeds with
even excellence from one class to another. There are relapses, as,
at least, in part (not all) of the business of Launce and his dog,
in *The Two Gentlemen*; there are failures to advance or even
thoroughly to 'know where he is,' as in that part of Helena which
has been very differently judged. It does not matter very much
whether those are right who consider her a touching example of
a wronged and loving woman, conquering through constancy and
wisdom, or those who think her 'Shakespeare's only disagreeable
heroine'—one who makes confusion of marriage and something
very different, who practically swindles a man into indissoluble
connection with her, and who, in short, when we contrast her,
say, with Cleopatra, is the more really vicious of the pair. Either
view may be right; but, if this play were of a later date, Shakespeare would have taken more care to prevent the uncertainty—or
would, at any rate, have left the worse interpretation on the
shoulders of the interpreters, as he has done in the case of Ophelia.
Still, there are great things in both these plays, though, emphatically, they are experiments still, and experiments in which the ill
success is more conspicuous from the very fact that they aim higher.
The poetical beauties in *The Two Gentlemen* are, occasionally, of
all but the very highest kind, while in *All's Well* there is much fine
verse, Lafeu is a comic, not burlesque, character of great interest,
and there is a further advance towards the Shakespearean clown
proper.

There is, however, another candidate for the *alias* of *Love's
Labour's Won* which seems to have much less claim to it, but
which, undoubtedly, is early—in fact, in all probability, one of

Shakespeare's earliest adaptations of other men's work. This is the popular, and, in parts, very amusing, but only in parts original, *Taming of the Shrew*. A play entitled *The Taming of a Shrew* appeared in 1594, and, from this, the Shakespearean piece is adapted, with not a little of 'his own sauce,' as Mrs Tibbs would say, in the main or Petruchio portion, an addition in the shape of the doubly contrasted sister Bianca, and some very curious local allusions (in the induction) to Shakespeare's own country. The Bianca part of the subject had been taken from the Italian much earlier by Gascoigne. The story was sure to catch the public taste, and the play was actually taken up long afterwards by Fletcher for the purpose of reversing it and showing 'the tamer tamed.' The situations, though in the farcical division of comedy, are of general appeal, and Shakespeare has made the very utmost of them—indeed, there are few more remarkable instances of his power of transforming marionettes into men and women than Petruchio and Katharine. But much of the verse, even in the added portions, is of quite early 'university wit' character—singly-moulded lines, the trick of repetition of the speaker's own name instead of 'I,' 'my,' and so forth, Latin tags and the like. Indeed, some have questioned whether this part of the addition is Shakespeare's at all. In any case, what is his cannot be late; and, as the original play appears not to be older than 1594, the rehandling, if it be rehandling, must have followed very quickly. And there is very little to say for the identification with *Love's Labour's Won*. Petruchio's is an odd 'labour of love,' and Lucentio seems to be a rather doubtful winner.

As to the other seven named plays in the Meres list, there are practically no means of certain chronological arrangement. Those who choose to do so may, of course, observe that, in *Romeo and Juliet*, the nurse says ''Tis since the earthquake now eleven years,' discover that there was an earthquake in 1580 and point to 1591. There was, doubtless, also salmons caught in both years. So, also, in dealing with *The Merchant of Venice*, it has been observed that the queen's physician, Lopez, of Jewish descent, was tried and executed in 1594. And there is an *o* in Lopez and an *o* in Shylock; likewise an *l* in both. There were marriages in 1595, and there are marriages in *A Midsummer Night's Dream*. Let these things appeal to those to whom they do appeal. Others, perhaps, more happily, may be content to abide by Meres and 'before 1598,' except in so far as—without positiveness but making suggestions for what they may be worth—they rely on the kind

of internal evidence already outlined. For reasons of convenience,
we may take the three plays just mentioned first, leaving the
histories for the moment.

For all reasons, *Romeo and Juliet* seems likely to be the
earliest. It has not, indeed, quite such a mixture of metres as
A Midsummer Night's Dream has, and the mere 'picture of young
love' may easily deceive us. But, on the other hand, there is
much of Marlowe's 'single-moulded' line; and, together with
many things among the most magnificent in Shakespeare, there
are crudities and inequalities of the kind natural to a beginner.
On the other hand, such a beginner as this is not frequent in
literature; and he is already far, in more than one or two respects,
from his beginnings. Already, we have seen something of that
astonishing power of vivification which distinguishes him from all
his predecessors; already, the characters have begun to take the
play into their own hands, as it were, and to work it out, not
regardless of the story, by any means, but in a way that gives to
that story a tenfold power and interest. But it has been only in
touches—the whole story has never been treated in this way,
still less have all the characters undergone this peculiar transforming influence. In *Romeo and Juliet*, much further advance
has been made. As before—as always—Shakespeare takes a given
story and does not vary the mere incidents much, or add very
much to them. But the personages become persons; and this
personality extends throughout the drama. Independently of
Romeo and Juliet themselves—the very opposites and contradic-
tions of the stock hero and the stock heroine—of Mercutio and
the nurse, the whole houses of Montague and Capulet almost
down to Antony and Potpan, are alive. There is hardly a figure
in the play, except, perhaps, the unfortunate count Paris, to
whom Shakespeare has not communicated this vivacity: and Paris
had to be a contrast to Romeo. Here, too, not for the first time—
for we have seen it in *Love's Labour's Lost*, in *The Two Gentlemen* and even in *Titus Andronicus*—but in far larger measure and
intenser form, is the splendid poetry which Shakespeare puts at
the service of the drama, as (save in a few flashes of Marlowe and
Peele) it had not been put since the great days of Greek tragedy.

There is hardly less of this in *A Midsummer Night's Dream*;
though, as comports with comedy, it is of a less poignant and
transporting nature. And this play, as was remarked above, is
more of an olio of metres. But, in certain respects, it still marks
progress. If not in all parts, in the whole, it is the most original

of Shakespeare's plays in point of subject up to this time; in fact, it is one of the most original of all in that respect. And this subject is worked up into action with a skill not yet displayed— indeed, Shakespeare here depends more on incident than on character. It is not always fully recognised how artfully the several motives—the Theseus and Hippolyta story, the quarrel of Oberon and Titania, the fortunes of the lovers and the 'tedious brief play'— work into each other and work out each other. Popular as fairy mythology had, in a manner, been, nobody had made anything like this use of it; it is only necessary to name Gloriana and Titania, in order to prove any *rapprochement* of Spenser and Shakespeare on this head to be out of the question. Puck 'was feared in field and town' long before Shakespeare; but Shakespeare's Puck is something very different from a mere 'lob of spirits.' The multiplicity of the interests and beauties in this short play is almost bewildering: there is the stuff of half a dozen poetical comedies in it, yet not in the least confusedly disposed.

The Merchant of Venice presents a somewhat different problem. Here, also, there are many actions: nor, perhaps, are they much less well connected than those of the *Dream*, though they lack the subtle excuse for rapid and interfluent metamorphosis which the very title 'A Midsummer Night's' *Dream* supplies in the other case. There need be no cavilling on this score—in fact, on the 'relief' system, the system of tragic and comic interchange and conflict which makes English drama, the chequers are even better placed. The plot of Shylock against Antonio, the casket scenes, the trial and the trick on the husbands, with the Lorenzo and Jessica 'trace-horse' or 'outrigger' interest, provide a vivid wave-like change of intensity and relief, which even the fierce vexation of Puck's persecution of the midsummer lovers does not give. But, from another point of view, the *Merchant* is less mature than the *Dream*; or, rather, some of its parts are. The Morocco and Arragon sections, at least, of the casket scenes are quite of the Marlowe period in verse, and, to some extent, in handling; the bantering of the lovers behind their backs, part of the Gobbo business and other things belong to the unripe clowning which is at its greenest in the *Errors* and has ripened consummately in, say, *As You Like It*. On the other hand, the trial is admittedly among the *apices* of dramatic poetry; and the whole characters of Shylock and Portia are among the *dramatis personae* of eternity. To the present writer, it has for many years been a moral certainty that these different parts are of different dates, and that a similar difference prevails much more largely in Shakespeare's work than is sometimes thought. The single-plot drama, with its beginning, middle and end, could, perhaps, not easily be written in this way. But the drama which, though not patchwork, is interwoven, can be thus written.

The chronicle plays, *King John*, *Richard II* and *III* and *Henry IV*, which are certainly early because mentioned by Meres, introduce a new division of Shakespeare's work, to which we shall take the liberty of adding *Henry VI pro tanto*. In the opinion of the present writer, the *tantum* is considerable; but something has already been said in the preceding chapter[1] as to the authorship of *The Contention* and *The True Tragedie*, on which *Parts II and III of Henry VI* were based. In the case of all these plays, with the possible exception of *Richard II* (both the *Richards* were actually published in 1597), there were previously existing pieces on the subject; whether in all cases these were the actual pieces that we have is another question. But in no kind of drama would the specially Shakespearean method find better exercise than in the chronicle history. That remarkable species, though it was to receive its perfect development only in England, and (in absolute perfection) only at the hands of Shakespeare himself, had, as has been seen, made its appearance as a modernised and practicalised development of the mystery and morality, much earlier in the sixteenth century. The advantages of the species, when it discards allegory altogether and at least affects to be frankly historical, are obvious: subjects that 'come home,' copiousness and variety of interest, given outlines of striking figures, and the like. Its dangers—hardly less obvious—are those of the prosaic and the promiscuous; of a mere decoction of chronicle facts and speeches, fortified by bombast and frothed with stock horseplay. And these are abundantly exemplified in the earliest Elizabethan specimens, while they are by no means absent from the curious later attempts of Dekker, Middleton and others to combine a more or less historical mainplot with a purely fictitious underplot, romantic or classical. Now, Shakespeare's two greatest gifts, that of sheer poetic expression and that of character creation, were exactly what was needed to turn these 'formless agglomerations' into real organisms, possessing life and beauty. If *Richard II* be quite original (which, as has been hinted, it would not be wise to assume too absolutely) it must be a good deal earlier than its publication, but later than *Titus Andronicus*, with which, however, it may be

[1] See *ante*, chap. VII.

classed as exhibiting the Marlowe influence more strongly than anything else, save some parts of *Henry VI*, which one would be inclined to place between them.   In yet other respects, *Richard II* makes a very fair pair with *Romeo and Juliet* in its far different division.   The curious immature splendour of the conception of the title part is like nothing else in Shakespeare.   The parallel with, and the suggestion given by, Marlowe's *Edward II* are, of course, unmistakable.   But, where Marlowe has given three Edwards, not perhaps irreconcilable with each other but not actually reconciled, Shakespeare's Richard *sibi constat* throughout, in weakness as in strength—he is sincere in his insincerity.   Still, the part is not well supported—even of 'time-honoured Lancaster' it may be said that he rather makes great speeches than is a great character; and so of others.   The chronicle sequence, encroaching rather on dramatic connection, is also noticeable; as is the fact (especially to be considered in view of *Titus Andronicus* and Marlowe) that there is practically no comic element whatever.   Of the extreme beauty of the poetry (almost always, however, of the 'purple patch' or 'fringe' kind and, it would seem, purposely so) in the king's part, it is almost unnecessary to speak.

King John and *Richard III*, on the other hand, are examples—documented, as we may say, and almost acknowledged—of adaptation, of the working up of existing materials.   But not many impartial and competent critics will adopt Greene's very unkind simile of the crow and the feathers.   It is much rather a case of grafting the fairest and most luscious fruit on a crab-tree or a sloe, though no metaphor of the kind can be satisfactory.   The processes and results of the adaptation, however, are rather different in the two cases.   In *King John*, Shakespeare took and kept more of the original; but he heightened the presentation incomparably.   The famous part of Constance is almost wholly his own; he has done much to the king, not a little to the bastard, hardly less to Arthur and Hubert.   Above all, he has (to quote an absurd boast of another person a century later) 'made it a play'—a piece of life and not a sample of chronicling.   Hardly anywhere will the student find better examples of Shakespeare's craftsmanship in verse and phrase—of the way in which, by slightly adding, cancelling, smoothing, inspiriting, he turns a lame line or passage into a beautiful one—than in *King John*, compared with its original.

Richard III, on the other hand, bears very much less resemblance to its predecessor, *The True Tragedie of Richard III*, and some have regarded it as almost an independent following of Marlowe's *Edward II.* It certainly resembles that play in bursts of poetry of a somewhat rhetorical kind, in the absence of purely comic episodes or scenes and in the concentration of character interest on the hero. Not quite, however, in this latter point. For the character of Margaret (which seems to the present writer to be definitely connected with the Angevin princess's part in *Henry VI,* and Shakespearean throughout) is greater than any secondary part in *Edward II. Richard III,* too, in the famous wooing scene, has a scene of character, as distinguished from a mere display of it, which is unmatched elsewhere. And, perhaps, as a whole, the play has been too much and too commonly regarded as a mere melodrama or popular blood-and-thunder piece, with Clarence's dream and some other *placebos* thrown in. It is, at any rate, full of life—with nothing in it either of the peculiar dream quality of Marlowe or of the woodenness of certain other early playwrights.

As was above observed, the part due to Shakespeare in *Henry VI* cannot be minutely discussed here. It seems to the present writer to be probably large. There is, at least, no doubt that many of the passages which it used to be the fashion to dole out to the university wits, like beef bones at a buttery door in ancient days, are quite like those in Shakespeare's plays of the period which we have already surveyed. And it may seem to some that many scenes—some of them, no doubt, not wholly or originally from his pen—many of the battle pieces, French and English; the starting of the rose dispute; the quarrel of Winchester and Gloucester and the deaths of both; all, as has been said, of the scenes where Margaret appears; much of the Cade part; the deaths, again, of York and Clifford; of prince Edward and king Henry—smack of Shakespeare in their altered forms. But it would be altogether uncritical to be positive here. It may be sufficient to say that *Part I* exhibits least change; *Part II* most; and *Part III* somewhat less than *Part II,* but still a very considerable amount; while, independently of positive changes, the whole composition of *Part I* is very much less Shakespearean, even as compared with his earliest probable work, than that of the other two. At any rate, we may safely return to the position that, in this chronicle work, Shakespeare had new and admirable opportunities for developing his grasp of character and for getting into complete working order that remarkable and, in fact, unique, conception of the loose, many-centred drama kept together by character itself, which was to be his—and ours.

Last of the Meres-warranted batch comes *Henry IV*, like the others worked up from an earlier production, *The Famous Victories of Henry the fifth*, but more remarkable than any of them, if not for passages of pure poetry (for which its theme gives but rare opportunity), for complete transformation of the merest brute material into magnificent art. The first assignment of the world-famous part of Falstaff—one of the very greatest of dramatic creations, and practically a creation, in the precise sense of the word—to the luckless Lollard Oldcastle was a mistake; but it was speedily rectified—though not without further protest on the part of the prosaic in favour of the historical warrior Fastolf. The actual play (for its two parts are practically one) is, undoubtedly, with the reservation above stated, one of Shakespeare's very greatest achievements; and, seeing that he had already proved himself able to supply pure poetry in unlimited quantities and in any required degree of strength, no drawback or shortcoming could possibly be urged. The entwining and enforcing of the purely historical part receives, and, probably, has always received, less attention from readers and spectators; but it is wonderful in itself. The prince (the famous key-soliloquy, 'I know you all' and the other on the crown excepted) is designedly kept undeveloped in his public capacity. But the king, the Percies, Glendower, the younger princes and wiser noblemen, are all vivified and spirited up in the inscrutable Shakespearean manner. Still, 'the general' are not wrong in preferring to dwell on the Bohemian society of which the prince is the rather Mephistophelian centre, but of which Falstaff is the real master and king. Not a member of it, male or female, but has the certain, vital touches. 'Bowdlerising' is seldom less justified of its works than when it here prevents readers from appreciating the curious and universal humanity of Shakespeare's portraiture, and its contrast with the artificial efforts of modern realism. The supremacy of Falstaff does not disparage the exemplary virtue of Pistol or the modest adequacy of Bardolph and of Nym; and, in the same way, Nell and Doll make each the other *deformitate formosam videri*. Everyone has noticed how, in this most genial, if not most poetical, of his cycles (anticipating, for a moment, *The Merry Wives*), Shakespeare has been prodigal of home memories—of Warwickshire and Gloucestershire detail. But everybody, perhaps, has not noticed the singular fashion in which, once more, this yoking of almost domestic minutiae with public affairs passes itself off, in contrast with the strident discord of *Poetaster* and *The Mayor of Quinborough*. Shallow, immortal in his own way, is a planet in a greater system only; and all the parts combine to work this out.

We are now deprived of the safe, if not in all ways definite, assistance of Meres in respect of chronology; and, for the rest of the contents of the folio as well as for *Pericles* (the single play outside of it which will be considered in the present chapter) we have, in a majority of cases, nothing but guesswork to guide us. But, using the same general principles as heretofore—the internal evidence of versification and dramatic craftsmanship, with such positive aids as may bear investigation, we can continue this history of Shakespeare's work on the same general lines. Only, it will be desirable to adhere to the usual folio order with one single exception, that of *The Tempest*, which, in accordance with general practice (to be critically examined later) we shall keep to the end, putting *Pericles*, which has no folio order, in its place, though by no means asserting that it certainly deserves priority over all the others.

That the whole of *Pericles* is not Shakespeare's is extremely probable; but the allocation of parts to other dramatists, named or unnamed, is as hazardous a piece of 'hariolation' as has been tried even in this hazardous game. It is not too much to say that there is no part which might not be his; the very choruses which have been denied him are extremely Shakespearean, and group excellently with similar things in *A Midsummer Night's Dream* and *As You Like It*. The brothel scenes can be similarly, if not so completely, paired with passages in the *Errors* and in *Measure for Measure*; and divers examples of stiff Marlowe verse and handling with others in *Titus Andronicus* and the early chronicles and elsewhere. On the other hand, some of the best things throughout the play are *aut Shakespeare aut Diabolus*, and it must have been a most superior fiend who forged the shipwreck passage. Still, nothing is heard of the play till 1606, when it was licensed; and it is pretty certain that, whether the whole was written by Shakespeare or not, the whole was not written by Shakespeare at or near that time. The present writer would be prepared to take either side on the question: 'Did Shakespeare about this time complete an early immature sketch of his own; or did he furnish, voluntarily or involuntarily, scenes to one which was vamped up and botched off by another or others?' But he rather inclines to the first alternative, because of the distinct similarity of the phenomena to those shown in others of Shakespeare's plays actually contained in the folio. That the scheme of the play is not of a mature period is shown by the fact that it has little character, and that what it has is still less concerned with the working out of the action. The contrast here, not merely with *A Winter's Tale* but with the much abused *Cymbeline*, is remarkable.

To cast back to the earlier, but not yet discussed, plays of the canon, *The Merry Wives of Windsor*, as most people know, is a play with a legend—that the queen wished to see Falstaff 'in love,' and that it was written in fourteen days to please her. This, however (the later part of which is one of the curious Shakespeare-Molière coincidences), comes only from Dennis, a hundred years after date. The play was actually licensed in 1601, and imperfectly printed next year—dates which suit well enough with the inclusion of *Henry IV* in the Meres list of 1598 and its completion by *Henry V* in that year or 1599. With his usual preference of artistic convenience to prosaic exactitude, Shakespeare has not troubled himself about niching this episode very carefully in his precedent history of the fat knight. Shallow appears duly, but Slender replaces Silence; 'the wild prince and Poins' are referred to, but vaguely. You neither need, nor are you intended, to make a 'harmony' of the four pieces. So, too, it seems to be lost labour and idle sentimentality to lament the decadence and defeat of Falstaff. Men are generally decadent, and frequently defeated, when dealing with women in such circumstances; and Falstaff's overthrow does not make him fall very hard after all. On the other hand, the *vis comica* of the piece is perfect; its exuberant invention and variety are unsurpassed; and the actual construction is more careful than usual. In character and dialogue, it is not surpassed by the very greatest of the plays, allowance being made for kind and atmosphere. Everybody is alive and everything is vividly illuminated—not with the extra-natural, if not non-natural, Congreve rockets, but with a lambent easy light of air. Sir Hugh Evans must have been meant as a brother in dramatic arms to Fluellen, and it is difficult to prefer Roland to Oliver or *vice versa*. The attractive grace—though given in outline merely—of sweet Anne Page is masterly; and, in her mother and Mistress Ford, Shakespeare has given, as hardly another writer has ever succeeded in doing, in *bourgeois* condition and deliberately prosaised tone, the same high but perfectly human standard of wifeliness which, elsewhere, he has carried to the court of poetical quintessence in Hermione and in Imogen. There are few things more amusing to a liberally catholic student of literature than the half patronising, half apologetic, tone adopted, sometimes, towards *The Merry Wives*, as a 'farce.' And, here again, one is reminded of Molière.

Measure for Measure is a more difficult play—one not so liable to be undervalued from inability to perceive that a comic microcosm may be thoroughly cosmic, but more apt to disconcert, if not actually to disgust, by reason of its singular apparent discords, its unusual scheme of conduct and character and its scant reconcilableness with that un-puritan, but fairly severe, system of poetical justice which Shakespeare generally maintains. Its 'disagreeableness'—to use a word often laughed at but expressive and without a synonym—is less to some tastes than that of *All's Well that Ends Well*; but, to a certain extent, it exists. On the other hand, its power is unquestionable, and it contains some of the greatest things in Shakespeare. It was certainly (or almost certainly) performed in 1604, and it has been customary to accept that year as the approximate date of the composition. To the present writer, this seems very improbable, and he would select *Measure for Measure* as the strongest instance of the suggested earliness, in a more or less incomplete form, of many more plays than are contained in Meres's list. Shakespeare, indeed, has improved immensely on the original Italian story and on Whetstone's two English versions, in novel and drama. He has not only added the magnificent scenes between Isabella and Angelo, and Isabella and her brother, and the character (dramatically important, inasmuch as it helps to save Isabella and provides a *dénouement*) of 'Mariana in the moated grange'; he has lavished his nepenthe of poetry on a not particularly attractive theme. But, in the first place, it seems very unlikely that he would have chosen that theme so late; and, in the second, it is nearly certain that, if he had, he would have worked it up with different results. His seventeenth century plays generally contain nothing so crude as the cruder parts of *Measure for Measure*, while these are very like parts of the early certainties and of *Pericles*. Moreover, even if Pompey and Lucio were cleaner-mouthed, they would still be unfinished studies, companions of Launce and Launcelot, not of Touchstone and Feste. The play, as a whole, gives one the idea of an early, half finished piece which the writer has resumed, which he has improved immensely, but on which he has rather hung additional and separate jewels than spent the full labour of thorough refashioning and refounding. Had it come straight from the hands of the Shakespeare of 1604, we should surely have had a much more defensible and, in fact, intelligible duke, than the person who runs his state and his servants into difficulties in order that he may come to the rescue as a rather shabby Providence—an Angelo more of

a piece, less improbably repentant (not to say so improbably
flagitious) and less flagrantly 'let off.' If one cared to conjecture, it
might be possible to show a strong case for an original intention to
adopt the story in its blackest shape, *Titus* fashion; a disgust with
this leading to the abandonment of the thing for a time; an
inspiration to create a 'Saint Isabel' and a consequent adaptation and transformation to 'happy ending' and poetical injustice.
But even a Shakespeare cannot reshape ends in a manner entirely
contrary to their rough-hewing, without some loss of accomplishment, verisimilitude and effect.

Measure for Measure was never printed in Shakespeare's lifetime; *Much Ado about Nothing*, which (with the much earlier
Errors between them) follows it in the folio and which, like it, is
founded on an Italian story, had been actually printed four years
before the alleged date of *Measure for Measure* and is thought to
have been written even a year earlier than this. Here, there is
neither necessity nor probability for any theory of partial composition. The play is all of a piece; and the best things in it are
entirely original. The trick played on Hero had appeared both in
Bandello's prose and in Ariosto's verse; and there seems actually
to have been an English play on the subject so early as 1583. But
Shakespeare added Benedick and Beatrice; he added Dogberry
and Verges and he made the whole thing into one of the most
remarkable instances of the kind of tragicomedy where no actual
tragedy is permitted, but where it is only just avoided, and where
tragic motives are allowed to work freely. The play is of extraordinary merit, and Shakespeare has only left one loose stitch—
a stitch which he might have picked up with very little trouble—
in the entirely unexplained, and very nearly inexplicable, behaviour
of Margaret, who, being certainly not a traitress and as certainly
not a fool, first lends herself to a proceeding obviously prejudicial
to her mistress, and then holds her tongue about it. Except in
this point, the play works with perfect ease of action; and, if one
does not envy Hero her husband, and does grudge her very much
to him, that is no uncommon case. As for Benedick and Beatrice,
they are, perhaps, as good touchstones as any in Shakespeare. No
one but an 'innocent' can possibly fail to like them; no one but
a charlatan will ever pretend not to do so. The authorities of
Messina are more 'farcical'; but the farce, again, is superfarcical.

It might well have been thought that nothing better in the way
of romantic comedy would be written. But this was to be triumph-
antly contradicted by two plays, *As You Like It* and *Twelfth Night*,

which are believed to have followed *Much Ado* very quickly, and which, in the folio (with plays already mentioned intervening), observe the order in which they have been named. But it is not positively known which appeared first. *Twelfth Night* was acted on 2 February 1601/2; *As You Like It*, on less certain grounds, is put some two years before. So far as one can judge from internal evidence, *Twelfth Night* would seem to be a little the earlier, or, at any rate, to retain a little more of the characteristics of Shakespeare's earliest comedies. But, in reality, *Much Ado About Nothing*, *As You Like It* and *Twelfth Night* form a trio of which the best thing to say is that only the man who wrote the other two could have written any one of them. Still, *As You Like It* has a certain pre-eminence, and may put in a claim to be the greatest of Shakespeare's comedies—the typical romantic comedy—excluding *The Tempest* as belonging rather to that middle kind for which there is no English name, but which is inexactly designated *drame* in French. There is hardly more than one fault in it—a fault which, oddly enough, is very rare in Shakespeare, though extremely common in his contemporaries—the fault of concluding the play with a violent 'revolution' merely communicated by a messenger. That an 'old religious man' of Shakespeare's creation might have converted even such an exceedingly unpromising subject as duke Frederick need not be denied: it is very difficult to say what any one of Shakespeare's creation might not have done. But it would have been very interesting to hear the arguments used on the occasion. With this exception, there is nothing that exceeds the licence of romantic character comedy. That was the way they lived in Arden—there can be no doubt of it. And the other things had to happen in order that they might so live. A fresh qualm, succeeded by a fresh desire, may, indeed, be aroused by the announced intention of Jaques to seek duke Frederick's company: the qualm as to his probable reception, the desire to have Shakespeare's account of it. But Jaques himself, with whom some have quarrelled, is a perfectly allowable, and a perfectly admirable, foil to the lovers and the fleeters of the time. The vividness of almost every scene and passage is unmatched even in Shakespeare; there are no *longueurs*; and, if there were, Rosalind and Touchstone would save them. The poet has not here, as he did earlier in *A Midsummer Night's Dream*, and, later, in *The Tempest*, resorted to supernatural machinery to help his glamour. We are no further from ordinary life than romance always is, and in the least extraordinary regions of romance itself. But 'Arden' is none the less made an enchanted ground without spells or incantations, an earthly Paradise, with nothing that is not within reach of almost any human being. Wit, wisdom and poetry are the only trans-figurers. Shakespeare, of course, had certainly for canvas Lodge's Euphuist romance of *Rosalynde*; perhaps (it would be pleasant to think so) the *Tale of Gamelyn* itself—but it was merely canvas. The charm of Rosalind, the marrowy moralising of Jaques, the unfailing fool-wisdom of Touchstone, are all his own. By this time, too, he had arrived at that complete command of verse of which something will be specially said later, and had perfected his wonderful prose. Both the blank verse and the lyric in *As You Like It* are in absolute perfection, each for its special purpose; and there is, perhaps, no play (for *Hamlet* lacks the lyric) in which all three media are so perfectly displayed.

As You Like It, with Rosalind as Ganymede, had taken advan-tage of that habit of representing women's parts by boys which has been supposed to possess advantages in itself. Cleopatra, played by a boy (as with true Shakespearean audacity she is herself made to suggest) must have been absurd, but Shakespeare could not help himself and the custom of the country. Here, he could help himself; and he did so with admirable success. Moreover, the success could evidently be repeated (if the artist were strong enough) in a different key. The artist was strong enough and he repeated it in Viola; relying here on the custom to emphasise and make probable the confusion of brother and sister. *Twelfth Night or What You Will*—the latter title an obvious pendant to *As You Like It*; the former, perhaps unnecessarily, supposed to refer to the time of production—is the purest comedy of all Shakespeare's plays. We know that the captain is in no danger; none, even apparently, threatens any one else. To make Malvolio, as has sometimes been attempted, an almost tragic personage, virtuous and deeply wronged, is an absurdity. The duke is, and is meant to be, a feeble person; but he can talk exquisite poetry, is a gentleman, probably made exactly the sort of husband that Viola wanted and so is one of those subtlest, because most faintly nuanced, criticisms of life which only the greatest masters dare to allow themselves. Feste is not Touchstone's equal—but who is? and, besides, it would not have done for the clown to be wittier than the knight when both were witty—in *As You Like It* things are different. The rest are of the Upper House almost without an exception. Viola, no Rosalind or Beatrice, but a jewel of the other type and differenced exquisitely from such sisters as Juliet

and Miranda; Olivia, stately, but perfectly human; Maria, not
elaborately, but sufficiently, drawn in the other vein for contrast—
form an extraordinary triad even for Shakespeare; and it is afflict-
ing that some commentators should forget that 'the youngest wren
of nine' was no 'waiting maid' in the modern sense. On the other
side, Sir Toby Belch is one of those doubles that are no doubles,
over which nearly all artists stumble. He is of the same genus as
Falstaff, but of a different species; and almost entirely different as
an individual; just as Sir Andrew is of the tribe of Silence and
Slender, but quite other than they. As for Malvolio, he has no
parallel anywhere save Molière's Alceste, who, like him but more
commonly, has been travestied into a *persona tragica* by incom-
petent criticism. A gentleman, a man of honour and of his duty,
of parts and of merit, his comic ἁμαρτία is compounded of vanity,
sourness of temper, lack of humour, a little jack-in-officeship, much
ambition and, probably, not a little downright jealousy—and it
brings the comic punishment upon him most completely and con-
dignly. Sebastian, no doubt, has extraordinary, but not impossible, luck.

From this point, we may take a liberty—of which we have
already given warning—with the folio arrangement. *The Winter's
Tale* would come next, according to the division of 'Comedies,
Histories and Tragedies,' and several histories, earlier according
to the Meres *point de repère*, would come next after that. But,
according to that class of internal evidence which we have allowed,
The Winter's Tale is distinctly later; some more plays regarded
as 'histories' in Shakespeare's time are, not merely to us, but
essentially, romantic tragedies; and the arrangement, according to
logic and literature must, in other ways, be altered. We shall
rearrange the scene from this point, therefore, recording all certain,
or even probable, data as to individual plays as they arise, under
four heads—the remaining English histories, the classical plays
subsequent to *Titus Andronicus*, the romantic tragedies and the
three final *drames*.

The first of the histories is *Henry V*, which was partly drawn
from the same originals as *Henry IV*, and followed it closely. It
was published (imperfectly) and 'stayed' in 1600; and is supposed
to have been acted the year before. The magnificent death of
Falstaff almost necessitated the previous turning upon him of the
king, which, indeed, had been foreshadowed in *Henry IV*. Partly
this, and partly other things, have prejudiced some critics against
this 'patriot king,' who, nevertheless, is one of the greatest, if not

the most attractive, of Shakespeare's creations. The fresh presentment of Pistol and the addition of Fluellen demonstrate the in-
exhaustibleness of the poet's comic *prosopopoeia*, and, besides the
fine tirades which figure in all the extract books, there are in-
numerable passages of literary excellence. But, in a panoramic
survey of Shakespeare's plays, *Henry V*, perhaps, with one exception to be dealt with presently, stands forth most conspicuously as
almost the deftest of his spiritings up of chronicles—as a pattern
of the difficult accomplishment of vitalising chronicle by character.
Here, it is by character diffuse rather than compact—by the
extraordinary vivacity of the different personages rather than by
interest concentrated in a hero. So far as he is concerned, it is
the triumph of Henry of England, rather than that of Harry of
Monmouth, in which we rejoice.

The last remaining, and, probably, the last written, of the English
group, *Henry VIII*, presents remarkable peculiarities; and it has
been usual to take it as Shakespeare's only in parts—Fletcher's,
and, perhaps, Massinger's, in others. A play on Henry VIII was
represented in 1613 and interrupted by the burning of the playhouse. The piece which, ten years later, appeared in the folio is a
loose composition (though, perhaps, not much looser than *Cymbeline*); and, though there are points of great and truly Shakespearean
interest of character in the king and, still more, in Wolsey and
queen Katharine, it cannot be said that the character in any one
instance, or in all put together, unifies the play as it generally does
with Shakespeare. Still, there is no doubt about his authorship in
whole or part. No reasonable critic will attempt to go behind the
folio as regards plays—though no such critic need accept either
'the whole folio' as regards passages or 'nothing but the folio'
in any way. The play is patchy, and some of the patches are
inferior; while there are hardly any marks in it of that early and
'first draft' character which we have detected in others.

With the classical plays, we come to a new and very interesting
group. In a sense, of course, *Titus Andronicus* belongs to it; but
nothing like the extreme earliness of that piece belongs to any of
the others, and none of them is mentioned by Meres. Two of them,
however, are, internally as well as externally, of very uncertain
date; the other three are of Shakespeare's very meridian.

For *Troilus and Cressida*, a licence to print was obtained in
1602/3; but the players objected, and it was not published till half
a dozen years later, and then surreptitiously. It is extremely
difficult not to believe that it is much older than the earlier date

would show. Some of the blank verse, no doubt, is fairly mature: but the author may have furbished this up, and much of it is not mature at all. Instead of transcending his materials, as Shakespeare almost invariably does, he has here failed almost entirely to bring out their possibilities; has not availed himself of Chaucer's beautiful romance so fully as he might; and has dramatised the common Troy-books with a loose yet heavy hand utterly unsuggestive of his maturer craftsmanship. If it were not for certain speeches and touches chiefly in the part of Ulysses, and in the parts of the hero and heroine, it might be called the least Shakespearean of all the plays.

Timon of Athens, again a puzzle, is a puzzle of a different kind. It is usual to resort to the rather Alexandrine suggestion of collaboration and then to put it as late as 1607. To the present writer, the first theory seems unnecessary and the last impossible. There is nothing in *Timon* that Shakespeare, at one time or another, may not have written; there are some things which hardly anybody but Shakespeare can have written; but that he wrote this piece just after *Lear*, even with somebody, not to help, but to hinder, him, is not, from the point of view from which the present survey is written, conceivable. The play is as chaotic as *Troilus*, or more so; and, except Timon himself, it has no character of interest in it. But Timon himself must be Shakespeare's own; he has so much of good in him, and might have been made so much better, that it is impossible to imagine Shakespeare, in his maturity, turning over such a character to be botched by underlings, and associated with third rate company. On the other hand, he might have written the whole play in his nonage and—as in the other case—have thrown in some 'modern touches' to freshen it up and get it off his hands. At any rate, the two plays (which may be called Greek) stand in the sharpest contrast to the great Roman trio, based, in Shakespeare's most easy-going fashion, on North's *Plutarch* for matter, and, sometimes, even for words, but made his own, absolutely and for ever.

None of the three was printed till the folio appeared, though licence appears to have been obtained for *Antony and Cleopatra* in 1608. It is usual to select that date for it and for *Coriolanus*, and to put *Julius Caesar* seven years earlier, because of an apparent allusion to it in that year. Internal evidence does not, perhaps, supply any valid reason for such a separation in date; and, as they are all taken from the same source, they may very well all have been written about the same time. This could not have been very early, from the complete mastery of the blank verse, but might be anywhere after the close of the sixteenth century. All three are masterpieces, but curiously different in kind; though there is an equally curious agreement between them in the manner in which the author, at one time, simply arranges the very words not merely of Plutarch but of North, while, at another, he will add or substitute passages of absolute originality.

Julius Caesar has, at least, this mark of an earlier date that its interest is of a diffused character, and that there is a certain prodigality of poetic passages put in everybody's mouth. The titular hero perishes before half the play is done; and his place is taken, first by Antony and then by Brutus. Nor does he make any very copious appearance even before his murder. Further, the marvellous Shakespearean impartiality seems to take delight in doing the best for each of these heroes in turn; while the prodigality above referred to furnishes not merely the three, Cassius, who is all but a fourth hero, and Portia, but quite insignificant people —Marullus, Casca, Calpurnia—with splendid poetical utterance. The magnificent speech of Antony—all Shakespeare's own ; the great exchange of mind between Brutus and Cassius, both as friends and as (almost) foes; the dialogue of Brutus and Portia: these, and many other things, with the surpassing majesty and interest of the theme, have always made the play a great favourite, and deservedly so. Moreover, its central interest from the point of view of romance—the death and revenging of Caesar—is perfect. But, from the point of view of unity of character, which is Shakespeare's general appeal, it may be thought somewhat lacking. Brutus is the only person whose character can supply a continuous tie rod—and, except to those who take the old French Revolution or Roman declamation line of admiration for tyrannicide *per se,* Brutus, admirably as he develops, is rather thin at first. It may plausibly be argued that either he should not have required Cassius's blend of personal and pseudo-patriotic hatred of Caesar to ferment his own patriotism, or he should have detected the insufficiency of the 'lean and hungry' conspirator. Practically, however, *Julius Caesar* is of the panoramic, if not of the kaleidoscopic, order of drama—its appeal is of sequence rather than of composition.

With the other two Roman plays, it is quite different. *Coriolanus* is certainly not deficient in variety of incident, or of personage, but every incident and every personage is, in a way, subservient to the hero. The ordinary descriptions of the *dramatis personae*—

'friend to Coriolanus,' 'mother to Coriolanus,' 'wife to Coriolanus'—acquire a new appositeness from this feature. Menenius and Volumnia are no shadows; the 'gracious silence' herself is all the more gracious for her unobtrusiveness. But it is in relation to Coriolanus that they interest us most. The sordid spite of the tribunes—types well known at this time and at all times—helps to bring out the arrogance, at its worst not sordid, of Caius Martius. The inferior generals set him off. And that interesting, and not very easy, character, Tullus Aufidius, whose psychical evolution Shakespeare has left in obviously intentional uncertainty, furnishes yet another contrast in his real changes from enmity to friendship, and then from hospitality to treachery, with the changes of Coriolanus from the height of Roman patriotism to actual hostility against his ungrateful and degraded country, and from that hostility to semi-reconciliation, at least to the foregoing of his vengeance in obedience to his mother. Most of all do the various mobs—the mob of Rome above all, but, also, the rank and file of the army, the Volscian conspirators, the officers, the senators, the very servants of Aufidius—throw up against their own vulgar variety and characterless commonness the 'headstrong beauty' of the great soldier's mind and will—his hatred of the *vulgus* itself, of its malignity, of its meanness, of its ingratitude. He is, of course, no flawless character: he need not have been rude to the people (one cannot blame him for being so to their misguiders); and, because they committed virtual treason to Rome by banishing its defender, he was certainly not justified in himself committing the overt act. But he remains one of the noblest figures in literature, and his nobility is largely the work of Shakespeare himself. What is more, he has provided Shakespeare with the opportunity of working out a 'one-man' drama, as, except in inferior specimens like *Timon*, he has done nowhere else. For, even in *Hamlet*, the single and peculiar life of the hero does not overshadow all the others, as is done here.

Great as *Coriolanus* is, however, it is not nearly so great as *Antony and Cleopatra*. Coriolanus, personally, is a great figure, but rather narrowly great and hardly as provocative of delight as of admiration. The interest of his story is somewhat lacking in variety, and, cunningly as the comic or serio-comic aspects and interludes are employed to lighten it up, the whole play is rather statuesque. *Antony and Cleopatra* has nearly as infinite a variety as its incomparable heroine herself: its warmth and colour are of the liveliest kind; its character drawing is of the Shakespearean best;

the beauties of its versification and diction are almost unparalleled
in number, diversity and intensity ; and, above all, the powers of
the two great poetic motives, love and death, are utilised in it to
the utmost possible extent. Even this long list of merits does not
exhaust its claims. From the technical side, it is the very type and
triumph of the chronicle play—of the kind which dramatises whole
years of history, solid portions of the life of man, and keeps them
dramatically one by the interwoven threads of character interest,
by individual passages of supreme poetry and by scenes or sketches
of attaching quality. Here, again, Shakespeare follows North, at
times very closely indeed ; and here, more than ever, he shows how
entirely he is able not to follow his leader when he chooses. The
death of Cleopatra, with the ineffable music of the words that
follow 'Peace, Peace,' is only the strongest example of a pervading
fact. But the central interest of character and the side portraits
which accompany and enforce it are the greatest points about the
play. Nowhere has even Shakespeare given such a pair, hero and
heroine, as here. Antony, at once ruined and ennobled by the
passion which is both his ἁμαρτία and his abiding title to sympathy,
which completes his friendship for Caesar in the earlier play ;
Cleopatra, her frailty sublimated into the same passion—both
heroic in their very weakness and royal in the way in which they
throw away their royalty : there is nothing like them anywhere.
There is no palliation of fault or of folly ; both are set as plainly
before the spectator as may be, and he will imitate them at his
peril. But the power of romantic tragedy in this direction can go
no further.

It might be questioned whether this power actually went further
in any other direction. But, possibly, between *Julius Caesar* and
the other two Roman plays—certainly in the same general period,
and, according to popular reckoning, between 1602 and 1605—
Shakespeare produced, it is thought in the order to be named,
what are pre-eminently the four wheels of his chariot, the four
wings of his spirit, in the tragic and tragicomic division,
Hamlet, Othello, Macbeth and *Lear*. To condense the enormous
mass of discussion on these, and especially on the first, were
here impossible. The puzzles of the text of *Hamlet* (which differs
most remarkably in the quarto of 1602, apparently pirated, in
that of 1604, which at least claims authenticity, and in that of the
folio), though perhaps less than they seem, and much less than
they have been thought to be, are considerable ; and the problems
of the play are infinite. Its immediate, lasting and now world-wide

popularity is not surprising. For, though Hamlet himself is capable of being problematised to the nth, he is a sufficiently taking figure (especially as introduced by the ghost scenes) to persons who care little indeed for problems. The enormous length of the play is diversified by the most varied, and, at times, most exciting, action. In the common phrase, there is something for everyone—the supernatural, the death of Polonius, that of Ophelia, the fight or almost fight in the churchyard, the duel, the final slaughter scene (simply an exciting moment for the mere vulgar)—the pity of all these things for the sentimental, the poetry of them for those who can appreciate it. And, above all, and with all, there is the supreme interest of the character presentment, which informs and transforms the incidents, and which, not merely in the central figure, is the richest and most full to be found in Shakespeare. This may be developed in one instance.

It has been impossible, in the scale and range of the present notice, to dwell on individual characters. But, putting sheer poetical expression aside, the Shakespearean character is the Shakespearean note; and, for more reasons than one, it would be an incorrectness not to offer a specimen of dealing with this feature. No better suggests itself than the character of Claudius. For it seems to have escaped even some elect wits; and it is very typical. There were at least two ways in which an ordinary, or rather more than ordinary, dramatist might have dealt with this other 'majesty of Denmark.' He could have been made a crude dramatic villain—a crowned 'Shakebag' or 'Black Will,' to use the phraseology of his creator's own day. He could have been made pure straw—a mere common usurper. And it would appear that he has actually seemed to some to be one or other of these two. Neither of them is the Claudius which Shakespeare has presented; and those who take him as either seem to miss the note which, putting sheer poetic faculty once more aside, is the note of Shakespeare. It is not to be supposed that Shakespeare liked Claudius; if he did, and if he has produced on respectable readers the effect above hinted at, he certainly was as ineffectual a writer as the merest *crétin*, or the merest crank, among his critics could imagine. But neither did he dislike Claudius; he knew that, in the great Greek phrase, it was the duty of creators to 'see fair'— τὰ ἴσα νέμειν—in the handling of their creations. It would appear that the successor of Hamlet I might have been a very respectable person, if his brother had not possessed a kingdom and a queen that he wanted for himself. But this brother did, unluckily, possess these

things and the Claudian—not ἁμαρτία, not 'tragic frailty,' but outrageous, unforgivable, fully punished—crime was that he would not
tolerate this possession. He put an end to it, and—let those laugh
at him who like—he seems to have thought that he could trammel
up the consequence. Macbeth was wiser. If it were not for the
ugly circumstances and the illegitimate assistance of the ghost, we
might be rather sorry for Claudius at first. There was nothing
out of the way in the succession of brother before son. There was
nothing (except, perhaps, undue haste) out of the way, under the dispensation of dispensations, in the successive marriage of one woman
to two brothers. Fifty years before Shakespeare's birth, queen
Katharine did it, and few people thought or think her other than
a saint. A hundred years after Shakespeare's birth, Louise de
Gonzague, queen of Poland, did it, and nobody thought the worse
of her at all. It is clear that there was not much likelihood of
offspring from the second marriage : even Hamlet himself, in the
very scene where his abusive description of the king ('not evidence,'
if ever anything was not) has prejudiced many against Claudius,
seems to admit this. Claudius himself would probably—his very
words could be cited—have been most happy to regard Hamlet as
crown prince, would not have objected to receive Ophelia (perhaps
with a slight protest against derogation) as crown princess and,
after a due enjoyment of his kingdom and his wife, to assign the
former to them and die quite comfortably.

But this could not be : the gods would not have 'seen fair' if they
had allowed it, and the πρώταρχος ἄτη of the crime in the orchard
bears its fruit. Yet Claudius behaves himself by no means ill. He
meets Hamlet's early, and, as yet, ungrounded, or only half grounded,
sulks with a mixture of dignity and kindness which is admirable
in a difficult situation. There does not appear any prejudice against
Hamlet (though, of course, guilt makes the king uneasy) when
Polonius first tells him of the prince's antics. When he has eaves-
dropped, a proceeding fully justified by the statecraft of the time,
his desire to get rid of Hamlet, somehow, is natural, and it does
not yet appear that he has any design to 'get rid' of him in criminal
kind. Even after the play—an outrageous insult in any case—
there is no sign of murderous purpose either in his words to
Rosencrantz and Guildenstern or in the prayer soliloquy. Only
after the killing of Polonius, which might have alarmed an innocent
man, does he decide on the *literae Bellerophontis*. Few who have
paid any attention to it have denied the combined courage and
skill with which he meets the *émeute* headed by Laertes. Even

thenceforward, he is not pure villain, and, though it endangers all his plans, he tries to save the queen, between whom and himself it is quite certain that a real affection exists. He is a villain, but he is a man; and there are probably lesser villains who are rather poorer personages as men. Now, is this mere whitewashing on the critic's part, or the puerile and sneaking kindness for villany which is not quite unknown in men of letters? Not at all. No better deserved swordthrust was ever given than Hamlet's last; and Shakespeare never palliates the crime of Claudius in the very least degree. But he knows that a criminal is not necessarily bad all through; and he knows that there is no cheaper or falser morality than that which thinks that you must represent a criminal as bad all through lest you tempt people to sympathise with his crime. May it be added that, at this time of his career, he simply could not 'scamp' his work in the direction of character any more than in the direction of poetry? Others might throw in 'supers' to fill up a play—he would not. Claudius, of course, in no way disputes the position of hero; but there is stuff in him, as he is presented, for half a dozen heroes of the Racinian type.

Of Ophelia, and Polonius, and the queen and all the rest, not to mention Hamlet himself (in whose soul it would be absurd to attempt to discover new points here), after this we need not say anything. But it is observable that they are not, as in the case of Coriolanus, interesting merely or mainly for their connection with the hero, but in themselves. And it must be added that, not merely in the soliloquies and set speeches, but in the dialogue, even in its least important patchwork, Shakespeare's mastery of blank verse has reached complete perfection.

If *Othello* came next, as it may very well have done—it has been asserted, on the faith of a document not now producible, to have been acted at court on 1 November 1604—there was certainly no falling off. The pity, if not the terror, is made more intense than even in *Hamlet*. And, though for complexity Iago cannot approach Hamlet, he is almost as interesting. Once more, the Shakespearean impartiality is shown in this character. Iago, in the ordinary sense, is a much 'worse' man than Claudius; and, unlike Claudius, he has no compunction. But you see his point of view. It is by no means so certain as some critics have thought that his suspicions of Othello and Emilia are merely pretended; it is quite certain that he has never forgiven, and never will forgive, Othello or Cassio for the preference accorded by the former to the latter. Against Desdemona, he probably has no

personal spite whatsoever; but she is the most convenient instrument that suggests itself for embroiling his two foes with each
other and plaguing them both; so he uses her, once more without
compunction of any kind.   Roderigo is another instrument and
a useful pigeon as well.   But this newer 'ancient'—very different
from Pistol !—has an admirable intellect, a will of steel and a
perfectly dauntless courage.   'I bleed, sir; but not killed' is one
of the greatest speeches in Shakespeare, and the innocent commentators who have asked whether Shakespeare 'did not hate
Iago' can never have apprehended it.   As for Desdemona herself,
an interesting point arises in connection with another of Shakespeare's most pity-claiming figures, Cordelia, and may be noticed
when we come to her.

Those who (if there be any such) believe that Shakespeare
wrote the whole of *Macbeth* and that he wrote it about 1605, must
have curious standards of criticism.   To believe that he wrote the
whole of it is quite easy—indeed, the present writer has little or
no doubt on the matter; but the belief is only possible on the
supposition that it was written at rather different times.   The
second scene, that in which the 'bleeding sergeant' appears, and
some few other passages, are, in verse and phrase, whole stages
older than the bulk of the play, which, in these respects, is fully
equal to its great companions.   The character interest is limited
to the hero and heroine.   But in the thane and king—who is
a marvellous variant sketch of Hamlet, except that *he* can never
leave off, while Hamlet can never begin, and that, also, he can never
leave off metaphysicalising on the things he does, while Hamlet's
similar self-indulgence is confined to those he does not do—its
intensity and variety yield only to that of Hamlet himself; while
Lady Macbeth is quite peerless.   And the fresh handling of the
supernatural illustrates, fortunately not for the last time, the
curious fertility of the writer in a direction where, especially
when it is blended with events and motives not supernatural,
failure is not so much the usual, as the invariable, result.   That the
Shakespeare of one play, or part, should be the Shakespeare of
another, is a constantly repeated marvel; but it is scarcely anywhere more marvellous than in the fact that the same writer
wrote *A Midsummer Night's Dream, Hamlet, Macbeth* and *The
Tempest.*

Early British history seems at this moment to have had a
fascination for Shakespeare; for *Macbeth* appears to have been
followed pretty quickly by *King Lear*, and the date of *Cymbeline*

cannot have been very distant as it was certainly a stage play in 1610. *King Lear*, like its companions in the great *quatuor*, has special virtues, but it resembles them and *Antony and Cleopatra* in a certain regality of tone which hardly appears elsewhere. It resembles *Othello*, also, in being a tragedy of pity above all things; and it offers, perhaps, the most notable opportunity for the examination of the Shakespearean ἁμαρτία, which at once agrees and contrasts strikingly with the Aristotelian. The terrible fate of Lear—which the poet wisely introduced instead of the happy (or differently unhappy) ending which occurs in the chronicles and in a worthless contemporary play, a little earlier than his own—may seem excessive. As a punishment for his selfish abandonment and parcelling out of the kingdom, his general petulance and his blind misjudgment of his daughters, it may be so; as the consequence of his frailty, not. So, too, Cordelia's disinheritance and her ultimate fate are caused (whether deserved or not is, as before, a different question) by her self-willed and excessive want of compliance with her father's foolish, but not wholly unnatural, craving for professions of affection. The calamities of Gloster are a little more in the way of strict poetical justice of the ordinary kind; but they coincide well enough. The character of Edmund is a pendant to that of Iago, and his final speeches 'The wheel is come full circle: I am here,' and 'Yet Edmund was beloved,' are even more revealing than the stoical finale of the ancient. The extraordinary success of the fool has never been denied save by his unofficial successors; nor the superhuman poetry of the heath scenes. That the tragedy is too tragical, may be an argument against tragedy, or against the theatre generally; but not against this play. The one accusation of some weight is the horror of the Gloster mutilation scene, a survival of the old *Andronicus* days which, in a way, is interesting, but which, perhaps, could have been spared. The fact that it actually is a survival is the most interesting thing about it, except the other fact that it shocks, as, in an earlier play, it certainly would not. Nothing can show better the enormous lift which Shakespeare had himself given to the stage in, at most, some fifteen years, than the demand made on him, by modern criticism, not to do what everyone had been doing.

Last come the famous three: *Cymbeline, The Winter's Tale* and *The Tempest*, where no idle fancy has seen 'the calmed and calming *mens adepta*' of which one of all but the greatest of Shakespeare's contemporaries, Fulke Greville, speaks in a great passage of prose. The first and second were seen by Simon Forman, an astrologer of the day, in 1610 and 1611; *The Tempest* was certainly performed in 1613, and may have been written one or two years earlier—a theory which makes it not a late play at all is absurd and rebutted by the whole internal evidence. But internal coincides with external in allotting the three to the latest period possible: the versification supporting the general tone, and the intense romantic influence corroborating both. In respect of construction, however, there is a remarkable difference between *Cymbeline* and *The Winter's Tale*, on the one hand, and *The Tempest*, on the other.

Cymbeline has by some been reproached with being, and by others regretfully admitted to be, the loosest and most disorderly play in Shakespeare. Not only does he take his largest romantic licence of neglecting unity of time and place—to that the reader must long have been accustomed. Not only does he mix plots and interests with the most *insouciant* liberality, as if he were making a salad of them. But he leaves his materials, his personages, his incidents, at a perfect tangle of loose ends. Still, the interest is maintained, partly because of the actual attraction of many of his episodes; partly because of the exquisite poetry which is showered upon the play in every direction; but, most of all, because of the perfect charm of the character of the heroine. That Shakespeare has equalled Imogen is certainly true; but he has never surpassed her, and he has never repeated or anticipated her.

Perhaps there is nothing more remarkable in these three plays, even among Shakespeare's work, than the extraordinary beauty—both in phrase, passage and scene—of their separate parts. The word beauty is used advisedly. Here, in *Cymbeline*, for instance, fault may be found—irrelevantly, perhaps, but not ungroundedly—with construction, with connection of scenes and so forth. But those who look, not at the skeleton, but at the body, not at the mathematical proportion of features, but at the countenance, will hardly be disturbed by this. The two Imogen and Iachimo scenes; the whole episode of Belarius and his supposed sons; the miraculous song dirge which Collins, though he made a pretty thing of it, merely prettified—these are things impossible to conceive as bettered, difficult to imagine as equalled, or approached.

The Winter's Tale has something, but less, of the same sublime neglect of meticulous accuracy of construction; it has, perhaps, a more varied interest; it has even more lavishness of poetical appeal. The 'sea coast of Bohemia' is nothing; but the story, merely as a story, is certainly more romantic than dramatic. There is no character that approaches Imogen; for Perdita, exquisite as she is, has no character, properly speaking. The jealousy of Leontes, though an interesting variant on that of Othello and that of Posthumus, not to say on that of Master Ford, has a certain touch of ferocious stupidity, which Shakespeare probably intended, but which is not engaging. Hermione, admirable so far as she goes, is not quite fully shown to us; and, though Paulina is a capital portrait of what Ben Jonson declared his own wife to be—'a shrew but honest'—she does not go far. Autolycus, perhaps, is the only figure who fully displays the Shakespearean completeness. But the fascination of the play is quite independent of these knots in the reed. The abundance of it—the cheerful beginning and sombre close of the first Sicilian scenes; the partly tragic opening and pastoral continuation of the Bohemian; the tragicomedy and *coup de théâtre* of the end—is very great. But the suffusion of the whole with quintessenced poetry in the fashion just mentioned is greater. It appears chiefly in flash of phrase for the first three acts till the great storm scene at the end of the third, with the rather severe punishment of Antigonus and the contrasted farce of the shepherds. But, in the fourth, where comedy and romance take the place of farce and tragedy, and especially in Perdita's famous flower speech, it overflows; and there is plenty of it in the fifth. Had Greene lived to see this dramatising of his story, he might have been more angry than ever with the upstart crow; if, as sometimes, though too seldom, happens, his stormy spring had settled into a mellow early autumn, he ought to have been reconciled.

But, while the charms of *Cymbeline* and *The Winter's Tale* appear in even greater measure in *The Tempest*, this astonishing swan song is open to none of the objections which, from some points of view, may lie against them. It is almost regular, so far as 'time' is concerned; its violation of 'place' is very small, being confined to the limits of one little island; and its 'action' though, of course, of the English multiple kind, can be plausibly argued to be almost single in its multiplicity. The working of the spells of Prospero on all the important members of the shipwrecked crew in their diverse natures, qualities and importance—for correction on Alonso, Antonio and Sebastian (though these last two were probably incorrigible); for trial and reward on Ferdinand; for well deserved plaguing on Stephano and Trinculo—might have given more pause to Aristotle 'if he had seen ours,' as Dryden says, than anything else. The contrast of Caliban and Ariel is almost classical in conception, though ultraromantic in working out. The loves of Ferdinand and Miranda at once repair and confirm according to justice the acquisition of Milan by Naples, which has been unjustly accomplished before the opening. In the management of the supernatural, too, Shakespeare once more shows that unique combination of power and economy which has been noted. But he has not, because of this extra expenditure—if, indeed, it was an extra expenditure—of trouble, in the very least stinted the outpouring of beauty on individual character, scene, passage, phrase or line. Ariel and Caliban among super- or extra-natural personages, and Miranda, even among Shakespeare's women, occupy positions of admitted supremacy. Prospero is of extra-ordinary subtlety; the butler and the jester are among the best of their excellent class. It is curious that this play makes a kind of pendant to *Much Ado About Nothing* in the nearness with which comedy approaches tragedy, though the supernatural element relieves the spectator of the apprehension which, in the other case, is not unjustified. The inset masque, too (to which there is a faint parallel in *Cymbeline*), is a remarkable feature, and adds to the complicated, and yet not disorderly, attractions of the piece. But these attractions are all-pervading. The versification, though in part of Shakespeare's latest style, is of his best, in song and dialogue alike, throughout; and there are curious side interests in Gonzalo's citation of Montaigne, and in other matters. But the main charm is once more in the poetry, to which the prose adds not a little. The vividness of the storm; the admirable *protasis* of Miranda and Prospero; Ariel, whenever he speaks, and Caliban not seldom—give this charm, while Prospero himself is always a master of it. Indeed, in the great parallel with Calderon of 'life's a dream,' led up to by the picture of the vanishing universe, it reaches one of the 'topless towers' of poetry. To refuse to see an actual leavetaking in this perfect creation with its (to say the least) remarkable prophecy of the 'burial of the book' is, surely, an idle scepticism, considering the weight of positive evidence of all kinds which supports the idea. At any rate, if it were not the last, it ought to have been; and, though there are too many instances of non-coincidence between what ought to be and what is, we need hardly lay it down as a rule that what ought to have been could not be. *The Tempest* is not all Shakespeare: only all Shakespeare is that. But it may, at least, be pronounced a diploma piece of Shakespeare's art.

The foregoing survey of Shakespeare's plays has been made rather from the results of a long and intimate familiarity with their contents, than in reference to traditional opinion in their favour, or to recent efforts in the opposite direction. Some of these latter, such as the attacks of the very remarkable young Breton critic Ernest Hello not long since, and those of Tolstoy, only the other day, have been made, seriously and in good faith, from points of view which, when allowed for, deprive them of most of their effect. Others have come from mere mountebankery, or from the more respectable, but not much more valuable, desire to be unlike other people. But, apparently, they have had the effect of inducing some critics who are nearer to the truth to make provisos and qualifications—to return, in fact, to something like the attitude of George III, that 'a great deal of Shakespeare is sad stuff, only one must not say so,' but to put on more show of courage than the king and dare to 'say so,' with more or less excuse for theatrical necessities, 'faults of the time,' journeyman's work executed as a mere matter of business and the like. Perhaps this is only a new form of cant. For the characteristics of the time something, of course, must be allowed; with, however, the remembrance that, after all, they may not be faults when brought *sub specie aeternitatis*. But, except in the very earliest plays—not half a dozen out of the whole seven and thirty—and in passages of the middle division, it may almost be said that there is *no* 'sad stuff' in Shakespeare, though there is a great deal of very sad stuff in what has been written about him. In particular, both the impugners and the defenders on the theatrical side seem to protest too much. It is, of course, quite true that all Shakespeare's plays were written to be acted; but it may be questioned whether this is much more than an accident, arising from the fact that the drama was the dominant form of literature. It was a happy accident, because of the unique opportunity which this form gives of employing both the vehicles of poetry and of prose. But, though in a far milder degree, it was unlucky, because nothing has varied more or more quickly than the popular taste in drama, and, therefore, dramatic work has been exposed to even greater vicissitudes than those which necessarily await all literary performance. Even here, its exceptional excellence is evidenced curiously enough by the fact that there has been no time—the last forty years of the seventeenth century are not a real exception—at which Shakespeare has not (sometimes, it is true, in more or less travestied forms) retained popularity even on the stage.

But, if we regard his work from the far more permanent, and less precarious, standpoint of literary criticism, his exceptional greatness can be shown in divers and striking ways. The chain of literary dictators who have borne witness to it in their several fashions and degrees—Ben Jonson, Dryden, Pope, Samuel Johnson, Coleridge—has been pointed out often enough. It has not, perhaps, been pointed out quite so often that the reservations of these great critics, when they make them, and the more or less unqualified disapproval of others, can always be traced to some practically disabling cause. Ben Jonson held a different theory of the drama; Dryden, for a time, at least, was led aside by the heroic play and, for another time, by the delusion that the manners, language and so forth of 'the present day' must be an improvement on those of yesterday; Pope, by something not dissimilar to that which worked in Dryden's case, and Johnson, by something not dissimilar to that which worked in Jonson's; Coleridge, by 'his fun'—that is to say, by occasional crotchet and theory. On the other hand, Voltaire, with all who followed him, differed partly in point of view, and partly was influenced by the half concealed, half open conviction that French literature must be supreme. Patriotism worked in another way on Rümelin, vexed at the way in which his countrymen, led by the Schlegels (from the earlier, and too much forgotten, John Elias onwards) and Goethe, had deified foreigners. Hello was affected by that strange dread and distrust of great human art which has influenced the Roman Catholic church almost as much as the extreme protestant sects, and which descends from Plato through the Fathers. The mere dissident for the sake of dissent need hardly be noticed; still less the mountebanks. But it is a certificate of genuineness to have mountebanks against you; and the heretic, by the fact of his heresy, goes further than he knows to establish the orthodoxness of orthodoxy.

Except from the historical side, however, it is unnecessary to dwell on this part of the matter. What establishes the greatness of Shakespeare is the substance of Shakespeare's work. 'Take and read is the very best advice that can be given in reference to him. It is not necessary, nor at all desirable, to disparage at least part of the enormous labour that has been spent upon him by others. But it is quite certain that anyone who, with fair education and competent wits, gives his days and nights to the reading of the actual plays will be a far better judge than anyone who allows himself to be distracted by comment and controversy. The important thing is to get the Shakespearean atmosphere, to feel the breath of the Shakespearean spirit. And it is doubtful whether it is not much safer to get this first, and at first hand, than to run the risk of not getting it while investigating the exact meaning of every allusion and the possible date of every item. The more thoroughly and impartially this spirit is observed and extracted, the more will it be found to consist in the subjection of all things to what may be called the romantic process of presenting them in an atmosphere of poetical suggestion rather than as sharply defined and logically stated. But this romantic process is itself characterised and pervaded by a philosophical depth and width of conception of life which is not usually associated with romance. And it is enlivened and made actual by the dramatic form which, whether by separable or inseparable accident, the writer has adopted. Thus, Shakespeare—as no one had done before him, and as people have done since far more often in imitation of him than independently—unites the powers and advantages of three great forms: the romance (in verse or prose), pure poetry and the drama. The first gives him variety, elasticity, freedom from constraint and limit. The second enables him to transport. The third at once preserves his presentations from the excessive vagueness and vastness which non-dramatic romance invites, and helps him to communicate actuality and vividness.

It is in the examination of his treatment, now of individual incidents and personages, now of complicated stories, by the aid of these combined instruments, that the most profitable, as well as the most delightful, study of Shakespeare consists. But there is no doubt that, as a result of this study, two things emerge as his special gifts. The first is the coinage of separate poetic phrases; the second is the construction and getting into operation of individual and combined character. In a third point—the telling of a story or the construction of a drama—he is far greater than is often allowed. After his earliest period, there is very little in any play that does not directly bear upon the main plot in his sense of that word. Even in so very long, so very complicated, a piece as *Hamlet*, it is almost impossible to 'cut' without loss—to the intelligent and unhasting reader, at any rate, if not to the eager or restless spectator. But plot, in his sense, means, mainly—not entirely—the evolution of character; and so we may return to that point.

Two features strike us in Shakespearean character drawing

which are not so prominent in any other. The one is its astonishing prodigality, the other its equally astonishing thoroughness, regard being had to the purpose of the presentation. On this latter head, reference may be made to the examination of the character of Claudius above given; but it would be perfectly easy to supplement this by scores, nay, literally, by hundreds, of others, were there space for it. Shakespeare never throws away a character; but, at the same time, he never scamps one that is in any way necessary or helpful to his scheme. But this thoroughness, of course, shows itself more fully still in his great personages. It has been almost a stumblingblock—the bounty of the describing detail being so great that interpreters have positively lost themselves in it. Nor was this probably unintended; for Shakespeare knew human nature too well to present the narrow unmistakable type character which belongs to a different school of drama. His methods of drawing character are numerous. The most obvious of them is the soliloquy. This has been found fault with as unnatural—but only by those who do not know nature. The fact is that the soliloquy is so universal that it escapes observers who are not acute and active. Everybody, except persons of quite abnormal hebetude, 'talks to himself as he walks by himself, and thus to himself says he.' According to temperament and intellect, he is more or less frank with himself; but his very attempts to deceive himself are more indicative of character than his bare actions. The ingenious idea of the 'palace of truth' owes all its ingenuity and force to this fact. Now, Shakespeare has constituted his work, in its soliloquies, as a vast palace of truth, in which those characters who are important enough are compelled thus to reveal themselves. Nothing contributes quite so much to the solidity and completeness of his system of developing plot by the development of character; nor does anything display more fully the extraordinary power and range, the 'largeness and universality,' of his own soul. For the soliloquy, like all weapons or instruments which unite sharpness and weight, is an exceedingly difficult and dangerous one to wield. It may very easily be overdone in the novel (where there are not the positive checks on it which the drama provides) even more than in the drama itself. It is very difficult to do well. And there is a further danger even for those who can do it well and restrain themselves from overdoing it: that the soliloquies will represent not the character but the author; that they will assist in building up for us, if we desire it, the nature of Brown or Jones, but will not do very much for the construction

or revelation of that of Brown's or Jones's heroes and heroines.
Shakespeare has avoided or overcome all these points. His
soliloquies, or set speeches of a soliloquial character, are never, in
the mature plays, overdone; they are never futile or unnatural;
and, above all, they are so variously adapted to the idiosyncrasies of
the speakers that, while many people have tried to distil an
essence of Shakespeare out of them, nobody has succeeded. From
Thackeray's famous *parabases* (even when they are put in the
mouths of his characters as they sometimes are) we learn very little
more about these characters than he has told us or will tell us in
another way; but we learn to know himself almost infallibly. From
Shakespeare's soliloquies we hardly see him even in a glass darkly;
but we see the characters who are made to utter them as plain
as the handwriting upon the wall.

It remains, before concluding with a skeleton table of dates
and facts which may serve to vertebrate this chapter, to consider
three points of great, though varying, importance—Shakespeare's
morality in the wide sense, his versification and his style.

In dealing with the first, there is no necessity to dwell much on
the presence in his work of 'broad' language and 'loose' scenes.
That he exceeds in this way far less than most of his contemporaries will only be denied by those who do not really know the
Elizabethan drama. Of the excess itself, it seems rather idle to
say much. The horror which it excites in some cases is, perhaps,
as much a matter of fashion as the original delinquency. But this
is only a miserable specialisation and belittlement of the word
'morality.' In the larger sense, Shakespeare's morals are distinguished and conditioned almost equally by sanity, by justice
and by tolerance. He is not in the least squeamish—as has been
said, he shocks many as not being squeamish enough—but he
never, except in *All's Well that Ends Well*, and, perhaps, *Measure
for Measure*, has an unhealthy plot or even an unhealthy situation.
His justice is of the so-called 'poetical' kind, but not in the least
of the variety often so misnamed. In fact, as a rule, he is rather
severe—in some cases, decidedly so—and, though too much of an
artist to court the easy tragedy of the unhappy ending, is, except
in his last three plays, equally proof against the seductions of the
happy sort. But this severity is tempered by, and throws into
relief, the third quality of tolerance in which he excels every other
author. This tolerance is not complaisance: justice prevents
that, and sanity too. Shakespeare never winks at anything.
But, as he understands everything, so, without exactly pardoning it

('that's when he's tried above'), he invariably adopts a strictly impartial attitude towards everything and everybody. In this, he stands in marked contrast to Dante, who, with almost equal sanity and fully equal justice, is not merely unnecessarily inexorable, but distinctly partisan—not merely a hanging judge, but a hanging judge doubled with an unsparing public prosecutor. It was once observed as an *obiter dictum* by a Dante scholar of unsurpassed competence[1] that 'Dante *knows* he is unfair.' It might be said that the extraordinary serenity and clarity of Shakespeare's mind and temper make it unnecessary for him to think whether he is fair or not. He gives the character as it is—the other characters and the reader may make what they can of it. He allows Malcolm to call Macbeth a 'dead butcher' and Lady Macbeth a 'fiendlike queen,' because it is what Malcolm would have done. But he does not attach these tickets to them; and you will accept the said tickets at your own risk. Another contrast which is useful is, again, that of Thackeray. The author of *Vanity Fair* and *The Newcomes* has a power of vivifying character not much inferior to Shakespeare's. But, when he has vivified his characters, he descends too much into the same arena with them; and he likes or dislikes them, as one likes or dislikes fellow creatures, not as the creator should be affected towards creations. Becky Sharp is a very fallible human creature, and Barnes Newcome is a detestable person. But Thackeray is hard on Becky; and, though he tries not to be hard on Barnes, he is. Shakespeare is never hard on any of his characters—not merely in the cases of Lady Macbeth and Cleopatra, where there is no difficulty; but in those of Iago and Edmund, of Richard and of John, where there is. The difficulty does not exist for him. And yet he has no sneaking kindness for the bad, great person as Milton has. The potter has made the pot as the pot ought to be and could not but be; he does not think it necessary to label it 'caution' or 'this is a bad pot,' much less to kick it into potsherds. If it breaks itself, it must; in the sherds into which it breaks itself, in those it will lie; and 'there is namore to seyn.'

Equally matter subject to opinion, but matter much more difficult to pronounce upon with even tolerable distinctness and trenchancy, is the feature of style. It is, perhaps, in this point that Shakespeare is most distinguished from the other greatest writers. He has mannerisms; but they are mostly worn as clothes—adopted or discarded for fashion's or season's sake. He has no mannerism in the sense of natural or naturalised gesture which is

[1] [A. J. Butler.]

recognisable at once. When we say that a phrase is Shakespearean, it is rather because of some supreme and curiously simple
felicity than because of any special 'hall-mark,' such as exists in
Milton and even in Dante. Even Homer has more mannerism
than Shakespeare, whose greatest utterances—Prospero's epilogue
to the masque, Cleopatra's death words, the crispest sayings of
Beatrice and Touchstone, the passion of Lear, the reveries of
Hamlet, others too many even to catalogue—bear no relation to
each other in mere expression, except that each is the most appropriate expression for the thought. Euphuism and word play, of
course, are very frequent—shockingly frequent, to some people,
it would seem. But they are merely things that the poet plays
at—whether for his own amusement or his readers', or both, is
a question, perhaps of some curiosity, but of no real importance.
The well ascertained and extraordinary copiousness of his vocabulary is closely connected with this peculiar absence of peculiarity
in his style. The writer given to mannerism necessarily repeats, if
not particular words, particular forms of phrases—notoriously, in
some cases, particular words also. The man who, in all cases, is to
suit his phrase to his meaning, not his meaning to his phrase,
cannot do this. Further, Shakespeare, like almost all good English
writers, though to the persistent displeasure of some good English
critics, coins words with the utmost freedom, merely observing
sound analogy. He shows no preference for 'English' over 'Latin'
vocabulary, nor any the other way. But, no doubt, he appreci-
ates, and he certainly employs, the advantages offered by their
contrast, as in the capital instance of

> The multitudinous seas incarnadine
> Making the green one red,

where all but the whole of the first line is Aristotle's *xenon* and the
whole of the next clause his *kyrion*. In fact, it is possible to talk
about Shakespeare's style for ever, but impossible in any way to
define it. It is practically 'allstyle,' as a certain condiment is
called 'allspice'; and its universality justifies the Buffonian
definition—even better, perhaps, that earlier one of Shakespeare's
obscure Spanish contemporary Alfonso Garcia Matamoros as
habitus orationis a cujusque natura fluens.

There is no need to acknowledge defeat, in this way, as regards
the last point to be handled, Shakespeare's versification. This,
while it is of the highest importance for the arrangement of his
work, requires merely a little attention to the prosody of his prede-

cessors, and a moderate degree of patient and intelligent observation, to make it comparatively plain sailing. In no respect is the Meres list of more importance than in this; for, though it does not arrange its own items in order, it sets them definitely against the others as later, and enables us, by observing the differences between the groups as wholes, to construct the order of sequence between individual plays. Hardly less valuable is the practical certainty that *The Winter's Tale, Cymbeline* and *The Tempest* are the latest plays, and, to say the least, the extreme probability of the grouping of the greatest of the others as belonging to a short period immediately before and a rather longer period immediately after the meeting of the centuries.

Putting these facts together with the certain conditions of prosody in the plays of the Marlowe group, and in the nondescripts of the third quarter of the sixteenth century, we are in a condition to judge Shakespeare's progress in versification with fair safety. For the earliest period, we have pieces like *Love's Labour's Lost* and *The Comedy of Errors* on the one hand, like *Titus Andronicus* on the other. In this last, we see an attempt to play the game of the Marlowe heroic, the unrimed 'drumming decasyllabon,' strictly and uncompromisingly. The verses are turned out like bullets, singly from the mould; there is little condescendence (though there is some) to rime, even at the end of scenes and tirades; there is no prose proper. But there is considerable variation of pause; and, though the inflexibility of the line sound is little affected by it, there is a certain running over of sense in which, especially when conjoined with the pause, there is promise for the future.

The two other plays represent a quite different order of experiment. *Love's Labour's Lost*, especially, is a perfect *macédoine* of metres. There is blank verse, and plenty of it, and sometimes very good, though always inclining to the 'single-mould.' But there is also abundance of rime; plenty of prose; arrangement in stanza, especially quatrain; doggerel, sometimes refining itself to tolerably regular anapaests; fourteeners; octosyllables or, rather, the octosyllable shortened catalectically and made trochaic; finally, pure lyric of the most melodious kind. The poet has not made up his mind which is the best instrument and is trying all—not, in every case, with a certain touch, but, in every case, with a touch which brings out the capacities of the instrument itself as it has rarely, if ever, been brought out before.

In the other early plays, with a slight variation in proportion to subject, and with regard to the fact whether they are adaptations or not, this process of promiscuous experiment and, perhaps, half unconscious selection continues. The blank verse steadily improves and, by degrees, shakes off any suggestion of the chain, still more of the tale of bullets, and acquires the astonishing continuity and variety of its best Shakespearean form. Still, it constantly relapses into rime—often for long passages and, still oftener, at the ends or breaks of scenes and at the conclusion of long speeches; sometimes, perhaps, merely to give a cue; sometimes, to emphasise a sentiment or call attention to an incident or an appearance. The very stanza is not relinquished; it appears in *Romeo and Juliet*, in *A Midsummer Night's Dream*, even in *The Merchant of Venice*. The doggerel and the fourteeners, except when the latter are used (as they sometimes are) to extend and diversify the blank verse itself, gradually disappear; but the octosyllabic, and more directly lyrical, insets are used freely. The point, however, in that which is, probably, the latest of this batch, and in the whole of the great central group of comedies and tragedies, is the final selection of blank verse itself for reliance, and its development. Not only, as has just been noticed, do the deficiencies of the form in its earlier examples—its stiffness, its want of fluency and symphony, the gasps, as it has been put, of a pavior with the lifting and setting down of his rammer—not only do these defects disappear, but the merits and capabilities of the form appear contrariwise in ways for which there is no precedent in prosodic history. The most important of these, for the special dramatic purpose, if also the most obvious, is the easy and unforced breaking up of the line itself for the purpose of dialogue. But this, of course, had been done with many metres before; even medieval octosyllable writers had had no difficulty with it, though the unsuitableness of rime for dialogue necessarily appeared. But Shakespeare enlarged greatly and boldly on their practice. In all his mature plays—*Hamlet* is a very good example to use for illustration—the decasyllabic or five-foot norm is rather a norm than a positive rule. He always, or almost always, makes his lines, whether single, continuous, or broken, referable to this norm. But he will cut them down to shorter, or extend them to greater, length without the least hesitation. Alexandrines are frequent and fourteeners not uncommon, on the one hand; octosyllables and other fractions equally usual. But all adjust themselves to the five-foot scheme; and the pure examples of that scheme preponderate so that there is no danger of its being confused or mistaken.

Secondly, the lines, by manipulation of pause and of *enjambe-*

ment or overrunning, are induced to compose a continuous sym-
phonic run—not a series of gasps. In some passages—for instance,
the opening lines of *Antony and Cleopatra*—the pause will hardly
be found identical in any two of a considerable batch of verses.
As to its location, the poet entirely disregards the centripetal rule
dear to critics at almost all times. He sometimes disregards it to
the extent—horrible to the straiter sect of such critics—of putting
a heavy pause at the first or at the ninth syllable. Always, in
his middle period, he practises what he taught to Milton—the
secret of the verse period and paragraph—though in drama he has
a greater liberty still of beginning this and ending it at any of his
varied pause places, without troubling himself whether these places
begin and end a line or not. Sometimes, indeed, he seems to prefer
that they should not coincide.

But the third peculiarity which distinguishes the accomplished
blank verse of Shakespeare is the most important of all. It is the
mastery—on good principles of English prosody from the thirteenth
century onwards, but in the teeth of critical dicta in his own day
and for centuries to follow—of trisyllabic substitution. By dint of
this, the cadence of the line is varied, and its capacity is enlarged,
in the former case to an almost infinite, in the latter to a very
great, extent. Once more, the decasyllabic norm is kept—is, in fact,
religiously observed. But the play of the verse, the spring and
reach and flexibility of it, are as that of a good fishing-rod to that
of a brass curtain-pole. The measure is never really loose—it
never in the least approaches doggerel. But it has absolute
freedom: no sense that it wishes to convey, and no sound that
it wishes to give as accompaniment to that sense, meet the slightest
check or jar in their expression.

In the latest division, one of the means of variation which had
been used even before Shakespeare, and freely by him earlier,
assumes a position of paramount and, perhaps, excessive importance,
which it maintains in successors and pupils like Fletcher, and which,
perhaps, carries with it dangerous possibilities. This is what is
sometimes called the feminine, or, in still more dubious phrase,
the 'weak,' ending; but what may be better, and much more
expressively, termed the redundant syllable. That, with careful,
and rather sparing, use it adds greatly to the beauty of the
measure, there is no doubt at all: the famous Florizel and Perdita
scene in *The Winter's Tale* is but one of many instances. But it
is so convenient and so easy that it is sure to be abused; and
abused it was, not, perhaps, by Shakespeare, but certainly by

Fletcher. And something worse than mere abuse, destruction of the measure itself, and the substitution of an invertebrate mass of lines that are neither prose nor verse, remained behind.

But this has nothing to do with Shakespeare, who certainly cannot be held responsible for the mishaps of those who would walk in his circle without knowing the secrets of his magic. Of that magic his manipulation of all verse that he tried—sonnet, stanza, couplet, lyric, what not—is, perhaps, the capital example, but it reaches its very highest point in regard to blank verse. And, after all, it may be wrong to use the word capital even in regard to this. For he is the *caput* throughout, in conception and in execution, in character and in story—not an unnatural, full-blown marvel, but an instance of genius working itself up, on precedent and by experiment, from promise to performance and from the part to the whole.

APPENDIX

TABULAR CONSPECTUS

I

BIOGRAPHICAL

1564 April 26. Shakespeare baptised.

1582 November 27. Licence granted for marriage of William Shakespeare and Anne *Whateley*. 28. Bond entered into in reference to marriage of William Shakespeare and Anne *Hathaway*.

1583 May 26. Susanna Shakespeare baptised.

1585 February 2. Hamnet and Judith Shakespeare baptised.

1587 Michaelmas Term. Shakespeare appears in deed concerning Asbies mortgage.

1592. Referred to (?) by Greene as 'Shake-scene.' Apology by Chettle to the person thus referred to at end of this year or beginning of next.

1593. *Venus and Adonis* published.

1594. *The Rape of Lucrece* published. Shakespeare concerned in Christmas entertainments before the queen at Greenwich. *The Comedy of Errors* simultaneously acted on Innocents' day at Gray's inn.

1596 August 11. Hamnet Shakespeare buried. Shakespeare's father applies for coat of arms (20 October).

1597 May 4. Shakespeare buys New Place. References to him thenceforward by citizens of Stratford. He buys land and more houses.

1598. Meres mentions certain of Shakespeare's poems and plays. He acts (?) in Ben Jonson's *Every Man in His Humour*.

1599. Arms granted. Shakespeare acquires share in Globe theatre.

1601 September 8. John Shakespeare buried.

1604 March 15. Shakespeare takes part in procession at James I's entry into London.

1605. Augustine Phillips, a brother actor, leaves Shakespeare a thirty-shilling piece of gold in his will.

1607 June 5. Susanna Shakespeare marries John Hall.

1608 September 9. Shakespeare's mother buried. Soon afterwards, he establishes himself at New Place and has more business transactions of various kinds.

1609. The *Sonnets* published.

1616 January 25. Shakespeare makes his will, though it is not signed till March.

     February 10. Judith Shakespeare marries Thomas Quiney.

     April 23. Shakespeare dies, and is buried on the 25th.

1623. Shakespeare's widow dies. The first folio is published.

II

(The order followed is that of The Cambridge Shakespeare.)

The Tempest. Probably subsequent to 1610, certainly acted in May 1613, but not printed till first folio. References to Somers' shipwreck on the Bermudas (1609). Plot partly found in Jacob Ayrer's *Die schöne Sidea*. (This play is assigned to about 1595.)

The Two Gentlemen of Verona. Early. Story derived from Montemayor's *Diana*. Not printed till folio.

The Merry Wives of Windsor. After 1598. Licensed 1601: printed in part next year. Plot partly suggested by divers tales, Italian and other.

Measure for Measure. Produced December 1604(?). Not printed till folio. Story from Cinthio and Whetstone.

The Comedy of Errors. Early. Acted December 1594. Not printed till folio. Adapted from the *Menaechmi* of Plautus.

Much Ado About Nothing. After 1598. Printed in 1600. Part of story from Bandello and Ariosto.

Love's Labour's Lost. Early. First printed 1598. No direct source of story known.

A Midsummer Night's Dream. Middle early. Printed 1600. Story combined from Chaucer, Ovid, *Huon of Bordeaux* and many other sources. Practically original.

The Merchant of Venice. Late early, but before 1598. First printed (twice) in 1600. 'Casket' and 'pound of flesh' stories old medieval; frequently rehandled before Shakespeare separately and, perhaps, combined before him.

As You Like It. About 1600. Not printed till folio. Main story from Lodge's *Rosalynde*, which throws back to the medieval English tale of *Gamelyn*.

The Taming of the Shrew. Adapted from an older play printed in 1594. Not itself printed till folio. Partly drawn from Gascoigne's *Supposes*.

All's Well that Ends Well. Before 1598 (if identical with *Love's Labour's Won*). Not printed till folio. Story from Boccaccio through Painter.

Twelfth Night. About 1600. Acted at Middle Temple, February 1601/2. First printed in folio. Origin Italian either from play or novel, but perhaps directly from Barnabe Rich's translation of Bandello.

The Winter's Tale. Acted in May 1611. Not printed till folio. Story from Greene's novel of *Pandosto* (*Dorastus and Fawnia*).

King John. Early. Not printed till folio. Directly adapted from earlier play on same subject.

Richard II. Early. Printed 1597. Matter from Holinshed.

Henry IV. Late early. *Part I* printed 1598. *Part II* printed 1600. Partly worked up from earlier play *The Famous Victories of Henry the fifth*, but all best things original.

Henry V. 1599. Printed imperfectly next year. Origin as above.

Henry VI. *Part I* was first published in folio and no part is mentioned by Meres. *Parts II and III* in folio had appeared in a different and much less elaborate shape under the titles *The First Part of the Contention betwixt the two famous Houses of Yorke and Lancaster,* and *The True Tragedie of Richard Duke of Yorke* in 1594 and 1595. The source of the matter, as in all English chronicle plays, is Holinshed; but he is here largely corrected from other authorities.

Richard III. Completing the series, apparently, but more original than the *Henry VI* plays. It was published in 1597. Source again Holinshed.

Henry VIII. Performed in 1613; not printed till folio.

Troilus and Cressida. Acted and licensed for publication in February 1602/3, was not actually printed till January 1608/9. It may have been suggested by Chaucer whom it follows in the main lines of the love story; but owes much to other forms of the tale of Troy—perhaps most to Lydgate's.

Coriolanus. Appeared at an unknown date (*c.* 1608/9 is the favourite guess) but was never printed till folio. It follows Plutarch very closely—an observation which applies to all the Roman plays except

Titus Andronicus; which, one of the earliest, was acted in January 1593/4 and printed next year. The subject is quite unhistorical and its original source is unknown; it could have had little or nothing to do with a previous play on '*Titus* and Vespasian.'

Romeo and Juliet, which is certainly early, has been put as far back as 1591; was printed in 1597. Its source was a novel of Bandello's, already Englished by Broke in verse and Painter in prose.

Timon of Athens. Supposed to have been written in 1607, but was not printed till folio. A play on the same subject had been produced in 1600 and the suggestion of it was taken from Lucian and Plutarch through Painter.

Julius Caesar. Perhaps acted in 1601. Not printed till folio and is Plutarchian.

Macbeth. Has been conjecturally put as early as 1605. It was certainly acted in 1610: but was not printed till folio. The matter comes from Holinshed.

Hamlet. First acted and entered on the register 1602; first extant edition 1603; again printed in 1604 and, finally, in folio—the three forms differing much. The story came from *Saxo Grammaticus* through Belleforest, and, apparently, had been dramatised in English. [But see Bullen, A. H. in *The Times,* 3. XII. 1913.]

King Lear. Acted on 26 December 1606, was printed in 1608 and again later, before folio. It comes from Holinshed, whose story had been (more exactly but much worse) dramatised in 1605 by someone else.

Othello. Acted, apparently, in November 1604 but was not printed till 1622. The story comes from Cinthio.

Antony and Cleopatra. Licensed for publication, but not published, in 1608. Like *Julius Caesar,* to which it is a sequel, it did not appear in print till folio, and is again Plutarchian.

Cymbeline. Acted in 1610 or next year, but not printed till folio. Its matter comes partly from Holinshed, partly from Boccaccio.

Pericles. Though not included in folio, was printed in 1609 and no less than five times again before 1635. It was included among Shakespeare's works thirty years later in the third folio of 1664. The story comes from Gower.

Poems. Venus and Adonis, published 1593, is, apparently, Ovidian in origin; and *Lucrece,* published 1594, may be so or may only go back to Chaucer. The *Sonnets* were referred to by Meres in 1598. Next year, two were printed in Jaggard's *Passionate Pilgrim,* and all appeared in 1609. *The Phoenix and The Turtle* dates from 1601.

For editions and for commentaries on Shakespeare, reference must be made to the bibliography; but this chapter would be incomplete without some reference to the history of his fame in his own country. That his reputation was considerable already in his lifetime is proved by the references of Chettle probably, certainly of Meres, of *The Returne from Pernassus,* of

Webster, of Heywood and of others. But the two famous passages in verse and in prose of Ben Jonson have an importance greater than anything else. As was partly seen by Samuel Johnson, whose critical acuteness, when unprejudiced, was of the highest order, and who was certainly no Shakespeare fanatic, the testimony of these passages disproves most of the common errors and should preclude most of the doubts which have at different times existed on all the most important questions relating to the poet. For no man's work was better known than Jonson's, and, when he died, there were still living numerous men of letters who must have known the facts more or less fully, and would pretty certainly not have failed to correct or contradict Ben if there had been occasion to do so. In the succeeding generation, the admiration of Charles I, of John Hales and of Suckling—men as different as possible and yet all representative and all of unusual capacity—takes up the tale. After the Restoration, the expressions of a man like Pepys, who had no faculty of literary criticism whatever, merely set off those of Dryden, who was the best critic of the time; while the fact that Dryden's admiration is chequered itself enhances its value—especially as the unfavourable utterances can be easily explained. Almost more remarkable than this is the way in which, at the close of the seventeenth century and after the issue of the four folio editions, without any known attempt to edit, this attempt was made by a series of men of letters sometimes of the very highest literary eminence and always of some special ability. But the principal English editors of Shakespeare, beginning with Rowe, will be discussed in a later chapter (XI), while the chapter succeeding it (XII) will be devoted to the consideration of Shakespeare's reputation and influence abroad, and especially in France and Germany, from the seventeenth century onwards. Nor did the tide which rose steadily through the eighteenth century show any signs of ebb at its close. On the contrary, in Germany, with the younger Schlegels and Tieck; in England, with Coleridge, Lamb, Hazlitt and many others; in France, all the main promoters of the romantic movement with Victor Hugo, later, at their head, joined in exalting Shakespeare to a higher position than he had ever held and in deliberately reversing the previous estimate of his supposed faults and drawbacks. Nor has an entire century arrested the progress of his fame.

At many times, indeed, there have been gainsayers; but, in almost every case, from Rymer, and, indeed, from Ben Jonson himself in his carping mood to the remarkable Breton critic named above, it has been obvious that the objections came from theories, sometimes demonstrably erroneous, always resting ultimately upon opinion, and, therefore, no more valid than their opposites. And for the last half century or more, in accordance with a prevailing tendency of the criticism of the age, attempts have been made to question in larger or lesser extent the claim of William Shakespeare of Stratford to the personal authorship of the plays called by his name, special efforts being used to transfer the credit to Bacon. The latest of these fantastic suggestions has fixed on Roger Manners, earl of Rutland, ambassador to Denmark, and son-in-law of Sir Philip Sidney. To give an account of these attempts, and to deal with them adequately, would oblige us to outrun our limits altogether. It is sufficient to say that, up to the present time, they have not commended themselves to a single person who unites accurate knowledge of Elizabethan and other literature with the proved possession of an adequate critical faculty.

CHAPTER IX

SHAKESPEARE: POEMS

INTRICATE as are the complications which have been introduced into the study of Shakespeare's plays by attempts to use them as supplements to the missing biography, they are as nothing to those which concern the non-dramatic poems, especially the *Sonnets*. The main facts, with which we shall begin, are by no means enigmatical; and, save in regard to the small fringe or appendix of minor pieces—*A Lover's Complaint*, and the rest—there can be no doubt of their authenticity, except in the minds of persons who have made up their minds that, as Shakespeare cannot possibly have written Shakespeare's works, somebody else must have done so. Something has been said in the preceding chapter concerning these poems, in connection with what is known of the general course of Shakespeare's life, and with the plays; but it seems expedient to treat them also, and more fully, by themselves.

Venus and Adonis, the earliest published, was licensed on 18 April 1593, and appeared shortly afterwards with a fully signed dedication by the author to the earl of Southampton, in which he describes the poem as 'the first heire of my invention.' It was followed a year later by *Lucrece*, again dedicated to Southampton. Both poems were very popular, and were praised (sometimes with the author's name mentioned) by contemporaries. Four years later, again, the invaluable Meres referred, in the famous passage about the plays, to their author's 'sugared sonnets among his private friends' as well as to *Venus* and *Lucrece*; and, a year later still, in 1599, Jaggard the printer included two of these sonnets, numbers 138 and 144, in *The Passionate Pilgrim*. The whole was not published till ten years later, in 1609, by Thomas Thorpe, with Shakespeare's full name, but without any dedication or other sign of recognition from him. The circumstances make it quite clear that Shakespeare did not wish to undertake any ostentatious responsibility for the publication; but it is, perhaps, rather rash to assume that this publication was carried out against his will or even without his privity. There is no evidence on either point; and the probabilities must be estimated according to each man's standard of the probable. What is certain is that he never repudiated them.

Thorpe subjoined to them *A Lover's Complaint*, about which we know nothing more. But, in *The Passionate Pilgrim*, Jaggard had not merely included the two sonnets referred to, but had assigned the whole of the poems, of which three others were actually taken from *Love's Labour's Lost*, to 'W. Shakespeare.' Others had already appeared under the names of Marlowe, Ralegh, Barnfield, Griffin and others. Nine have no further identification. It appears that, in this instance, Shakespeare did protest; at any rate, the dramatist Thomas Heywood, from whom Jaggard, in a later edition, 'lifted' two more poems to add to the original twenty, says that Shakespeare was 'much offended'—a little piece of evidence of a wide ranging effect, both positive and negative, which, perhaps, has never been quite fully appreciated.

Some of the *adespota* are quite worthy of Shakespeare; and his 'offence' would, of course, be quite sufficiently explained by the imputation to him of plagiarism from such men as the living Ralegh, and the dead Marlowe. Lastly, there exists a rather obscure, very curious and, in parts, extremely beautiful, poem called *The Phoenix and the Turtle*, which, in 1601, was added to Robert Chester's *Love's Martyr*, as a contribution by Shakespeare: Jonson, Chapman, 'Ignoto' and others contributing likewise. This was reprinted ten years later, and we hear of no protests on the part of any of the supposed contributors, though, whatever Shakespeare might be, neither Jonson nor Chapman could be described as 'gentle' or likely to take a liberty gently. We may take it, then, that, as regards the two classical pieces, the *Sonnets, A Lover's Complaint* and *The Phoenix and the Turtle*, we have at least the ordinary amount of testimony to genuineness, and, in the case of the first three, rather more than this ; while some of *The Passionate Pilgrim* pieces are certainly genuine, and more may be. *Sonnets to Sundry Notes of Music*, it should, perhaps, be mentioned, though they often are separately entered in the contents of editions, merely form a division, with sub-title, of *The Passionate Pilgrim*.

There is nothing, therefore, so far, in what may be called the external and bibliographical history of the work, which justifies any special diversion from the study of it as literature. But, beyond all question, there is perilous stuff of temptation away from such study in the matter of the *Sonnets*. And, unfortunately, Thomas Thorpe stuck a burning fuse in the live shell of this matter by prefixing some couple of dozen words of dedication: 'To the only begetter of these ensuing sonnets Mr W. H. all happiness and that eternity promised by our ever-living poet wisheth the well-wishing adventurer in setting forth T. T.' It would be rash to guess, and impossible to calculate, how many million words of comment these simple nouns and verbs have called forth. The present writer has never seen any reason to abandon what has been, on the whole, the view most generally accepted by those who have some knowledge of Elizabethan literature and language, that this may be translated 'T. T., publisher of these sonnets, wishes to the sole inspirer of them, Mr W. H., the happiness and eternity promised by Shakespeare.' Moreover, though feeling no particular curiosity about the identification of 'Mr W. H.,' he has never seen any argument fatal to that identification with William Herbert, earl of Pembroke, which has also been usual. He admits, however, the possibility that ' W. H.' may be designedly inverted for ' H. W., and that this may be Henry Wriothesly, earl of Southampton, which would bring the three great poem units into line. Nor, without attempting an impossible summary of theories and arguments on this head, must we omit to mention that there is one, commanding the support of Sidney Lee, to the effect that 'Mr W. H.''s 'begetting' had nothing whatever to do with the inspiration of the *Sonnets*; and that he himself was merely a sort of partner in their commercial production. And so, having solidly based the account of the poems on known facts and known facts only, let us pursue it in reference to their actual contents and literary character.

The author could hardly have chosen a happier sub-title for *Venus and Adonis* than 'first heire of [his] invention.' It is exactly what a child of youth should be, in merit and defect alike; though, as is always the case with the state of youth when it is gracious, the merits require no allowance, and the defects are amply provided with excuse. In general class and form, it belongs to a very large group of Elizabethan poetry, in which the combined influence of the classics, of Italian and, to a less degree, of recent French, literature are evident. For the particular vehicle, Shakespeare chose the sixain of decasyllabic lines riming *ababcc* which had been used by Spenser for the opening poem of *The Shepheards Calender*. This, like its congeners the rime royal and (in its commonest form) the octave, admits of that couplet, or 'gemell,' at the end which, as we know directly from Drayton and indirectly from the subsequent history of English prosody, was exercising an increasing fascination on poets. It is, perhaps, the least effective of the three, and it certainly lends itself least of all to the telling of a continuous story. But Shakespeare's object was less to tell a story than to draw a series of beautiful and voluptuous pictures in mellifluous, if slightly 'conceited,' verse; and, for this, the stanza was well enough suited. As for the voluptuousness, it stands in need of very little comment either in the way of blame or in the way of excuse. The subject suggested it; the time permitted if it did not positively demand it; and there is evidence that it was not unlikely to give content to the reader to whom it was dedicated. If it were worth while it would be easy to show, by comparison of treatments of similar situations, that Shakespeare has displayed his peculiar power of 'disinfecting' themes of this kind even thus early. 'He who takes it makes it' is nowhere truer than of such offence as there may be in *Venus and Adonis*.

Its beauties, on the other hand, are intrinsic and extraordinary. Much good verse—after the appearance of 'the new poet' (Spenser) thirteen, and that of his masterpiece three, years earlier—was being written in this last decade of the sixteenth century. As was pointed out in the summary of prosody from Chaucer to Spenser[1], the conditions of rhythm, in accordance with the current pronunciation of English, had been at length thoroughly mastered. But, in Spenser himself, there are few things superior—in Drayton and Daniel and Sidney there are few things equal—at this time, to such lines as

> Ten kisses short as one, one long as twenty,

or as

> Leading him prisoner in a red-rose chain,

or the passages which have been wisely pounced upon by musicians, 'Bid me discourse,' and 'Lo! here the gentle lark,' with many others. To pass from mere melody of line and passage to colour and form of description, narrative, address and the like: the pictures of the hare and of the horse and of the boar, the final debate of the pair before Adonis wrenches himself away, the morning quest—these are all what may be called masterpieces of the novitiate, promising masterpieces of the mastership very soon. If some are slightly borrowed, that is nothing. It is usual in their kind; and the borrowing is almost lost in the use made of what is borrowed. Naturally, this

---

[1] See vol. III, chap. XIII.

use does not, as yet, include much novelty of condition, either in point of character, or of what the Greeks called *dianoia*—general cast of sentiment and thought. It is a stock theme, dressed up with a delightful and largely novel variety of verse and phrase, of description and dialogue. But it is more charmingly done than any poet of the time, except Spenser himself, could have done it; and there is a certain vividness—a presence of flesh and blood and an absence of shadow and dream—which hardly the strongest partisans of Spenser, if they are wise as well as strong, would choose, or would in fact wish, to predicate of him.

It has been usual to recognise a certain advance in *Lucrece*; which was thus entitled at its publication, though it had been licensed as *The Ravishment of Lucrece* and has, later, been generally called *The Rape of Lucrece*. The reasons for this estimate are clear enough. There is the natural presumption that, in the case of so great a genius, there will be an advance; and there is the character, and, to some extent, the treatment, of the subject. This latter still busies itself with things 'inconvenient,' but in the purely grave and tragic manner, the opportunities for voluptuous expatiation being very slightly taken, if not deliberately refused. The theme, as before, is a stock theme; but it is treated at greater length, and yet with much less merely added embroidery of description and narrative, which, at best, are accidentally connected with the subject. There is little pure ornament in *Lucrece* and a great deal of the much desiderated and applauded 'high seriousness,' 'thoughtfulness' and the like. Moreover, to suit his more serious subject, Shakespeare has made choice of a more serious and ambitious vehicle—the great rime royal, which had long been the staple form of English poetry for serious purposes. The special qualities of this stanza, as it happens, are especially suited to such a theme as that of *Lucrece*; for, while it can do many things, its character of plangency—not for monotonous wailing but for the varied expression of sorrow and passion—had been magnificently shown by Chaucer and by Sackville. Nor is Shakespeare unequal to the occasion. The first two stanzas weave the more complicated harmony of rhythm and rime in which the septet has the advantage over the sixain to excellent effect; and there are fine examples later. The length of the piece—1854 lines—is neither excessive nor insufficient; the chief, if not the only, episode (Lucrece's sad contemplation of the painted tale of Troy) is not irrelevant, and is done almost as vigorously as the best things in *Venus and Adonis*. And, if the unbroken sadness of the piece, which is not disguised even in the overture, is oppressive, it can hardly be said to be unduly oppressive.

On the whole, however, while allowing to it an ample success of esteem, it is difficult to put it, as evidence of genius and as a source of delight, even on a level with *Venus and Adonis*, much more to set it above that poem. It is a better school exercise, but it is much more of a school exercise, much more like the poems which were being produced by dozens in the hotbed of late Elizabethan poetic culture. Though it is half as long again, it contains far fewer single lines or line batches of intense and consummate beauty than the *Venus*. Though there is more thought in it, there is less imagery, and even less imagination; the prosodic capacities (higher as they have been granted to be) of line and stanza are less often brought out; the greater equality of merit is attained by lowering the heights as well as by filling up the depths. What is specially remarkable, in the work of the greatest character monger and character master of all time, Lucrece is still very little of a *person*—rather less (one feels inclined to say) than either the lovesick goddess or her froward lover. She is a pathetic and beautiful type; she does and says nothing that is inappropriate to her hapless situation and much that is exquisitely appropriate; but she is not individualised. In short, the whole thing has rather the character of a verse theme, carefully and almost consummately worked out according to rule and specification by a very clever scholar, than that of the spontaneous essay of a genius as yet unformed. From *Venus and Adonis* alone, a cautious but well instructed critic might have expected either its actual later sequel of immensely improved work or, perhaps, though less probably, nothing more worth having. From *Lucrece*, the legitimate critical expectation would be, at best, a poet something like Drayton, but, perhaps, a little better, a poet whose work would be marked by power sometimes reaching almost full adequacy and competence, but rarely transcending, a poet somewhat deficient in personal intensity himself and still more in the power of communicating it to his characters and compositions.

Almost everyone who has any interest in literature is more or less acquainted with the interminable theories and disputes which have arisen on the subject of the *Sonnets*. Yet it should not be very difficult for anyone who has some intelligence to divest himself sufficiently of this acquaintance to enable him to read them as if they were a new book—uncommented, unintroduced, with nothing but its own contents to throw light or darkness upon it.

If they are thus read, in the original order (for long after Shakespeare's death this order, purposely or not, was changed, though
modern editions usually, and rightly, disregard this change), certain
things will strike the careful reader at once. The first is that, by
accident or design, the pieces composing the series are sharply, but
very unequally, divided in subject, design being, on further inspection, pretty clearly indicated by the fact that the dividing point,
sonnet 126, is not a sonnet at all, but a *douzain.* In this reading,
it will, also, have become clear that the direct and expressed
object of most of the first and far larger batch is a man, and
that those of this batch which do not specify person or sex fall
in with the others well enough; while the main object of the last
and smaller batch is a woman. The first score or so of the earlier
group, though containing expressions of passionate affection, are
mainly, if not wholly, occupied with urging the person addressed
to marry. Both batches contain repeated complaint—though it is
not always exactly complaint—that the friend has betrayed the
poet with the mistress and the mistress with the friend. (It is,
however, perhaps possible to argue that the identity of friend
and mistress in the two batches is not proved to demonstration.)
A large portion of the whole—perhaps nearly a third—is full of that
half abstract, and almost impersonal, meditation on the joys and
sorrows of love which is the special matter of the sonnet. One or
two special and particular points, however, emerge—such as the indication of jealousy of other poets in respect of the friend, expressions
of dissatisfaction with the writer's 'public means' of living or profession (which, most probably, is the actor's, but, it must be observed,
far from necessarily so), and, in regard to the mistress, special, and
repeated, insistence on the fact of her being a 'dark lady' with black
eyes and hair. There is a good deal of wordplay on the name ' Will,'
which, of course, it would be absurd to overlook, but which had
rather less significance in those days than it would have now.

All these things are quite unmistakable. That the friend was
a 'person of quality' is generally admitted, and need not be much
cavilled at, though it must be observed that the words 'so fair a
house,' in sonnet 13, do not necessarily bear the meaning of
'family.' But everything beyond is matter of doubt and question;
while the very points just enumerated, though unmistakable in
themselves, suggest doubt and question, to those who choose to
entertain them, almost *ad infinitum.* Who was the friend? Pembroke, Southampton, or another? Who was the lady? Mistress
Mary Fitton (who seems to have been a love of Pembroke, but

who, they say, was fair, not dark) or somebody else? Who was the rival poet? When the list of uncertain certainties is overstepped, and men begin to construct out of the *Sonnets* a history of the course of untrue love in both cases, and endeavour to extend this history into something like a cipher chronicle of a great part of Shakespeare's life, we have, obviously, passed into cloudland. There is no limit to the interpretations possible to a tolerably lively fancy; and the limitless becomes more infinitely unlimited in respect to the criticisms and countercriticisms of these interpretations themselves.

On the other hand, it is possible to lay rather too much stress on the possibility of there being no interpretation at all or very little, of the *Sonnets* being merely, or mainly, literary exercises. It is, of course, perfectly true that the form, at this time, was an extremely fashionable exercise; and, no doubt, in some cases, a fashionable exercise merely. It is further true that, great as are the poetical merits and capacities of the sonnet, historically it has been, and from its nature was almost fated to be, more the prey of 'common form' than almost any other variety of poetic composition. The overpowering authority of Petrarch started this common form; and his Italian and French successors, enlarging it to a certain extent, stereotyped and conventionalised it even still more. It is perfectly possible to show, and has been well shown by Sidney Lee, that a great number, perhaps the majority, of sonnet phrases, sonnet thoughts, sonnet ornaments, are simply coin of the sonnet realm, which has passed from hand to hand through Italian, French and English, and circulates in the actual Elizabethan sonnet like actual coin in the body politic or like blood in the body physical. All this is true. But it must be remembered that all poetry deals more or less in this common form, this common coin, this circulating fluid of idea and image and phrase, and that it is the very *ethos*, nay, the very essence, of the poet to make the common as if it were not common. That Shakespeare does so here again and again, in whole sonnets, in passages, in lines, in separate phrases, there is a tolerable agreement of the competent. But we may, without rashness, go a little further even than this. That Shakespeare had, as, perhaps, no other man has had, the dramatic faculty, the faculty of projecting from himself things and persons which were not himself, will certainly not be denied here. But whether he could create and keep up such a presentation of apparently authentic and personal passion as exhibits itself in these *Sonnets* is a much more difficult question to answer in the affirmative. The present writer is inclined to echo seriously a light remark of one of Thackeray's characters on a different matter: 'Don't think he could do it. Don't think anyone could do it.'

At the same time, it is of the first importance to recognise that the very intensity of feeling, combined, as it was, with the most energetic dramatic quality, would, almost certainly, induce complicated disguise and mystification in the details of the presentment. It was once said, and by no mere idle paradoxer, that the best argument for the identity of the dark lady and Mary Fitton was that Mistress Fitton, apparently, was a blonde. In other words, to attempt to manufacture a biography of Shakespeare out of the *Sonnets* is to attempt to follow a will-o'-the-wisp. It is even extremely probable that a number, and perhaps a large number, of them do not correspond to any immediate personal occasion at all, or only owe a remote (and literally occasional) impulse thereto. The strong affection for the friend; the unbounded, though not uncritical, passion for the lady; and the establishment of a rather unholy 'triangle' by a cross passion between these two— these are things which, without being capable of being affirmed as resting on demonstration, have a joint literary and psychological probability of the strongest kind. All things beyond, and all the incidents between, which may have started or suggested individual sonnets, are utterly uncertain. Browning was absolutely justified when he laid it down that, if Shakespeare unlocked his heart in the *Sonnets*, 'the less Shakespeare he.' That the *Sonnets* testify to a need of partial unlocking, that they serve as 'waste' or overflow, in more or less disguised fashion, to something that was not unlocked, but which, if kept utterly confined, would have been mortal, may be urged without much fear of refutation. We see the heart (if we see it at all) through many thicknesses of cunningly coloured glass. But the potency and the variety of its operation are, however indistinctly, conveyed; and we can understand all the better how, when the power was turned into other, and freer, channels, it set the plays a-working.

To pass to more solid ground, the *Sonnets* have some mechanical, and many more not mechanical, peculiarities. The chief of the first class is a device of constantly, though not invariably, beginning with a strong caesura at the fourth syllable, and a tendency, though the sonnet is built up of quatrains alternately rimed with final couplet, to put a still stronger stop at the end of the second line (where, as yet, is no rime), and at each second line of these non-completed couplets throughout. The piece is thus elaborately built up or accumulated, not, as sonnets on the octave and sestet system often are, more or less continuously wrought in each of their two divisions or even throughout. This arrangement falls in excellently with the intensely meditative character of the *Sonnets*. The poet seems to be exploring; feeling his way in the conflict of passion and meditation. As fresh emotions and meditations present themselves, he pauses over them, sometimes entertaining them only to reject them or to qualify them later; sometimes taking them completely to himself. Even in the most artificial, such as sonnet 66, where almost the whole is composed of successive images of the wrong way of the world, each comprised in a line and each beginning with 'and,' this accumulative character is noticeable; and it constitutes the strongest appeal of the greatest examples. While, at the same time, he avails himself to the full of the opportunity given by the English form for a sudden 'turn'—antithetic, it may be, or, it may be, rapidly summarising—in the final couplet. Of course, these mechanical or semi-mechanical peculiarities are not universal. He varies them with the same infinite ingenuity which is shown in his blank verse; so that, as for instance in the beautiful sonnet 71, the first two quatrains are each indissoluble, woven in one piece from the first syllable to the last. But the general characteristics have been correctly enough indicated in what has been said above.

Still, the attraction of the *Sonnets*, almost more than that of any other poetry, consists in the perpetual subduing of everything in them—verse, thought, diction—to the requirements of absolutely perfect poetic expression. From the completest successes in which, from beginning to end, there is no weak point, such as

> When to the sessions of sweet silent thought,

or

> Let me not to the marriage of true minds, .

through those which carry the perfection only part of the way, such as

> When in the chronicle of wasted time,

down to the separate batches of lines and clauses which appear in all but a very few, the peculiar infusing and transforming power of this poetical expression is shown after a fashion which it has proved impossible to outvie. The precise subject (or, perhaps, it would be more correct to say the precise object) of the verse disappears. It ceases to be a matter of the slightest interest whether it was Mr W. H. or Mistress M. F. or anybody or nobody at all, so that we have only an abstraction which the poet chooses to regard as concrete. The best motto for the *Sonnets* would be one taken from not the least profound passage of the *Paradiso* of Dante

> *Qui si rimira nell' arte ch' adorna*
> *Con tanto affetto.*

And this admiration of the art of beautiful expression not only dispenses the reader from all the tedious, and probably vain, enquiries into particulars which have been glanced at, but positively makes him disinclined to pursue them.

The lesser poems, if only because of their doubtfulness, may be dealt with more shortly. *A Lover's Complaint*, by whomsoever written, must have been an early poem, but shows good powers in its writer. The rime royal, of which it is composed, is of the same general type as that of *Lucrece*, but has a few lines superior to any in the larger and more certain poem, such as the well known last

> And new pervert a reconcilèd maid,

or the fine, and quite Shakespearean, second line in

> O father! what a hell of witchcraft lies
> In the small orb of one particular tear!

The jilted and betrayed damsel who is the heroine and spokeswoman has sparks of personal character. Of *The Passionate Pilgrim* pieces, not already known as Shakespeare's, or assigned to others, the two Venus and Adonis sonnets might be either suggested by the authentic poem to someone else or alternative studies for a different treatment of it by Shakespeare himself; and it is hardly possible to say of any of the rest that it cannot be, or that it must be, his. There are flashes of beauty in most of them; but, considering the way in which such flashes of beauty are shot and showered over and through the poetry of 1590—1610, this goes but a little way, or, rather, no way at all, towards identification. As for *The Phoenix and the Turtle*, the extreme metaphysicality of parts of it—

> Property was thus appalled
> That the self was not the same; etc.—

is by no means inconceivable in the Shakespeare of *Love's Labour's Lost* and of some of the *Sonnets*. The opening lines, and some of those that follow, are exceedingly beautiful, and the contrast of melody between the different metres of the body of the poem and the concluding *threnos* is 'noble and most artful.'

Inasmuch, moreover, as some of these minor and doubtful pieces draw very close to the songs in the plays, and actually figure in their company under the thievish wand of Hermes-Jaggard, it cannot be very improper to take them slightly into account, with the songs and certainly assigned poems, as basis for a short connected survey of Shakespeare's poetical characteristics in non-dramatic verse. One of these, which is extremely remarkable, and which has been also noted in his dramatic verse, is the uniform metrical mastery. This, when you come to compare the two classical narratives, the *Sonnets* and the songs with their possible companions among the doubtful minors, is extraordinary. Neither Chaucer nor Spenser was good at light lyrical measures, admirable and beyond admiration as both were in regard to non-lyrical verse, and accomplished, as was at least Spenser, in the more elaborate and slowly moving lyric. In fact, it may almost be said that neither tried them. Shakespeare tries them with perfect success; while his management of the sixain and septet is more than adequate, and his management of the English form of sonnet absolutely consummate. This lesser exhibition (as some would call it) of his universality—this universality in form—is surely well worth noting; as is, once more, the unusually lyrical character of some of his stanza work itself, and the likeness to his blank verse lines of not a few things both in stanza and in sonnet. This polymetric character has since become more and more common because poets have had examples of it before them. But it is first strongly noteworthy in Shakespeare.

Of the matter that he put into these forms, perhaps the first thing that ought to be remarked is that most of it certainly, and nearly all of it (except the later play songs) probably, dates from a very early period in his literary life; and the second, that the range of direct subject is not large. From this, enough having been said of the other productions, we may pass to the third observation: that in the *Sonnets* the absolute high water mark of poetry is touched, at least for those who believe with Patrizzi, and Hazlitt, and Hugo, that poetry does not so much consist in the selection of subject as in the peculiar fashion of handling the subject chosen. What their exact meaning may be is one question, with, as has been shown in practice, a thousand branches to it. It is a 'weary river,' and, probably, there is no place where that river 'comes safe to sea' at all. Whether or not we wish, with Hallam, that they had never been written must be a result of the personal equation. But that, in the Longinian sense of the Sublime, they 'transport' in their finest passages as no other poetry does except the very greatest, and as not so very much other poetry does at all, may be said to be settled. If anyone is not transported by these passages, it is not impertinent to say that he must be like 'the heavier domestic fowls' of Dr Johnson's ingenious and effective circumlocution—rather difficult to raise by external effort and ill furnished with auxiliary apparatus for the purpose.

The poems other than the *Sonnets* are either tentative essays or occasional 'graciousnesses' for a special purpose; the *Sonnets* themselves have such an intensity of central fire that no human nature, not even Shakespeare's, could keep it burning, and surround it with an envelope able to resist and yet to transmit the heat, for very long. Fortunately, experiment and faculty both found another range of exercise which was practically unlimited; fortunately, also, they did not find it without leaving us record of their prowess in this.

CHAPTER X

PLAYS OF UNCERTAIN AUTHORSHIP ATTRIBUTED TO SHAKESPEARE

THE foundations of the Shakespearean apocrypha were laid while the dramatist was still alive, when a number of plays, in the composition of most of which he could have had no hand, were entered upon the Stationers' register as his, or were published with his name or initials on the title-page. Against the laying of these foundations Shakespeare, so far as we know, raised no protest. In any case, it is upon them that the ascriptions of publishers and others in the generation that followed his death, and the theories advanced by students of the Elizabethan drama during the last two centuries, have built up a superstructure so massive that the total of the plays of more or less uncertain authorship attributed to Shakespeare already equals in quantity that of the accepted canon.

Disregarding those plays—six in all—which were claimed by their publishers as Shakespeare's, but which have since been lost, we may attempt the following classification. First, plays which were published during Shakespeare's lifetime with his name, or initials, upon the title-page: *Locrine* (published in 1595); *The first part of the ... life of Sir John Oldcastle* (1600); *The whole life and death of Thomas Lord Cromwell* (1602); *The London Prodigall* (1605); *The Puritane* (1607); *A Yorkshire Tragedy* (1608); *Pericles* (1609). Two of these plays do not concern us here: *Sir John Oldcastle, part I,* has been assigned, on the evidence of an entry in Henslowe's diary, to the joint authorship of Munday, Drayton, Wilson and Hathwaye; and certain parts of *Pericles* have been almost universally recognised as the work of Shakespeare.

A second class comprises three plays which were published after Shakespeare's death with his name, as sole or joint author, upon the title-page: *The Troublesome Raigne of John, King of England* (published as Shakespeare's in 1622, after having been issued anonymously in 1591); *The Two Noble Kinsmen* (published as the work of Fletcher and Shakespeare in 1634); and *The Birth of Merlin* ('written by William Shakespear and William Rowley,' 1662).

Again, three plays have been attributed to him on the very slender evidence that they were discovered bound up together in a volume in Charles II's library, labelled 'Shakespeare, vol. I.' These are *Mucedorus* (first published, anonymously, in 1598); *The Merry Devill of Edmonton* (1608); and *Faire Em* (1631)[1]. None of these was included in the third folio edition of Shakespeare's works, which appeared in 1664, and which added to the thirty-six plays of the first folio the seven plays first mentioned above.

The last class of plays of uncertain authorship attributed to Shakespeare will comprise those which have been assigned to him since the beginning of the eighteenth century on the basis of internal evidence. The number of plays which could be brought under this heading is very large, but only three of them—*Edward III*, *Arden of Feversham* and *Sir Thomas More*—can be included here. Two other plays—*The First Part of the Contention* and *The True Tragedie of Richard, Duke of Yorke*—also fall into this division; but these, like *The Troublesome Raigne of John, King of England* mentioned above, have been treated in a preceding chapter[2].

In considering the question of Shakespeare's share in any of the above plays, it is unfortunate that our main evidence has to be sought in the plays themselves. The appearance of his name on the Stationers' register, or on the title-page of a play, is of interest as showing the extent of his popularity with the reading public of his time, but is no evidence whatever that the play is his. On the other hand, it is uncritical to reject a play as Shakespeare's solely because it does not find a place in the first folio of 1623. Valuable as that edition is as a standard of authenticity, it does not include *Pericles*, portions of which are almost unanimously claimed for Shakespeare, while it includes *The First Part of Henry VI*, portions of which are just as unanimously believed not to be his. There remains, therefore, the evidence furnished by the plays themselves—evidence which, for the most part, consists in the resemblances which these plays bear, in respect of diction and metre, characterisation and plot construction, to the accepted works of Shakespeare. Such evidence, confessedly, is unsatisfactory and leaves the whole question under the undisputed sway of that fickle jade, Opinion.

But the question of Shakespearean authorship is not the only point of interest presented by the doubtful plays. So varied in

---

[1] There is an undated quarto edition of *Faire Em* which C. F. Tucker Brooke considers older than that of 1631 'by perhaps a generation or more' (*Shakespeare Apocrypha*, p. xxxviii).　　[2] Chap. VII.

character are the works which go to form the Shakespearean apocrypha, that they may fairly be said to furnish us with an epitome of the Elizabethan drama during the period of its greatest achievement. Almost every class of play is here represented, and one class—that of domestic tragedy—finds, in *Arden of Feversham* and in *A Yorkshire Tragedy*, two of its most illustrious examples. The Senecan tragedy of vengeance is represented by *Locrine*; the history or chronicle play by *Edward III*, *The First Part of the Contention*, *The True Tragedie*, *The Troublesome Raigne of John, King of England, Sir Thomas More* and *Cromwell*, and, less precisely, by *The Birth of Merlin* and *Faire Em*. The romantic comedy of the period is illustrated by *Mucedorus, The Merry Devill* and *The Two Noble Kinsmen*, while *The London Prodigall* and *The Puritane* are types of that realistic *bourgeois* comedy which, in Stewart days, won a firm hold upon the affections of the play-going community.

Of the apocryphal tragedies, the earliest in date of composition was, probably, *Locrine*, which, when published by Thomas Creede, in 1595, was described as 'newly set foorth, overseene and corrected, By W. S.' The initials, probably, were intended to convey the impression of Shakespearean authorship, but nowhere in the five acts is there the faintest trace of Shakespeare's manner. The words 'newly set foorth, overseene and corrected' indicate that *Locrine* was an old play revised in 1595; and in the number of revised passages must be included the reference in the epilogue to queen Elizabeth as

that renowned maid
That eight and thirty years the sceptre swayed.

A feature of the play, pointed out by Crawford[1] and by Koeppel[2], and discussed in an earlier chapter, is that some of its verses reappear almost unchanged in *Selimus* (1594), and, also, that both of these plays have imported a number of verses from Spenser's *Ruines of Rome*, published in 1591. But, if *Locrine*, as verse, diction and plot construction lead us to suppose, was written before 1590, it is probable that the lines borrowed from Spenser do not belong to the original edition, but only to the revised version of 1595.

The play, while yielding to popular taste in respect of stage action, neglect of the unities and the mingling of kings and

---

[1] *Notes and Queries*, 1901, Nos. 161, 163, 165, 168, 171, 174, 177.
[2] 'Locrine und Selimus,' *Shakespeare Jahrbuch*, vol. XLI, pp. 193—200. As to the relations between *Locrine* and *Selimus*, see *ante*, chap. IV.

clowns, is, in its main outlines, a Senecan revenge tragedy; and, in
its adaptation of a theme drawn from early British history to the
Senecan manner, it is the direct successor of *Gorboduc* and *The
Misfortunes of Arthur*. The story of Locrine, which is also told
by Lodge in his *Complaint of Elstred* and by Spenser in his
Faerie Queene[1] was found by the playwright in Geoffrey of
Monmouth's *Historia Britonum* and the *Chronicles* of Holinshed.
Weak in characterisation, and somewhat loose and episodic in
plot construction, the play, however, is by no means the *caput
mortuum* which Lamb declared it to be.   It is full of youthful
vigour, and, amid much turgid declamation and a too ready indulgence in Senecan horrors, contains passages of splendid rhetoric.
Sabren's lament to the mountain nymphs, the 'Dryades and light-
foot Satyri,' and the

> gracious fairies which at evening tide
> Your closets leave, with heavenly beauty stored[2],

is a noble anticipation of *Comus*, and Locrine's farewell to Estrild
in the same scene—

> Farewell, fair Estrild, beauty's paragon,
> Fram'd in the front of forlorn miseries;
> Ne'er shall mine eyes behold thy sunshine eyes.
> But when we meet in the Elysian fields—

advances with the pomp and rhythmic splendour of a legionary
march. The comic scenes, too, are full of vitality, and there are
elements in the character of Strumbo the clown that foretell both
Don Armado and Falstaff.

At different times, the play has been ascribed to Marlowe,
Greene and Peele respectively, and, of late, opinion has veered
strongly in the direction of Peele.   But, while there are certain
resemblances of style to *The Battell of Alcazar*—if, indeed, that
anonymous play be Peele's—there are still more striking resemblances to the tragedies of Kyd, past master of that type of
Senecan revenge tragedy to which *Locrine* very closely approaches.
A comparative study of *Locrine* and *The Spanish Tragedie*
brings so many points of resemblance to light as to make it seem
probable that they are the works of the same author; and, in
support of this view, it may be noticed, incidentally, that the
two plays are coupled together in the ridicule which Jonson
metes out to Kyd in *Poetaster*[3].   *Locrine* resembles *The Spanish
Tragedie* in the introduction of the goddess of Revenge, before
each act, in the notable use which is made of the Senecan

---

[1] Book II, canto 10, stanzas 13—19.   [2] Act v, sc. 4.   [3] Act III, sc. 1.

ghost, in the constant appeal to, or tirade against, Fortune and in the countless references to the horrors of the classic underworld, with its three judges, Minos, Aeacus and Rhadamanth. The Senecan rodomontade of *The Spanish Tragedie*, with its lurid imagery and wild cries for vengeance, reappears, if possible with heightened colours, in *Locrine*, together with the introduction of Latin verses and even a stray phrase in the Spanish tongue. There is, too, an affinity between the two plays in situation and sentiment: just as, in *The Spanish Tragedie*[1], Horatio and Lorenzo strive against each other for the possession of the captured prince of Portugal, so, in *Locrine*, two soldiers dispute over the captured Estrild; while the outraged Hieronimo's appeal to nature to sympathise with him in his sorrow is echoed in the speech of the ghost of Corineus[2].

Arden of Feversham, apparently the earliest, and, beyond all question, the highest, achievement of the Elizabethan age in the field of domestic tragedy, was first claimed for Shakespeare by Edward Jacob, a Faversham antiquary, who re-edited the play in 1770. Since then, it has passed through numerous editions, and, engaging the notice of almost every Shakespearean critic, it has called forth the most divergent views as to its authorship. The play was entered on the Stationers' register as early as 3 April 1592, and was published anonymously in the same year with the title, *The Lamentable and True Tragedie of M. Arden of Feversham in Kent*; later quarto editions, also anonymous, appeared in 1599 and 1633. The tragic incident upon which the drama is based took place in 1551, and left so lasting a mark upon the minds of men, that Raphael Holinshed, in the publication of his *Chronicles of England, Scotland and Ireland*, twenty-six years later, devoted five pages to the story and recorded the details with considerable dramatic power. The dramatist, although he makes a few slight alterations and adds the character of Franklin, follows Holinshed's narrative in all its essential aspects with scrupulous fidelity. Writing, too, at a time when the exuberant style of Marlowe and Kyd was in the ascendant, he exercises a marked self-restraint. Here and there, the spirit of the age lifts him off his feet—as, for instance, where he makes the ruffian Shakebag discourse in superb poetry[3]; but, for the most part, he preserves that austerity of manner which, he felt, the sordid theme demanded. The exercise of this self-restraint, which often amounts to a

---

[1] Act I, sc. 2. [2] Act V, sc. 4. As to *Locrine*, cf. *ante*, chap. IV.
[3] Act III, sc. 2, 1—9.

cynical indifference to the principles of art, pertains to much besides diction. The plot of the play, judged by the standard of Shakespearean tragedy, is singularly devoid of constructive art; it advances not by growth from within but by accretion from without. One murderous plot against Arden's life follows another in quick succession, and, as we see each attempt baffled in turn, our sense of terror is changed to callousness, and the tragic effect of the actual murder is, thereby, blunted. The repeated attempts at murder, again, are merely so many episodes, and, as the drama proceeds, we are not made to feel that the meshes of the conspirators' net are closing upon their prey. Except for the exigencies of a five-act play, and the author's determination to abridge none of the details of Holinshed's story, the murder of Arden might very well have occurred at the end of the first act. If our sense of terror is blunted by the nature of the plot, so, also, is our pity for the victim. By reason of his stupidity and insensate credulity, his avarice and his cruelty to Bradshaw and Reede, Thomas Arden fails altogether to win our sympathy. The dramatist, it is true, leaves unnoticed some of the charges brought against him by Holinshed; but he makes no attempt whatever to render him attractive, or to awaken our pity at his death. In all this, we recognise the contrast to the manner of Shakespeare as displayed, for example, in *Macbeth*. Holinshed's Duncan arouses as little sympathy as Holinshed's Arden, but Shakespeare, in his regard for tragic pity, has made of Macbeth's victim a hero and a saint. Apart from the work of mere journeymen playwrights, there is no play in the whole range of Elizabethan dramatic literature which disregards tragic *katharsis*, alike in its terror and its pity, so completely as *Arden of Feversham*.

But are we to ascribe this neglect of tragic *katharsis* to obtuseness of dramatic vision? The marvellous power which the playwright reveals in the handling of certain situations and the deftness with which he introduces, now a touch of grim humour and now a gleam of tragic irony, are sufficient indications that his treatment of the story was deliberate. And, if any doubt remains in our minds, we have only to turn to the closing words of the play, in which the author defends his craftsmanship against all attack:

> Gentlemen, we hope you'll pardon this naked tragedy,
> Wherein no filed points are foisted in
> To make it gracious to the ear or eye;
> For simple truth is gracious enough,
> And needs no other points of glosing stuff.

The author of *Arden of Feversham* is not only the creator of English domestic tragedy; he is, also, the first English dramatic realist, and the first who refused to make nature bend beneath the yoke of art. Delighting in the 'simple truth' of Holinshed's narrative, he refused to alter it—refused to reduce the number of attempts on Arden's life or to make the victim of the tragedy a martyr. And, in all this, he stands as a man apart, neither owning allegiance to the recognised masters of English tragedy, Kyd and Marlowe, nor claiming fellowship with the rising genius of Shakespeare. It is impossible to believe that the author of *Arden* is the author of *Romeo and Juliet.* True, there are lines, sometimes whole speeches, in the play which have something very like the Shakespearean ring in them; and it is also true that the play reveals, especially in the famous quarrel scene between Alice Arden and Mosbie[1], a knowledge of the human heart which the Shakespeare of 1592 might well have envied. But, in 1592, the temper of Shakespeare was not that of the austere realist: he was ardent and romantic, a lover of rime and of 'taffeta phrases,' a poet still in his pupilage, well content to follow in the steps of his masters; and, in each of these respects, he differs widely from the creator of *Arden.* Nor, finally, was it the principle of Shakespeare, either in 1592 or at any other period of his life, to place the record of history above art in the way that the *Arden* dramatist has done. There is no rigidity in the materials out of which Shakespeare has fashioned his plays; to him, all things were ductile, and capable of being moulded into whatever shape the abiding principles of the playwright's craft demanded.

A Yorkshire Tragedy resembles *Arden of Feversham* in its unflinching realism, as well as in being a dramatisation of a tragic occurrence in the annals of English domestic life. The event which it memorises took place at Calverley hall, Yorkshire, early in 1605, and was recorded very fully by an anonymous pamphleteer, very briefly by Stow in his *Chronicle,* by a ballad writer and, lastly, by two dramatists—the authors of *The Miseries of Inforst Mariage* and *A Yorkshire Tragedy* respectively. The former play, which was first published in 1607, was by George Wilkins; the latter, after being acted at the Globe theatre, was entered on the Stationers' register on 2 May 1608, as 'by Wylliam Shakespere,' and published in the same year with his name upon the title-page. Wilkins, appalled by the tragic gloom of the story, alters the facts and brings his play to a happy ending; but the author of the ten short, breathless scenes which make up

[1] Act III, sc. 5.

A Yorkshire Tragedy spares us none of the harrowing details.
Keeping very close to the version of the pamphleteer, he furnishes
a record of the last act in a rake's progress to the gallows,
and, delighting in the relentless analysis of criminality, sacrifices
everything for the sake of the criminal. The wife—a faintly-
outlined Griselda of the Yorkshire dales—the various 'gentlemen,'
and the 'Master of a College,' are little more than lay-figures
grouped around the central character, the master of Calverley hall.

In him, we encounter a being of strange complexity of
character; at first sight a mere wastrel and ruffian, we realise,
as the play advances, the tragic fascination that he exercises.
Brought to a sense of his evil ways by the Master of a College,
he expresses in soliloquy thoughts which carry with them a
haunting power: 'O, would virtue had been forbidden! We
should then have proved all virtuous; for 'tis our blood to love
what we are forbidden.' The soliloquy ended, a tragic surprise
awaits the reader : remorse, which seems to be driving the husband
to repentance, is suddenly turned in a new direction by the impulse
of ancestral pride; and, instead of a repentant sinner, we are
confronted with a murderer, red-handed with the blood of his own
children, whom he slays lest they shall live 'to ask an usurer
bread.' The closing scene, though it contains Calverley's infinitely
pathetic speech, made over his children's corpses—

> Here's weight enough to make a heart-string crack, ...

is unequal to what has gone before.

There is no sufficient reason for ascribing the play to
Shakespeare. Powerful as it is, the workmanship is not Shakespearean, and the fact that a play written about 1606—7 should
introduce rime into some twenty-five per cent. of the total number
of verses is, in itself, it would appear, ample proof that the
ascription of the title-page is unwarranted[1].

Of the historical plays attributed to Shakespeare, but not
included in the first folio, the most important is *Edward III*.
The conjecture that he had a hand in this play was not put forward
during his lifetime, and rests entirely on internal evidence.
Edward III was first published, anonymously, in 1596, and a
second edition followed in 1599; but it was not until Capell
re-edited the play in his *Prolusions* (1760) that the claim for
Shakespearean authorship was seriously put forward.

Written in verse throughout, the play opens with a scene which
is similar to the first scene of *Henry V*; but no sooner are the

---

[1] As to the significance of *Arden of Feversham* and *A Yorkshire Tragedy* in the
history of English domestic drama, see *post*, vol. VI. chap. IV (Thomas Heywood).

preparations for king Edward's foreign campaign begun than the main action is impeded by the introduction of the romantic love story of the king and the countess of Salisbury, which occupies the rest of the first, and the whole of the second, act. Then, when the monarch has at last conquered his adulterous passion, the narrative of military conquest, with the prince of Wales as its hero, is resumed, and proceeds, without further break, along the path prescribed to the dramatist by Froissart and Holinshed. But, although the countess episode impairs the little unity of action which this desultory chronicle play would otherwise have, it must be remembered that that episode is no extraneous matter foisted into the play for the sake of dramatic effect; the author goes to Bandello, or, rather, to Bandello's English translator, William Painter, for the details of the story, but the main outlines of it are faithfully recorded by Froissart and subsequent chroniclers of English history. If, however, the double plot of the play furnishes, in itself, no reason for assuming double authorship, that assumption must, nevertheless, be made on other and more substantial grounds. In diction and verse, in the portrayal of character and in the attainment of dramatic effect, the author of the love scenes stands apart from the author of the battle scenes. The number of riming verses and verses with double endings in the love scenes, is considerably greater than in all the remainder of the play. Soliloquy is unknown in the battle scenes, whereas, in the countess episode, one-sixth of the total number of verses are spoken in monologue. The love scenes are also distinguished from the rest of the play by the strain of lyricism in which their author indulges; it would, indeed, be difficult to find in the whole range of Elizabethan drama a passage more completely imbued with lyric feeling than that in which Edward converses with Lodowick, his secretary[1]. It is not the tempestuous lyricism of Marlowe which we meet with here, but the elegiac lyricism of the sonneteers, the unfeigned delight in the play of amorous fancy and the fond lingering over airy sentiment. Characteristics such as these isolate the countess episode from the rest of the play, and, at the same time, associate it with much of the early work of Shakespeare, above all with *Romeo and Juliet*.

But, in the absence of all external authority, it would be unsafe to claim the episode for Shakespeare upon such evidence as this alone; and the same may be said for the resemblances of idea, imagery and cadence which many passages in these love scenes bear to passages in his canonical works. If the claim for Shakespearean authorship is to be put forward at all, it must be based

---

[1] Act II, sc. 1.

upon those elements of Shakespeare's genius which ever elude the grasp of the most skilful plagiarist—the creation of character, the reaching after dramatic effect and the impalpable spirit of dramatic art. It is in the person of the countess of Salisbury that the genius of Shakespeare first seems to reveal itself, and it has been well said that, without her, his gallery of female characters would be incomplete. She is a woman as resolute in her chastity as the Isabella of *Measure for Measure*, yet far more gracious and far less austere. We have only to compare her with the Ida of Greene's *James IV* to realise the masterly workmanship of the author of *Edward III*. The situation in which the two women are placed is almost identical; but, whereas Ida is a slight, girlish figure who, for all her purity, has little save conventional commonplace wherewith to rebut the Scottish king's proffers, the countess rises in the face of trial and temptation to supreme queenliness. And whereas, in his presentation of the story, Greene wastes every opportunity of bringing the love suit to a dramatic crisis, the author of the countess episode displays the highest art of plot construction.

When we compare the dramatic version of the story with that of the Italian novel, we realise at once the transforming touch of a master artist. The action in Bandello extends over a considerable period of time, during which the countess becomes a widow, but persists, in spite of the importunities of her mother, in rejecting the king's unlawful suit. At last, dagger in hand, she begs the king to slay her, or let her slay herself, in order that her chastity may be preserved. Then the king, impressed now by her fortitude as before by her beauty, offers her his hand in marriage, and the countess straightway accepts him as her husband. As we read the play, we realise how this Pamela ending offended the finer taste of the dramatist. Going carefully over the incidents of the story, he excises here, enlarges there, and, finally, brings his plot to a crisis and *dénouement* quite unlike, and infinitely nobler than, that of Bandello. The one dagger becomes two, and, in the countess's simple but burning words to the lascivious king, we feel ourselves in the presence of Shakespeare, and of Shakespeare rising at one genial leap to the full stature of his divinity:

> Here by my side do hang my wedding knives:
> Take thou the one, and with it kill thy queen,
> And learn by me to find her where she lies;
> And with this other I'll despatch my love,
> Which now lies fast asleep within my heart:
> When they are gone, then I'll consent to love [1].

[1] Act II, sc. 2.

A prime objection which has been brought against the Shakespearean authorship of these scenes is that they break in upon the action of the main story in a way that Shakespeare would not have tolerated. But a close study of the countess episode reveals the skill with which the dramatist has lessened this defect. Throughout the episode we are made aware that the preparations for the French campaign are proceeding, though the king is wholly absorbed in his amour. At the beginning of act II, sc. 2, Derby and Audley appear and inform their sovereign of the mustering of men and of the emperor's goodwill. The drum incident which follows, and which leads up to the entrance of the Black Prince, the hero of the main story, effects, in masterly fashion, the purpose of keeping the military scenes before the mind of the spectator. The king's soliloquies, too, as he beholds first his son all afire with military ardour, and then his secretary returning with a message from the countess, produce a feeling of true dramatic tension ; and, as we see the monarch borne this way and that by the impulse of contending passions, we realise once again the hand of the master.

If we ascribe the countess episode to Shakespeare, there still remains for consideration the difficult problem of determining the nature of his task. The choice lies between collaboration of Shakespeare with another dramatist and revision by Shakespeare of a play already in existence. The latter theory seems the more reasonable. The battle scenes, by virtue of their loose, episodic character, point to a date previous to that reform of the chronicle play which was effected by Marlowe's *Edward II* (*c.* 1590). If, then, we may conjecture the existence of a pre-*Edward III*, it may be further assumed that it contained already some rendering of the countess episode. Without it, the play would be too brief, and it is hard to believe that any dramatist, especially if he were Robert Greene or a member of Greene's school, would have allowed the romantic love story to pass unnoticed when reading the pages of Froissart. It is reasonable to believe that, at some time between 1590 and 1596, Shakespeare found himself engaged upon a revision of this pre-*Edward III* chronicle play, and that, in revising it, he left the story of the king's French wars practically unaltered, but withdrew entirely the rendering of the countess episode, substituting for it that pearl of great price which now lies imbedded in the old chronicle play.

The Life and Death of Lord Cromwell and *Sir Thomas More* are among the most notable examples in Elizabethan dramatic

literature of what has been called the biographical chronicle play—
an offshoot from the history or chronicle play proper, from which
it differs in that its theme is not the events of a reign but the
record of an individual life. Both of these plays have been
attributed to Shakespeare, the former because on the title-page
of the second edition of the play—that of 1613[1]—stand the words,
'written by W. S.,' and the latter, partly on internal evidence,
and partly on the curious theory, first advanced by Richard
Simpson, that some of the passages in the original manuscript
of the play (Harleian MSS 7368) are in Shakespeare's handwriting.

Cromwell is so devoid of genuine dramatic and poetic power
as to make its ascription to Shakespeare little better than an
insult. The scenes hang loosely together, nowhere is there any
sign of real grasp of character, and only the racy humour of Hodge,
Cromwell's servant, saves it from abject dulness. The desultory
plot is taken from Foxe's *Story of the Life of the Lord Cromwell*
in the second volume of *Actes and Monuments,* and there is no
reason to believe that the dramatist went to Bandello for his
account of Cromwell's dealings with the Florentine merchant,
Frescobaldi. Foxe had already borrowed this story from the
Italian novelist, and the dramatic version, throughout, is faithful
to Foxe's rendering of it. The conception of Cromwell as a popular
hero who, having risen to eminence, delights in remembering the
friends of his obscure youth, is, also, common to the biographer and
the dramatist, and both, again, agree in adopting a strongly, at
times blatantly, protestant standpoint. The studious omission
of Henry VIII from the characters of the play indicates that it
was written before the death of Elizabeth, and the general structure
and versification point to a date of composition anterior by some
years to its entry on the Stationers' register on 11 August 1602.

In every respect, *Sir Thomas More* is superior to *Cromwell.*
There is nothing to show that this play was ever published in
Elizabethan times; but the original manuscript is preserved in the
British Museum and was edited by Dyce for the Shakespeare
Society in 1844. The sources of the play, indicated by Dyce, are
Hall's *Chronicle,* and the biographies of More by his son-in-law,
William Roper, and his great-grandson, Cresacre More. The
dramatist shows considerable skill in the use of his materials, and
the plot, though episodic, approaches much nearer to dramatic
unity than that of *Cromwell.* The interest of the play lies chiefly
in the masterly and sympathetic portraiture of the great lord

[1] The first edition appeared in the year 1602.

chancellor. The idealism, the winning grace and fine sense of humour, the large humanity and the courage under affliction, which we associate with the name of Sir Thomas More, are admirably brought out. The quotations from Seneca and other Latin writers show that the author was a scholar, and the burden of some of More's speeches reveals a political thinker of no mean calibre. The introduction of the play within the play, together with More's speeches to the actors and his insertion into their scenes of an extempore speech of his own, is a curious anticipation of *Hamlet*. But those who attribute portions of the play to Shakespeare base their arguments not upon this, but upon the view that certain scenes are in his handwriting, and that the thought and diction of these scenes is unmistakably Shakespearean. As our knowledge of Shakespeare's handwriting is limited to five autograph signatures, it is difficult to attach great weight to the theory of Simpson and Spedding that 'hand D' in the *More* MS is the hand of Shakespeare; and there is also a good deal of difference of opinion among the experts as to how far 'hand D' extends. Simpson claimed for it act II, sc. 3 and 4, 1—172; act III, sc. 2 and 3. Subsequent investigators have detached some of these scenes, and the latest opinion—that of G. F. Warner, the keeper of MSS in the British Museum—is that only act II, sc. 4, 1—172 are in this hand. Since this passage is also that on which the literary claim for Shakespearean authorship mainly rests, a close examination of it is necessary. It tells the story of the insurrection of London citizens against the Lombard merchants settled in their midst, and contains the long and spirited speech with which More quells the riot. The talk of the rioters in the opening lines of the scene resembles, but is inferior to, that of Jack Cade's followers in *Part II of Henry VI* (act IV, sc. 2 and 3, and 6—8), and there was more than one dramatist in the last decade of the sixteenth century who, having the Jack Cade episode in mind, might have written these lines. The speech of More which follows is full of vigour, and is of peculiar interest as giving expression to the theory of the divinity of kings, which, in the late Tudor period, had come to be a widely accepted tenet of political faith. 'God,' says More,

> hath not only lent the king his figure,
> His throne and sword, but giv'n him his own name,
> Calls him a god on earth. What do you, then,
> Rising gainst him that God himself installs,
> But rise gainst God?...

It may be said that a similar view as to the divinity of the royal office is put forward by the aged bishop of Carlisle in *Richard II*; but can it seriously be contended that this was Shakespeare's own view? A scorner of democracy, he was far from being a believer in the divinity of kings. He treats the theory with mordant irony in *Richard II*, placing it on the lips of the hapless king[1] and proving its insufficiency by the remorseless logic of subsequent events. In *Henry V*, he returns to the same theme, and, in words which give forth no uncertain sound, makes his hero declare : 'I think the king is but a man, as I am ... all his senses have but human conditions; his ceremonies laid by, in his nakedness he appears but a man[2].'

The fact that *Sir Thomas More* was probably written about the same time as *Richard II*, and only a few years before *Henry V*, makes it hard to believe that such varying views as to the nature of the kingly office could have been held by the same man. Nor can escape from the difficulty be found by regarding More's speech as merely dramatic. It is more than this : it is lyrical in tone and *doctrinaire* in purpose ; and was probably intended to appease the master of the revels, who, when the first draft of the MS had been submitted to him, had demanded the excision of the whole of the insurrection scene.

The Birth of Merlin: Or, The Childe hath found his Father was first published in 1662 by the Restoration bookseller, Francis Kirkman, who ascribed it to 'William Shakespear and William Rowley.' The play is a medley in which legendary history, love romance, sententious praise of virginity, rough and tumble clown-play, necromancy and all kinds of *diablerie* jostle each other, and where British kings and English nobles, a hermit and a wizard, the wraiths of Hector and Achilles, the devil, Lucina and the three Fates, 'a little antick spirit' and Joan Go-to-'t, the mother of Merlin, are warring atoms contending for mastery over the spectator's attention, and combining to produce a play which defies classic rule utterly, but keeps at arm's length Pope's 'cloud-compelling queen,' Dulness.

It is almost certain that more than one hand was engaged in weaving this particoloured vesture ; but Kirkman's association of the play with the name of Shakespeare may be lightly dismissed. At no point in the course of the five stirring acts are we tempted, by plot construction, characterisation or style, to believe in Shakespearean workmanship. On the other hand, it is highly

---

[1] Act iii, sc. 2 and 3.   [2] Act iv, sc. 1, 105—110.

probable that William Rowley was one of its authors; the comic scenes, alike in their coarseness and racy humour, exhibit his manner, and it is also possible that some of the serious scenes are his. The question of authorship involves a comparison of the play with Middleton's *Mayor of Quinborough*, of which *The Birth of Merlin*, in its main plot, is both a sequel and a copy. An American scholar, F. A. Howe, has clearly shown that many of the scenes of the Merlin play were written in imitation of similar scenes in *The Mayor*, and that there is just as close an imitation in the elaboration of some of the leading characters. The dependence of the one play upon the other is certain; but, in spite of occasional resemblances of style, it is hard to believe that a dramatist of Middleton's acknowledged inventive power would have repeated himself in so abject a manner as he has done, if *The Birth of Merlin* be partly his work.

However this may be, it is probable that yet another hand may be detected in its composition. A notable feature in the play is the sacrifice which, in deference to the popular demand for realism, has been made of the romantic elements in the Arthurian legend. Yet, here and there, we are made aware of a certain consciousness on the dramatist's part of the glamour and magic beauty of the material under treatment. We feel this most in the presence of Uther Pendragon, the prince who, when we first encounter him, has disappeared mysteriously from his brother's court, in order to follow through forest wastes the quest of the unknown lady whose beauty has him in thrall:

> How like a voice that echo spake, but O!
> My thoughts are lost for ever in amazement.
> Could I but meet a man to tell her beauties,
> These trees would bend their tops to kiss the air,
> That from my lips should give her praises up...
> As I have seen a forward blood-hound strip
> The swifter of the cry, ready to seize
> His wishèd hopes, upon the sudden view,
> Struck with astonishment at his arriv'd prey,
> Instead of seizure stands at fearful bay;
> Or like to Marius' soldier, who, o'ertook,
> The eyesight-killing Gorgon at one look
> Made everlasting stand; so fear'd my power,
> Whose cloud aspir'd the sun, dissolv'd a shower [1].

In this and in other passages, drama is sacrificed to poetry, the verse grows lyrical and falls insensibly into rime. This romantic and lyrical strain is as foreign to Middleton as it is to Rowley,

[1] Act ii, sc. 2.

but it is singularly like what we meet with in the romantic work of Dekker. The passage quoted above is characterised not only by its lyricism, but, also, by frequent use of inversion, irregularity of verse and prevalence of rime; and, in each of these respects, it is thoroughly representative of the style of the more romantic scenes of the play, while, at the same time, it bears a marked resemblance to the authentic work of Dekker. The hand of the same dramatist can be detected in the Merlin scenes. Rowley may very well have created Joan Go-to-'t and her brother, and have acted as midwife to the marvellous boy prophet; but, when born, Merlin becomes the property of Dekker, and reveals his creator in the light-hearted *bravura* with which he performs his deeds of magic, no less than in the exercise of that strong moral sense by virtue of which he punishes the lust of his father the devil, makes a converted Bellafront of his mother and sends her to Salisbury plain, to waste away her offending flesh in groans and solitary sighs.

The sources of *The Birth of Merlin,* apart from *The Mayor of Quinborough,* are somewhat obscure. The story of Merlin was, of course, familiar enough in Elizabethan times, and a drama entitled *Uter Pendragon* is entered in Henslowe's diary under date 29 April 1597; the difficulty lies in determining what warrant, if any, the author had for degrading the circumstances of Merlin's birth.

The evidence in favour of the Shakespearean authorship of *Faire Em, Mucedorus* and *The Merry Devill of Edmonton* is of the slenderest. Francis Kirkman, the Restoration bookseller, having found in the royal library the three plays bound together in a volume on the back of which was the name of Shakespeare, accepted the word of the original owner—or the binder—of the volume without demur. The internal evidence of all three plays is strongly against the theory that Shakespeare had anything to do with their composition.

Faire Em is the work of some member of that early school of dramatists who, under the leadership of Greene, delighted in the union of fictitious English history with love romance. There are two distinct plots in this play, and they have almost nothing in common. That which furnishes the title is the story of the courtship by three knights of Fair Em, the daughter of an English noble who, robbed of his lands at the Norman conquest, is now plying the trade of a miller at Manchester. A ballad, entered on the Stationers' register on 2 March 1581, and entitled *The*

Miller's Daughter of Manchester, is the probable source of this portion of the play. The second plot is taken from Henry Wotton's *Courtlie Controversie* of *Cupids Cautels* (1578), a collection of five stories translated from Jacques Yver's *Le Printemps d'Iver*. This relates the unhistoric adventures of William the Conqueror, who, in order to win the hand of the Danish king's daughter, visits his court disguised as a knight and pursues his amours there under strange changes of fortune. The workmanship of the play is very poor, but certain allowances must be made for its early date. It seems to have been in existence in 1587, for, in Greene's introduction to his *Farewell to Folly*, registered in that year, he makes a satiric reference to *Faire Em*, and quotes, in a slightly altered form, two lines from the closing scene of the play.

The Merry Devill of Edmonton, although the earliest known edition of it is dated 1608, was certainly written by 1604, when T. M. (? Thomas Middleton) alludes to it, in company with *A Woman Kilde with Kindnesse*, in his *Blacke Book*; twelve years later, in the prologue to *The Divill is an Asse*, Jonson describes it as the 'dear delight' of the theatre-going public. The popularity which the play enjoyed was not unmerited; in the words of Charles Lamb, it 'seems written to make the reader happy.' In its blending of scenes of magic and the black art with a romantic love comedy, standing out against a pleasant background of English rural life, *The Merry Devill* recalls *Frier Bacon and Frier Bongay*. But the magic element in the play is little more than a sop to the popular taste of the day. After an induction, which is a serio-comic imitation of the famous closing scene in *Dr Faustus*, we hear little more of the doings of Peter Fabell, the Edmonton magician, and give ourselves up to the main story, which shows by what devices youth and true love overcome the treasonable counsels of age and prudence. The lovers are lightly conceived; but in their veins there flows the youthful spirit and romantic ardour of the early school of Elizabethan comedy, and Millicent, the heroine, who is willing to dare much lest love be 'smothered in foggy gain,' is worthy of a place not far below the early heroines of Shakespeare. The play is not Shakespeare's; but its author, alike in his love romance and in the humorous and realistic scenes in which Blague the host, Smug the smith and Sir John the priest appear, is one of Shakespeare's imitators. The character of the host of the George tavern at Edmonton is modelled, as Hazlitt pointed out, on that of the host of *The Merry Wives of Windsor*; and this fact furnishes us with a clue as to the period at which the play was written. The source of the story is unknown, but the adventures of Peter Fabell, who, in the district round about Enfield Chase, enjoyed something of the reputation of a Dr Faustus, had been already recorded. There was a poem, now lost but known to Warton, entitled *Fabyl's Ghoste*, written in octave stanzas and printed by John Rastell in 1533, which may be the same as *The Merry Pranks of Fabyl* mentioned by Weever; and, in the same year as that in which the play was published, Thomas Brewer's prose tract, *The Life and Death of the Merry Devill of Edmonton, with the Pleasant Pranks of Smug the Smith, Sir John and mine Host of the George about the stealing of Venison*, was entered at Stationers' Hall. These Fabell stories, doubtless, furnished the dramatist with some of the materials for the comic by-plot, but not for the romantic love story.

The popularity of *The Merry Devill of Edmonton* was as nothing compared with that of *A Most pleasant Comedie of Mucedorus, the kings sonne of Valentia and Amadine the kings daughter of Arragon, with the merie conceites of Mouse*. The earliest known edition of this play is dated 1598; but the words, 'newly set foorth,' on the title-page, indicate that it was first produced at some earlier date; numerous reprints followed, and W. W. Greg has succeeded in tracing no less than seventeen quarto editions of the play up to the year 1700. This popularity is the more remarkable since, as the epilogue makes clear, it was not written for popular representation, but for a performance at court. And, having delighted queen Elizabeth, it was revived, with numerous additions and an altered epilogue, for a Shrovetide performance at Whitehall early in the reign of James I. The text, thus enlarged and amended, was first published in 1610. The vogue of this 'very delectable' comedy, while it illustrates the uncritical temper of the age, is somewhat hard to understand; for the play, though doing credit to the infancy of Elizabethan romantic comedy, is, in respect of plot construction, characterisation and metric art, a very primitive piece of work. It teems, however, with action and romantic adventure, and these, with the crude wit and cruder folly of Mouse the clown, seem to have been deemed sufficient by courtier and groundling alike. A Spanish prince, who, in the prosecution of his love, disguises himself first as a shepherd and then as a hermit; a wild man of the woods, who combines cannibal instincts with a nice taste for romance; a rustic clown; and a bear that instructs the princess Amadine how to distinguish between the hero lover and the coward—these are the most notable ingredients of the play. The appearance of such morality figures as Envy and Comedy in the induction and epilogue is a sign of an early date of production, and it is hard to believe that the drama, in its original form, is later than 1590. The name Mucedorus, and the disguise of that prince as a shepherd, recall one of the two heroes of Sidney's *Arcadia*, and the probability is that the plot is taken from some half chivalrous and half pastoral romance of Spanish or Italian literature.

The London Prodigall and *The Puritane*, as already stated, are examples of realistic city comedy. At the hands of Heywood and Dekker, realism associated itself with romance; but, with Middleton and his successors, the romantic element was purged away, and nothing was allowed to interfere with the realistic, and often satirical, representation of contemporary manners. The authorship of these two plays is not easy to determine; but it can be stated without hesitation that neither is the work of Shakespeare, who, while interested in *bourgeois* comedy, rarely allowed it to force its way into the foreground. Both plays, probably, were written early in the seventeenth century, when Heywood and Middleton were making this type of drama acceptable to popular taste, and when Ben Jonson was also engaged in a close inspection of the social types of London life and in the discovery of humours.

The London Prodigall was first published in 1605, and the title-page of this edition informs us that the play was acted 'by the Kings Majesties servants' and that its author was William Shakespeare. It is full of bustling life, but is wholly wanting in the higher elements of dramatic art, and, also, in poetic beauty. The most striking feature in the plot is the resemblance, pointed out by A. W. Ward, which it bears to the Charles Surface story of Sheridan's *School for Scandal*. The wealthy father, Flowerdale senior, who has just returned to England after long years of absence, and who, under the disguise of a servant, attaches himself to his prodigal son and, in the end, pardons his excesses, is a crude prototype of uncle Oliver. But the author of the Elizabethan play fails, where Sheridan succeeds, in winning the reader's sympathy for the prodigal. Flowerdale junior's career of riot and neglect has no redeeming feature in it, and his final repentance, so far from convincing us of its reality and endurance, only deepens our pity for the outraged and extravagantly patient wife, Luce, who takes the repentant sinner to her bosom. The humour of the play is chiefly to be sought among the serving-men of the wealthy city knight, and in the persons of Sir Launcelot Spurcock, Weathercock the parasite and the Devonshire clothier Oliver, whose west country talk and manners have the homely honesty of the rough kersey cloth which he makes and wears. The disguise of Luce as a Dutchwoman, and the pigeon English by which, when thus disguised, she conceals her identity, may, very possibly, have been suggested by the similar disguise of Lacy in Dekker's highly popular play, *The Shoemaker's Holiday.*

The Puritane Or The Widdow of Watling-streete was one of the plays acted by the choristers of St Paul's, and it was published in 1607 as 'written by W. S.' It is a realistic comedy of intrigue, bordering, at times, upon farce, and its main object is ridicule of the puritan party and of London citizens. The scenes are mainly in prose, and the few passages in verse are wholly wanting in poetic feeling. The five acts are constructed out of a number of episodes of shrewd knavery, which follow one another in swift succession, but hardly form a plot. The moving spirit in these knavish tricks is a certain George Pyeboard, who makes the puritan family in Watling street his dupes up to the very last scene of the play, when the intervention of the nobleman as a *deus ex machina* exposes the chain of fraud. At least one of Pyeboard's knaveries is taken from the so-called *Merrie Conceited Jests of George Peele*[1], and it has long since been pointed out that, under the name of George Pyeboard, George Peele was intended[2].

There is no reason whatever for associating the play with Shakespeare; but its author, doubtless, was familiar with that dramatist's work, and refers in act IV, sc. 3 to the appearance of Banquo's ghost in *Macbeth.* It has been argued, with considerable show of reason, that it was written either by an Oxford student, or by a dramatist newly come from that university. The hero of the play is a student adventurer, who is acquainted with the academic phraseology of his university, while the author exhibits a fondness for Latin phrases, and lays much stress on the fact that a university scholar is a gentleman. Tucker Brooke ascribes the play to Middleton, and compares it with *Eastward Hoe.*

The only other play which calls for notice in this chapter is *The Two Noble Kinsmen,* the question of Shakespeare's share

---

[1] See Dyce's introduction to Peele's *Works*, p. viii.

[2] 'Peel' and 'pieboard' are synonymous terms for the flat wooden shovel used in taking pies out of a brick oven.

in which has evoked more discussion than all the remaining doubtful plays together. It was first published in 1634 as the work of 'the memorable worthies of their time, Mr John Fletcher and Mr William Shakespeare, Gent,' and the title-page of this edition also informs us that it had been performed by the king's players at the Blackfriars theatre. The famous Palamon and Arcite story which it reproduces had been dramatised before. Richard Edwards had written a *Palamon and Arcyte* as early as 1566, which was performed before Elizabeth by Oxford students on the occasion of the queen's visit to the university in that year; but the account of this lost academic comedy, preserved in Anthony à Wood's manuscripts and published in Nichols's *Progresses of Elizabeth,* suggests that it was very different in character from *The Two Noble Kinsmen.* Nothing is known of the *Palamon and Arsett* mentioned by Henslowe as having been acted at the Newington theatre in 1594.

The Two Noble Kinsmen follows Chaucer's *Knight's Tale* as closely as an Elizabethan play can be expected to follow a fourteenth century verse romance; but the dramatists, deferring to the seventeenth century taste for a realistic underplot to a romantic theme, have added the story of the gaoler's daughter, of which there is but the faintest hint in *The Knight's Tale.* The element of divine caprice which lurks in Chaucer's romance is by no means eliminated from the play. In the closing speech of the last scene, Theseus would fain convince us that, of the two rival kinsmen, Palamon has the better right to the lady—because he saw her first!—but the enduring impression which the play leaves upon the reader's mind is that man is but the puppet of fortune. And if the *dénouement* of the play is unsatisfactory, so, also, are the characters. Palamon and Arcite, except in the scene in which they first appear, are not well distinguished from each other; Theseus, though he discourses fine poetry, is a stilted and a vacillating figure, and Emilia, a poor faded copy of Chaucer's 'Emelye the sheene,' would be more in her place as Hotspur's comfit-maker's wife than as a warrior's bride. Finally, the underplot, the author of which endeavours to make up for his lack of invention by imitating familiar incidents in the plays of Shakespeare, is both unskilful and indelicate. Yet, with all these shortcomings —shortcomings which are largely due to the fact of double authorship—*The Two Noble Kinsmen* abounds in elements of greatness. It is a play which needs to be seen in order that the masque-like splendour of some of its scenes may be fully realised; but a mere perusal of it suffices to reveal its imaginative power, the ripeness and energy of the thought and the luminous colour of high romance in which it is steeped. Into it are poured the riches of classic legend, medieval romance, Elizabethan comedy and Jacobean masque, and, in the union of these varying elements, we recognise the genius of a dramatist who could subdue all things to harmony.

The problem of authorship is beset with difficulties, for, while it is certain that the play is the work of more than one author, it seems also probable that the workmanship of the two men is not sharply sundered, but that, in places, the hand of the one has been engaged in revising what the other had written. With the exception of Delius, who propounded the fanciful theory that *The Two Noble Kinsmen* is the work of an anonymous dramatist who deliberately set himself to imitate now the manner of Shakespeare and now that of Fletcher, critics are agreed that one of the two authors was Fletcher, and that to him may be allotted most of acts II, III and IV, including the whole of the underplot, with the possible exception of the two prose scenes[1], but only a small, and comparatively unimportant, part of the main story. The whole of the first act, the first scene in act III, and almost the whole of the last act are clearly not by Fletcher in the first instance, and in the determination of the authorship of these scenes lies the chief problem of the play. The choice seems to lie between Massinger and Shakespeare; it has been argued by Robert Boyle that the handling of the characters in these scenes is singularly unlike that of Shakespeare and singularly like that of Massinger, and that the frequent medical allusions, and the echoes of passages in Shakespeare's authentic works, furnish further evidence in favour of Massinger and against Shakespeare. Arguments such as these, though not without force, are outweighed by others on the opposite side. A comparison of the play with Massinger's scenes in *The Lover's Progress*, a play which introduces the similar theme of the love of two friends for one woman, shows the greatest variance in the application of the principles of dramatic art. The resemblance, too, between the verse of Massinger and that of the non-Fletcherian portions of *The Two Noble Kinsmen*, on which Boyle lays considerable stress, is only superficial. In the mechanical elements of poetic rhythm, Massinger comes very near to Shakespeare; but, when we look deeper, and come to the consideration

---

[1] Act II, sc. 1 and act IV, sc. 3.

of those features of style which do not admit of tabular analysis, we find the widest difference. The diction of Massinger is, above all things, orderly and lucid. He shows, at times, passion and imagination; but he never allows these to check the stately decorum and even flow of his verse. Now, the diction of *The Two Noble Kinsmen* is of a peculiar nature, and Spalding, in his famous *Letter*, with others after him, naturally directed his attention to this, above all other things, in attributing these non-Fletcherian scenes to Shakespeare. In the profusion of striking metaphors, the copious outpouring of profound thoughts and the extreme concision, often involving harshness and obscurity, of the utterance, these scenes bear a marked resemblance to the plays of Shakespeare's final period, and to nothing else in literature. Moreover, the very defects of these scenes are the same defects which we meet with in Shakespeare's so-called romances. The sacrifice of dramatic probability to the attainment of magnificent spectacular effects, the intrusion of the *deus ex machina* to cut the Gordian knot which human effort cannot disentangle and the triumph of the poetic and intellectual interests over the strictly dramatic—these are all features common to *The Two Noble Kinsmen* and the products of Shakespeare's genius in the last phase of his dramatic career.

CHAPTER XI

THE TEXT OF SHAKESPEARE[1]

THE text of Shakespeare is as uncertain as are the facts of his life. In neither case are we in possession of any real authorities. But, while there is evidence to establish the certainty of some of the incidents in his career, we cannot be sure of the accuracy of a single line in his plays. Not only are we without Shakespeare's manuscript, but we do not even possess an authorised edition of any play, such as we have of *Venus and Adonis* and *Lucrece*. The conditions under which plays were produced in the Elizabethan age supply us with two reasons for this, at first sight, extraordinary fact. Shakespeare, like his fellow dramatists, wrote for the stage and not for publication. The playwright's sole ambition was to see his play on the stage. Hardly any play was published by its author without some apology. Marston, in his preface to *The Malcontent* (1604), actually complains that he is detracting from the value of his work by publishing it; and he goes on to state that his reason for consenting to this is that, if he did not publish it, others would, thus inflicting upon him still greater injury. All rights in a play were tacitly, if not legally, surrendered to the acting company, and the author's interest in it ceased. No more striking proof of this attitude could be desired than the fact that Shakespeare himself described *Venus and Adonis* as 'the first heire of my invention,' at a time when he had certainly written several plays.

On the other hand, companies refrained from publication. They sought by this means to increase the profit from their performances. Thus, Thomas Heywood speaks of some of his plays being 'still retained in the hands of some actors, who think it against their peculiar profit to have them come in print.' But

[1] The references throughout are to *The Cambridge Shakespeare*, ed. Wright, W. Aldis, 1894.

this shortsighted policy on the part of the companies did not prevent others from supplying the demand for printed copies which naturally existed. In the absence of any strict laws of copyright[1], it is not surprising that publishers were found ready to snatch a profit by the surreptitious publication of the more popular plays of so favourite a writer as Shakespeare.

This explains the origin of the quartos, in which form the text of nineteen plays[2] first saw the light. As all these plays appear again in the folio edition (*Pericles* for the first time in the third folio), the relative value of the quarto and folio texts becomes the fundamental question for textual discussion. No generalisation is possible with regard to the quarto text, owing to its unequal character. But, for textual purposes, the quarto plays may be classified as duplicate, variant and doublet. The duplicate quarto plays are those in which the text of the first folio has been derived from that of one of the quartos. The first quarto, therefore, is entitled to rank as the only authoritative text for these eight plays[3]. The printing of some of these plays is equal to anything in the first folio ; that of *A Midsummer Night's Dream* is excellent. Their comparative freedom from corruption and their adoption by the editors of the first folio suggest that they were drawn from copies not far removed in date from Shakespeare's manuscript. The spelling of the quarto text is more archaic than that of the first folio. In many cases, it resembles that of the first quarto of the *Poems,* which may fairly be taken to represent Shakespeare's own spelling.

The text of the remaining quarto plays diverges to a very large extent from that of the folio, not only in respect of verbal differences, but by the addition or omission of passages amounting, in some cases, to thirty or forty lines, and even to whole scenes. In *Parts II and III of Henry VI, Henry V* and *The Merry Wives,* the omissions are all made by the quarto, as are also the most

---

[1] Companies gradually had their rights acknowledged, and, in 1637, the lord chamberlain issued an injunction to the Stationers' company, prohibiting the publication of plays without consent of the players.

[2] *Part II of Henry VI* (*First Part of the Contention,* Q_1 1594), *Part III of Henry VI* (*True Tragedie of Richard, Duke of Yorke,* Q_1 1595), *Richard II* (Q_1 1597), *Richard III* (Q_1 1597), *Romeo and Juliet* (Q_1 1597), *Love's Labour's Lost* (Q_1 1598), *Part I of Henry IV* (Q_1 1598), *Much Ado* (Q 1600), *A Midsummer Night's Dream* (Q_1 Q_2 1600), *The Merchant of Venice* (Q_1 Q_2 1600), *Part II of Henry IV* (Q 1600), *Henry V* (Q_1 1600), *Titus Andronicus* (Q_1 1600), *The Merry Wives* (Q_1 1602), *Hamlet* (Q_1 1603), *King Lear* (Q_1 1608), *Troilus and Cressida* (Q 1609), *Pericles* (Q_1 1609), *Othello* (Q_1 1622).

[3] *Love's Labour's Lost, A Midsummer Night's Dream, The Merchant of Venice, Part I of Henry IV, Much Ado, Pericles, Titus Andronicus* (with exception of one scene added in F_1), *Richard II* (part of scene added in Q_3).

serious omissions in *Part II of Henry IV*; in *Troilus and Cressida*, *King Lear* and *Othello*, they are fairly evenly divided. The greater completeness of the folio text constitutes it the chief authority for these variant quarto plays. An exception has to be noted in the case of *Richard III*. Here, the omissions in the folio are trifling, compared with those in the quarto; but textual evidence conclusively proves that the folio text follows two different quarto texts and contains systematic alterations. The first quarto, therefore, becomes the authoritative text for all except the omitted passages[1]. *Romeo and Juliet* and *Hamlet* are unique in possessing doublet quarto texts. The first quarto, in both cases, is very defective; but, in the case of the former play, the folio text was derived from the second quarto, while, in the case of the latter, the folio text was taken from a copy which was considerably less complete.

The great discrepancies in these texts demand some explanation. There can be little doubt that they are due, in the main, to the fact that the defective texts were based on copies which had been adapted for the stage. From the fact that Shakespeare wrote for the stage, it must not be inferred that he allowed himself to be bound by the exigencies of stage performance. The need of adaptation for stage purposes has always made itself felt in the case of the texts of plays, even to the present day; and it is highly probable that none of the longer plays of Shakespeare were ever produced in the theatre exactly as they were written. There is, moreover, definite evidence that the plays of other dramatists were shortened for the stage. It is in this sense that we are to understand the statement made on the title-page of the second quarto of *Hamlet*, 'newly imprinted and enlarged to almost as much againe as it was, according to the true and perfect Coppie,' and similar statements in the quartos of other plays.

The references in the prologue to *Romeo and Juliet* to 'the two hours traffic of our stage,' and in that of *Henry VIII* to 'two short hours,' fix the average length of a performance. The mere length of such plays as *Richard III*, *Hamlet*, *Othello*, *King Lear*, *Troilus and Cressida*, *Part II of Henry IV*, *Henry V*, necessitated curtailment. Thus, of the long scene in *Richard III*[2], numbering five hundred and forty lines in the folio, nearly eighty are omitted (including a passage of over fifty lines); the quarto text of *Hamlet* omits sixty lines of Hamlet's interview with Rosencrantz

---

[1] The genealogy of the text of *Richard III* is described in an appendix to this chapter.
[2] Act IV, sc. 4.

and Guildenstern concerning the players; and the folio text of *King Lear* lacks a whole scene, as well as a passage of nearly fifty lines.

Not only, however, the length of a play, but also the number of characters called for adaptation. Companies were often so thin that one player had to act two or three parts. A clear case of curtailment on this ground is the omission in the folio text of the dialogue between Hamlet and a lord, who comes to urge him to the rapier contest with Laertes. This is the only occasion on which this character appears. The folio text of *King Lear* omits the conversation between two servants after the putting out of Gloucester's eyes, probably for the same reason. Sometimes, speeches are put into the mouths of other characters, instead of being omitted altogether. In *Henry V*, Westmoreland's wish for ten thousand more men is transferred to Warwick.

A different reason for the omission of passages in the performance of a play was political expediency. Both Elizabeth and James I frequently witnessed stage performances, and a natural consequence of this personal patronage was a strict censorship of plays presented before them. Precarious as is any attempt to point out political allusions in Shakespeare, the magnificent compliment paid to 'the fair vestal throned by the west,' and 'her single blessedness,' would suffice to show that such allusions were, on occasion, introduced by him. The suppression of the deposition scene in the first quarto of *Richard II* was doubtless made out of deference to the queen's well known susceptibilities on the subject. In *King Lear*, Edmund's allusions to the results of the 'prediction,' in which James is said to have had some faith, and the reference to nobles acting as spies in France may have been suppressed on similar grounds. Portia's description of the 'Scottish' lord contains a satirical allusion to the alliances of Scotland with France against England. After the accession of James, the players, instead of omitting the passage, altered 'Scottish lord' to 'other lord,' which is the reading of the folio.

The legal restrictions with regard to the use of oaths and the profane use of Scripture account for the excision of a great number of passages and the modification of many expressions, especially in *Part II of Henry IV*. A few seem to be omitted in both quarto and folio on account of their lewdness. Other passages were struck out by the players because of their inherent obscurity. The corrupt passages in *Hamlet*, containing 'stars with trains of fire,' 'dram of eale,' 'that monster custom,' omitted entirely in the folio text, very likely owe their corruption to the tampering of the players.

The process of adaptation caused passages to be added as well as omitted. The clown's duty was to afford amusement to the spectators after the play was finished; but he was also expected to add specimens of his own native wit to his regular part in a play. This practice is referred to by Hamlet in a well known passage of his address to the players, to which the first quarto adds samples— 'Cannot you stay till I eate my porridge? and you owe me a quarters wages, my coat wants a cullison; And your beere is sowre.' The fool in *King Lear* is no mere clown[1]. It is probable that for portions of this, and for 'poor Tom's' parts, buffoonery was often substituted; which would account for the disturbed state of the text both in quarto and folio in these passages. The omission of the prologue to *Troilus and Cressida* in the folio may be explicable in the same way. The omission from the folio text of several other passages seems to confirm doubts as to their genuineness.

The mangled state of the text in the first quartos of *Parts II and III of Henry VI, The Merry Wives, Henry V, Romeo and Juliet* and *Hamlet* shows another disintegrating factor at work besides adaptation. Publishers who could not secure a copy of a play by any other means would employ a shorthand writer to report it, while it was being acted. This report, naturally, would be very imperfect; some poetaster would patch it up as best he could, and thus it found its way into print[2]. The numerous mistakes due to imperfect hearing confirm this view of the origin of these texts, such as 'tigers of Arcadia' for 'tigers of Hyrcania,' 'Cophetua' for 'Caveto' etc.

The first quartos of these plays have been regarded as earlier drafts subsequently revised by the poet. This theory is plausible with regard to *The Merry Wives*, where the quarto contains passages which evidently do not go back to the same original as the corresponding passages in the folio, and to the two parts of *Henry VI*, which appear under a different title. But the causes already enumerated are sufficient to account for the state of the quarto text; and, wherever this is admitted to be not only an

---

[1] The difficulty of acting this part has been often felt on the modern stage. Cf. Macready, W. C., *Reminiscences*, vol. ii, p. 97.

[2] Cf. the well known passage in Thomas Heywood, cited *post*, vol. vi, ch. iv. A specimen of the 'stenographer's' work is to be found in the first quarto version of Hamlet's famous soliloquy:

> To be or not to be, I there's the point,
> To Die, to sleepe, is that all? I all :
> No, to sleepe, to dreame, I mary there it goes, etc.

adaptation of the supposed earlier draft, but a garbled version of the adaptation, it is difficult to see how the question of revision can be fruitfully discussed.

Numerous minor omissions in the quartos are due to carelessness in copying either on the part of the players or the printers. In this way, a whole scene was omitted in earlier impressions of the quarto of *Part II of Henry IV*, but restored in later copies. The very numerous half-lines which still remain in the text may be attributed to this cause. Sometimes, a passage drops out owing to similarity of expressions at the beginning and end[1].

The text of the first folio has a more uniform value than that of the quartos. But, in two respects, it is, on the whole, hardly any more trustworthy. For the punctuation and metre of the plays, we are largely dependent on the work of modern editors. In individual cases, however, the metrical arrangement of the folio is vastly superior. In *King Lear,* the verse of the folio, to a large extent, is represented by prose in the quarto. The duplicate quarto plays, in which the folio text was drawn from one of the quartos, afford a test of its conjectural emendations. They are of little importance and generally for the worse. Where real corruption exists (*e.g.* 'perttaunt-like,' in *Love's Labour's Lost*) it is usually left alone.

Alternative readings are very common in the variant quarto plays. There is sometimes very little to choose between them; but, in such cases, the folio text is to be preferred, as having better authority. But, ordinarily, it is better in itself[2]. The quarto text, though often substituting a more usual word or phrase[3], occasionally preserves the unmistakable words of Shakespeare[4]. The inimitable 'Love's thrice *repured* nectar[5]' appears, in the folio, as 'reputed.'

Some critics have held that Shakespeare was responsible for

---

[1] For an example see *Othello*, act IV, sc. 2, 74—7.

[2] Thus, the pregnant line in *King Lear* (act II, sc. 4, 119) 'O me, my heart, my rising heart! But down' is, in the quarto, the commonplace 'O my heart, my heart!' 'Come unbutton here' (act III, sc. 4, 107—8) is, in the quarto, the nonsensical, 'Come on, be true.'

[3] Thus, Othello's striking words (act. v, sc. 2, 13),

I know not where is that Promethean heat
That can thy light relume,

are robbed of their force by the substitution of 'return' for 'relume.' Lear's no less striking epithet, 'cadent' tears, becomes the meaningless 'accent' tears.

[4] Othello's 'She gave me for my pains a world of sighs' (act I, sc. 3, 159) is, for instance, turned by the folio into the hackneyed 'a world of kisses.'

[5] *Troilus and Cressida*, act III, sc. 2, 21.

corrections and additions in the folio text of these plays. This assumption leaves out of account two important facts. In certain cases, it is unquestionably the quarto text which has been altered, and which has received additions. Moreover, it is obvious that these changes could not have been made for stage purposes. They must, therefore, have been made with a view to printing the plays; but it is surely inconceivable that Shakespeare should have made these minute corrections without also authorising an edition of the revised plays.

In the case of the doublet quarto plays, the folio text, as we have seen, is subordinate to that of the second quarto. The first quarto of *Romeo and Juliet* is a valuable corrective. In spite of its *lacunae*, it was evidently made by a skilful reporter, for it contains many unquestionably genuine readings, where all the rest have gone astray[1]. In *Hamlet*, when the readings of the first quarto and folio coincide, they are to be preferred[2]. The intrinsic value of the first folio lies in the fact that it contains the only extant text of eighteen plays; but its merits are unequal. The text of some of the plays is as good as that of the duplicate quartos; that of the rest recalls the characteristics of the text of the variant quartos. *Measure for Measure, All's Well, Cymbeline, Coriolanus* and *Macbeth* are among the worst texts in the folio. It is practically hopeless to determine the metre of *Timon*, in large portions of which it is impossible to tell whether verse or prose is intended. *Julius Caesar* holds the same position among the folio plays which *A Midsummer Night's Dream* has among the quartos. The text is free from any serious error and might well have been printed from the original manuscript.

The value of the later folios is comparatively small. They take great liberties with the text, though, it must be admitted, not beyond those taken by some of the later editors. When the second folio makes an alteration, this is, as a rule, perpetuated in the third and fourth. Where the second or third stands alone, it is nearly always wrong. The fourth folio is not so free in making alterations, except in order to modernise the spelling. Were it not for the legacy of errors inherited from the second and third, the

---

[1] Thus, Romeo's wish (act i, sc. 4, 113),

> But He, that hath the steerage of my course,
> Direct my sail,

is preserved by it, when the other quartos and the folio read 'sute' for 'sail.'

[2] Thus, the 'fretful porpentine' of the ghost's speech (act i, sc. 5, 20) has greater textual authority than the 'fearfull porpentine' of the later quartos, because it is supported by two independent copies.

fourth would often be nearer a modern text than either. The later folios, however, have all made some happy restorations of the text[1]. In the case of the variant quarto plays, where a later folio agrees with the quarto against the first, we have a better attested reading. There are some remarkable cases of this co-incidence[2].

One cause of variation between the different quarto and folio texts remains to be noted. It is the most prolific and the most modern of all—the mistakes of editor and printer.

Special causes for these mistakes are to be found, first, in differences of spelling in vogue in the Elizabethan age, *e.g.* 'antique' and 'antick,' 'rights' and 'rites,' 'symboles' and 'cymbals.' Again, an uncommon word sometimes caused the substitution of one more usual: 'moe' and 'more'; 'intentively' and 'instinctively'; 'foy-sons' and 'poisons'; 'prescience' and 'patience'; 'unprevented' and 'unprepared.' This practice was a thoroughly characteristic licence at a time when an editor had no hesitation in substituting a word which he considered more suitable to the context—'unprofit-able' for 'improbable'; 'the way to study death' for 'the way to dusty death'; 'phlegmatick' for 'choleric.' Thirdly, contractions commonly used in manuscripts often caused variations in the endings of words: 'h'as' and 'hath'; w^c = which; y^e = the; y^t = that; y^u = thou or you; I = ay; 'ignomie' and 'ignominy'; 'conster' and 'con-strue.' The abbreviation 'L.' doubtless accounts for such variations as 'liege' and 'lord.' Finally, there were the ordinary misprints with which everyone is familiar—due to the dropping out of letters ('contradict' and 'contract'; 'remuneration' and 'remura-tion'); to the omission of words ('his trusty Thisby's' Qq, 'his Thisby's' F_1, 'his gentle Thisby's' $F_2 F_3 F_4$); to wrong letters ('Loue' Q_1 (Duke of Devonshire's copy), 'Ioue' Q_1, 'Ioane' $F_1 F_2$, 'Joan' $F_3 F_4$); to wrong punctuation (the first folio reads 'Dispatch Enobarbus.' As Enobarbus is not present, the second, third and fourth read 'Dispatch Eros.' The right punctuation solves the difficulty: 'Dispatch. Enobarbus!'); to permutation of letters ('Athica' for 'Ithaca'); to repetition of letters ('involverable' F_1,

---

[1] One of the best is to be found in *Coriolanus* (act II, sc. 3, 18). The third citizen says: 'not that our heads are, some brown, some black, some auburn, some bald, but that our wits are so diversely coloured.' The fourth folio was the first to suggest 'auburn' for 'Abram,' which is read by the first three.

[2] Thus, an uncommon word 'renege' is restored by the second folio in *King Lear*, act II, sc. 2, 73, where the first folio reads 'Revenge' and the quartos have 'Reneag.' In *Othello*, act V, sc. 2, 350, 'base Indian,' the reading of the quartos and later folios, has greater textual authority than the 'base Judean' of the first folio.

'invaluerable' $F_2 F_3 F_4$, for 'invulnerable'). Such is the process by which the text of Shakespeare has been evolved—a process precisely similar to that undergone by any classical text. The quartos and folios represent the work of copyists—that of editing follows.

The subsequent history of Shakespeare's text falls, naturally, into two divisions—a period of conjecture, during which the great bulk of accepted emendations were made, and a period of consolidation, in which a fuller knowledge of the old copies and a firmer grasp of textual principles combined to produce the received text of today.

It was fitting that a poet laureate should be the first to give to the world an edition of Shakespeare—whether or not poetic gifts are an advantage to an editor. At all events, Nicholas Rowe (1709)[1] was engaged on a more profitable task when he attempted to edit the works, than when he endeavoured to emulate the style, of Shakespeare. Rowe's main object, as Johnson says, was to publish an edition of Shakespeare, 'like those of his fraternity, with the appendages of a life and a recommendatory preface.' Therefore, it is not surprising that his work shows little critical method. He based his text on the latest and worst copy—the fourth folio. This error affected all editions before Capell, for each of the succeeding editors was as uncritical as Rowe in basing his text on the edition immediately preceding his own. Although Rowe says, 'I have taken some care to redeem him from the injuries of former impressions,' and speaks of comparing 'the several editions,' he can hardly have possessed any acquaintance with old copies. His corrections of the fourth folio, sometimes, coincide with the readings of the first, as where he reads 'dread trident' for 'dead trident' of the later folios. In general, however, he follows the fourth, even where the first obviously contains the genuine reading. He occasionally consulted a late quarto: textual evidence shows that he used the quarto of 1676 for the additions in *Hamlet*. His alterations were made simply with a view to rendering the plays more intelligible, and he did much useful pioneer work to this end. His knowledge of the stage enabled him to add lists of *dramatis personae* to each play, to supply stage directions and to make divisions into acts and scenes, which, to a large extent, have been followed by modern editors. Many proper names were restored by him (as 'Plutus' for 'Platus').

---

[1] The date mentioned, in each case, is that of the first edition.

Others, which had been manufactured by his predecessors, were unmasked (thus 'Cyprus' grove becomes 'cypress'). Thanks to his linguistic attainments, he was able to make sense of a good deal of nonsense, which did duty in the folios for French or Italian. Dr Caius's 'green-a-box' of ointment appears in the folios as 'unboyteene' instead of '*un boitier*,' as in Rowe. But his work for the text rises above that of a proof corrector. Some of his conjectures deserve a place beside those of his more eminent successors. Few quotations are more firmly established than 'Some are born great.' (The folios have 'are become.') And 'the temple-haunting martlet' in *Macbeth* is not likely to be ousted from the place occupied in the folios by 'Barlet.'

No one will dispute Rowe's modest claim that he has 'rendered many places intelligible that were not so before.' It is his unique distinction that he did not stir up any controversy. His emendations were silently introduced into his text, and as silently appropriated by his successors.

To Pope belongs the unenviable distinction of having introduced into the study of Shakespeare's text that controversial acrimony of which echoes were heard far on into the nineteenth century. But his edition (1723—5) is quite free from this blemish. Instead of expanding his notes, which are models of brevity, he curtailed the text to suit his 'private sense,' and filled his margin with rejected passages. Some of these, it is true, were no great loss, though Pope was hardly qualified for expurgating Shakespeare. Others, however, seriously interfere not only with the sense, but with the conceptions of the dramatist. Mercutio is robbed wholesale of his jests. Much of Caesar's distinctive braggadocio is struck out. Again, the porter's soliloquy in *Macbeth* is dispensed with, and so are several lines of Richard's soliloquy before the battle. *Romeo and Juliet* fares worst of all ; many passages being omitted on the pretext that they do not occur in the defective first quarto, while others are inserted because they appear in the second, and others, again, are struck out simply because they are 'nonsense' or 'trash' or 'ridiculous.' It is difficult to understand how a poet could deliberately reject such a line as 'Sleep that knits up the ravell'd sleave of care.' Occasionally, a line is dropped out altogether, without warning or comment. Pope's text is further marred by hundreds of verbal alterations for which no justification is even attempted. A small proportion of these may be regarded as legitimate conjectures ; but the great majority are arbitrary corrections, not of copyists' errors, but of

Shakespeare's own composition. We are left to guess the reasons for his changes. In many instances, they are obviously made to harmonise the metre with the ideal of rigid uniformity which dominated the Augustan age ('brest' for 'bosom,' 'lady' for 'gentlewoman,' 'foes' for 'enemies'). Monosyllables are omitted or inserted with the utmost licence to produce a regular line. Uncommon forms of expression, or words employed in an unusual sense, are rarely allowed to stand. (The 'untented woundings of a father's curse' become 'untender'; 'I owe you no subscription' is altered to 'submission'; 'to keep at utterance,' that is, to the last extremity, has to make way for 'to keep at variance.') Such reckless alterations have obscured Pope's real contribution to the study of Shakespeare's text. Compared with the work of Rowe, his services may justly be called great. That he thoroughly understood the nature of his task is abundantly clear. His preface—the only part of his work which he brought to perfection—contains a careful and accurate characterisation of the quarto and folio texts. The theory that 'the original copies,' referred to by the editors of the first folio, were 'those which had lain ever since the author's day in the play-house, and had from time to time been cut or added to arbitrarily,' is there found for the first time. Pope evinces an acquaintance with all the most important quarto texts. If he was too ready to suspect interpolations, nevertheless he was responsible for the insertion of most of the passages in the variant quarto plays, which were omitted in the first folio. Although he made havoc of the text of *Romeo and Juliet* by his excisions, he instinctively introduced a number of undoubtedly genuine readings from the first quarto. He has often unravelled Shakespeare's verse from the prose of the old copies, and in almost every play the metrical arrangement of the lines owes something to him. Many of his conjectures have been generally accepted. He restored a realistic touch in 'Tarquin's ravishing strides' where the first folio has 'sides,' and he recovered Falstaff's '*oeillades*' from the 'illiads' of all the folios. On the other hand, the cause of Pope's failure is revealed in his own phrase: 'the dull duty of an editor.' He had been invited to undertake the work as the first man of letters of his day; and he deals with the text in the spirit of a dictator. But the laborious task of collating texts could not be accomplished by the sheer force of poetic genius. Had he possessed an army of collaborators for doing the drudgery, Pope's edition of Shakespeare might have achieved as great a success as his translation of Homer. As it was, the work was only half done.

Yet it might still have brought him some fame, had it not been doomed to pass through the ordeal of criticism at the hands of one who has few rivals as a textual critic. All its defects were laid bare by Lewis Theobald in his *Shakespeare Restored* (1726). No one could read this work—monumental in the history of Shakespeare's text—without acknowledging that here, at any rate, Pope had met more than his match. Pope was too wise to attempt to defend himself against criticism, which he, better than anyone else, knew to be unanswerable. In his second edition, he calmly adopted many of Theobald's corrections ; and, then, he began a campaign of misrepresentation and abuse which culminated in his making Theobald the hero of *The Dunciad.* The power of satire, wielded by genius, has never been more strikingly displayed. Pope's caricature of the foremost of all textual critics of Shakespeare as a dull, meddling pedant without salt or savour not only led astray the judgment of the sanest critics of the eighteenth century, but infected the clear reason of Coleridge, and has remained the current estimate to this day. Theobald's method of retaliation was unfortunate. He remained silent while Pope was exhausting every mean device to ruin his projected edition. But, when that edition (1733) became a triumphant fact, he emptied the vials of his wrath into his notes. Those who are aware of the unprecedented provocation which he received and of the superiority of which he must have been conscious find no difficulty in acquitting him ; but the majority who read only Theobald's notes must perforce join with Johnson in condemning his 'contemptible ostentation.' Every correction adopted by Pope from *Shakespeare Restored* in his second edition is carefully noted, although Theobald himself appropriated many of Pope's conjectures without acknowledgment. Every correction of Theobald's own, if but a comma, is accompanied by shouts of exultation and volleys of impotent sarcasm. But he overreached himself. Though smarting under the 'flagrant civilities' which he received from Pope, he paid him the unintentional compliment of taking his text as the basis of his own. Had he been as anxious to adhere faithfully to his authorities as he was eager to dilate on the faithlessness of Pope, he would hardly have fallen into the error of following the edition which he himself classed as 'of no authority.' It has sometimes been stated that Theobald based his text on the first folio. But the very numerous instances in which he has perpetuated Pope's arbitrary alterations in his own text show that this was not the case. Yet the multitude of readings which he restored both from the quartos

and from the first folio largely neutralised the effect of this error[1].   It
is in dealing with real corruption that Theobald is seen at his best,
and remains without a rival.   His acuteness in the detection of
errors is no less admirable than is the ingenuity shown in their
correction.   His thorough knowledge of Shakespearean phraseology,
his sound training in 'corrupt classics,' and also his fine poetic
taste, were qualifications which contributed to his success.   The
importance of Theobald's conjectures may be gathered from the
words of the editors of *The Cambridge Shakespeare*: 'Where the
folios are all obviously wrong, and the quartos also fail us, we
have introduced into the text several conjectural emendations;
especially we have often had recourse to Theobald's ingenuity[2].'
It is not surprising that the gift of conjecture revealed in these
brilliant restorations led Theobald to make many unnecessary
changes in the text.

Some of these abortive attempts were adopted by Sir Thomas
Hanmer in his edition (1744), which was based, however, on that of
Pope.   He provided an *édition de luxe* for gentlemen of his own
class.   The print and binding were magnificent, and caused its
value to rise to nine guineas, when Warburton's edition was going
for eighteen shillings.   Pope has celebrated this, its chief feature,
in the well known picture of Montalto and his 'volume fair[3].'
On its title-page, the text is said to have been 'carefully revised
and corrected by the former editions'; but there is no evidence
that the old copies were consulted.   Hanmer is nearer the mark
when he says in the preface that it was only 'according to the best

---

[1] One example may be taken out of hundreds. Bolingbroke compares the meeting
of himself with king Richard to that

> Of fire and water, when their thundering shock
> At meeting, tears the cloudy cheeks of heaven.

This is the reading of the first quarto. The later quartos, followed by the folios and
Rowe and Pope, read 'smoak' (smoke) for 'shock.' Theobald's note reads: 'This is
the first time, I believe, we ever heard of a *thundering smoak*: I never conceived
anything of a more silent nature. But this is a *nostrum* of the wise editors, who
imagine, I presume, that the report and thundering of a cannon proceed from the
"smoak" and not from the explosion of the powder.'

[2] We could hardly imagine the fat knight dying unless ' a' babbled o' green fields.'
Yet this touch of mingled humour and pathos is due to the bold and brilliant conjecture of Theobald—bold, because the quartos entirely omit the passage; brilliant,
because never did an emendation more aptly fit both text and context. The folios
read 'and a table of green fields.' No less brilliant, though less familiar, is the
restoration of the true poetry of Shakespeare in the image of the opening flower which
'dedicates its beauty to the sun.' Quartos and folios read 'same.' The very name
of the 'weird' sisters comes from him. He did not think the 'weyward' of the folios
a very suitable epithet, and, on searching Holinshed, he found the word which, doubtless, Shakespeare used.

[3] *The Dunciad*, bk. iv, ll. 105 ff.

of his judgment' that he attempted 'to restore the genuine sense and purity' of the text.   He relegated to the bottom of the page all the passages which Pope had thus degraded, and added several others, thinking it a pity that 'more had not then undergone the same sentence.'   His emendations are numerous, and are generally made in the reckless spirit of Pope; but his natural acuteness produced some conjectures of value[1].   William Warburton had corresponded with both Theobald and Hanmer on the text of Shakespeare.   He had sympathised with the former in his controversy with Pope, whom in some of his letters he attacked with such vigour that, had Pope been acquainted with them, the subsequent friendship between them would have been impossible. Theobald inserted some of Warburton's conjectures in his text, and printed his notes with his name.   After the appearance of Theobald's edition, Warburton thought it well to quarrel with him; he also quarrelled with Hanmer, when he discovered that he was contemplating an edition of Shakespeare.   In the preface to his own edition (1747), he accused both of plagiarism, a charge which might have been made with more justice against his own edition. He eulogised Pope, whose name he placed by the side of his own on the title-page, only, however, to depart from his text; while he denounced Theobald, only to adopt his edition as a basis.   The title-page blatantly boasts that 'the Genuine Text (collated with all the former editions, and then corrected and emended) is here settled.'   If we naturally wonder how 'the genuine text' can require correction, all wonder ceases when we have become acquainted with Warburton's methods.   His knowledge of the old copies was mostly gained from Pope and Theobald.   In the opening scene of *King Lear,* he comments on Theobald's reading ''tis our fast intent'—'this is an interpolation of Mr Lewis Theobald, for want of knowing the meaning of the old reading in the quarto of 1608, and first folio of 1623; where we find it "'tis our first intent."' Unfortunately for Warburton's reputation, Theobald's 'interpolation' is simply the reading of the first folio.   His ignorance of the old texts is only exceeded by his ignorance of Shakespeare's language.   His conjectures would furnish a curiosity shop of unused and unheard of words.   He strains at a gnat, it may be, and then swallows his own camel.   'Following' is changed to 'follying,' which we are told means 'wantoning'; 'jewel' becomes

---

[1] Polonius's 'I'll sconce me even here,' is due to Hanmer's conjecture for 'silence,' and Helena's 'Yours would I catch,' for the reading of the quartos and folios, 'Your words I catch,' in *A Midsummer Night's Dream.*

'gemell,' from the Latin *gemellus* 'a twin'; 'Venus' pigeons' ought to be called 'Venus' widgeons'; for 'beauty's crest,' Shakespeare, without question, wrote 'beauty's crete' *i.e.* beauty's white, from *creta*; 'shall damp her lips' is nonsense which should read 'shall trempe' *i.e.* moisten, from French *tremper*; Lear's 'cadent tears' should be 'candent' *i.e.* hot. For 'black-corner'd night,' we must read 'black-cornette' night, *cornette* being a woman's headdress for the night. 'My life itself and the best heart of it' is denounced as a 'monstrous' expression. 'The heart is supposed the seat of life; but as if he had many lives and to each of them a heart, he says his "best heart." A way of speaking that would become a cat rather than a king.'

Bentley is reported to have said that Warburton was a man of 'monstrous appetite but very bad digestion.' At any rate, this description is true of his work as an editor. There is, however, a halfpennyworth of bread with this intolerable deal of sack. 'Like a God, kissing carrion' of the sun, in *Hamlet*, Johnson called a 'noble' emendation for the 'good kissing carrion' of the quartos and folios. 'The wolf behowls the moon,' for 'beholds'; 'eyeless night' for 'endless night,' and 'gentle fine' for 'gentle sin,' are other favourable specimens. But, in spite of these, Warburton's false criticism of Theobald, that 'he left his author in a ten times worse condition than he found him,' is not far from the mark, when applied to his own performance. Warburton's edition was very effectively criticised by 'Another gentleman of Lincoln's Inn'— Thomas Edwards—who made 'tragical mirth' out of his 'genuine text.' John Upton, Zachary Grey and Benjamin Heath also joined in the onslaught.

Nearly twenty years elapsed before another edition appeared. But there were two men busy with the text, in the interval. One was Samuel Johnson; though his critics were wondering when the subscribers would get their book[1]. It appeared, at last, in 1765. The text was based on Warburton's edition; but all his ἅπαξ λεγόμενα were carefully excised. Ill as Johnson was equipped physically for the arduous work of collating texts, he was responsible for restoring many readings from the old copies, which had escaped Theobald's vigilance. Some of these are of the minutest character (such as 'momentany' for 'momentary,' 'fust' for 'rust'). He also brought back several passages from the quartos, which were

---

[1]
He for subscribers baits his hook
And takes your cash, but where's the book?

Churchill, *The Ghost*, book III.

wanting in the folio. He made no striking conjectures, but several useful emendations by him have passed into the text of today. He was attacked with uncalled-for vehemence by William Kenrick, who undertook to expose his 'ignorance or inattention.' As a matter of fact, Johnson's text had a distinct value, due to his own restorations; this, however, was speedily eclipsed by the publication of Capell's edition in 1768.

Scientific criticism of the text begins with Edward Capell. He was the first to base his text actually on the quartos and folios; and later editors, even when they go back to the original authorities, owe an incalculable debt to his painstaking and remarkably accurate collation of the old copies. Ever since the publication of Hanmer's edition, Capell had been silently laying his foundations. He is said to have transcribed the whole of Shakespeare ten times. His services, like those of Theobald, have been greatly underrated. An involved style obscured the value of his preface, quite the best piece of textual criticism in the eighteenth century. An unfortunate method, which caused him to avoid noting anything at the foot of the page, except the original reading which had been changed in the text, failed to reveal the prodigious labour which he underwent to form his text, and transferred the credit of it to others. His discrimination between the quarto and folio texts, on the whole, is remarkably accurate. He rightly gave the preference to the first quarto in the case of the duplicate quarto plays; but he certainly underestimated the value of the folio text when he said that 'the faults and errors of the quarto are all preserved in the folio, and others are added to them: and what difference there is, is generally for the worse on the side of the folios.' He did not, however, act on this opinion, for he often adopts the folio reading, after taking the quarto as his basis. He made a thorough investigation of Shakespeare's versification, and his arrangements of lines are often those which are now generally adopted[1]. His care for the metre led him to introduce many words into the text. In fact, he was far too free in introducing conjectures. The original readings are always given at the bottom of the page; but neither these nor the conjectures are assigned to any one. Although he adopted the most important of Theobald's conjectures, it is remarkable that he should speak of Theobald's edition as 'only a little better than Pope's by his having a few more materials, of which he was not a better collator than the other, nor did he excel him in

---

[1] An example is to be found in the opening scene of *Hamlet*, 'Give you good night,' etc.

use of them.' His own conjectures (distinguished by black type), as a rule, are not happy; but there was no justification for Johnson's slighting opinion that his abilities were 'just sufficient to select the black hairs from the white for the use of the periwig makers.' Three quarto volumes of notes published after his death gave some idea of the labour which his neat little edition had cost.

George Steevens, who, in 1766, had done good service by printing twenty old quartos, was, in 1773, associated with Johnson in bringing out a new edition of Shakespeare. The text of this edition was the best that had yet appeared. It contained all the most important conjectures hitherto made, and, owing to the removal of many unnecessary emendations which Capell had introduced, was more faithful to the original copies than that editor's text had been. But it is quite certain that Capell's text formed the basis of Steevens's collation, and that to it was largely due the accuracy of the resultant text. In his advertisement, Steevens says

The Second Part of King Henry VI is the only play from that [Capell's] edition which has been consulted in the course of this work; for as several passages there are arbitrarily omitted, and as no notice is given when other deviations are made from the old copies, it was of little consequence to examine any further. This circumstance is mentioned, lest such accidental coincidences of opinion, as may be discovered hereafter, should be interpreted into plagiarism.

The criticism of Capell's text here offered by Steevens is sheer misrepresentation. The only 'passages' omitted by Capell are a few lines inserted by Theobald from the defective quarto and also omitted by Malone and the editors of *The Cambridge Shakespeare*. All Capell's deviations from the folio, except the most trifling, are scrupulously noted by him. Thus, Steevens's statement as to the use made by him of Capell's text, while suspicious in itself, must be altogether rejected; as a matter of fact, he follows Capell, in the main, even to his punctuation, and also adopts some of his conjectural emendations.

A second edition of Johnson and Steevens's text appeared in 1778, Edmond Malone contributing an *Essay on the Chronology of Shakespeare's Plays* and a few notes. In 1780, he published a supplement to this edition, containing the *Poems* and an intimation of his intention to bring out a new edition of the whole of the poet's works. Steevens had now retired from the field and cast his mantle on Isaac Reed, who brought out the third edition in 1785. To this, Malone contributed some notes occasionally opposing the *dicta* of Steevens, whereupon the latter demanded that his original notes should be printed word for word in any future edition. Malone, of course, would not listen to such a proposal, and the usual separation ensued. Malone's edition appeared in 1790. There can be no doubt that he went back to the old copies for his text, which shows a scrupulous fidelity to the quartos and folios, and a preference for the first folio in the case of the variant quarto plays. Indeed, it may be said that 'faith unfaithful kept him falsely true,' for he rejects such obviously certain conjectures as Theobald's 'dedicate its beauty to the sun.' He did not study the text of previous editors with the care which he devoted to the old copies, and, in several cases, he assigns an emendation to the wrong person. Malone made a careful investigation of the relative value of quartos and folios. He is not far wrong when he says that the editor of the second folio and Pope 'were the two great corrupters of our poet's text.' Steevens now once more comes upon the scene; but his reappearance ruined his reputation as a textual critic. He published a new edition in 1793, with the sole object of displacing that of Malone. It was obviously impossible for Steevens to surpass Malone in fidelity to the quartos and folios; hence, he declares

it is time instead of a servile and timid adherence to the ancient copies, when (offending against sense and metre) they furnish no real help, that a future editor, well acquainted with the phraseology of our author's age, should be at liberty to restore some apparent meaning to his corrupted lines, and a decent flow to his obstructed versification.

Steevens took this liberty and emulated Pope in 'indulging his private sense.' Hallam's estimate of the two editors is just:

Malone and Steevens were two laborious commentators on the meaning of words and phrases; one dull, the other clever; but the dulness was accompanied by candour and a love of truth, the cleverness by a total absence of both.

A new edition of Malone's text was brought out by a son of James Boswell, Johnson's biographer, in 1821. It contains an accumulated mass of information, which has been of great service to later editors. But the confused arrangement of its contents and the bulk of its notes entailed upon Malone a reputation for dulness and stupidity which approaches that of the first hero of *The Dunciad.* Walpole said that Malone's notes were an 'extract of all the opium that is spread through the works of all the bad playwrights of that age'; and, among later writers, G. H. Lewes has endeavoured to exaggerate this censure[1].

---

[1] Boswell's chief service to the text was his final vindication of the reading 'like

Of detached criticism on Shakespeare's text, the *Observations and Conjectures* of Thomas Tyrwhitt (1766) is worthy of mention. Joseph Ritson shows some acquaintance with the original authorities in his *Remarks* (1783) and in *The Quip Modest* (1788), in which he criticises Johnson and Steevens's edition and Reed's revision. Monck Mason's *Comments* (1785) and further *Comments* (1807) contain some of the best detached criticism of the time. Malone's text left nothing to be done which faithful adherence to the old copies could achieve. But the variant quarto plays still afforded scope for critical discrimination between the readings of quarto and folio.

Nineteenth century editors may be distinguished broadly by their attitude to these two texts. Samuel Weller Singer (1826) mainly followed the text of Malone. He led a revolt against superfluous notes and bulky volumes ; but he went to the opposite extreme. Out of scores of emendations incorporated in it, chiefly from Theobald, only a few are assigned to their authors, while, in the *Life* prefixed to the edition, we are told that 'Theobald did not wholly abstain from conjecture, but the palm of conjectural criticism was placed much too high for the reach of his hand.' Singer was the first to attempt a refutation of Collier's 'corrector.' Hudson followed in his footsteps with another well printed and convenient edition (1851—2). His introductions deal ably with textual questions, but his chief merits lie on the literary side. Payne Collier, in his first edition (1844), shows distinct bias in favour of the quartos[1]. The text is marred by the retention of many errors, owing to a slavish adherence to the old copies. Collier is quite supercilious towards former editors, expressing doubts about 'a' babbled o' green fields,' and retaining 'strange companions' for 'stranger companies' in the passage in *A Midsummer Night's Dream*, to the detriment of rime, metre and sense. When he does adopt a conjecture, he speaks of it as though it were only the correction of an obvious misprint. Collier now underwent as sudden and as complete a conversion as Steevens

the base Indian,' in *Othello*, by quoting, together with a passage from Habington's *Castara*, from *The Women's Conquest*, by Edward Howard (1671):

—Behold my queen—
Who with no more concern I'le cast away
Than Indians do a pearl that ne're did know
Its value.

[1] Thus, where Othello says

[Let] all indign and base adversities
Make head against my estimation !

he is almost alone in reading ' reputation ' with the quartos.

had passed through before him. From a hopeless Tory among editors, he now developed into a confirmed Radical. His own *Notes and Emendations* appeared in 1853. Certain of these conjectures are amongst the best produced in the nineteenth century, and some among them are quite in Theobald's style[1]. But most of the emendations in his book recall Warburton's eccentricities. Nevertheless, had they been given to the world as his own suggestions, Collier's fame would still be untarnished. As a matter of fact, he deceived the very elect into believing that these emendations were corrections in a seventeenth century hand in his copy of the second folio (the 'Perkins folio'), until Nicholas Hamilton, of the British Museum, proved them to be fabrications.

A magnificent folio edition was begun in 1853 and completed in 1865 by James Orchard Halliwell(-Phillipps). The text is very conservative, but contains more conjectures than Collier had admitted. Its chief value lay in the fact that, for the first time, full materials for the study of the text were embraced in one edition. Several old quartos are here reprinted, and facsimiles of parts of other old texts; and the notes give a very full account of variant readings. Though Halliwell-Phillipps will chiefly be remembered by his antiquarian researches, his reproductions of the first folio and the quartos were of immense service to the textual study of Shakespeare.

Nikolaus Delius (1854) adopted the first folio as the standard authority for the text of all the plays, and carried out his work with a critical sagacity which makes his text valuable to all scholars. This principle has been shown to be unsound, so far as the duplicate and doublet quarto plays are concerned. The first quarto, from which the folio text was derived, ought to be the basis of the text of the duplicate quarto plays, and Delius is compelled, at times, to depart from his principle. Thus, in *The Merchant of Venice* (act II, sc. 5, 29), folios have 'the vile squealing of the wry-neck'd fife.' Delius reads 'squeaking,' with the first quarto. So, again, with the doublet quartos. In *Hamlet* (act I,

---

[1] In Polonius's speech (act I, sc. 3, 109), Collier reads:

> Tender yourself more dearly;
> Or—not to crack the wind of the poor phrase,
> Running it thus—you'll tender me a fool.

(Quartos 'Wrong' and folios 'Roaming.') Again, Coriolanus says (act III, sc. 1, 131) (according to the folios)

> How shall this bosome multiplied digest
> The senate's courtesy?

Collier conjectured 'beson multitude,' which Dyce improved to 'bisson.'

sc. 1, 65), the quartos (including the defective quarto) read 'jump at this dead hour.' The folios have 'just.' Delius followed the quartos in his first edition, though he comes round to the folio in his second. On the other hand, his principle rightly applies to the variant quarto plays. His text of these plays is probably the best extant from a critical point of view. But, in two pamphlets on *Richard III* and *King Lear*—the best studies extant of the relations between the quarto and folio text—he rejects the theory of a later revision by Shakespeare. The quarto and folio text, he concludes, both represent the same original; but the quarto is an inferior pirated copy. Howard Staunton introduced many improvements into his edition (1860) from the text of Dyce. He shows a sound judgment on textual questions, and considerable resource in emendation. His notes contain a fairly full textual apparatus in very brief compass. He followed the folio text in the main for the variant quarto plays, except in the case of *Richard III*, and introduced several fresh readings from the defective quarto in *Romeo and Juliet*.

Grant White (1861) may be mentioned in the same connection, inasmuch as he professed that his text was founded 'exclusively upon that of the first folio,' which marks him as a disciple of Delius.

'The superior antiquity of the quarto texts,' he remarks, 'is not infrequently brought to the attention of the critical reader of Shakespeare in support of a reading taken from some one of those texts—as if the age of a surreptitiously printed edition could supply its lack of authenticity!'

The plays in which the folio text is taken from the 'surreptitious' edition are here entirely ignored. Yet his text draws on the quartos almost as much as on the folios. He is often even one of a minority who follow the quarto. In spite of this inconsistency, however, his textual studies have a distinct value. His opinions, though always vigorously expressed, have often been hastily formed, as when he prints 'Judean' in his text, but favours 'Indian' in his notes.

Alexander Dyce's acuteness and soundness of judgment enabled him to produce what his reviewer called 'the best text which has yet been given to the world' (1857). He showed a fine discrimination, with regard both to the quarto and folio readings, and to the conjectures which he admitted into the text. He was well versed in Elizabethan literature, and thoroughly conversant with his authorities. He had already given evidence of his ability in his *Remarks* on Collier's and Charles Knight's editions; and, in 1859, he mercilessly exposed the absurdity of many of the 'corrections' put forward by Collier. His conjectures are never wide of the mark, and some have been generally adopted. One example may be given from *Part III of Henry VI*, where the folios make Henry say:

> Let me embrace the sower Adversaries
> For wise men say it is the wisest course[1].

Dyce restored a certain reading in 'Let me embrace thee, sour Adversity.'

He paved the way for what has now become the standard text of Shakespeare—*The Cambridge Shakespeare*, 1863—6, edited by W. G. Clark and W. Aldis Wright. The introductions contain the safest guide as to authorities for the text, and the notes form a complete *apparatus criticus* of the text. The variant and doublet quartos whose texts differ too widely from the folio to allow of collation in the notes are printed in full. If this edition errs at all, it is in exhibiting too great a partiality for the quartos in the case of the variant quarto plays, and in giving to modern (mostly futile) conjectures too much valuable space in the notes, which might have been better filled by recording the coincidences of the chief editions with the folio or quarto text—small flaws in a work which is a monument of editorial judgment and accurate scholarship, as well as of careful typography.

[1] Act iii, sc. 1, 24.

APPENDIX

GENEALOGY OF THE TEXT OF *RICHARD III*

This play offers quite the most difficult problem in the criticism of Shakespeare's text. It contains the variations usually found in the variant quarto plays, but in far greater numbers (act I, sc. 1, 13 lute F₁ love Qq; 26 see F₁ spy Qq; 133 play F₁ prey Qq; 138 St John F₁ St Paul Qq; act I, sc. 2, 11 wounds F₁ holes Qq; 28 young F₁ poore Qq; 76 crimes F₁ euills Qq; 94 murd'rous F₁ bloudy Qq; 105 better F₁ fitter Qq; 175 brest F₁ bosom Qq; act I, sc. 3, 5 eyes F₁ words Qq; 67 children F₁ kindred Qq; 125 spent F₁ spilt Qq; 147 soueraigne F₁ lawful Qq; 273 peace, peace F₁ have done Qq; 305 muse why F₁ wonder Qq; act I, sc. 4, 18 falling F₁ stumbling Qq; 46 sowre F₁ grim Qq; act II, sc. 2, 46 nere changing night F₁ perpetuall rest Qq etc.).

The folio text seems to show that the editors not only introduced many emendations but made some collation of the quarto copies.

(1) In act II, sc. 3, 43 ensuing dangers Qq Pursuing danger F₁ the catchword in the folio is 'ensuing.' The editor therefore had the quarto text before him, but altered it.

(2) In act I, sc. 2, 19   to adders spiders toads

         Or any creeping venom'd thing that lives Qq

                 to Wolves to Spiders toads etc. F₁

The context plainly shows that the alteration has been made in the folio.

(3) Act I, sc. 2, 212; act III, sc. 1, 190 Crosby Place Qq is altered to Crosby House F₁. But in act I, sc. 3, 345 Crosby Place Qq Ff. Act II, sc. 4, 35 perilous or perillous of Qq is altered to parlous F₁; act III, sc. 1, 154 F₁ reads perillous as Q₁ Q₂. Act I, sc. 2, 27-28; act IV, sc. 1, 76-77 As ... As is altered to More ... then F₁. 137 slew Qq kill'd Ff; act I, sc. 3, 119 slewest Qq killd'st Ff. 282 princely Qq noble Ff; act III, sc. 4, 66 noble Qq princely Ff. These examples point to systematic alteration, which was sometimes omitted through oversight.

(4) Oaths and sacred names are, as usual, modified in the folio. But a very unusual phenomenon is their presence in the folio, in some cases where they are either omitted or toned down in the quartos (act II, sc. 3, 46 Marry F₁ om. Qq; act III, sc. 4, 99 God F₁ Heaven Qq). These must have come from the other copy, from which the additional passages came.

(5) The coincidences between F₁ and Q₁ show that the first quarto was used (act I, sc. 1, 21 scarse Q₁ Q₂ F₁ om. the rest; act I, sc. 2, 115 keen Q₁ keene F₁ kind or kinde the rest; 206 devoted suppliant Q₁ devoted servant F₁ suppliant the rest; act I, sc. 3, 26 false accusers Q₁ Q₂ F₁ accusers the rest; 178 faultless Q₁ Q₂ F₁ om. the rest; 246 poisonous Q₁ F₁ poisoned the rest; act I, sc. 4, 139 purse Q₁ Q₂ F₁ piece or peece the rest; act II, sc. 4, 30 biting or byting Q₁ F₁ pretie, pretty, etc. the rest; act III, sc. 4, 45 sudden F₁ sodaine Q₁ soone the rest; 59 looks Q₁ F₁ face the rest; act III, sc. 5, 42 form Q₁ Q₂ F₁ course the rest; act IV, sc. 4, 25 Harry Q₁ Q₂ F₁ Mary the rest; 170 Thy prime of manhood daring bold and venturous Q₁ Q₂ F₁ om. the rest).

(6) F_1 agrees with Q_3 in many cases in act III and act v, showing that Q_3 was probably collated for parts of the play (act III, sc. 1, 63 seems Q_1 Q_2 thinkst Q_3 think'st F_1; 78 all-ending Q_1 ending Q_2 Q_3 F_1; 96 loving Q_1 Q_2 noble Q_3 F_1; 97 dread Q_1 Q_2 deare Q_3 F_1; 120 heavy Q_1 waightie or weightie Q_2 Q_3 F_1; act v, sc. 3, 351 helmes Q_1 Q_2 helpes Q_3 F_1; 255 sweate Q_1 Q_2 sweare Q_3 F_1; 82 loving Q_1 Q_2 noble Q_3 F_1; 125 deadly Q_1 om. Q_2 Q_3 F_1; 222 see Q_1 Q_2 heare Q_3 F_1; 338, Fight Q_1 Q_2 Right Q_3 F_1; act v, sc. 5, 7 enjoy it Q_1 Q_2 om. Q_3 F_1).

The omissions in the quarto text show that it was adapted for the stage (act I, sc. 2, 16; 25; 155-166; act I, sc. 3, 116; 167-9; act I, sc. 4, 36-37; 69-72; 84; 113-4; 166; 213; 257-260; 266; act II, sc. 1, 25; 140; act II, sc. 2, 16; 89-100; 123-140; act II, sc. 4, 67; act III, sc. 1, 172-3; act III, sc. 3, 7-8; 15; act III, sc. 4, 104-7; act III, sc. 5, 7; 97; 103-5; act III, sc. 7, 8; 11; 24; 37; 98-99; 120; 127; 144-153; 202; 245; act IV, sc. 1, 2-6; 37; 98-104; act IV, sc. 2, 2; act IV, sc. 4, 20-21; 28; 52-53; 103; 159; 172; 179; 221-234; 276-7; 288-342; 387; 400; 429; 432; 451; 523; act v, sc. 3, 27-8; 43). The text of the first folio was probably drawn from a library copy in the theatre, from which the quarto text had been adapted. The omissions in it are (with one exception) unimportant (act I, sc. 2, 202; 225; act I, sc. 3, 114; act I, sc. 4, 133-4; 147; 148; 185-6; 209; 234; act II, sc. 2, 84-85; 145; act III, sc. 3, 1; act III, sc. 4, 10; 60; act III, sc. 7, 43-44; 83; 220; act IV, sc. 1, 19; act IV, sc. 2, 103-120; act IV, sc. 4, 39; act v, sc. 3, 212-4).

CHAPTER XII

SHAKESPEARE ON THE CONTINENT

It is a tribute to the force and originality of the Elizabethan drama that, while still at its prime, it should have found its way to the continent. The conditions of the time could hardly have been less favourable for interest to be felt in English drama outside England itself; for all continental opinion, or, at least, the continental opinion that prided itself on the possession of good taste, had fallen under the spell of the classic traditions of the renascence, and, in poetry, irregularity and lack of clearness were abhorred above all things. There was, thus, no possibility of compromise between Shakespearean drama and the literary ideals of Europe at the beginning of the seventeenth century. But, as a matter of fact, English drama did not reach the continent by way of literary channels at all. It was conveyed, not by books, but by actors, and had little to do with literature in the strict sense of that term.

Towards the end of the sixteenth century, and throughout the seventeenth, English actors from time to time crossed the channel and played in Dutch, German and Scandinavian towns, wandering as far north as Copenhagen and Stockholm, as far east as Danzig, Königsberg and Warsaw and as far south as Vienna and Innsbruck. They took with them the masterpieces of Elizabethan drama in garbled acting versions, the more garbled, undoubtedly, owing to the fact that the foreign audiences before whom they played came to see even more than to hear. From the evidence of the *répertoire* lists, as well as from German versions of English plays, we are able to say with certainty that, of Shakespeare's works, *Titus Andronicus, Hamlet, King Lear, Romeo and Juliet* and *The Merchant of Venice* were played in some form on the continent in the course of the seventeenth century; and it is highly probable that this list may be increased by the addition of *The Comedy of Errors, A Midsummer Night's Dream* (or, at least, the comic interlude of that drama), *The Taming of the Shrew,*

Othello and *Julius Caesar.* The success of these English companies induced German actors to adopt their methods and to translate their *répertoire,* and, in 1620, and again in 1630, there appeared at Leipzig collections of German versions of the plays which the *Englische Comoedianten* had in their list.

That English actors should also have tried their fortune in France was natural, but we have only the vaguest references to such visits; in 1604, an English troupe performed at Fontainebleau, but it is impossible to say with what plays they attempted to win the interest of the French court. In the absence of proof and the still more significant absence of any knowledge of the English drama on the part of French critics who had never visited England, it seems probable that, in the metropolis of seventeenth century culture, the main attractions on which English players relied were acrobatic tricks and buffoonery.

In spite of the comparative popularity of Shakespeare's plays in Germany in this early period, there is no evidence that the English poet's name was known to any of his adapters or translators, or to any member of the public before whom the pieces were acted. This, perhaps, is not surprising, so far as the crude and vulgarised versions of the *Comoedianten* were concerned; but it is not unreasonable to expect that native dramatists, who were eager enough to imitate the new English models, might have evinced some curiosity with regard to the author or authors of these models. This, however, was not the case; no trace of Shakespeare's name is anywhere to be found. 'The only German of the seventeenth century,' says Creizenach, 'who can be proved to have taken an interest in the works of Shakespeare and his contemporaries was the elector Karl Ludwig of the Palatinate, who had been in England in the years 1635—7.' In his correspondence with his sister, duchess Sophia of Hanover, he quotes from *The Merry Wives of Windsor,* and she, in one of her letters, uses the English words 'he leads apes in hell,' which have been assumed to refer to a passage in act II, sc. 1 of *Much Ado about Nothing.* But even in this correspondence there is no mention of Shakespeare's name.

The influence of Shakespeare on both the German and the Dutch drama of the seventeenth century is, however, clearly demonstrable, notwithstanding the lack of curiosity as to the name and personality of the English poet. In the case of the oldest German dramatist who imitated the methods of the *Comoedianten,* the Nürnberg notary Jacob Ayrer, there are chronological difficulties in the way of describing this influence as Shakespearean; the resemblance which his *Comedia von der schönen Sidea* bears to *The Tempest,* and his *Schöne Phoenicia* to *Much Ado about Nothing,* seems to point rather to common sources than to actual borrowing. It is, however, just possible that Shakespeare obtained some knowledge of *Sidea* from English actors. In any case, Ayrer did not stand on a much higher level than the nameless German adapters, and it was hardly likely he should have any greater curiosity as to the authorship of his models. About a generation later, Andreas Gryphius based his comedy or, rather, farce, *Absurda comica, oder Herr Peter Squentz,* on the interlude of *A Midsummer Night's Dream.* The nature and method of Gryphius's borrowing are still wrapped in mystery; but it seems clear that his knowledge of the English comedy was not immediate. He himself, if his statement is to be trusted, obtained the materials for his *Peter Squentz* from the learned Daniel Schwenter, professor at the university of Altdorf; but it is not possible to say whether Schwenter actually knew Shakespeare's work, or, as is more likely, became acquainted with *A Midsummer Night's Dream* in a Dutch adaptation. Here again, however, we find no mention of Shakespeare's name. Still later, at the very end of the seventeenth century, Christian Weise, a prolific writer of school dramas in Zittau, made a lengthy version of *The Taming of the Shrew,* under the title *Comödie von der bösen Catherine,* which goes back directly or indirectly to Shakespeare. But he, too, is silent with regard to his source. The hypothesis of a Dutch intermediary in the case of both Gryphius and Weise receives some support from the fact that the two comedies by Shakespeare which they adapted are also to be found in Dutch seventeenth century literature. The Pyramus and Thisbe episode from *A Midsummer Night's Dream* forms the basis of Matthus Gramsbergen's *Kluchtige Tragedie of den Hartoog van Pierlepon* (1650), and *The Taming of the Shrew* was reproduced by A. Sybant in alexandrines as *De dolle Bruyloft, Bley-eyndend-Spel,* in 1654.

A second period in the history of Shakespeare's fame and influence outside England begins with the awakening of an interest in the poet's name and personality. Jusserand has discovered what is probably the earliest occurrence of the name Shakespeare on the continent, in a manuscript entry in the catalogue of the French king's library (1675—84) by the royal librarian, Nicolas Clément. But the first printed mention of the

name is to be found in a German book published in 1682, *Unter-
richt von der Teutschen Sprache und Poesie*, by the once famous
Polyhistor of Kiel, Daniel Georg Morhof. Three or four years
later, the name appears for the first time in a printed French
book. So far, however, it is merely a question of Shakespeare's
name and nothing more; and, for the next few years, the continent's knowledge of Shakespeare extended little beyond isolated
remarks copied from Temple's *Essay on Poetry*, which had been
translated into French in 1693. The earliest biographical lexicon
which took notice of Shakespeare was Johann Franz Buddeus's
Allgemeines Historisches Lexicon (1709); and, from Buddeus, the
ludicrously inadequate notice—copied from that in Collier's *Historical Dictionary* (1701—21)—passed into the various editions
of Johann Burckhard Mencke's *Gelehrten-Lexicon* (1715, 1725,
1733). Shakespeare, however, is not mentioned either in Bayle's
Dictionnaire historique et critique (1697, 1702, 1740), or in the
German translation of Bayle published by Gottsched and his
coterie in 1741—4 ; but Moréri made good the deficiency by
briefly mentioning him in the 1735 edition of his *Supplément*.

The chief factor in spreading a knowledge of English literature
on the continent at the end of the seventeenth, and beginning of
the eighteenth, centuries was the revocation of the edict of Nantes,
in 1685, which, by expelling the French Huguenots from France,
forced them to settle in Holland, England and Germany. Such of
these men as were interested in literature turned their attention
to the books of the people among whom they were thrown,
thus opening up avenues for the exchange of ideas between the
different nations of Europe, and placing at the very outset a cos-
mopolitan stamp on the thought and literature of the eighteenth
century. The printing presses of Holland were especially called
into requisition in this 'internationalising' process ; English
literature was reprinted and translated into French at Amsterdam and the Hague; French journals, especially those published
in Holland, contained regular correspondence from abroad on
literary matters, and their example was soon followed by German
and Italian learned periodicals. It would have been strange had
Shakespeare not benefited by this interchange of ideas between
England and the continent, and his name—in strangely varying
orthography—occurs with increasing frequency in French periodicals of the time. Addison's *Spectator*, of which the first French
translation was published at Amsterdam in 1714 (frequently
reprinted in succeeding years), although not fully elucidatory

about Shakespeare, was at least adapted to awaken curiosity; the '*Dissertation sur la poésie anglaise*,' published in *Le Journal littéraire*, in 1717, helped materially; and Béat de Muralt had also something to say of Shakespeare in his *Lettres sur les Anglois* (1725). But all these beginnings were soon to be eclipsed by Voltaire; and, with the appearance of that writer's *Lettres philosophiques* (or *Lettres sur les Anglais*), in 1733, the tentative period of Shakespeare's continental fame comes to a close.

Voltaire's attitude to Shakespeare is one of the most difficult problems calling for notice in the present chapter. On the one hand, there is no doubt that Voltaire did more than any other writer of the eighteenth century to familiarise the continent with Shakespeare; on the other, it is exceedingly difficult to do justice to his pioneer work, by reason of the foolish, and often flippant, antagonism to the English poet which he developed in later years. The tendency of recent writers on the subject has been to ascribe too much in that antagonism to purely personal motives and injured vanity, and to overlook the forces that lay behind Voltaire. For, after all, it was hardly a personal matter at all; it was the last determined struggle of the classicism of the seventeenth century, with its Cartesian lucidity and regularity, to assert itself against new and insidious forces which were making themselves felt in literature and criticism. It was Voltaire's lot to fight in this losing battle to the bitter end; he was himself too much immersed in the spirit of the seventeenth century to discover, like his contemporary Lessing, a way of reconciling new ideas with the old classic faith.

Voltaire came over to England in 1726 without any direct knowledge of Shakespeare, but prepared, to some extent, by the utterances of emigrant journalism, to find English tragedy not merely in childish ignorance of the rules of polite literature, but, also, barbarous and sanguinary. He was filled with curiosity, however, and eager to learn. He had opportunities of seeing Shakespeare's dramas on the English stage, he noted the enthusiasm of English audiences and—in spite of the inward protests of his better 'taste'—he himself shared in that enthusiasm for the wayward errors of genius. Either because of the exceptional opportunities he had of seeing *Julius Caesar* on the stage, or because that play, owing to its classic analogies, was more accessible to a mind that had been nurtured on seventeenth century tragedy, it appealed with special force to Voltaire. Possibly, another reason for his interest in *Julius Caesar* was the fact that two writers of the time, the duke of Buckingham and the Italian abbé, Antonio Conti (*Il Cesare*, 1726), had already shown the possibility of adapting that tragedy to the 'regular' stage. However that may be, Voltaire was convinced that the best means of conveying some knowledge of the English form of tragedy to his countrymen was by a Roman drama. He began by writing *Brutus*, which was played towards the end of 1730, and published in the following year with a lengthy preface addressed to his friend Bolingbroke. Here, his earlier assertions about Shakespeare were repeated with more emphasis and point. A more direct attempt to familiarise France with Shakespeare was *La Mort de César* (published in 1735, but written in 1731), in which, within the space of three acts, he reproduced the gist, and at least some of the glaring 'improprieties,' of the Shakespearean tragedy. After *Julius Caesar*, the play which seems to have attracted Voltaire most—his knowledge of Shakespeare, it must be remembered, was exceedingly limited— was *Hamlet*. And just as the crowd in the former play had a peculiar fascination for him, so the ghost scenes in *Hamlet* suggested to him another means of widening the conventions of the pseudo-classic stage by what was, after all, a return to a favourite element of the early renascence tragedy on the Senecan model. He introduced a ghost into the unsuccessful tragedy *Ériphyle* (1732), and, again, into *Sémiramis* (1748). It was the latter that gave Lessing the opportunity for his famous criticism, in which he proved what might surely have occurred to Voltaire himself, that the introduction of the supernatural was inconsistent with the canons of French classic art, and only possible in the *chiaroscuro* of a naturalism untrammelled by artificial rules. In his *Zaïre* (1733), Voltaire endeavoured to utilise *Othello* for the purposes of classic tragedy ; and, in *Mahomet* (1742), he laid some scenes of *Macbeth* under contribution.

For a time, Voltaire had it almost entirely his own way with regard to Shakespeare on the continent. He had awakened curiosity ; and, henceforth, every one who crossed the channel— Montesquieu among others—was expected to bring back with him impressions of England's interesting poet. In prefaces to his tragedies and in his correspondence, Voltaire rang the changes on the views he had already expressed in his *Lettres philosophiques*, with more or less piquant variety. These views were familiar to the entire continent, and the periodical press, especially in France and in Holland, felt obliged to take up a critical attitude towards them, either refuting Voltaire's modest claims in the interests of 'good taste,' or espousing Shakespeare's cause with a warmth which awakened mixed feelings in Voltaire himself. Voltaire's dramas, too, were played on all stages that made any pretension to be in touch with literature ; and, although the author himself was by no means ready to acknowledge his indebtedness, his *Mort de César* was generally regarded as the one accessible specimen of a Shakespearean tragedy.

Among French admirers of Shakespeare, however, there was one, abbé Prévost, whose knowledge of England and the English was more profound than Voltaire's and whose enthusiasm was much less equivocal. He visited England in 1728; he wrote of the English theatre with warm appreciation in his *Memoirs*; and, in 1738, he devoted several numbers of his journal *Le Pour et Contre* solely to Shakespeare, whom he discussed with a freedom from classic prejudice to be found in no other continental writer at that time. But Prévost seems to have been a little in advance of his age, and his views made little impression compared with the interest shown everywhere in Voltaire's utterances on the subject of English tragedy. Louis Riccoboni, however, in his *Réflexions historiques et critiques sur les différents Théâtres de l'Europe* (1738), a book that was widely read throughout the continent, gave Shakespeare—in spite of a rather distorted account of the poet's life—his place at the head of English dramatic literature. Abbé Le Blanc devoted a number of his *Lettres d'un Français* (1745) to Shakespeare ; and, although his views are essentially bounded by the pseudo-classic horizon, he at least, as Jusserand has pointed out, attempted to do justice to the charm of Shakespeare's style. Lastly, mention should be made of Louis Racine, son of the poet, who, in an essay on his father's genius (1752), vindicated the greatness of the classic drama by a comparison of Shakespeare with Sophocles.

In Italy, so far as the Italy of this period had any views about Shakespeare at all, Voltaire's opinions dominated. Abbé Conti's *Cesare* has already been mentioned, and, in the introductory epistles to that tragedy, he acknowledged his indebtedness, through the duke of Buckingham, to the famous English poet 'Sasper'; Scipione Maffei referred to Shakespeare in 1736, while Francisco Quadrio, who first really introduced Shakespeare to the Italians, merely repeated in his *Della Storia e della Ragione d' ogni Poesia* (1739—52) what Voltaire had written. In Germany, on the other hand, there were some attempts, if not to subvert, at least to modify, the Voltairean dogma. In fact, Germany stole a march on France, in so far as she possessed, as early as 1741, a real translation—the first translation of a Shakespearean drama into any language—of *Julius Caesar*. The author, Caspar Wilhelm von Borck, was Prussian ambassador in London between 1735 and 1738, and, doubtless, like Voltaire himself, experienced the piquant charm of English representations of that tragedy. Possibly, the translation may have been, in some measure, due to a desire on Borck's part to show his countrymen that Voltaire's *Mort de César*, in spite of its author's protestations, gave a very imperfect idea of the original. But it is not to be supposed that, at heart, Borck was at variance with the standard of dramatic excellence set up by Voltaire, and he conformed to that standard by translating Shakespeare into the German alexandrines which did service for translations of Voltaire's tragedies. This version, *Der Tod des Julius Caesar*, however, not merely gave men like Lessing, and, doubtless, Herder also, their first glimpse of the English poet, but it also led to the earliest German controversy on Shakespeare's art. Johann Christoph Gottsched, the representative of classicism in Germany at that time, asserted the superior standpoint of Voltaire, with an intellectual arrogance beyond even that which distinguished the French critic's methods ; but, in so doing, he awakened a certain respect for the 'drunken savage' in one of his own disciples, Johann Elias Schlegel. This young writer—Voltairean as he was—presumed to detect merits in Shakespeare which, although admittedly at variance with the requirements of French classicism, were at least justified by the practices of a German dramatist of an older generation, Andreas Gryphius. In Switzerland, about the same time, Johann Jakob Bodmer instinctively felt that the 'Sasper' with whom his Italian authorities had acquainted him, and whom he had found praised in *The Spectator*, might be a useful ally in his controversy with the Leipzig classicists concerning the legitimacy of the 'marvellous' in poetry ; but of Shakespeare's works, Bodmer, at this time, seems to have known little or nothing.

A new development of the Shakespeare question on the continent began with the publication of the earliest French translation of his works. In 1745, the year in which Le Blanc's letters appeared, Pierre Antoine de La Place began his series of translations of English plays by publishing two volumes containing *Othello, The Third Part of Henry VI, Richard III, Hamlet* and *Macbeth*. So acceptable were these volumes to the public that they were followed by other two, containing *Cymbeline, Julius Caesar*,

Antony and Cleopatra, Timon of Athens (according to Shadwell)
and *The Merry Wives of Windsor.* In but one case, however,
did he translate the entire play, namely *Richard III*; for the
rest, he was content to summarise in a connecting narrative what
seemed to him the less important scenes. He also gave an
abstract of the plots of twenty-six other Shakespearean plays.
Moreover, he prefaced his translation with an introduction on the
English stage, in which he expressed very liberal views on the
legitimacy of Shakespeare's art. This work attracted wide attention, not merely in France, but on the continent generally,
and the *Mémoires de Trévoux* devoted no less than seven articles
to its discussion. In one respect, La Place's translation brought
about an immediate effect; it awakened Voltaire's resentment.
Always sensitive where his personal vanity was concerned, he was
hurt to the quick by the presumption of this unknown author,
who wrested from him his laurels as the European authority
on Shakespeare and the sole judge of how much the continent
ought to know of the barbarian poet, and—what was worse—
who ventured to speak of Shakespeare in terms of praise which he,
Voltaire, regarded as dangerous. As a matter of fact, La Place's
translation helped materially to undermine Voltaire's authority as
a Shakespearean critic; henceforth, Voltaire fell more and more
into the background, and was looked upon, even in otherwise
friendly quarters, as cherishing an unreasonable prejudice against
the English poet. And, as the years advanced, his antagonism to
Shakespeare became increasingly embittered and violent.

A more liberal spirit—thanks, mainly, to the initiative of
Voltaire himself—was making itself felt in French criticism; and,
from about the middle of the century onwards, there was an appreciable body of educated opinion, especially among the younger
writers, which regarded Shakespeare in a favourable light, and
cherished the hope that his example might break the stiffening
bonds of the classic canon. The *anglomanie* which set in with
considerable force after the middle of the century, the frequent
visits to England of Frenchmen interested in literature, and the
fame of Garrick, who had many French friends and correspondents,
were all in favour of a sympathetic attitude towards Shakespeare, or,
at least, ensured that the controversy about him should be carried
on with some kind of mutual understanding. On the whole, however,
the French standpoint towards the English poet held its own in
these years, and the drawing together of the two countries had
resulted in a nearer approach of English criticism to that of France,

rather than the reverse. Still, Frenchmen began now to study the English theatre historically; *Le Nouveau Dictionnaire historique* (a supplement to Bayle) devoted, in 1756, no less than six pages to an article on Shakespeare, and the authors of the *Encyclopédie* mentioned him repeatedly. It was thus no wonder that a few bold spirits had even the temerity to prefer Shakespeare to Corneille. Such, at least, was the implication in an anonymous article, professedly translated from the English, entitled '*Parallèle entre Shakespear et Corneille*,' which appeared in *Le Journal Encyclopédique* in 1760. This article, together with a second one in which Otway was held up as superior to Racine, offended Voltaire deeply; he felt that the honour of France must be vindicated at all costs, and, in the following year, he launched his *Appel à toutes les Nations de l'Europe*. This 'appeal' does not appear, however, either then or in 1764, when it was re-published under the pseudonym of 'Jérôme Carré,' to have awakened any widespread desire among the nations to bring the rival poets before a French tribunal of Voltaire's making.

Meanwhile, the sentimental movement, which set in in full force with Rousseau, was distinctly favourable to Shakespeare's reputation in France; Diderot felt the power of the 'Gothic colossus' and expressed his views with that fervent emphasis which was characteristic of him; and, in Sébastien Mercier, there arose a critic of power and originality, whose influence was not restricted to France. Mercier's treatise *Du Théâtre, ou Nouvel Essai sur l'Art dramatique* (1773), in fact, put the entire Shakespeare question in a new light; and, while Voltaire was still fencing with Horace Walpole and others about La Place and that translator's shortsighted policy in undermining good taste by making the English '*Gille de la foire*' unnecessarily accessible to French readers, another blow fell on him which kindled his wrath anew. This was a new and much more ambitious translation of Shakespeare by Pierre Félicien Le Tourneur; with this publication, the French appreciation of the poet entered upon a new phase.

The first volume of Le Tourneur's work appeared in 1776; it is a sumptuous quarto and opens with an imposing list of subscribers headed by the king and queen. The quality of the translation— which is in prose—is not of a very high order; but, compared with that of La Place and other contemporary efforts, it marks a very considerable advance. The introduction expatiates in no measured terms on the greatness and universality of Shakespeare's genius, on his insight into the human heart and his marvellous powers of painting nature. In this eulogy, Le Tourneur had not omitted to mention as Shakespeare's equals the French masters of the seventeenth century, Corneille, Racine and Molière; but not a word was said of the French theatre of the translator's own time. Voltaire was not merely indignant at the disgrace to France implied in placing Shakespeare on this pinnacle: he was incensed that his own name should not even have been mentioned on the French roll of dramatic fame. The *Appeal to all the Nations of Europe* had failed; he felt he must now approach the custodian of the nation's good name, the Academy. D'Alembert, secretary of the Academy, was not unwilling to meet Voltaire's wishes; and it was ultimately agreed that d'Alembert should read before a public meeting a letter by Voltaire on the dangers of Shakespeare to French taste. This actually took place on 25 August 1776. The old battery was drawn up anew, and once more the untutored mountebank was successfully routed; d'Alembert's eloquent de-livery of his friend's appeal to the good sense of France was received with acclamation (broken only by an English boy of twelve who wanted to hiss Voltaire). But to Voltaire even this protest did not seem sufficient. A second letter followed on 7 October, and was published as the preface to his last tragedy, *Irène*, the performance of which had been Voltaire's final triumph in Paris. 'Shakespeare is a savage with sparks of genius which shine in a horrible night.' This was Voltaire's last word on the Shakespeare controversy. As Jusserand finely remarks, he who, all his life long, had been the champion of every kind of liberty refused it to tragedy alone.

The dust raised by Voltaire's last skirmish was long in subsiding. From England, naturally, came several protests: Mrs Montague, who had been present at the meeting of the Academy when Voltaire's letter was read, had her *Essay on the Writings and Genius of Shakespear* (1764) translated into French, with a reply to Voltaire; Giuseppe Baretti, an Italian residing in London, wrote his *Discours sur Shakespeare et M. Voltaire* (1777); Lessing's *Hamburgische Dramaturgie* was translated in the interests of Voltaire's opponents, while La Harpe, on the other side, staunchly upheld the classic faith. But nothing could now undo the effects of the new force which had made itself felt in the French theatre, and even dramatists of unimpeachable 'taste,' who abhorred irregulari-ties, introduced elements—death on the stage, infringements of the unities and the like—which pointed unmistakably to Shakespeare.

In the later years of the eighteenth century, his plays were adapted to the French stage by several hands and in many different ways ; but only one of these adapters need be mentioned here, Jean François Ducis, who occupied Voltaire's seat in the Academy. In his *Hamlet* (1769), *Roméo et Juliette* (1772), *Le Roi Lear* (1783), *Macbeth* (1784), *Jean sans Terre* (1791) and *Othello* (1792), Ducis succeeded in reconciling a very genuine enthusiasm for Shakespeare with what now seems to us an extraordinary lack of taste, in adapting him for presentation to the French theatre-goer. He was himself, however, ignorant of English and obliged to draw exclusively from French translations. But, in spite of these disadvantages, Ducis succeeded where no one had succeeded before him : he made Shakespeare—mutilated, it may be, but still Shakespeare—popular on the French and on the Italian stage ; and it was in the *Othello* of Ducis that Talma achieved one of his greatest triumphs. However we may condemn these distorted adaptations, we should at least remember to the credit of Ducis that his stage versions of Shakespeare's plays outlived the French revolution, were still popular under the first empire and were remembered when Marie-Joseph Chénier's *Brutus et Cassius* (1790), a play that may be described as the last attempt to reduce *Julius Caesar* to the law and order of classic taste, was forgotten.

In the years when the French literary world was torn asunder by controversies as to what should be admired and imitated in Shakespeare, Germany was rapidly outdistancing France as the real leader of continental appreciation of Shakespeare. A critic had arisen here—a greater than Voltaire—who not merely made Shakespeare a power of the first magnitude in his own literature, but also discovered the formula which was to reconcile the un-classic art of Shakespeare with the classic and humanitarian strivings of the eighteenth century. This was Gotthold Ephraim Lessing. We must, however, avoid the mistake of overestimating either Lessing's services to the appreciation of Shakespeare in Germany, or his originality in judging the English poet. It is usual to scoff at the slender knowledge with which Voltaire presumed to pass judgment on Shakespeare ; but, so far as Lessing's printed work is concerned, he, also, gave no proof of any intimate familiarity with the poet's works. To begin with, there is no doubt that, until at least the year 1753, Lessing's actual acquaintance with Shakespeare was limited to Borck's translation of *Julius Caesar* ; of critical judgments of Shakespeare he had read nothing more authoritative than Voltaire's *Lettres philosophiques*, of which he had just translated and published in his journal, *Beiträge zur Historie und Aufnahme des Theaters*, the two letters on tragedy and comedy. From about the year 1753, however, Germany made rapid strides in her knowledge of Shakespeare; indeed, this was inevitable, considering how carefully Germans, in these years, followed the opinions of French writers and the French press. An article vigorously remonstrating against Gottsched's standpoint appeared in *Neue Erweiterungen der Erkenntnis und des Vergnügens*, in 1753, and was followed, three years later, by a prose translation of *Richard III*; while, in 1755, Lessing's friend and later colleague, Nicolai, boldly put in a plea for the irregularity of the English stage in preference to the artificial regularity of the French stage. Lessing was willing enough to subscribe to these opinions and to echo them in his writings; his own interest in the English theatre at this time, however, was directed not to Shakespeare, but to the 'tragedy of common life'; and, when, in the winter of 1756—7, he devoted himself seriously to the study of tragedy and its aesthetic basis, it was to Aristotle and to Sophocles he turned in the first instance. Lessing's acquaintance with Shakespeare in the original seems to date from the year 1757, and fragments of dramas which have been preserved from that period bear testimony to the deep impression which Shakespeare had then made upon him. By 1759, Lessing had arrived at two conclusions of far-reaching significance with regard to the English poet. Neither was altogether new; but they were both expressed with a vigour and piquancy which at once riveted the attention of his contemporaries. One of these was that the drama of Shakespeare was akin to the German *Volksdrama*; and, on the ground of this affinity, Lessing hoped that Germany might be assisted to a national drama of her own by imitating Shakespeare. The other conclusion, which was similar to opinions that were being freely expressed by iconoclasts in France itself, was particularly attractive to the German literary world, weary as it was of the tyranny of classicism: it was to the effect that Shakespeare, in spite of his irregularities, was a greater and more Aristotelian poet —in other words, more akin to Sophocles—than the great Corneille. 'After the *Oedipus* of Sophocles, no piece can have more power over our passions than *Othello*, *King Lear*, *Hamlet*.' These bold assertions, which form a landmark in the history of German Shakespeare appreciation, are to be found in number 17 of *Briefe die neueste Literatur betreffend*, published on 16 February 1759.

With this famous letter, Lessing's significance as a pioneer of

Shakespeare in Germany reaches its climax. After 1759, he occasionally turned to Shakespeare to demonstrate a point of dramatic theory, or to clinch an argument, or to discredit the French; in the *Hamburgische Dramaturgie*, which has disappointingly little to say about Shakespeare, he insisted on Shakespeare's mastery as a delineator of character, on his kinship with the Greeks and on his essential observance of the Aristotelian canon; not for a moment would Lessing have admitted that Aristotle was a critic for all time because his theory of tragedy could be shown to be equally applicable to Sophocles and Shakespeare; rather, Shakespeare was a great poet because he could be proved to have obeyed the Greek lawgiver instinctively. In his later years, however, Lessing—as his own *Nathan der Weise* shows—was, at heart, more in sympathy with Voltaire's conception of tragedy than with Shakespeare's. Leadership in matters of Shakespearean criticism passed rapidly into other and younger hands.

A very few years after Lessing's famous letter, the Germans were themselves in a position—and in a better position than their French neighbours—to form some idea of the English poet. Between 1762 and 1766, appeared Christoph Martin Wieland's translation of Shakespeare into prose. It was very far from being adequate; it was suggested, doubtless, in the first instance, by La Place's French translations, and, like these, was in clumsy prose; but, compared with what had preceded it in Germany—Borck's *Caesar*, a few fragmentary specimens of Shakespeare's work in periodicals and a bad iambic translation of *Romeo and Juliet*—it was an achievement no less great than Le Tourneur's French translation at a somewhat later date. And, in one respect, no subsequent translation could vie with Wieland's, namely, in its immediate influence upon German literature. Its faults are obvious enough; it is ludicrously clumsy, often ludicrously inaccurate. Wieland was himself too good a Voltairean to extend a whole-hearted sympathy to Shakespeare's irregularities and improprieties, and he grasped at every straw which contemporary French criticism or the notes of Pope and Warburton offered him, to vindicate the superiority of classic taste. At the same time, his private correspondence would seem to indicate that his feelings for Shakespeare were considerably less straitlaced than his commentary would imply. The consequences of the translation were more far-reaching than Wieland had anticipated; indeed, he, no less than Lessing, was filled with dismay at the extravagances which followed the introduction of Shakespeare to the German literary world—

perhaps this is even a reason why, in his *Dramaturgie*, Lessing is reserved on the subject of Shakespeare. In that work, Lessing had published a kindly recommendation of Wieland's translation; but, a few months earlier, another and more subversive critic, Heinrich Wilhelm von Gerstenberg, under the stimulus of the new ideas of genius propounded in England by Young and Home, had made claims for Shakespeare of which Lessing could not have approved.

The new generation was no longer, like the latter critic, interested in 'Shakespeare the brother of Sophocles': 'Shakespeare the voice of nature' was the new watchword. The young writers of the German *Sturm und Drang* did not criticise at all; they worshipped; they sought to 'feel' Shakespeare, to grasp his spirit. They had not patience to study his art, to learn how to write from him, as Lessing had recommended them to do, when, in the *Dramaturgie*, he had lectured his quondam friend Weisse on the lessons to be learned from *Richard III*. The five letters on Shakespeare in Heinrich Wilhelm von Gerstenberg's *Briefe über Merkwürdigkeiten der Literatur* are, perhaps, the most important contribution to continental Shakespearean criticism of the entire eighteenth century. It is not that much real critical discrimination is to be found in them; but Gerstenberg's whole attitude to Shakespeare's works is new; he regards them as so many '*Gemälde der sittlichen Natur*'—as things that we have no more business to question than we should question a tree or a landscape. Judged purely as criticism, Gerstenberg's letters on Shakespeare could not have carried much weight in circles unaffected by the *Sturm und Drang*; but his ideas fell on fruitful ground in Herder's mind, and Herder, stripping them of their excesses and extravagances, made them acceptable even beyond the pale of the literary revolution. His essay on Shakespeare was one of the chief constituents of the little pamphlet entitled *Von deutscher Art und Kunst* (1773), with which the new movement was ushered in. Herder had an advantage over Gerstenberg in not approaching the subject in quite so naïve a frame of mind; he had studied the *Hamburgische Dramaturgie*; and, from 1769 to 1772, he had busied himself zealously with the English poet. Unlike Lessing, who attempted unconditionally to reconcile Shakespeare with the Aristotelian canon, Herder brought his conception of historical evolution to bear on the Greek, and on the English, drama; he showed that, while both Sophocles and Shakespeare strove to attain the same end, they necessarily chose very different ways; the historical conditions under which they

worked were totally unlike.   In this way, Herder sowed the seeds
of the German romantic criticism of a later date.

Meanwhile, however, the younger dramatists of the day were
moved to enthusiasm by Gerstenberg.   Goethe expressed their
views in his perfervid oration *Zum Schäkespears Tag*; Lenz, in
his *Anmerkungen übers Theater*, developed Gerstenberg's ideas;
and later critics joined hands with Sébastien Mercier.   When
Wieland had led the way, the translating of Shakespeare became
more and more common;   Christian Weisse, who has just been
mentioned, produced in 1768 his German version (in alexandrines)
of *Richard III*—or, rather, of Cibber's adaptation of *Richard III*
—and, in the same year, he converted *Romeo and Juliet* into
a 'tragedy of common life.'   Versions of *Othello* and *Cymbeline* by
other hands followed; while, in Vienna, *Hamlet* and *Macbeth*,
A Midsummer Night's Dream and *The Merry Wives of Windsor*,
were adapted to the stage with a freedom which rendered them
almost unrecognisable.   In 1775—7, the naturalisation of Shakespeare in Germany was advanced another important stage by
the publication of *William Shakespear's Schauspiele*, in twelve
volumes, by Johann Joachim Eschenburg, professor in the Caro-
linum at Brunswick and one of the most active workers of his
day in introducing English literature to the Germans.   Eschenburg's *Shakespear* is a revised and completed edition of Wieland's
translation; but so thorough was the revision that it is practically
a new work.

The chief importance of the age of *Sturm und Drang* for the
history of Shakespeare on the continent lies in the fact that it led
to the permanent incorporation of his plays in the *répertoire* of the
German national stage.   Wieland had made the earliest beginning,
by arranging a performance of *The Tempest* in Biberach in 1761;
but the most memorable date in this connection is 20 September
1776, when Germany's greatest actor, Friedrich Ludwig Schröder,
produced *Hamlet* in Hamburg, he himself playing—like Garrick in
England in 1741—the ghost.   This was followed in the same year
by a production of *Othello*; in 1777, by *The Merchant of Venice* and
Measure for Measure; and, in 1778, by *King Lear*, *Richard II*
and *Henry IV*; *Macbeth* was produced in 1779 and *Much Ado
about Nothing* in 1792.   The chief impression we obtain from
Schröder's Shakespeare versions nowadays is their inadequacy to
reproduce the poetry of the originals; but it would be unfair to
condemn them.   Compared with the travesties of Ducis, a little
later, they are masterpieces of reverent translation.   The fact

must be recognised that the real Shakespeare, that is to say, the Shakespeare Schlegel gave to Germany twenty years later, would have been impossible on Schröder's stage; and it was Schröder's unquestionable merit—just as it was that of Ducis in France—that he realised clearly in what form Shakespeare could be made palatable to the theatre-goers of his time. In fact, the extra-ordinary success of Schröder's Shakespeare over the German speaking continent from Hamburg to Vienna—in the latter city, the performance of *Lear* on 13 April 1780 was again a landmark in the history of the theatre—is the best justification of his method of treating Shakespeare; and we have only to compare his work with the versions in which, before his time, German theatres had ventured to perform Shakespeare, to appreciate the magnitude of Schröder's achievement. In these years, the English poet was accepted by the Germans as one of the chief assets of their national stage, and he has never since lost his commanding position in the German *répertoire*.

There is little to record in the history of Shakespeare in Germany between Schröder's first triumphs and the publication of Shakespeare's works in what may be called their permanent and final form, the translation of August Wilhelm Schlegel and his fellow-workers. The starting-point for the preoccupation of the romantic school with Shakespeare was the famous criticism of *Hamlet* which Goethe put into the mouth of his hero in *Wilhelm Meisters Lehrjahre*. The fine comparison of Hamlet to an oak-tree in a costly jar kindled the new criticism as with an electric spark, and contained implicitly, one might say, the whole romantic attitude to Shakespeare. Like its predecessors of the *Sturm und Drang*, the romantic school looked up to Shakespeare with unbounded reverence; like them, it recognised the impossibility of applying the old canons of *a priori* criticism; but an advance is to be seen in the fact that the members of the school were not satisfied with mere open-eyed wonder: they endeavoured to interpret and under-stand. In 1796, Ludwig Tieck made a prose version of *The Tempest*; and, in the same year, August Wilhelm Schlegel published, in Schiller's *Horen*, his essay *Etwas über William Shakespeare bei Gelegenheit Wilhelm Meisters*, and also specimens of the new translation of Shakespeare which, with the help of his gifted wife Caroline, he had just begun. The translation itself, *Shakespeare's Dramatische Werke, übersetzt von August Wilhelm Schlegel*, began to appear in 1797; and, between that year and 1801, eight volumes were published containing the following dramas: *Romeo and Juliet*,

A Midsummer Night's Dream, Julius Caesar, Twelfth Night, The Tempest, Hamlet, The Merchant of Venice, As You Like It, King John, Richard II, Henry IV, Henry V and *Henry VI.* The ninth volume, *Richard III*, did not appear till 1810. With this marvellous translation, which has been deservedly called the greatest literary achievement of the romantic school, German labours to naturalise the English poet, which had been going on since 1741, reach their culmination. Whatever has been said to impugn the accuracy and faithfulness of Schlegel's work, the fact remains that no translation of Shakespeare can vie with this in the exactitude with which the spirit and the poetic atmosphere of the original have been reproduced; to Schlegel, in the main, belongs the credit of having made Shakespeare the joint possession of two nations. A word remains to be said about the attitude of Germany's two greatest poets to Shakespeare at the turn of the century. The period in Goethe's life which followed the publication of *Wilhelm Meister* was not favourable to a sympathetic understanding of Shakespeare, and Schiller was even less accessible. In the course of their friendship, the two poets had arrived at a theory of classicism, which, although less dominated by rules than the French classicism of earlier times, was no less opposed to the irregularities and subjectivity of Shakespeare's art ; their attitude is to be seen most clearly from the carefully pruned and polished versions of *Macbeth* by Schiller, and *Romeo and Juliet* by Goethe, produced in Weimar in 1800 and 1812 respectively. Goethe's own most definite pronouncement on the subject of Shakespeare in these later years was his essay entitled *Shakespeare und kein Ende!* published in 1815, a kind of apology for his adaptation of *Romeo and Juliet.*

The foregoing account of Shakespeare's gradual naturalisation in Germany in the eighteenth century would be incomplete without some indication of what Shakespeare meant for the development of German literature itself. His influence in Germany from Borck to Schlegel can hardly be exaggerated ; and it may be said without paradox that the entire efflorescence of German eighteenth century literature would have been otherwise—have stood much nearer to the main movement of European literature in that century—had it not been for Shakespeare. It was he who awakened the Germanic spirit in modern German literature and pointed out to Germany how the traditions of the renascence poetics might be abandoned; it was he who freed the intellectual growth of northern Europe from the clogging presence of influences Latin in their origin. With Lessing, Shakespeare first became a mighty force in Germany, and, with Goethe, whose *Götz von Berlichingen* appeared in 1773, and the group of gifted playwrights who followed in Goethe's footsteps, he brought the tyranny of the 'rules' in Germany to an end. Wieland's translation, with all its defects, gave the German theatre a new language and a new form of expression ; and, under Shakespeare's guidance, the drama found its way into a romantic fairy-world of which the French classic stage knew nothing—above all, plays like *Romeo and Juliet*, *Othello* and *The Merchant of Venice* first revealed to the Germans the poetic charm of Italy. There was thus hardly a question round which controversy raged in the German literature of the eighteenth century with which the English poet was not in some way bound up.

If we turn to the nineteenth century, a certain analogy to the influence of Shakespeare in Germany just discussed is to be found in his influence on the French romantic school ; in this period, Shakespeare might be said to have deflected for a time the literature of France from its normal development, or, at least, from the development defined by the literary history of previous centuries. It might have been expected that the precursors of the *école romantique*, the representatives of the so-called emigrant literature, should have had a special sympathy for the sombre, misty side of Shakespeare's genius. But this was only the case in a limited degree ; there was no question of his seizing them and bending them, as it were, to his will, as in the contemporary literary movement in Germany ; indeed, in Chateaubriand (*Shakespeare*, 1801), we find a revival of the old Voltairean standpoint. On the other hand, Madame de Staël (*De la littérature*, 1800) wrote with a certain enthusiasm of Shakespeare, and Charles Nodier, in his *Pensées de Shakespeare* (1801), reflected the attitude of his German masters. Meanwhile, on the stage, Népomucène Lemercier borrowed freely from the English dramatist, and the mutilations of Ducis found even less scrupulous imitators than Ducis himself. It seemed as if the labours of the *anglomanes* of the eighteenth century were to be wholly undone ; the gulf between French and English taste was wider than ever ; and, in the summer of 1822, English actors, who attempted to present *Hamlet* and *Othello* in Paris, were actually hissed off the stage. But a better time was not far off ; in the very next year, Stendhal (Henri Beyle) published his *Racine et Shakespeare*, and took his side very emphatically against the classicists. Guizot, together with other fellow workers, had, in 1821, resuscitated Le Tourneur, republishing his translation in a revised form, and thus enabling the

younger generation of poets and critics to put to the test those
enthusiastic eulogies of English poets which they found in German
romantic writers. In the following year, Guizot vindicated the
English poet in his essay *De Shakspear et de la Poésie dramatique*.
In 1827, the attempt to produce Shakespeare in English in the
French capital was renewed, this time with the cooperation of
Charles Kemble, Macready and Edmund Kean, and awakened the
enthusiasm of all literary Paris ; and, under the influence of these
impressions, Victor Hugo wrote his famous manifesto of the new
movement, the preface to *Cromwell* (1827). It seemed as if the
intoxication to which the English poet had given rise more than a
generation earlier in Germany were about to repeat itself in France.
Alfred de Vigny, in an admirable translation, transferred the
English triumphs of *Othello* to the stage of the Théâtre Français
itself (1829); Alexandre Dumas translated *Hamlet* (played 1847);
while Alfred de Musset's whole dramatic work is permeated and
coloured by Shakespearean influence. The press of the day echoed
the emotional interest which the romantic school felt in Shakespeare;
and the enthusiasm of Charles Magnin (in *Le Globe*, 1827—8)
and of Jules Janin helped to counteract such spasmodic attempts
as, for instance, were made by Paul Duport (*Essais littéraires sur
Shakespeare*, 1828), to resuscitate the antagonistic criticism of
Voltaire and La Harpe. The peculiarly emotional nature of this
enthusiasm of 1827 distinguished it from the *anglomanie* of the
previous century, and it shows itself still more clearly in the
remarkable influence of the English poet on French romantic art—
for example, on Eugène Delacroix—and on French music as represented by Hector Berlioz. From this time, the supremacy of
Shakespeare in modern literature was not seriously questioned in
France ; the romantic fever passed, romanticism assumed other
forms, but the controversies which Shakespeare had stirred up in
the previous century were no longer possible. Except in the case
of Victor Hugo, who, so late as 1864, repeated the old fervid notes
of *Cromwell* in an essay inspired by his son's success as a translator
of Shakespeare, romantic criticism ripened and matured as time
went on. Guizot, towards the end of his career, devoted another
volume to Shakespeare (*Shakespeare et son temps*, 1852); a work
by Alfred Mézières, *Shakespeare, ses œuvres et ses critiques*, appeared in 1860. Lamartine published his *Shakespeare et son œuvre*
in 1865. Translations of Shakespeare's works were published by
Francisque Michel in 1839, by Benjamin Lariche in 1851, by Émile
Montegut in 1867 and, as already mentioned, by François Victor

Hugo from 1859 to 1866. And yet, in spite of the continued occupation with Shakespeare on the part of literary classes, it must be confessed that the interest in him in France, otherwise than in Germany, where Shakespeare was completely naturalised, remains a matter only of intellectual curiosity. French criticism of Shakespeare cannot belie the fact—and, perhaps, the absence of any attempt on its part to do so may attest its justness of perception—that his kind of greatness lies outside the pale of the national ideas and the national taste. He has won no permanent place in the national theatre, and the many performances of Shakespearean dramas which have taken place from time to time in Paris have been viewed as literary experiments appealing to the cultured few, rather than as dramatic fare for the general public.

The *rôle* which Shakespeare played in the Germany of the nineteenth century was much more important, but, so far as literary history is concerned, perhaps less interesting, than that which he played in France. A kind of zenith had been reached in German appreciation of Shakespeare at the close of the eighteenth century. The translation then begun by Schlegel, was, in later years, completed under the direction of Ludwig Tieck, with the help of his daughter Dorothea and of count Baudissin; and it may at least be said that these later translations, although inferior, are not unworthy to stand beside Schlegel's. Germany, like France, went on producing new translations—a complete Shakespeare, for instance, was published by the poet Johann Heinrich Voss and his two sons in nine volumes in 1818—29, and another by Friedrich von Bodenstedt, with the cooperation of Ferdinand Freiligrath, Otto Gildemeister, Paul Heyse and others, in 1867—but the romantic translators had done their work so well that these new productions could only have a subordinate and supplementary value. In German literature, Shakespeare has remained a vital and ever-present force. The problem which Schiller had first tentatively approached, namely, the reconciliation of Shakespeare with the antique, could not be evaded by his successors; Heinrich von Kleist took it up with abundant zeal and solved it in an essentially romantic way; and, notwithstanding the romantic tendency to place Calderon on a higher pinnacle than Shakespeare, the romantic dramatists were all, in the first instance, Shakespeareans. Christian Grabbe was as zealous a Shakespeare worshipper as the Lenzes and Klingers of earlier days; and even Franz Grillparzer—with all his love for the Spaniards—had moments when he saw eye to eye with the English dramatist.

It was not before Christian Friedrich Hebbel, about the middle of the century, that the German drama began to feel its way to a conception of dramatic poetry more essentially modern than Shakespeare's; and even Hebbel sought to justify by the example of Shakespeare that accentuation of the psychological moment in which his own peculiar strength lies. On the other hand, Hebbel's brother-in-arms, Otto Ludwig, was a more uncompromising Shakespearean than any German before him; he not merely Shakespeareanised his own dramas, but struck an original note of Shakespeare criticism in essays unfortunately not printed until several years after his death. On the whole, however, Shakespeare had expended his fructifying influence on German literature in the previous century; to none of these later writers did he bring— as to Goethe and Herder—a new revelation; and the subversive forces of the modern German drama have little in common with Elizabethan ideals.

The consideration of Shakespeare in Germany in the nineteenth century falls into two main divisions: German Shakespearean scholarship and the presentation of Shakespeare on the German stage. The former of these is a long and difficult chapter which has still to be written; in the present survey, it is only possible to indicate its general features. The beginnings of German scholarly work on Shakespeare might be traced to Wieland's investigation of the source of *Othello*, in 1773; but this was more or less isolated; what men like Eschenburg had to say, somewhat later, was little more than a reproduction of English criticism. A significant moment in the development was Goethe's analysis of *Hamlet* in *Wilhelm Meister*, to which reference has already been made. Then came Friedrich Schlegel, with his marvellous insight into the workings of genius, and kindled a new light on the poet; Tieck laboriously and patiently investigated the whole Shakespearean world—defining that world, perhaps, too vaguely and loosely—and it is assuredly a loss that the life of Shakespeare which he planned was never written; lastly, August Wilhelm Schlegel, in his famous lectures *Über dramatische Kunst und Literatur* (1809—11), popularised the romantic criticism of Shakespeare, and, in this form, it reacted on our own Coleridge and influenced profoundly the theory of the drama in France, Italy and Spain. As the romantic movement passed away, the place of its followers was taken by a new race of critics, who followed the dictates of Hegel; and, during the first half of the nineteenth century, Hegelianism lay particularly heavy on German Shakespeare scholarship, one obvious reason being that Shakespeare's life offered no opportunity for that pragmatic investigation and criticism which, for instance, was the saving element in extricating Goethe from Hegelian metaphysics. The influence of Hegel's aesthetics, which was essentially anti-romantic in its tendency, is to be seen in Hermann Ulrici's *Über Shakespeares dramatische Kunst und sein Verhältnis zu Calderon und Goethe* (1839), and, in a less accentuated form, in Georg Gottfried Gervinus's *Shakespeare* (1849—52), in Friedrich Kreyssig's *Vorlesungen über Shakespeare und seine Werke* (1858) and in the recently published *Shakespeare-Vorträge* of the famous Swabian Hegelian, Friedrich Theodor Vischer. On the whole, the influence of Hegelianism on German Shakespeare criticism has not been favourable; it has led to an excessive preoccupation with metaphysical theories of tragic guilt and tragic purpose, to a misleading confusion of moral and aesthetic standards and to a too confident reliance on *a priori* theories of literary genius. It has also made it difficult for Shakespeare's countrymen to appreciate at their true value the learning and scholarship which lay behind the metaphysical veil. With the labours, however, of Karl Simrock, Gustav Rümelin, Karl Elze, whose biography, *William Shakespeare*, appeared in 1876, Nikolaus Delius and Alexander Schmidt, not to mention more recent workers, the speculative method has been in great measure discarded in favour of scientific investigation of facts. Germans can now point to a magnificent record of patient and careful work, to which, since 1865, the *Shakespeare Jahrbuch* has borne eloquent testimony.

The importance of Shakespeare for the history of the German theatre in the nineteenth century can hardly be overestimated; it might, indeed, be said that (with the single exception of the Bayreuth festival, dating from 1876) Shakespeare has been associated with every advance that the national theatre has made. Shakespearean types of character have formed an important factor in the staff organisation of theatres and, in large measure, have supplanted in poetic drama the French distribution of *rôles*; Shakespearean representations are the test of dramaturgic ability of every *régisseur*, and Shakespearean impersonations the keystone of every actor's reputation. The schemes of a reformed stage with which Tieck busied himself and which he outlined in his novel *Der junge Tischlermeister* were based on the requirements of the English drama; plays by Shakespeare were included in the remarkable representations at Düsseldorf with which Karl Immermann endeavoured to stay the decay of the post-classical stage; and, in the golden days of the Vienna Hofburgtheater, under Heinrich Laube's direction, and with actors like Sonnenthal, Lewinsky, Bauermeister and Charlotte Wolter, Shakespeare was acted as probably never before in any land. At the Shakespeare tercentenary in 1864—the occasion of the founding of the German *Shakespeare-Gesellschaft*—Franz Dingelstedt, then intendant of the court theatre in Weimar, produced the first complete cycle of Shakespeare's *Königsdramen*, that is to say, dramas from English history ; and it was with Shakespeare that Duke George II of Saxe-Meiningen, from 1874 onwards, attracted the attention not only of all Germany but of other lands, to stage representations of rare pictorial beauty and historical accuracy. The Meiningen 'reforms,' which gave a great stimulus to the representation of classic dramas in Germany, were akin to what was being done, much about the same time, by Henry Irving in London ; but they had an advantage over the English performances due to the stronger bond which has always united theatre and literature in modern Germany. In 1889 *King Lear* served for the inauguration of the *Shakespeare-Bühne* in Munich, which, notwithstanding other recent attempts in England, Germany and France, remains the only experiment of the kind which avoided the temptation to be only antiquarian, and succeeded in winning the approval of a wider public over a period of many years.

The question of Shakespeare's influence and appreciation in continental lands, other than France and Germany, is, necessarily, one of minor interest. The Latin peoples followed more or less in the footsteps of France, the Germanic peoples of the north of Europe in those of Germany. What Italy knew of Shakespeare in the eighteenth century, as has been shown, was drawn exclusively from Voltaire, and the same is true of Spain ; and both countries made their first acquaintance with the poet as an acted dramatist through the medium of the mutilated French versions by Ducis. The real work of translating and studying Shakespeare was not begun in either land until the nineteenth century. A translation of Shakespeare's tragedies into Italian verse by Michele Leoni was published at Pisa in 1814—5 ; this was followed by the complete works in Italian prose by Carlo Rusconi (1831), and selected plays by the Milanese poet, Giulio Carcani (1857—9), ultimately increased to a complete edition (1874—82). Spain, on the other hand, has had to wait until comparatively recently for satisfactory translations of Shakespeare's works. Considering the kinship between Shakespeare and the masters of the Spanish drama—a kinship which Germans recognised at an early date—it seems strange that

Spaniards should have been thus late in showing a curiosity about the English poet. It should be added that Italy has contributed in no small degree to the interpretation and popularisation of the greater tragedies by the impersonations of Salvini and Rossi, of Adelaide Ristori and Eleanora Duse, while Italian music has drawn extensively on Shakespeare for the subjects of operas.

It is only natural to find in Germanic lands a more intense interest in Shakespeare, and a higher development in the translation and interpretation of his works. Here, the influence of Germany is paramount. Even Holland, which, at an earlier stage, had been immediately influenced by England, fell back ultimately almost wholly on German sources. The difficulty of naturalising English drama in languages like Dutch, Danish and Swedish is more subtle than appears at first glance; there was no want of interest or will at a comparatively early period, but Shakespeare's language and style presented obstacles that were not easy to surmount. This aspect of the question did not concern Latin peoples in the same degree, for the only method of translation which the genius of their tongues allowed them to follow was to bend and adapt Shakespeare to their own style. But, as has been seen in the case of German itself, where Wieland first succeeded in overcoming the difficulty of creating a language and style suited to Shakespeare, and where Schlegel first made the German tongue 'Shakespeare-ripe,' this initial problem was a serious one. Just as the south of Europe learned from Voltaire, Ducis and Talma, so Holland and Scandinavia learned the art of translating Shakespeare from Wieland and Schlegel, and the art of playing him from Schröder. Between 1780 and the end of the century, more than a dozen dramas had appeared in Dutch, but it was late in the nineteenth century before Holland possessed satisfactory and complete translations, namely, those by Abraham Kok (1873—80) and Leendert Burgersdijk (1884—8). What had happened in Hamburg in 1777 virtually repeated itself in Copenhagen in 1813, that is to say, Shakespeare first won a firm footing on the Danish stage with *Hamlet*. The translator was the actor Peter Foersom, who was naturally influenced strongly by Schröder. At his death in 1817, he had published four volumes of what was intended to be a complete translation of Shakespeare, and it was completed at a later date by Peter Wulff and Edvard Lembcke. The chief Swedish translation of Shakespeare's works is that by Carl August Hagberg (12 volumes, 1847—51). Scandinavia's contribution to Shakespearean literature is much more important than that of Holland ; mention need only be made here of the admirable Swedish life of Shakespeare by Henrik Schück (1883), and *William Shakespeare* (1895) by the industrious Danish critic Georg Brandes. The latter work, in spite of a desire to reconstruct Shakespeare's life and surroundings on insufficient materials, is, unquestionably, one of the most suggestive biographies of the poet.

In Russia and Poland, the interest in Shakespeare is no less great than in the more western countries of Europe. Here, the influence of France seems to have predominated in the earlier period, Ducis introducing the English poet to the Russian and the Polish stage. Several plays were translated into Russian in the eighteenth century, and the empress Catherine II had a share in adaptations of *The Merry Wives of Windsor* and *Timon*. The standard Russian translation is that of Gerbel (1865). In Poland, where Shakespeare is a favourite dramatist both with actors and public, the best translation is that edited by the poet Józef Ignacy Kraszewski (1875). Reference must be made, in conclusion, to the great interest which Hungarians have always shown in the English poet, and the powerful influence he has exerted on their literature. A very high rank among translations of Shakespeare is claimed for those by the eminent poet Michael Vörösmarty, especially for that of *Julius Caesar*.

It seems supererogatory to add to this survey of Shakespeare abroad a word on Shakespeare in America; so far as our literature is concerned, America is not, and never has been, 'abroad,' and, in the case of Shakespeare especially, it would be invidious to set up any limits within the area of the earth's surface where the English tongue is spoken. But some tribute ought at least to be paid to the independence and originality of American contributions to Shakespearean criticism and research. By borrowing the best elements in English critical methods and combining them with German thoroughness and patience, American scholars, in recent years, have thrown much light on dark places and contributed very materially to our understanding of Shakespeare's work. In the first line stands the admirable *Variorum Edition* of Shakespeare's plays founded by Howard Furness in 1873. The leading American actors, too, such as Edwin Booth, J. B. Booth and Edwin Forrest have distinguished themselves by fresh and stimulating interpretations of Shakespeare's greater tragedies on the stage.

CHAPTER XIII

LESSER ELIZABETHAN DRAMATISTS

THE Elizabethan drama emerges as a distinct form of imaginative art shortly after the defeat of the Armada, and its first masterpieces are the work of a group of university writers of whom Marlowe and Greene are the greatest. There are no 'lesser dramatists' of this date. The lesser dramatist is the result of the extraordinary interest in the drama which these authors created, and the assiduous effort made by patrons, managers and players to produce plays in the new style which took the town. Moreover, we have to wait some years before the work of lesser writers survives sufficiently to enable us to appraise it. As a consequence, the lesser Elizabethan dramatists, as a group, belong to the last years of Elizabeth's reign ; and we owe it to the lucky chance of the survival of Henslowe's diary that we can eke out our knowledge of a few extant plays by the notices in that diary of the large mass of work done by the writers of them. It is important that the student of Elizabethan drama should appreciate justly the meaning and the value of Henslowe's record. We have no such light upon the proceedings of the company for which Shakespeare wrote and played. But it seems quite clear that Shakespeare was never under the harrow of a Henslowe.

The players of his company obtained the control of their own affairs and managed their business on cooperative principles. The system of the Chamberlain's men tended to produce a limited number of dramatists of proved ability, who were encouraged to write plays of a quality that would ensure a run at their first production and justify reproduction afterwards. The system of Henslowe's company, on the contrary, tended to produce quantity rather than quality. The public was attracted by variety and novelty rather than by excellence, and, in order that new plays might be produced quickly, very imperfect revision of old plays was allowed to pass, and the system of collaboration between three or four writers was freely encouraged. For these reasons, we may feel some confidence that the group of lesser dramatists who wrote for Henslowe during the years covered by his diary is representative of the body of lesser dramatists writing during those years for the London stage.

But, before we fix our attention upon individual writers whose plays have come down to us, two facts must be noticed which affect them as a body. In the first place, because they were lesser dramatists, and because the printing of a play, in those days, was an altogether secondary matter to the acting of it, their work can hardly be said to have survived. The fragments that have come down to us are so few and so mutilated that, in many cases, we are not justified in regarding them as characteristic. It is impossible, for instance, to decide whether *The Tragedy of Hoffman* is truly representative of the large dramatic output of Henry Chettle. We may feel reasonably sure that no important play of Shakespeare has been lost. We cannot be sure that the substance of Chettle's or Munday's work has survived. What we have of it may not be in any sense characteristic. The second fact that has to be reckoned with by the critic of the lesser dramatists in Henslowe's employ is the system of collaboration under which they wrote. Not the least of the fascinations of the Elizabethan era is that it affords remarkable instances of a collaboration by which two writers of genius stimulate and supplement each other's powers. But the collaboration which is possible because the minds of those taking part in it are commonplace is a different matter altogether. Among lesser writers, collaboration tends to suppress individuality and distinction of style, and makes still more confusing and difficult the task of ascribing to individual writers any qualities truly their own. Moreover, all Elizabethan dramatists may be said to have collaborated in a special sense with their predecessors. Broadly speaking, the Elizabethan drama was a process of re-writing and re-constructing old plays. The Elizabethan author stood in much closer relation to his 'origins' and sources than did later English writers. But this, again, tended to suppress the individuality of second-rate poets. The lesser dramatist does not set his own stamp on the 'old play' as Shakespeare does. There is no vital connection between *King Lear* and *The True Chronicle History of King Leir* : Shakespeare's play is a new thing. But, in reading Munday's *Downfall of Robert, Earle of Huntington,* the question continually suggests itself whether the play is much more than an alteration—an alteration which remains at the same artistic and imaginative level as the thing altered. The conclusion is that the student must not expect to distinguish lesser dramatists from each other as greater dramatists are distinguished. The attempt to characterise them involves the use of a critical microscope which magnifies their merits.

At the same time, it must be allowed that the lesser dramatist whose main work belongs to the last years of Elizabeth's reign has an individuality of his own which he loses after Shakespeare and Ben Jonson have impressed their age. A lesser dramatist, however rough, formless and incoherent, is more interesting when he is himself, or when he is the product of the general mind of his time, than when he is a 'son' of Ben Jonson or, palpably, a student of some particular aspect of the art of Shakespeare. The lesser Jacobean dramatist nearly always derives from some acknowledged master, and is an echo as well as an inferior. The Elizabethan lesser dramatist, on the contrary, does not interest us as an echo, but very much more deeply as the commonplace companion of the great master, his surrounding and background. It is much more interesting to find in Munday's *John a Kent and John a Cumber* clumsy work on a theme which, in Shakespeare's hands, is magically effective, than to notice how patiently and even skilfully 'Dick' Brome follows the manner of Jonson. And, therefore, it is disappointing to the student that, because of the conditions under which they respectively worked, much more of Brome should be extant than of Munday.

Henslowe's diary begins to record payments made to authors for writing plays at the end of 1597. The entries come to an end, for the most part, in 1603. During this time, twenty-seven authors are named as composers of plays or parts of plays. The work of ten of these is trifling. Of the remaining seventeen, six are writers of force and distinction, not to be reckoned as 'lesser.' These are Chapman, Dekker, Heywood, Jonson, Middleton, Webster[1]. We may note that, of these six, only Chapman refuses to collaborate with inferior men; that none of Jonson's work done in collaboration is extant, except his additions to *Jeronimo*; and that Middleton and Webster do not occur in the diary till 1602. Eleven writers are left whom we may describe as the main group of Elizabethan lesser dramatists. These, in alphabetical order, are Henry Chettle, John Day, Michael Drayton, Richard Hathwaye, William Haughton, Anthony Munday, Henry Porter, William

---

[1] Perhaps Maxton, 'the new poete,' is John Marston.

Rankins, Samuel Rowley, Wentworth Smith, Robert Wilson. Rowley and Smith begin writing in 1601; Rankins is mentioned only in 1599 and 1601; the remaining eight constitute the main group of lesser men who were writing for the Elizabethan stage between the end of 1597 and the beginning of 1603.

The comments of Francis Meres, in 1598, upon English contemporary writers, give us some means of checking the results of an examination of Henslowe's records. Of Henslowe's men, Meres names, among 'our best for tragedy,' Drayton, Chapman, Dekker, Jonson; among 'the best for comedy,' Heywood, Munday, Chapman, Porter, Wilson, Hathwaye, Chettle. From his place in the list, we conjecture that Wilson—son of the more famous Robert Wilson, the elder—is the writer for Henslowe. One writer, Chapman, shares with Shakespeare the honour of occurring in both lists. All the writers whom we have noted as doing a substantial amount of work for Henslowe's companies are mentioned by Meres, except Day and Haughton.

In considering the work of these men, upon whose output for six years a sudden light is thrown by Henslowe's papers, we propose to follow a chronological order so far as may be, and to begin with the older men who were practised hands at the date when Henslowe's payments are first recorded. Fortunately, there is one whom we may safely look upon as the senior of our group, and choose as a natural centre round which the work of the rest may be grouped, or from which it may be derived. This is the comedian Anthony Munday, spoken of by Meres as 'our best plotter,' perhaps because of his seniority and experience as a hewer and trimmer of plays rather than with any reference to his faculty for conducting a plot in the modern sense of the term. Of the lesser Elizabethan dramatists, Munday is the most considerable, interesting and typical. In his general versatility, his copiousness and his reliance upon himself and upon life for his learning and culture, he corresponds, on his own level, to Shakespeare and Ben Jonson on the heights. His long life, moreover, of eighty years (1553—1633) covers the whole of the Elizabethan and Jacobean era of dramatic activity. He was born before Shakespeare; Jonson survived him only by four years. He was a Londoner, and had some experience as an actor before his apprenticeship, in 1576, to John Allde, stationer and printer. In 1578, he undertook a journey to Rome, to see foreign countries and to learn their languages, according to his own account; but, also, with the less creditable object of spying upon English Catholics abroad, and

getting together materials for popular pamphlets against them on
his return to England. After interesting adventures on the way,
he reached Rome, and was entertained at the English college,
so that he came to describe himself as 'sometime the Pope's
scholar.' His experiences were detailed in a pamphlet published
in 1582, with the title *The English Romayne Life*. This was a
rejoinder to a tract, printed in 1581, in the Catholic interest, from
which we get some interesting lights upon Munday's early connection with the stage. He was 'first a stage player,' says the
pamphlet, 'after' (*i.e.* afterwards) 'an apprentice.' On his return
from Italy, 'this scholar did play *extempore*' and was 'hissed from
his stage,' 'Then being thereby discouraged he set forth a ballad
against plays; but yet (O constant youth) he now again begins to
ruffle upon the stage[1].'

This is to say that Munday attempted to achieve fame in that
special department of the Elizabethan player's art of which Robert
Wilson and Richard Tarlton[2] were the most distinguished ornaments. The extemporising clown not only supplied the humorous
element of the interlude, but, also, he was frequently called for
after the play was over, when he performed a jig, accompanied
by some kind of recitative of his own composing in prose or
verse. The audience might challenge him to rime on any subject,
and Tarlton's facility was so remarkable that 'Tarletonising' is
used as equivalent to extemporising. There is extant a 'platt' or
programme of the second part of *The Seven Deadly Sins*, which is
said to have been the composition of Tarlton ; and, probably,
such skeleton plays, in which actors were expected to fill in their
parts extempore, were not uncommon in the early days of the Elizabethan drama. Tarlton's successor in the esteem of the public as
a clown actor was William Kemp. It is easy to see from 'Kemp's
applauded Merriments of the Men of Gotham,' which is inserted in
A Knack to Know a Knave, how inevitably the improvising clown,
with his licence to introduce his own additions, was a discordant

---

[1] Consult 'A Caveat to the Reader touching A.M. his discovery,' printed at the
end of the pamphlet. The interesting theory (cf. *post*, vol. VI, chap. XIV) attributing to
Munday the anonymous authorship of *The Third Blast of Retreat from Plays and
Theatres* (1560) has to meet the difficulty that its author declares himself to have
'bene a great affecter of that vaine art of Plaie-making, insomuch that I have thought
no time so wel bestowed, as when exercised in the invention of these follies.' The
writer of the preface, Anglo-phile Eutheo, quotes these words and confirms them—
'yea, which I ad, as excellent an Autor of these vanities, as who was best.' We must
revise existing opinion on the subject altogether, if we are to treat Munday as a well
known writer of plays so early as 1580.

[2] As to Tarlton, cf. *ante*, vol. IV, p. 360, and *ibid.*, bibl., p. 531.

and incalculable element in the play, and hindered the development of artistic drama. The extempore clown of real genius usually failed as an author; but Robert Wilson was a remarkable exception. His two interludes, *The Three Ladies of London*, and *The Three Lords and Three Ladies of London*, are specimens of belated interludes modified in the direction of true drama by the life and the reality imported into the interlude by the extempore actor. It is from these interludes that Munday's work derives.

Munday's ballad writing is an important part of his earlier career. It put him into contact with the folklore of England, and had an appreciable influence on his dramatic work. It was so energetic that, by 1592, he looked upon himself as having some sort of monopoly of the art. Another of his activities, which was not without its influence upon the dramatists of the age, was his diligent translation of French romances, such as *Amadis de Gaule* and *Palmerin of England*. When Ben Jonson satirises him as Balladino, there is a double allusion to his ballad writing and to his *Palladino of England*, translated from the French.

A translation from the Italian may be given as the beginning of Munday's work as a dramatist, although it must be borne in mind that his authorship is not more than highly probable. This is *Fedele and Fortunio, The Deceits in Love discoursed in a Comedy of two Italian Gentlemen: translated into English*, printed in 1584[1]. This play must have had some vogue, for one of the characters, captain Crackstone, is alluded to by Nashe as well known in a tract printed in 1596[2]; and its influence as an admirably translated example of Italian comedy must have been considerable upon English drama. It is annoying, therefore, that the piece, which both Collier and Halliwell-Phillipps saw and quoted, has disappeared[3], and that we must judge of it by Halliwell's meagre extracts[4]. These present the humorous low life of the play rather than the romantic part, which was clearly of the character of Shakespeare's earlier comedies, in which pairs of lovers are fantastically at cross purposes:

> Lo! here the common fault of love, to follow her that flies,
> And fly from her that makes pursuit with loud lamenting cries.
> Fedele loves Victoria, and she hath him forgot;
> Virginia likes Fedele best, and he regards her not.

[1] In Stationers' register, 12 November 1584; Arber, vol. II, p. 202.
[2] *Have with you to Saffron Walden.*
[3] [See, however, bibliography, *post*, p. 474.]
[4] Halliwell(-Phillipps), J. O., *The Literature of the Sixteenth and Seventeenth Centuries*, 1851, No. 2, pp. 18, 19, 24.

Victoria's song at her window and Fedele's in answer are of real poetic charm, and Fedele's denunciation of woman's fickleness is exactly in the strain, as it is in the metre, of the riming rhetoric of *Love's Labour's Lost*. But the comic scenes are not less interesting. Their combination with the romantic intrigue is organic, and, in clear strong outlines, the play gives us two motives which receive elaborate development in English drama. Crackstone is the prototype of Bobadill and Tucca and all the braggadocios of the Elizabethan stage—but of Falstaff, also, for every one is glad of his company : 'I have such a wild worm in my head as makes them all merry.' And, secondly, the witchcraft scenes of the play deserve careful notice[1]. Medusa, the witch, is capable of development, either romantically and tragically, or humorously and by the method of realism. The witches of *Macbeth*, as well as the charlatans of Jonson and Brome, may be derived from this germ ; but, in the main, the witchcraft, in Munday's play, is realistic, in actual connection with the vigorous low life characters. Victoria's maid Attilia, who is wooed by Pedante and Crackstone, and is the confidante and champion of her mistress, is put before us in clear English speech, and, of course, stands at the beginning of a long gallery of familiar creations. She is indispensable in nearly all ensuing species of the drama. There seems to be no blank verse in the play. Riming alexandrines and four-teen-syllabled lines are generally employed ; but, in Fedele's speech already referred to, special seriousness and dignity of style are attained by the use of riming ten-syllabled lines in stanzas of six lines[2]. This might be expected in 1584 ; what is unexpected is the idiomatic English vernacular of the translation, which stamps Munday as much more than a translator in the ordinary sense. His prose translations do not display any special power in transforming the original into native English ; so that the mere style of *Fedele and Fortunio* is an argument for its having been translated in order to be acted, and for the translator having expected himself to be one of the actors. Nashe's allusion makes it highly probable that captain Crackstone had appeared upon the Elizabethan stage.

Munday, in 1580[3] and in his earliest published work, is anxious

---

[1] Presumably, Halliwell alludes to these when he says that one scene 'might by possibility have been the germ of one in *Macbeth*'; and yet he seems to imply that he has not printed this scene.

[2] Compare Biron's speech, *Love's Labour's Lost*, act I, sc. 1, 92—94.

[3] *A View of Sundry Examples*, &c., 1580: pp. 71 and 75 of the reprint in Collier's *John a Kent and John a Cumber*.

to proclaim himself 'servant to the Earl of Oxford.' The earl of Oxford's company of players acted in London between 1584 and 1587. Fleay, therefore, claims for Munday the authorship of *The Weakest goeth to the Wall*, a play printed in 1600, 'as it hath bene sundry times plaide by the right honourable Earle of Oxenford, Lord great Chamberlaine of England his servants.' It is in favour of this claim that the story of the play is found in Rich's *Farewell to the Military Profession*, printed 1581. But the play is very different from *Fedele and Fortunio*. Its chief merit is the force and fluency of portions of its blank verse, which must be later than *Tamburlaine*. On the other hand, there are signs of an older style in the play. We have frequent passages of rime, and, in one place, the six-lined stanza occurs. The humorous scenes are a great advance upon Kemp's applauded 'Merriments' already referred to. They are excellent examples of the low life comedy that grew out of the part of the extempore clown in earlier interludes. Barnaby Bunch the 'botcher'[1], and Sir Nicholas the country vicar, are vigorously etched from contemporary English life, and speak a fluent vernacular prose which, in one or two places, recalls Falstaff. Jacob Smelt the Dutchman requires a date nearer to 1600 than to 1580, but all this might be Munday's work, and is certainly the work of his fellow craftsmen. Moreover, the general looseness of construction is characteristic of 'our best plotter'; but he cannot have written the sonorous blank verse of the historic scenes, or made Emmanuel reproach Frederick—

> That from the loathsome mud from whence thou camest,
> Thou art so bold out of thy buzzard's nest,
> To gaze upon the sun of her perfections!
> Is there no beauty that can please your eye,
> But the divine and splendant excellence
> Of my beloved dear Odillia[2]?

The first extant play which is certainly Munday's is *John a Kent and John a Cumber*, of which we have a transcript dated December 1595. Fleay has very plausibly conjectured that this is identical with *The Wiseman of West Chester*, which was produced at the Rose by the Admiral's men on 2 December 1594, and was very popular. Henslowe mentions thirty-one performances within three years. On lines laid down by Greene in *Frier Bacon and Frier Bongay*, it describes the 'tug for maistree' between the two wizards John a Kent and John a Cumber. When the play

---

[1] *I.e.* tailor.   [2] C. 4⁰.

opens, the two heroines, Sidanen and Marian, are preparing a
strong confection of deadly aconite, which they propose to drink
with the husbands presently to be forced upon them, the earls of
Morton and Pembroke. But the romantic side of the story is entirely
subordinated to the wiles and disguisings by which the wizards
succeed in getting possession of the heroines, first for one set of
lovers and then for the other. Finally, by the subtlety of John a
Kent, Sir Griffin and lord Powis win their brides. The power of
the wizards to disguise and transform, and the masking of the
'antiques,' make the play a maze of errors not easy to follow. With
this main action, the comic scenes of 'Turnop with his Crewe
of Clownes and a Minstrell' are mingled in pleasant confusion.
'Turnop and his Crew' are not unworthy of being mentioned in
the same breath with Bottom and his mates. Munday's play is a
humble variation of the dramatic type of *A Midsummer Night's
Dream*. But another parallel with Shakespeare's work is even
more interesting. Shrimp, John a Kent's familiar, makes himself
invisible and, by music in the air, leads his master's enemies astray
till they lie down to sleep from weariness. It throws light upon
Shakespeare's mind and imagination rather than upon Munday's
to suppose that Munday's play gave hints for the character of
Ariel and the exquisite poetry of *The Tempest*; but the earlier
play, in its brightness and sweetness and wholesomeness, was
worthy of supplying the ground upon which Shakespeare's feet
stood—the point of departure for his mind—when he created
his own masterpiece.

This play shows that Munday was interested in English folk-
lore. His next play is a further incursion into the same type of
drama, which may be looked upon, in some respects, as a variety of
the chronicle play, and, in others, as a variety of the romantic play
of which *Fedele and Fortunio* was a specimen. As in *John a Kent
and John a Cumber*, historical characters are brought into the
play and mixed up with folklore. Munday's new subject is the
Robin Hood cycle of legends and ballads, which had been connected with dramatic representations early in the sixteenth, and
even in the fifteenth, century. It is worth noticing that a line in
Fedele and Fortunio, 'Robin-goodfellowe, Hobgoblin, the devil
and his dam[1],' cannot have been a literal translation from the
Italian. Munday's treatment of the Robin Hood story ran into
two parts. Part I, when the plays were printed in 1601, was

---

[1] Quoted by Collier, *History of Dramatic Poetry*, 1879, vol. III, p. 60. But for
'dam' we ought probably to read 'dame.'

entitled *The Downfall of Robert, Earle of Huntington*; part II
was called *The Death of Robert, Earle of Huntington*; but both
title-pages describe the earl as 'called Robin Hood of merrie
Sherwodde.' It would seem probable that, in a passage in the
first play, we have a description of an earlier play, of which
Munday's aspires to be a reconstruction. This contained 'mirthful
matter full of game' and confined itself strictly to the pranks and
pastimes of Robin Hood, Maid Marian, Friar Tuck and the other
familiar personages of the Robin Hood May game. Munday
prides himself upon adding to this the story of 'noble Robert's
wrong' and ' his mild forgetting' of 'treacherous injury.' Fleay
thinks that the old play was *The Pastoral Comedy of Robin Hood
and Little John*, written in 1594. It cannot be claimed that the
attempt to identify Robin Hood with Robert earl of Huntington,
and Maid Marian with the 'chaste Matilda' whom king John
persecuted, is artistically successful ; the two elements of history
and folklore are not satisfactorily fused together. On the whole,
John a Kent and John a Cumber has more artistic unity than *The
Downfall of Robert, Earle of Huntington*. But the effort to work
in the historical element is due to a true artistic instinct and
aspiration. Munday wishes to raise his subject above farce and
horseplay to a romantic and even tragic level. He gropes, also,
after some sort of organic unity which shall make his play more
than a series of incidents. An effort is made to produce sustained
blank verse, which is most successful in the earl of Leicester's
account of the prowess of Richard I. For a moment, the dramatist
touches the epic note of the history play, when he is fired by the
thought of the deeds of Richard Cœur de Lion. But, as a whole,
the historical side of the play is weak and feebly conceived. On
the romantic and imaginative side, it is stronger. When Fitzwater
comes upon the stage seeking 'the poor man's patron, Robin Hood,'
and the life of the greenwood is described, Munday uses the riming
verse which he seems always to handle more easily than blank
verse, and the result may be called a pleasant and intelligent
attempt to express the soul of the old English Robin Hood story.
This is the soundest and best part of the play and was deservedly
popular. We find in the play phrases that may have rested in the
mind of Shakespeare : such are 'heaven's glorious canopy,' 'made
the green sea red' and, in the second part, 'the multitudes of seas
died red with blood'; but a more general influence upon Shakespeare's work of Munday's attempt to idealise and dignify the
Robin Hood legend may, probably, be found in *As You Like It*.

Munday was paid £5 for the first part of his play in February 1598, and its vogue may have prompted Shakespeare's picture of the forest 'where they live like the old Robin Hood of England ... and fleet the time carelessly as they did in the golden world.' The first part of Robin Hood was immediately succeeded by a second part, in which Munday was assisted by Henry Chettle. When the two parts were printed in 1601, *The Downfall* was Chettle's revision of Munday's play for performance at court at the end of 1598. This revision clearly consisted of the induction in which the play is set and the 'Skeltonical' rimes. *The Death* presents a more difficult problem. Up to the death of Robin Hood, it is, in the main, Munday's work and continues the style and tone of Munday's combination of the Robin Hood legend with a history ; but this occupies less than one third of the play, and, when Robert is dead, a new play begins dealing with the 'lamentable tragedy of chaste Matilda,' and striking a tragic note quite different from anything written by Munday. At the end of *The Downfall*, a second play is promised us, which is to describe the funeral of Richard Cœur de Lion; and this was written in 1598, but is no longer extant. It is tempting to suppose that the opening section of *The Death* was written originally as a part of *The Funeral of Richard Cœur de Lion* ; and that Chettle, when he 'mended' the play for the court, cut down Munday's work as much as he could.

In Henslowe's diary, Munday is mentioned in connection with fifteen or, perhaps, sixteen plays, between December 1597 and December 1602. Of these, only two—*The Downfall of Robert, Earle of Huntington* and *The Set at Tennis*—are ascribed to his sole authorship. Munday's most frequent collaborators are Drayton, Chettle, Wilson, Hathwaye and Dekker; Smith, Middleton and Webster are mentioned as collaborating once. Of the lost plays in which Munday had a share, we know that *The Funeral of Richard Cœur de Lion* continued the Robin Hood plays, while *Mother Redcap* and *Valentine and Orson* belonged almost certainly to the same type of play, which used sources more popular than those of either the Italian romance or the literary chronicle. These plays were founded upon ballads and chap-books and folk-lore. They make a clumsy use of historical motives and romantic motives and generally fail to fuse them successfully with low life scenes—with the 'crew' of peasants, or 'sort' of artisans—which are often the salt of the play. *Sir John Oldcastle* is another play in which Munday collaborated. The first part of this play has survived. It shows a distinct advance towards the 'history' in the Shakespearean sense, and helps us to realise the special achievement of a genius which, on the one hand, was to create the Shakespearean romantic comedy and, on the other, the Shakespearean history[1]. But these plays of Munday, just because there is no genius in them, are more easily perceived to be natural developments of the interlude as written by the elder Wilson. In drawing the tree of our drama's descent, we must insert them between Shakespeare and the interludes.

A play of exactly the same genre as Munday's plays is the anonymous *Looke about you*, printed 1600 ; and it requires some notice because, in some respects, it is the best specimen of its class. We find Robin Hood and Robert earl of Huntington identified in this play as in *The Downfall* and *The Death*. But Robin is a youth remarkable for his good looks and the ward of prince Richard, afterwards Cœur de Lion ; his action in the play is subordinate. Chronologically, therefore, our play would seem to come between *John a Kent* and *The Downfall*. We are in exactly the same atmosphere of mixed history and folklore, recorded, probably, in ballads and chap-books. Some of the amateurish mannerisms of *The Downfall*, such as the use of 'too-too,' and the doubling of words and phrases to obtain emphasis, occur in *Looke about you*, while the relation to the play of the two tricksters, Skink and the 'humorous' earl of Gloster[2], is a repetition of the use made of the rival wizards in *John a Kent*. The earl of Gloster is, perhaps, a reminiscence in the popular mind of Robert earl of Gloster, natural son of Henry I and father-in-law of Ranulph earl of Chester, who is connected with the meagre historical element in *John a Kent*. The historical part of *Looke about you* deals with the quarrels of the sons of Henry II and is exceptionally naïve, undignified and clownish. Skink and Gloster are a sort of double Vice. Skink is tacked on to history as the agent who administered the poison to fair Rosamond. The play opens by his appearance before parliament, where Gloster strikes him in the king's presence. Gloster is committed to the Fleet prison for striking Skink and, after this perfunctory historical opening, the real business of the 'pleasant comedy' begins with the intricate succession of disguises, personations and tricks by which Skink and Gloster deceive and bewilder their pursuers. There are reminiscences of *The Comedy of Errors* in the play

---

[1] As to the ascription of this play to Shakespeare see chap. x above.
[2] He is called 'Robin' once or twice in the play which suggests the possibility that, at one time, he was Robin Goodfellow.

and, still more clearly, of the Falstaff scenes in *Henry IV*. Old
Sir Richard Fauconbridge is a far-away echo of Falstaff; there is
a drawer who answers 'anon'; but the glimpses of the inside of
the Fleet and of London taverns are at first-hand, and bring
Elizabethan London pleasantly before us. The stammering runner
Redcap is a humorous character of real originality, whose tireless
activity adds delightfully to the bustle and rush of the play. We
should like to claim this play for Munday; but, in the historical
scenes and especially in the character of prince John, we have
a style which cannot be Munday's and was, perhaps, Chettle's. It
is abrupt and extravagantly emphatic. Munday's tragical note in
The Downfall and *The Death* is smooth, sentimental and lachry-
mose; this writer's is rough, fierce and gloomy. It is very tempting
to discern in the clumsily boorish quarrels of Henry's sons and in
the fierce rant of prince John early work of Henry Chettle.

From about 1592, Munday was in the city's service, and probably began to write pageants about that date, although his extant
pageants date from 1605 to 1616. His historical and antiquarian
interests brought him the friendship of Stow, and, in 1606, after
Stow's death, he was instructed by the corporation to revise the
Survey of London, which revision was printed in 1618. It is
probable, therefore, that Munday left off writing for the stage
about 1603. His earlier career is excellently illustrated by the
attacks made upon him in the course of the 'war of the theatres,'
which broke out at the end of the century. In *The Case is
Altered*, Jonson introduces him as Antonio Balladino, the 'pageant
poet,' 'when a worse cannot be had,' and makes him describe his
own style as eminently 'wholesome'—

I do use as much stale stuff, though I say it myself, as any man does
in that kind I am sure.... Why, look you, Sir, I write so plain and keep
that old decorum that you must of necessity like it.

As for the new, more elegant play, 'the common sort they care
not for it.' This, no doubt, was true. We must not assume that
the typical Elizabethan cared only for Shakespeare and Ben
Jonson. There was a large public to whom inferior plays appealed,
and for whose tastes Henslowe's group of writers very largely
catered. Munday has reason when he declares, 'an they'll give
me twenty pounds a play, I'll not raise my vein.' Besides Jonson's
admirable raillery, we have the equally interesting lampoon of
Munday in *Histrio-Mastix*, an early allegorical play, revised, probably by Marston, in 1599. The sketch of the 'sort' of players

is a vivid picture of an Elizabethan 'company,' scratched hastily together, and not quite clear whose men they are :

> Once in a week new masters we seek,
> And never can hold together.

Posthast, the 'pageanter' and writer of ballads, is the poet of the company, very anxious to show his skill in 'extempore' riming. There is no 'new luxury or blandishment' in his style, but 'plenty of old England's mothers words.' But the writings of such 'ballad-mongers' and 'apprentices,' says Marston, 'best please the vulgar sense[1].'

It is natural, after considering Munday's work and personality, to proceed to the consideration of Henry Chettle's dramatic activity ; but this implies discussing the tragedy of our group of dramatists before we treat of their comedy. Both tragedy and comedy are natural developments from such a play as *The Downfall* ; but, on the whole, we should expect what is actually the case, that the group of plays we have been considering would lead rather to comedy than to tragedy, and that, on the whole, the comedies would be better than the tragedies. *The Death of Robert, Earle of Huntington,* Chettle's play on Matilda's death, is a complete contrast in tone and spirit to the work of Munday which preceded it.

If, from the scope of his activities and the length of his life, Munday may be placed at the head of those lesser Elizabethan dramatists whose work was not strong enough to survive except in fragments, we must place next to him, for mere amount of literary output, Henry Chettle, whom Henslowe associates with some fifty plays. His personality can be made out with tolerable clearness. He was the son of a London dyer, apprenticed in 1577 to a stationer, and free of the company in 1584. In writing to Thomas Nashe, he signs himself 'Your old Compositor,' which means that, in 1589—90, he set up Nashe's tracts against Marprelate. In 1591, he entered into partnership with two not very reputable stationers, William Hoskins and John Danter. They published a good many ballads, some of which may have been from Chettle's pen; and some plays—one of Peele's, one of Lodge's, a *Titus Andronicus* in 1594 and, in 1597, the surreptitious first quarto of *Romeo and Juliet.* Only one tract by Chettle himself was issued by Danter ; but, in 1592, Chettle edited *Greens Groatsworth of Wit,* and,

---

[1] R. Simpson's *School of Shakespere*, vol. II, pp. 21, 31, 33, 39, 40, 51, 62, 67.

soon after, wrote his *Kinde Hart's Dreame*, both of them memorable for their references to Shakespeare. These facts establish very definitely Chettle's connection with playwrights and the stage. Danter's presses were confiscated in 1597 for printing *Jesu's Psalter* without authority, and he printed no more ; but it is interesting to find Munday's *Palladino of England* licensed to Danter shortly before he was suppressed as a printer. Upon the failure of the printing business, Chettle would seem to have turned to the writing of plays for a livelihood. In 1598, Meres names him among ' our best for comedy,' which is disconcerting, inasmuch as his comedies have not survived. From *Kinde Hart's Dreame* (1593), we can gather that the humours of early comedy did not come amiss to him, and, if we may ascribe to him the Welsh scenes of *Patient Grissill*, we have in them a good example of a rather boisterous, though, at the same time, arid, comedy which suits his tragic vein[1]. But Chettle was the most copious of Henslowe's collaborators. For about a dozen plays, he alone receives payment, and we may suppose that these were his own work. In the early months of 1598, a regular partnership was carried on between Chettle, Dekker, Drayton and Wilson. In 1599, Dekker is most frequently Chettle's collaborator. In 1600, Day begins to work with him. On two occasions, he collaborates with Jonson. But of all his work very little has survived. We have conjectured that his tragic style is to be detected first in the melodramatic rant of prince John in *Looke about you*. The allusion in that play to the ' burning crown of red-hot iron,' with which prince Henry threatens to sear Gloster's brain, is found again in the single play extant which is ascribed to Chettle alone—*The Tragedy of Hoffman*. But, before we discuss this, we must examine Chettle's work in *The Death of Robert, Earle of Huntington*, written in 1598. The few scenes in that drama which bring us to the death of Robin Hood are described as a ' short play,' and the audience is asked to have patience while Matilda's tragedy is ended. After three dumb-shows, the story of king John's pursuit of Matilda is taken up, and with it is combined the story of the starvation of lady Bruce and her little son. The epilogue describes this play as ' Matilda's story shown in act,' and ' rough-hewn out by an uncunning hand.' That is to say, our play is the ' old compositor's ' first tragedy in which he works alone. He succeeds in striking a note of gloom and grief which marks the play off very clearly from the tamely cheerful work of Munday. But the style

[1] As to *Patient Grissill*, cf. vol. VI, chap. II.

is extremely 'uncunning' and amateurish. Sometimes, it is merely jejune and pedestrian, as when Leicester, surrendering to John,

> humbly begs his Highness to beware
> Of wronging innocence as he hath done.

At other times, it is almost comically naïve and undignified, as in the scene where the earl of Oxford tries to persuade queen Elinor not to take too seriously the king's infidelities. But the dramatist struggles manfully to rise above commonplace, and, though he produces mainly rant and fustian, there are occasional glimpses of dignity and power: as when king John says of his nobles

> Of high heroic spirits be they all;

and when he breaks out to Fitzwater,

> Old brands of malice in thy bosom rest.

Moreover, Chettle has the conception in his mind of an atmosphere of horror and grief as necessary to tragedy. But the elaborate account of the starving of lady Bruce and her boy is a clumsy failure, more painful to the reader because he must recall Dante's canto on Ugolino's death. Only in one place, where lord Bruce shows his murdered mother to the nobles, does the rant approach poetic force and suggest to us the style which gives some merit to *The Tragedy of Hoffman*. If Chettle copies any master in Matilda's tragedy, it is Marlowe in his most inflated vein; in one or two places, the influence of Shakespeare's *Richard II* is, perhaps, to be detected.

Could we be certain that the second play in the *Two Lamentable Tragedies* is Chettle's work, we should have an interesting example of the development of his tragic manner. If we may take Henslowe's writers as representative of the lesser dramatists and, therefore, as reflecting the dramatic tastes and capacities of the less cultured patrons of the drama, we perceive that, just at the end of the sixteenth century, a definite taste for tragedy was setting in. In 1598 and 1599, we find in Henslowe's lists a series of plays which were domestic tragedies founded upon actual murders as they were recorded in the ballads and pamphlets of the day. It was natural that, if plays were being made out of folklore ballads upon Robin Hood and other national heroes, mythical or historical, the murder ballad should be seized upon for stage purposes, and such a use could not but convey into serious drama a new strain of realism and vitality. Tragedy would thus be prevented from losing itself in the imaginative incoherence of the 'revenge' plays which Kyd's genius, catching fire from Seneca, had brought into vogue. *Arden of Feversham*, printed in 1592, proves that the possibilities of domestic tragedy had been perceived before Henslowe's day—perhaps even as early as 1578/9, when *The Creweltie of a Step-mother* and *Murderous mychaell* are mentioned in the accounts of the revels[1]. In 1598 and 1599, Henslowe's collaborators produced two parts of *Black Bateman of the North, Cox of Collumpton, The Stepmothers Tragedy* and *Page of Plymouth*, all of which have been plausibly classed as 'murder' plays. About the same date, if not earlier, the extant *Warning for Faire Women* must have been written, a play composed with more pains than Henslowe's writers usually bestowed upon their productions. The author had no dramatic or poetic genius; but his play is a transcript from the daily life of the people. It neither exaggerates nor idealises; it makes no effort to be tragic or comic, but is so steeped in English lower class sentiment and feeling that it will always possess interest and value. In 1599, Day and Haughton collaborated for Henslowe in *Thomas Merry, or Beech's Tragedy*. The murder of Robert Beech by Thomas Merry took place in London in 1594, and was duly recorded in a pamphlet and in ballads. This murder is the subject of the first of the two murders commemorated in *Two Lamentable Tragedies*, printed as by Rob. Yarington in 1601. The second murder is an Italian version of the story of the babes in the wood. Now, when we look at Chettle's work for Henslowe, at the end of 1599, we find him at work upon a certain *Orphan's Tragedy*, for which, in November, he receives two payments of 10*s.* Much later, in September 1601, he receives another 10*s.* for the same play. Moreover, in January 1600, a payment of £2 is made to John Day in earnest of *The Italian Tragedy*. It is a plausible explanation of these entries that Chettle wrote the main part of *The Orphan's Tragedy*, being helped by Day, and that, in 1601, he was again employed to throw into a single play Day and Haughton's *Thomas Merry* and Day and Chettle's *Orphan's Tragedy*. He had done similar work in the case of the Robin Hood plays; *The Death of Robert, Earle of Huntington* is just as clumsy and mechanical an amalgamation as *Two Lamentable Tragedies*. This view supposes that Robert Yarington is a pseudonym, or that he merely prepared Chettle's work for the press. Chettle's style is to be looked for mainly in the second of the *Two Lamentable Tragedies*, which represents *The Orphan's Tragedy*, otherwise called *The Italian Tragedy*, of Henslowe's diary. In these scenes, we find repeated with greater

[1] Cf., as to the development of English domestic drama, vol. VI, chap. IV.

force and more concentration those qualities which we have noted in Chettle's part of *The Death of Robert, Earle of Huntington.* But Marlowe is more obviously and definitely imitated.   The rant of the incredible villain Ithamore, the familiar of Barabas in *The Jew of Malta,* is almost copied by the first murderer[1], whose character is sketched with a horrible intense vigour which is the aim and goal of Chettle's art.   But there are, also, echoes of the style of Shakespeare's *Richard II,* and of the peculiar note of exquisite self-pity to which the deposed king gives perfect expression.   The second of the *Two Lamentable Tragedies* may, very plausibly, be set down as Chettle's work ; but the first play is quite different in character.   In parts, it is extraordinarily bald and pedestrian in its realism, taking out of prose pamphlets all that is trivial and brutal with unintelligent accuracy.   On the whole, it lacks the emotional and imaginative vehemence of the Chettle drama.   Is this the tragic style of Haughton after Day's work has been stripped away ?   It is noticeable that the inartistic faithfulness of the realism which we find here follows the method of the writer of *A warning for Faire Women,* which play must be supposed to have prompted the writing of *Thomas Merry* and, probably, of Chettle's play also.   But there are occasional intrusions into the *Merry* play of Chettle's heightened emotionalism, due, probably, to his revision as amalgamator ; and the induction and chorus scenes, suggested by similar scenes in *A warning for Faire Women,* are, probably, also by Chettle.   These are more nearly passionate and tragic than those in *A warning,* where the reader is mainly interested in the faithful description of the actual figures of Comedy and Tragedy, with drum, bagpipes and other stage properties.   As personifications, they are wooden and lifeless, while Chettle's Homicide, Avarice and Truth have in them some breath of life and imagination.   In every way, then, Chettle's power improves and develops in the *Two Lamentable Tragedies.*   His style gains in compression, and there are fewer lapses into roughness and banality ; and, as a reviser, he shows more judgment and neatness in joining together his two plays than he did in the case of the Robin Hood plays.   At the same time, it must be granted that these revisions and amalgamations are not in any sense fusions ; the two plots are merely tied together without any true coherence in a manner essentially inartistic.

The *Tragedy of Hoffman, or A Revenge for a Father* survives in an edition of 1631.   Unfortunately, the text is much corrupted.

---

[1] Bullen's *Old English Plays,* vol. IV, p. 48.

The play is one of revenge and murder of the type first made popular by Kyd; but it has none of Kyd's fluency and lucidity. It follows very naturally upon the plays we have just been considering. It is written with a concentration and energy of language and metre, lapsing continually into obscurity, which approximate to the stabbing ferocity of style conspicuous in the work of Marston and Tourneur. The dramatist's power of creating a tragic atmosphere, already noted in Chettle's treatment of Matilda's story, is matured in *Hoffman*. His imagination collects and groups together a succession of scenes which are consistently gloomy and horrible. It is worth noticing that Henslowe mentions Chettle twice in 1602 as collaborating with Webster. *Hoffman* was composed at the end of 1602; so Chettle may have stimulated the genius of Webster and himself received some inspiration from that great tragedian. *Hoffman* is a second part, probably of *The Danish Tragedy* which Henslowe mentions earlier in 1602. When the play begins, the hero, Hoffman, is discovered lurking in a cave on the sea-shore with his father's skeleton. The father, admiral Hoffman, has been executed as a pirate by the duke of Lunenburg, who destroyed him by fastening a burning crown of red-hot iron on his temples. The duke's son, Otho, is conveniently shipwrecked near Hoffman's cave, and becomes his first victim. Hoffman, by the help of Lorrique, Otho's valet, personates Otho and continues his riot of revenge with considerable ingenuity and entire success, until he falls in love with Otho's mother and, in consequence of this weakness, is entrapped and himself perishes by the torture of the burning crown. There are many correspondences between this play and *Hamlet*, but no real similarity. Shakespeare is human and sympathetic in a species of art which Chettle makes inhuman and almost insane. Hoffman, the revenge-mad hero of Chettle's tragedy, is a special development of Marlowe's tragic type ; but Chettle is without Marlowe's sense of the beautiful. Marlowe's type is hardened and coarsened. Chettle, however, by the time he wrote *Hoffman*, had improved upon the workmanship of *Matilda's Tragedy*, and his coarse but powerful melodrama was appreciated, probably, by a large public. Chettle died before 1606. In that year, his friend Dekker represents him as joining the poets in Elysium—Chaucer, Spenser, Marlowe and the rest; 'in comes Chettle sweating and blowing by reason of his fatness.' If Dekker felt that the 'old compositor' belonged to the company of which Marlowe, Greene and Peele were notable members, we need not doubt that he had reason for his judgment, and that Chettle's capacity is inadequately represented in what has survived of his work. Chettle was never so well to do as Munday. He belongs to the needy band of poets who were dependent upon Henslowe for loans and were occasionally rescued from prison by his help. Ben Jonson looked upon such dependents as 'base fellows'; but we must beware of exaggerating their degradation. The writers of Elizabeth's reign, high and low, rich and poor, great and small, were very close to each other. Chettle's *Mourning Garment*, written to commemorate queen Elizabeth's death, is excellent prose, and contains descriptions of contemporary poets in verse, which are as melodious as they are judicious. The whole piece is eminently respectable and shows considerable literary culture. It is Chettle in court dress. No doubt, like Shakespeare, he would consider such a composition more truly an 'heire of his invention' than his not altogether reputable plays.

We have seen reason to think that, in the *Two Lamentable Tragedies*, a glimpse is given us of the tragic style of William Haughton. This writer, when he first appears in Henslowe's diary, is called 'Yonge Harton,' and we may suppose, therefore, that he belonged to a group of younger men than are represented by Munday and Chettle. Like Richard Hathwaye, he is known to us only from Henslowe's notices, where he appears most frequently in collaboration with John Day; but some six plays are referred to his sole authorship. One of these, *A Woman will have her Will*, was entered on the Stationers' register in August 1601, but the first extant edition was printed in 1616 as *English-Men For my Money*. For another extant play, printed in 1662 as *Grim The Collier of Croyden*; *Or, The Devil and his Dame : With The Devil and Saint Dunston*, Henslowe made a payment to Haughton in 1600. Both these plays, like *Looke about you*, were originally named from a proverb or pithy phrase which is used with more or less frequency in the play; but, if we may take them as examples of Haughton's comedy, they represent him at the beginning and the end of his development. *The Devil and his Dame* belongs in all its characteristics to the sixteenth century, when a clear species of comedy had not yet been evolved. *A Woman will have her Will*, on the contrary, is regular comedy, with all the characteristics of the earlier interlude, or earlier chronicle history, definitely discarded. *The Devil and his Dame* is of the same type as the extant Munday plays, although the claim may be urged that it exhibits more constructive ability in grafting upon a quasi-historical ground a comic plot, which almost squeezes out of existence an earlier element of confused folklore and history. Morgan, earl of London, and Lacy, earl of Kent, are colourless historical characters. Robin Goodfellow is introduced from English folklore. The comic scenes introducing Grim the collier, Clack the miller and Joan, are good examples of the comedy which was developed from the improvisations of clowns like Kemp and Tarlton. But these familiar elements are mixed with others which, perhaps, are Haughton's. The play opens with a prologue from St Dunstan, who, 'on a sudden,' is 'o'ercome with sleep,' and dreams that he sees Pluto and three other 'judges of black hell' sitting as 'justice-benchers'

> To hear th' arraignment of Malbecco's ghost

—the Malbecco of the ninth and tenth cantos of the third book of Spenser's *Faerie Queene*. Malbecco urges that his wife is to blame for his suicide, and the judges decide that Belphegor shall be sent among men to discover whether the many tales 'of men made miserable by marriage' have any truth in them. Thus, the real subject of the play is introduced, St Dunstan wakes up and we proceed, with him as chorus, to watch the fortunes of the too much married fiend. The conception of a single comic idea dominating and unifying a succession of incidents is realised in this play as it never is by Munday or even by the anonymous author of *Looke about you*. In 1576, we hear of *The Historie of the Collier*, which may have been the original upon which Haughton worked. His play, in itself, is a good specimen of lesser Elizabethan drama; but it is also interesting as a link between the early amorphous type of play and the later comedy of manners, of which his second extant play, *A Woman will have her Will*, is a notable example.

This play, in its general style, savours so fully of the seventeenth century that we are inclined to wonder whether any revision of it took place before 1616, the date of the first extant edition. There is no mark of any such revision in the play as we have it. A London merchant, whose rather unamiable characteristics are excused by his supposed Portuguese extraction, has three daughters whom he wishes to marry to three foreigners, a Frenchman, an Italian and a Dutchman. The comedy describes how the three girls, with the help of their three English lovers, succeed in outwitting the father and the three foreigners. There is a brisk succession and variety of comic incident; but the incident is not managed so cleverly or neatly as to justify us in classing the play as a comedy of intrigue. Nevertheless, this is the stuff out of which the genius of a Jonson could produce his comedies of intrigue and manners, and which holds us back from regarding his work as so absolutely original as he thought it. The three foreigners, each speaking a special variety of broken English, seem, today, stupid and tedious ; but the minute picture of the lanes of the old city of London, in which, for a night, the characters play hide and seek, and the homely and lively reproduction of citizen life, are full of movement and naturalness, and give the play an attractiveness of its own. The characters have no romantic charm ; the daughters and their lovers lack refinement of both manners and morals. Haughton has been claimed as a university man, and his writing implies some culture ; but his purposes are somewhat blunted by his personages. The serving man, Frisco, who is nearest of all the characters to the early clown type of humour, is the fullest and heartiest personality in the piece. The interest of the play, if we may date it in substance before 1600, lies in its being a comedy of mingled intrigue and manners, without any archaic intermixture, written unaffectedly and easily, alongside the romantic comedy of Shakespeare and, perhaps, before the humorous comedy of Jonson.

In this respect, *A Woman will have her Will* resembles another extant comedy, which it is surprising to find in existence before 1600. Henry Porter's first work for Henslowe is dated May 1598, and, in about eleven months, he took part in five plays, producing three alone, and cooperating in the others with Chettle and Jonson. Of these, there is extant only *The two angry women of Abington*, of which there were two editions in 1599. The most probable interpretation of Henslowe's entries is that this play was the *Love Prevented* of 1598. But Porter had probably served a short apprenticeship as a dramatist, since we have record of a payment to him of £5 in December 1596. It would, indeed, be hard to believe that he wrote *The two angry women of Abington* as his first piece of dramatic work. It is a comedy of such full-blooded gusto and such strength and decision of style that it lifts its author out of the ranks of lesser dramatists. 'Abington' is the village of Abingdon near Oxford, and the play is a strong and sturdy picture of rural life ; it smacks of the soil, and has in it something of the vigour and virility which stamp Jonson's best work. The two angry mothers of the play are not altogether pleasing characters, but they are alive and life-like ; and the husbands are delineated firmly and naturally, without any fumbling or exaggeration. The daughter Mall, no doubt, is an 'animal'; she is without the romantic charm of Juliet, but is an honest English lass for all that, living and breathing as Rubens might have painted her. The life in the writing of the play is what makes it remarkable. It does not smell of the lamp. The author has a native power of imparting substance and vitality to his characters, and he would have gone far if he had continued to write. The merit of Porter's play has caused the suggestion that it is to be identified with *The Comedy of Humours* of May 1597, and that he suggested to Jonson his theories of 'humours' in the composition of comedy; but there is clear evidence that the latter play is Chapman's *Humerous dayes Myrth*. Nevertheless, Jonson's stimulus from such work as Porter's need not be doubted. He collaborated with Porter in *Hot Anger soon Cold* in 1598, and produced his *Every Man in His Humour* in the same year—in which play it is not so much the theory of 'humours' that is remarkable as the sober forceful painting of English life and character. Ben Jonson was not so isolated as he supposed. Just as we can perceive a background to Shakespeare's genius in the work of Munday and Chettle, so the comedies of the younger men among our lesser dramatists—such men as Haughton and Porter —prove that Jonson's art was in the air when he began to write; and from Porter he need not have disdained to learn.

We reach now the lesser dramatists whose work was too insignificant to survive. Five of Henslowe's writers have one play each credited to their sole authorship with a considerable amount of work done in partnership. But, of this work, almost nothing is extant. Richard Hathwaye appears in Henslowe's diary from 1597 to 1603. The first play by him noted in the diary is *King Arthur*, the only play in which he has no collaborator. It can hardly have been his first work. Perhaps he was growing out of fashion; he is mentioned by Meres as a veteran. Of the seventeen plays in which he collaborated, only the first part of *Sir John Oldcastle* has survived. This play contains, also, the only extant work of Robert Wilson, who collaborated in sixteen plays, and has one ascribed to his sole authorship. W. W. Greg suggests that he is mentioned by Meres because his main activity was in 1598 and, therefore, his name was specially before the public when Meres wrote. Wentworth Smith is the third writer with one play to his name. He collaborated in fourteen others, of which not one has survived. But, apparently, he began dramatic work in 1601, and may, very possibly, be the Wentworth Smith whose play *The Hector of Germaine* was acted about 1613 and printed in 1615.

It is to be feared that Michael Drayton's dramatic work, also, must be conjectured to have lacked the force and personal impress by which plays were kept alive. Let us consider what Henslowe's records say of him. He, again, has but a single play to his sole credit, and this has perished. He takes part in twenty-three plays, of which but one, the first part of *Sir John Oldcastle*, is extant. Drayton, alone among Henslowe's writers, regarded the writing of plays as discreditable ; and this fact suggested to Fleay the theory that his plays could be safely appropriated by unprincipled printers, but that, as the printer could not use Drayton's name, Shakespeare's name or initials appear on the title-pages of plays really by Drayton. This theory assigns to him *Cromwell, The London Prodigall, The Merry Devill of Edmonton, A Yorkshire Tragedy* and *Sir Thomas More*. It is added that a great unevenness of activity is noticeable in the record of Drayton's work for Henslowe, and that, therefore, he could very well have written for other companies. The obvious weak point of this theory is that unprincipled printers stole none of the plays which Drayton wrote for Henslowe's company. If, in these plays, there was work of the rank of *A Yorkshire Tragedy* or *The Merry Devill of Edmonton,* it is reasonable to suppose that they would not have been let die. Drayton's genius, moreover, as we know it apart from his unknown plays, was essentially undramatic, and, in competition with writers like Dekker and Chettle, we should expect it to fail to assert itself. In spite, therefore, of the deference due to Fleay, we must reluctantly include Drayton among the dramatists whose work could not live[1].

John Day is represented by Henslowe as beginning work in 1598, receiving payment once only as sole author, and collaborating in twenty-one plays. Of all this work, we have left only the first part of *The Blind Beggar of Bednal Green*—for we have supposed that all Day's work was cut out ruthlessly from *Two Lamentable Tragedies.* The hasty vehement copious writing which formed a large part of the partnership plays of Henslowe's writers swamped the delicate and slowly flowing fountain of Day's art. *The Blind Beggar of Bednal Green* is a confused, hastily-written play, plotted on Munday's model, and taking its story and hue from the ballad-lore of the day, but not so pleasant and sweet as Munday would have made it. It may, probably, be taken as a specimen of Chettle's comedy, and gave no scope to Day's special gifts. Day's best work, *The Parliament of Bees*, dates from 1640,

[1] Compare Child, H., in vol. IV, chap. X, p. 183.

and is vitally connected in style and excellence with that small group of extant plays by Day which began in 1606 after king James's accession. We shall, therefore, treat Day's main work as Jacobean; as an Elizabethan, he cannot be shown to have achieved success.

Samuel Rowley wrote comparatively little for Henslowe. He was a player in the Admiral's company, and begins to receive payments as a playwright in 1601. He apparently showed capacity, for, in 1602, he received £7 for a play called *Joshua*, not extant, as well as £4 for additions to *Doctor Faustus*, written in conjunction with W. Birde. But we must not judge him by his attempts to introduce into Marlowe's masterpiece some comic relief which would help the play with the groundlings. Comic scenes of this nature were insisted upon by popular audiences, and it was probably this childish weakness which forced Shakespeare's imagination to that high flight which succeeded in harmonising these comic scenes with tragedy in *Hamlet, King Lear* and *Macbeth.* Rowley's capacity must be judged by *When you see me, You know me. Or the famous Chronicle Historie of king Henry VIII*, acted in May 1603. In all respects, the play is like the Munday plays discussed above, with this important difference, that it is more definitely a 'history' than are these plays. It leaves the region of folklore and chap-book and ballad, and attempts to dramatise actual history. This it does more clearly and effectively than *Sir John Oldcastle*, where the main character is dealt with as a popular favourite and not historically. Rowley's play is of great interest as the forerunner of *Henry VIII*; but, in itself, it has merits. There is force and movement in the verse, and Wolsey's character, as an embodiment of pride and ambition, is presented with decision. The soliloquy in which he states his intention 'To dig for glory in the hearts of men,' is the germ of his great speeches in the later play. But the scenes in which Will Sommers appears carry us back to the days when the leading clown was allowed to display his comic talents regardless of the progress of the play; and the element of popular tale and story is given full scope in the night rambles of Henry VIII, while the naïve indelicacy of the jokes at the end of the play is not to be paralleled in Munday's work. We cannot, therefore, claim that Rowley has produced a 'history' in Shakespeare's style, although, in this play, he may be said to have worked in that direction. There is extant, also, *The Noble Souldier*, printed in 1634 as 'written by S. R.' It is an interesting play, containing work by Day which he uses over again in his *Parliament of Bees*, and it probably had been worked over by Dekker. Rowley, very possibly, wrote a large part of the original play, and it adds to the impression of his talent produced by *When you see me, You know me*.

The Elizabethan drama was essentially popular. The lesser Elizabethan drama was popular in a double sense, as being that large part of the total output which appealed to the tastes of those who were not capable of rising to the imaginative and intellectual standards of Shakespeare and Jonson. But, if there was a lesser drama which was too popular to be artistic in the high sense, there was, also, a lesser drama which failed of the first rank because it was not popular enough; because it was pedantic and learned, and tied to classical methods and traditions. In France, this drama, which imitated Seneca, dominated the stage, and, through the French poet Robert Garnier, it exercised a fruitful influence upon a coterie of distinguished literary people in England. In 1590, lady Pembroke translated Garnier's *Marc-Antoine* into scholarly English blank verse, using lyrical measures for the choruses and reaching, in this part of her work, a high level of excellence. Daniel's *Cleopatra*, printed in 1594, was a sequel to lady Pembroke's play, and his *Philotas* was a second study in the same style. Both plays are meritorious and may be read with pleasure. Thomas Kyd, also, at a date which is uncertain, but under lady Pembroke's influence, translated Garnier's *Cornélie*. The extant play is dated 1594. But in touch with this circle of poets was a genius of very singular and rare quality, Fulke Greville, born 1554, who produced two plays which were probably written in the main before the end of the century— *Mustapha*, printed 1609, and *Alaham*, which was not printed till after lord Brooke's death[1]. While Greville imitates the Senecan model, he largely discards what was characteristic of Seneca, and evolves for himself a drama that is Greek in its intensity and severity of outline, but peculiar to itself in its selection of dramatic types and character from the world of politics and statesmanship. His two plays, which are planned on the same lines, are attempts

to trace out the high waies of ambitious governours and to show in the practice that the more audacity advantage and good success such Soveraignties have, the more they hasten to theire own desolation and ruine[2].

He tells us that his mind has been fixed more 'upon the images of Life than the images of Wit,' and that he writes for 'those only that are weather-beaten in the sea of this world.' But he has a

---

[1] Compare *ante*, vol. IV, chap. IX.   [2] *Works* (Grosart), vol. IV, pp. 222—3.

command of concentrated and often highly imaginative phrases, such as : 'Despair hath bloody heels'; 'Confusion is the justice of the devil'; 'Sickness mows down desire'; 'A king's just favourite is truth'; 'Few mean ill in vain.' In his choruses, his verse, occasionally, reaches a gnomic weight and solemnity, which rivals Milton's *Samson Agonistes*. His speculation, by its mere intensity, is essentially poetical. The originality of his work becomes clear when we compare it with the dull though able contemporary *Monarchick Tragedies* of Sir William Alexander, afterwards earl of Stirling. Greville is the seer or Hebrew prophet of the Elizabethan dramatists, and, therefore, he is a solitary figure. Although a practical politician of large experience, he was yet able to view politics *sub specie aeternitatis* and to declare his convictions with extraordinary sincerity in his two plays.

CHAPTER XIV

SOME POLITICAL AND SOCIAL ASPECTS OF THE LATER ELIZABETHAN AND EARLIER STEWART PERIOD.

THE present survey of English dramatic literature before the civil war has now been carried to a midway point where it may be permissible to pause in order to glance rapidly at some political and social aspects of a period which, in the history of English drama, may be said to have reached its height with the completion of Shakespeare's creative career. The later years of Elizabeth's reign, and the earlier part of her successor's, beyond which it is not proposed, except in some occasional remarks, to extend the range of this chapter, constituted an age of singularly marked characteristics in English political and social life. It was a period of high aspirations, of much turbulence and unrest, of deeds mighty in themselves and mightier in their results, and of numberless minor changes in the conditions of things, which, as it were, break the light in which the great achievements of the time display themselves to posterity. It was an age, too, of strong individualities, of men and women moved by their passions and their interests to think, speak and act without veiling their thoughts, words and deeds ; enjoying life to the full and not afraid of death ; ardent, revengeful, remorseless—it was, in a word, the height of the English phase of the renascence. Some of these phenomena are mirrored with more or less distinctness in the great stream of dramatic production of which the present volume and its successor seek to describe the course ; of others, though but dimly or intermittently reflected on the same surface, the presence is not to be ignored. What little can be said of any of them in this place may, at all events, serve to suggest closer and deeper research in fields of enquiry inexhaustible alike in their variety and in their special interest for students of the English drama.

Queen Elizabeth, we remember, had sat on the throne during seventeen or eighteen eventful years before the first theatre was erected in her capital; the passing of the ordinance of the lords and commons which put a stop to the performance of any stage-play was, within a few weeks, followed by the actual outbreak of the great civil war. Long before her decease, the person of the English queen who had 'swum to the throne through a sea of sorrow' had become, in very truth, the incarnation of the nation's highest hopes; twoscore years had not gone by after Elizabeth's death when the English parliament levied against the king an army 'in defence of' him and itself. In the last decade of the sixteenth century, England, whose foes, a generation earlier, had judged her easy to conquer 'because she wanted armor,' had successfully defied the Catholic reaction and the would-be world-monarchy of Spain; towards the middle of the seventeenth, the great war which had swallowed up all other European wars came to a close without England so much as claiming a voice in the settlement. Side by side with the series of events and transactions which prepared or marked these tremendous changes, the history of English drama and of English dramatic literature—hitherto a gradual growth, whether in the highways of popular life or in the tranquil habitations of scholars and their pupils—pursued its now self-assertive course. Those would err who, in this or in any other instance, should look for a perfect or precise correspondence between a particular chapter of a nation's literary history and contemporary national affairs directly connected with the condition of its government and with its action as a state. But it is not the less certain that, in a national life in which an intensification of impetus and a concentration of purposes have declared themselves as they had in Elizabethan England, it becomes impossible for any sphere of literary activity—least of all one which, like the drama, directly appeals to popular sympathies and expressed approval—to remain in isolation from the rest.

Thus (to follow the rough division already indicated), during the earlier half of Elizabeth's reign, while English literature could not be said to differ largely, in its general character, from that of the preceding generation, the drama, still moving slowly onward in more or less tentative forms, was only gradually finding its way into English literature at all. When, in 1581, Sir Philip Sidney, president of his own small Areopagus, composed *An Apologie for Poetrie*, in which he bestowed praise on a very restricted number of English poets, he had very little to say in the way of commendation of recent labours in the field of the drama; and, though among English tragedies he politely singled out *Gorboduc* for both compliment and criticism, he was more at his ease in censuring the 'naughtie Play-makers and Stage-Keepers' who had brought English comic pieces into disrepute. But the creative literary impulse attested by Sidney's immortal treatise was awakening the literary sense of a much wider public than that to which its appeal, at any point of time in his short life, could have been consciously addressed; and it had already given rise to a dramatic productivity which he could not foresee, but which had reached a considerable height at the time of his death. Thus, in this even more notably than in other spheres of the national literature, the process of growth was gradual; but, in the end, the shell was rapidly burst, and the new life issued forth into the vigour of freedom about the very time when the England of Elizabeth became conscious of its advance to a knowledge of its political purposes and of its means for accomplishing them.

In the history of English dramatic literature, the last decade but one of the sixteenth century covers the literary beginnings of nearly all the poets of high original power whose activity as playwrights began before Shakespeare's, and, possibly, some tentative dramatic efforts in which Shakespeare himself had a hand. In the last decade of the century, several of those whom, by an inaccurate use of the term, it was long customary to describe as 'Shakespeare's predecessors,' had passed away; when the new century opened, he was at the height of his creative energy, and the number of plays by him that had been acted amounted to more than half of the total afterwards included in the Shakespearean canon. Within the same ten years, some of the comic masterpieces of Jonson, and several other plays of relatively high importance, had been produced. Thus, the epoch extending from 1589 to the years on which falls the shadow of Elizabeth's approaching end is marked out with signal splendour in the history of English dramatic literature, as, indeed, it is, though not throughout in the same degree, in that of English literature as a whole[1]. Without, therefore, excluding from the scope of

[1] The penultimate decade of the sixteenth century opened in the year after that of the publication of Spenser's *Shepheards Calender*, and of Lyly's *Euphues*, and was ushered in by the year in which Sidney wrote his *Arcadia*. The beginning of the last decade of the century was marked by the dedication of the first three books of *The Faerie Queene* to Elizabeth in 1590. Drayton began his career as an original writer in 1591; Daniel his in the following year. Bacon's *Essays*, in their earliest form, appeared in 1597. The earliest of Ralegh's prose publications dates from 1591, and of his contributions in verse from 1593; Hooker's great prose work appeared in 1594. Donne and Hall in verse, and North and Hakluyt in prose, entered upon authorship in the course of the same period.

these remarks the period of the first two Stewart reigns, during which the drama, though still bringing 'fruit to birth,' was already, in accordance with the law of mortality proclaimed by Dante[1], showing signs of decline and decay, we shall be justified in giving our chief attention to some of the characteristic aspects of political and social life in what may properly be designated as the Elizabethan age.

It is not to the personality of queen Elizabeth, or even to the statesmanship of her chief advisers and to the acceptance almost always given by her, before it was too late, to their counsels, that should be ascribed, in the first instance, the great political results achieved by the Tudor monarchy of whose rule her own was the crown and the consummation. The primary cause of these results, without which the achievement of them is inconceivable, was the principle of that monarchy itself, which supplied unity and strength, and made possible the direct control of national action by individual intelligence. The Tudor monarchy in England, like the other strong monarchies of Europe of which the latter part of the fifteenth century had witnessed the consolidation, was a creation of the renascence[2]; but the conditions in which it sprang into life and, after a short period of cautious circumspection, established its system, acquired fresh force as it progressed. It was an aristocratic monarchy, but based, not on the doubtful consent of great nobles, their sovereign's peers in power and influence almost as much as in name, but on the assured support of far-seeing statesmen, learned and surefooted lawyers, and merchants whose ambition spanned seas and lands—all of whom were chosen and maintained in high place by the personal confidence of the monarch. The policy of the crown was not dictated by the will of the people at large, expressed by such representation as it possessed in parliament; yet, in the midst of all the changes through which troubles at home and abroad obliged this policy to pass, it contrived, while deliberately pursuing its own path, to remain in general harmony with popular sentiment.

The dramatists of the age were monarchists to a man; and, though, of course, their sentiments herein accorded with their interests, it would be shortsighted to ascribe the tenacity with which they adhered to the monarchical principle of government merely to a servile attachment to the powers that were; indeed,

[1] *Paradiso*, canto XXII.
[2] This point is well brought out by Erich Marcks, in his admirable popular essay, *Königin Elisabeth von England* (1897), p. 12.

with these they were not unfrequently in conflict[1]. The stedfast-
ness with which these popular poets upheld the authority of the
crown as the pivot on which the whole state machine turned
is evident from the fact that their whole-hearted loyalty was
transferred, without halt or hesitation, from Elizabeth to James, as
it afterwards descended from him to his successor. Its root, no
doubt, was some sort of belief in the 'divinity' that 'doth hedge
a king'; but, as the personality of the speaker who, in *Hamlet*,
makes use of this famous phrase, may, perhaps, serve to indicate,
the divine authority to which appeal is made was derived less
from any claim of birth than from the *fiat* of Providence, commanding the assent of the people. By means, as it were, of a
dispensation from on high, accepted by the 'countrymen' of
successive kings and dynasties, in the person of the sagacious
Henry IV and, still more, in that of his heroic son, the royal
authority of the house of Lancaster was established in disregard of
the principle of legitimate right, and, again, disestablished in the
person of Henry VI, the gentle scholar equally unfit to hold a
sceptre and to wield a sword. The sovereign ruling by such an
authority as this is he whom the people is bound to obey—not
the chief of some faction of turbulent barons using him either
as their captain or their puppet; for it is the fitness recognised
and acclaimed by the people which warrants the confidence with
which he assumes and maintains supreme control. Such seems
to be the cardinal principle of the English monarchy as it stood
under the Tudors, and the spirit to which the dramatists
remained true, even when they expressed it in the elaborate
forms proclaimed as orthodox under the first two Stewarts.

Nowhere, perhaps, is the interdependence of royal will and
popular sentiment in the Elizabethan age more conspicuous than
in two questions which it may not be altogether incongruous
to mention side by side—the queen's marriage and the religious
settlement of the country. The former issue directly included
that of the security of the throne; and, notwithstanding the
ruptures of dramatic and other Elizabethan poets, 'Diana's rose[2]'

---

[1] For examples, see *post*, vol. VI, chap. VI.

[2] Greene's *Frier Bacon and Frier Bongay, ad fin*. This, the most national, as it
must have been one of the most acceptable, of all the classical and semi-classical
similes applied to queen Elizabeth by the dramatists, recurs in a simpler, but more
attractive, form in *The Blessednes of Brytaine*, an overflowing outpour of patriotic
sentiment produced by the great outburst of loyalty in 1586—7, one of the *Fugitive
Tracts written in Verse*, etc., 1493—1600, privately printed by Huth, H., in 1875:
'Our kingly rooted rose fresh flow'ring stands.'

might have been won by a French suitor with the goodwill of many Englishmen, before the massacre of 1572 undid the effects of the treaty with France which had seemed on the eve of developing into a league of war against Spain. But, though the rose might have been won, she could hardly have been worn with the assent of the English people after the old hatred of France had, though only for a time, flared up again[1]. As a matter of fact, it may be confidently asserted that, save in passing, no thought either of a French or of any other foreign marriage—still less of a match with a subject of her own—was ever seriously entertained by Elizabeth. So long as her marriage was still a matter of practical politics, she humoured the popular hope that the question of the succession might find this easy solution; and, in the case of Leicester (who was cordially hated outside his own party) she gratified her own fancy, long after she can have entertained even a passing thought of actually bestowing on him her hand[2]. But she knew what her subjects would approve in the end, and that the fact of her remaining unmarried must become an integral element of her unique popularity. On the one hand, marriage with a foreign prince could not but have implied the definite adoption of a particular 'system' of foreign policy—a decision which Burghley and she were desirous of avoiding while it could be avoided; and, in the second place, it would have meant her subjection to the will of another—a consummation which had gradually become inconceivable to her.

[1] The Alençon-Anjou intrigue which followed was, as is known, very unpopular, and was denounced by representatives of patriotic protestant feeling so different as Philip Sidney and the heroic fanatic John Stubbs. The best account of both the important French marriage negotiations (for the idea of a match between Elizabeth and Henry of Navarre was little more than a happy thought) is to be found in Stähelin, K., *Sir Francis Walsingham und seine Zeit*, vol. I (1898), a book of much general value.

[2] Lyly's *Endimion*, even if the usual interpretation of the allegory be accepted, can, at the most, be regarded as a plea, assured of a kindly reception, for the restriction of Leicester to the queen's favour—not for anything beyond. *Creizenach* (vol. IV, part I, p. 59), repudiates the supposition that any particular person was allegorised in the character of Endimion, or that there is an allusion in the same dramatist's *Sapho and Phao* to Anjou's departure from England (1582). As to *Endimion*, however, see a full discussion of the whole subject in Feuillerat, A., *John Lyly, contribution à l'histoire de la Renaissance en Angleterre* (Cambridge, 1910), pp. 119 ff., where, while Cynthia is identified with queen Elizabeth, Tellus and Endimion are identified with Mary queen of Scots and her son James. Concerning Lyly's plays, cf. *ante*, chap. VI. Leicester, though he enjoyed the confidence of many puritans, was so constant a friend and patron of the drama, that he might not unnaturally have thought 'the play the thing'; but since, notwithstanding, his arrogance was tempered by the exercise of self-control, he would certainly have been very careful in his instructions, and we cannot know for certain what the queen would at any particular moment have liked to hear.

Of greater significance is the attitude of queen Elizabeth towards the religious problem of the age, in so far as the treatment of it contributed to shape the destinies of her kingdom. For herself, she at no time showed herself moved by any strong religious impulse, or obedient to the dictate of conclusions reasoned out so as to have taken a firm root in her mind. But the circumstances of her birth and early years drew her, perforce, into association with the great religious movement which, as it swept over a large part of Europe, absorbed so many currents of thought and feeling, so many passions and so many interests, that whoever was not against it must be for many of its axioms, and that she, for instance, was left no choice as to a series of opinions which, at all events, it behoved her to make her own. When, after suffering persecution *tanquam ovis* (more or less), on account both of her birth and of her faith, she succeeded to her ill-starred sister's throne, she thanked the lord mayor for the city of London's welcoming gift of a Bible as for 'the jewel that she still loved best [1].' To the tenets—elastic in one direction, unyielding in the other—of which the Scriptures (as distinct from a larger body of traditional authorities) were regarded as the symbol she adhered firmly throughout her reign; and, in so doing, she rightly read the signs of the times and the convictions which were more and more widely taking hold of her people [2]. The social changes, in this instance, came to the aid of the religious. In a population among which, already in the days of Elizabeth's youth, a well-instructed middle class—made up, mainly, of country gentry and town merchants, and with a not inconsiderable infusion of smaller tradesmen and yeomen—was fast becoming the dominant social element, the Scriptures in the vernacular, together with a few popular commentaries and expositions, were certain, if read at all, to be read widely ; and any attempt to interfere with their circulation must prove futile. Again, the generation which was in its prime when queen Elizabeth came to the throne consisted of the men whose childhood had coincided with the times of the first rise of the English reformation ; while some who were to be numbered among that

---

[1] The incident appears both in Thomas Heywood's *England's Elizabeth* and in *Part I* of his *If you know not me*, etc., act v, *ad fin.*

[2] Harrison relates that in every office at the queen's court was placed a Bible, chronicle or the like, so that the court looked more like a university school than a palace ; and he adds a pious wish that the houses of the nobility were furnished in similar fashion. *Description of England*, ed. Furnivall, F. J., p. 275.

generation's leaders had spent part of their adolescence in the continental homes of the new learning. Inevitably, too, those regions of England which naturally lay most open to influences from abroad were, together with the capital and (in a special way) the universities (Cambridge in particular), the home counties, including Kent, of which, during many a generation, it might fairly be said that they were wont 'to think today what all England would think tomorrow.'

Queen Elizabeth no more shared the ardour of many contemporaries of her own youth than she understood the temper of those puritans of the combative sort who grievously ruffled her serenity in her mature years. Far from being timid by disposition, she had been inured to caution by experience; and, during the earlier half of her reign, while her foreign policy, under the guidance of Burghley, continued to be, in the main, though not, of course, absolutely, a defensive policy, she manifested no intention of moulding the church of which she had become the supreme governor in the forms either of an aggressive protestantism or of a rigid Anglican exclusiveness. With the former current of thought, she had no sympathy, either moral or intellectual; and to that opposed to it, she came to incline more largely in her later years, doubtless because she, as honestly as the two Stewart kings who followed her, believed that the exercise of authority furnished a sufficient answer to searchings of heart and stirrings of mind into which it was not given to her to enter. In those latter days, however, much success had brought with it many illusions; and, as Ben Jonson told Drummond, the late queen 'never saw her self after she became old in a true glass[1].'

The dramatists of the Elizabethan age, taken as a whole, exhibit the willingness for conformity and the instinctive abhorrence of nonconformity which satisfied the queen's conception of a national religion. They were, of course, directly interested, and, on various occasions, personally implicated, in the perennial struggle of the stage against puritanism, of which a full account will be given in a later chapter, and which, in its final phase, if their traditional loyalty to church as well as state be taken into account, might be regarded by them as a campaign for altar as well as hearth[2]. In the earlier part of the

---

[1] *Notes of Ben Jonson's Conversations with William Drummond*, xiv. The remark is quoted in F. E. Schelling's *The Queen's Progress and other Elizabethan Sketches*, p. 249.

[2] Cf. *post*, vol. vi, chap. xiv, and see as to the replies and retorts to Prynne's *Histrio-Mastix*, Ward, vol. iii, p. 275 note.

period under survey, their own protestantism, where it obtrudes itself with unmistakable intention, still wears a militant and aggressive aspect, and is of the demonstrative anti-papist and anti-Jesuit variety[1]; this character it exhibits even in later times, on occasions when there was a sudden revival of the old dread of the machinations of Rome in association with the designs of Spain[2]. Nothing is more notable in Shakespeare than his detachment, even in a play which, like *King Henry VIII*, brought him into near contact with it, from this kind of popular current of feeling; though, on the other hand, nothing could be more futile than to seek in his plays for signs of a positive leaning towards the church of Rome, such as, in different ways and degrees, is shown by Chapman, Massinger and Shirley[3].

But, to go back for a moment to the days when Elizabeth's personal fate hung in the balance, together with the political independence of the nation which she ruled and the form of faith for which she stood. Both the queen and her counsellors long shrank from hastening the decision, and, for herself, it was part of her statecraft that she could never be induced to choose her side till she was quite certain of the support of the nation. When, in 1568—the year in which Alva set foot in the Low Countries in order to reduce their population to submission—Mary queen of Scots had taken refuge on English soil, the struggle for the English throne really became inevitable; but it was not till nineteen years later, when the head of the prisoner was laid on the block, and Philip of Spain had become the inheritor of her claims, that Elizabeth finally took up the challenge. That interval of time had witnessed the launching of the papal bull excommunicating Elizabeth; the massacre which, whether or not she would acknowledge it, had cut through her alliance with France; the invasion of Ireland; the participation by English volunteers in the rising of the Netherlands[4], of which, at a later date, the queen formally

---

[1] For a brief survey of plays displaying this spirit or colour, see *Creizenach*, vol. IV, part I, pp. 115—6. They extend from *The Troublesome Raigne of John, King of England*, and Marlowe's *Massacre at Paris*, to Samuel Rowley's *When you see me, You know me* and Thomas Heywood's *If you know not me*, etc., and include several of the works of Munday.

[2] So, in the instance of the wave of public excitement marked by Middleton's *A Game at Chesse*, and its anti-Jesuit polemics.

[3] Cf. *Creizenach, u.s.* pp. 116—7, where it is justly observed that Jonson's temporary conversion had no perceptible influence on him as a writer.

[4] Whether one of these, George Gascoigne, who, in more ways than one, is prominent in the early history of the English drama, was the author of the prose tract *The Spoyle of Antwerp*, on which was founded the play, *A Larum for London or The Siedge of Antwerpe*, printed in 1602, is more than doubtful. R. Simpson thought Shakespeare's hand visible in the play.

assumed the protection ; the Jesuit missions for the conversion of England, and the executions of priests and seminarists ; the legalisation of the Association for the protection of the queen's person ; Parry's plot [1] ; the expedition of Drake, this time with the queen's permission, into the Spanish main ; and the maturing of the Babyngton conspiracy, nursed by Walsingham with remorseless craft into the proportions which it bore in the final proceedings against Mary. Her execution was the signal for the formal declaration of a rupture which had long yawned wide. In 1588, the Armada sailed, and was dissipated [2].

In these years of suspense, preparation and contest, there had grown into manhood the generation which included the statesmen, soldiers and sailors, and various types of adventurers declining to be classified, who came to the front in the later years of the reign of queen Elizabeth. It was a new England on which she looked—full of men eager for glory as well as for gain, self-confident as well as self-seeking, ready to plunder the wealth of the Spanish coast and to go shares with the Dutch in appropriating the profits of the trade of the far east. And the character of the leaders seemed to have changed as the outlook of the country had become more ambitious and impatient. Burghley, indeed, who survived till 1598, was followed in his chief offices (sooner or later) by his son, a lesser man than himself, but one who proved able, before long, to command the confidence not only of the queen but of her probable successor. Walsingham, a puritan at heart [3], but (like the greatest of the parliamentary puritans of a later generation, Pym) not afraid of plunging his foot into the maze of court intrigues, passed away in 1590 ; and another partisan and affecter of puritanism [4], Leicester, the people's ' violent hate,' if he was the queen's chosen companion, died two years earlier, on the very morrow of the great victory. The men to whom, together with the indispensable Robert Cecil, the queen granted her confidence in her declining years, or on whom, when that confidence was but imperfectly given, she bestowed at least the waning sunshine of her

---

[1] Commemorated on the stage by John Dekker and Thomas Heywood.

[2] It is certainly curious that, as Creizenach notes, the name of Drake should not occur in any contemporary play, and that (with the exception of an allusion in Lyly's *Midas*, and the treatment of the subject, such as it is, in Heywood's *If you know not me*) the references to the Armada in the Elizabethan drama should be few and slight.

[3] Walsingham appears to have been, if not a friend of the theatre, at least fair-minded in his treatment of actors and plays. See *post*, vol. VI, chap. XIV; and cf. the reference to Harington ap. *Creizenach*, vol. IV, part I, p. 39.

[4] ' I never yet,' writes Sir Robert Naunton, ' saw a stile or phrase more seemingly religious ' (than Leicester's). (*Fragmenta Regalia*.)

smiles, were true children of their age. Instead of circumspectly and silently choosing their path between dangers on the right and on the left, they pressed forward in the race for honour and wealth 'outspoken and turbulent, overflowing with life and energy[1].'

Of these men, by far the most conspicuous was Essex, whom his kinsman Leicester, disquieted by the fear of being supplanted by some stranger, had introduced into the royal presence. Although Essex could hardly be said to have been born to greatness, and certainly in no sense achieved it, the *peripeteia* of his fate was tragic, and was recognised as such by more than one English dramatic poet[2]. Undoubtedly, there was much in the generous character and impetuous conduct of Essex to make him not only a favourite of the populace, but an object of attraction and interest to aspiring minds among his contemporaries, while there were many for whose speculative purposes his rapidity of action seemed to promise a multiplication of opportunities. He was a friend to letters and their votaries, and a hereditary patron of players[3]. As a Maecenas, and, perhaps, in real intellectual ability and insight, Essex was surpassed by his friend and fellow-plotter Southampton, a man, like him, self-willed and impatient of restraint both in his outbursts of high temper and in his serious passions. Southampton was fortunate or, perhaps, astute enough to escape the doom of Essex, and when, with the advent of the new reign, 'peace proclaimed olives of endless age,' he passed from prison into new prosperity and influence. His liberal patronage of men of letters, of books and of plays, blossomed out afresh ; but he was of the new age, full of eager ambition and intent upon increasing the abundance of his wealth. Thus, he

---

[1] See bishop Creighton's monograph, *Queen Elizabeth*, p. 241.

[2] Shakespeare unmistakably referred to Essex's Irish expedition as in progress, in the chorus before act v of *Henry V*. He cannot, of course, be brought into any direct connection with the significant performance, on the eve of the outburst of Essex's rebellion, of a play which (as J. W. Hales established beyond reasonable doubt) was no other than Shakespeare's *Richard II* ; but the dying speech of Essex was certainly worked up in Buckingham's speech on the way to execution in *King Henry VIII* (cf. Ward, vol. ii, pp. 104, 125, 203 ; also p. 133). Daniel denied before the privy council that the story or the chief character of his *Philotas* referred to Essex, and 'apologised' in the printed edition (*Schelling*, vol. ii, p. 10). *The Unhappy Favourite*, by John Banks (1682, again a 'ticklish' date), treats the story of Essex, with which Heinrich Laube familiarised the modern German stage.

[3] The first earl of Essex died in 1576, when his eldest son was nine years of age ; but, in 1578, the earl of Essex's company seem to have played at Whitefriars, though they did not perform at Christmas in that year at court. See Fleay, *History of the Stage*, pp. 40 and 34. This is the more curious, as the first earl's affairs were in disorder at the time of his death.

became one of the chief directors—one might almost use the word in its modern technical sense—of early colonial activity ; and there can be little doubt that the story of the play with which Shakespeare bade farewell to the stage was suggested by the narrative of an expedition organised by the earls of Southampton and Pembroke[1]. William Herbert earl of Pembroke, and his brother and successor Philip (Montgomery), nephews of Sir Philip Sidney, and 'the incomparable pair of brethren' to whom the first folio was dedicated, were alike warmly interested in colonial undertakings ; and, in their case also, the love of enterprise and an impatience of restraint which gave rise to many a scandal was united to a generous patronage of scholarship, literature[2] or art, though it is in the elder of the pair only that an actual love of letters seems traceable. Among other young nobles exemplifying the ambitious unrest characteristic of the last period of Elizabeth's reign and the inrush of the tide of the Elizabethan drama, may be mentioned here Charles Blount lord Mountjoy (earl of Devonshire), rival of Essex in the favours of the aging queen, and, with more signal success, in the subjection of rebellious Ireland. Blount's life, like the lives of many of these men, had its episode of tempestuous passion. He, too, was in close touch with several men of letters of his day[3]. Finally, there had stood forth among the most typical representatives of the spirit of adventure and ambition which pervaded the last years of the Elizabethan age, a man of action both intense and diverse, who, at the same time, was himself a man of letters and an intimate of the literary leaders of his times[4]. Long, however, before the many variations of Ralegh's career ended in his being sacrificed to the resentment of Spain, the Jacobean age had set in. The policy of the crown had now become that of a *Cabbala,* to which the nation and the parliament which sought to represent it were refused a key; and those who were admitted to the intimacy of the sovereign, wrapped up as he was in his shortsighted omniscience, either did not care, or, as in the case of Buckingham, the fruits of whose policy were as

---

[1] The expedition of the adventurers and company of Virginia, which was wrecked on the Bermudas in 1609. Fletcher's *Sea Voyage* (which Dryden unjustly described as a copy of Shakespeare's *Tempest*) is supposed by Meissner, *Untersuchungen über Shakespeare's Sturm* (1872), to have made use of the same source.

[2] Both brothers were patrons of Massinger.

[3] As to Ford's elegy on Mountjoy's death, see *post*, vol. VI, chap. VIII, where reference is also made to the connection between the story of Stella and the plot of *The Broken Heart.*

[4] As to Ralegh's intimacy with Ben Jonson and Beaumont, and his reported intercourse with Marlowe, cf. *ante*, vol. IV, chap. III, p. 55.

dust and ashes in patriotic mouths, did not know how to guide him in the ways in which England still aspired to be led. It would serve no purpose to carry the present line of comment further. Its object has been to indicate how, at the height of the Elizabethan age and that immediately ensuing, the main course of the national history imparted to the national life a new fulness of ideas and purposes certain to find reflection in the English drama, first and foremost among the direct manifestations of the national genius.

Queen Elizabeth's court, designated by William Harrison as 'one of the most renowm'd in Europe,' and, in a more full and pregnant sense in which the description could have applied to the English court at any other period of the national history, as 'the very centre' of the land, 'drawing all things to it,' was anything but a stationary institution ; and, in this respect, king James did his best to follow his predecessor's example. As the same authority puts it, every gentleman's house in England was the sovereign's for her progresses ; and her unflagging love of display and adulation combined with her inbred frugality to impose upon her subjects—greater and lesser nobles, and corporations both learned and unlearned—a constant endeavour to outdo each other in costly exhibitions of their loyalty. In her own palaces—many of them 'worthy the owner, and the owner it[1],' others built with a view to appearance rather than endurance, and most of them surrounded by those vast parks which were among the most distinctive inheritances of English royalty—she maintained a becoming splendour and dignity. And, with this, her court united an openness to intellectual interests such as only her unfailing regard for learning and letters could have long maintained in an atmosphere swarming with germs of greedy ambition and frivolous self-indulgence. No similar effort was made by king James, whose literary tastes, like most of his thoughts and impulses, were self-ended ; and it was only in the reign of Charles, who sincerely loved art, and of his refined though fanciful French consort, that the English court might, in more propitious circumstances, have recovered something of its former distinction. In the great days of Elizabeth, the outward and visible fact of its central position in English life corresponded to what may be called an ethical, as well as a political, conception which still held possession of the age, and might almost be described as the last afterglow of chivalry. The

---

[1] See the felicitous reference to Windsor castle in *The Merry Wives*, act v, sc. 5.

ideal which the famous *Cortegiano* of Baldassare Castiglione[1] had spread far and wide through the higher spheres of European civilisation—the ideal of a high-minded Christian gentleman—was directly or indirectly commended in many an Elizabethan or Jacobean treatise, often at the expense of less elevated 'plans of life.' On the same principle, a popular Elizabethan dialogue [2] belonging to this group admonishes its readers that arms and learning are alone fit professions for a gentleman, and that, for such a one, the proper course of life, after passing through school and university, is to qualify himself for the service of his country by the study of the common law, or, if that service is to take an official and, more especially, a diplomatic form, by the study of the civilians, or again, if it is to be cast in the form of military service at home or abroad, by application to the mathematical sciences. Such was the training thought fittest for those desirous of giving of their best for the noblest of purposes and of leading that 'higher life' which 'Astrophill' and the few who were capable of following in his footsteps were (nor altogether unjustly) credited with leading. Numberless heroes of tragedy and comedy dazzled the imagination of their public by the semblance of similar perfection; and, though never completely presented, the ideal, in some of the very noblest creations of the Elizabethan drama, might seem to have almost reached realisation:

> The courtiers, scholars, soldiers, eye, tongue, sword;
> The expectancy and rose of the fair state,
> The glass of fashion, and the mould of form,
> The observed of all observers[3].

In this sketch of the complete training of an English gentleman, as in the early life of the actual Sidney and the Hamlet of the tragedy, the element of foreign travel must not be overlooked. There was not much travelling at home (partly in consequence of

---

[1] Cf. *ante*, vol. IV, p. 7 *et al.*

[2] *On Civyle and uncivyle life* (1579), afterwards (1583) reprinted under the title *The English Courtier and the Countrey-gentleman.*

[3] Much might be added in illustration of these lines—*inter alia*—on the subject of duelling, long an integral part of the courtier's code, and, in its several aspects, the theme of celebrated treatises. The duel and the problems connected with it play a considerable part in Elizabethan and Jacobean drama; see, for the most striking example, Middleton and William Rowley's *A Faire Quarrell* in vol. VI, chap. III, *post.* As to the decline of the practice, see a note in *Ward*, vol. III, pp. 226-7. In general, it is noticeable how this court ideal sank under James I—never to recover itself. See, for instance, Barnabe Rich, *The Honestie of this Age* (p. 23, in Percy Soc. Publ., vol. X): 'It hath bene holden for a maxime that a proud court doth make a poore countrey, and that there is not so hatefull an enemie to the common wealth as those that are surnamed *the Moathes of the court*.'

the state of the roads, which forced even the queen to make most
of her progresses on horseback). Even more than in the earlier
days of the English renascence, Italy, with all its great memories
and treasures, and with all its charms and seductions, was the
favourite resort of English travellers, and such it remained during
the long reach of years which bridge the interval between the
times of Ascham and those of Milton[1]. The frequency with which
the Elizabethan and Jacobean dramatists lay the scenes of their
plays in Italy, no doubt, was originally due to the use made by
them of Italian fiction; but we often find a play localised in Italy
for no better reason than deference to custom, or the possibility of
greater freedom of movement[2].

The perfect courtier (we are apprised in the same dialogue),
who has put such a training as the above to the proof, should quit
the court which has been the scene of his self-devotion after his
fortieth year, having by that time reached the decline of his age.
Instead of making himself a laughing-stock by lingering in livelier
scenes, and among more aspiring companions, he should now
withdraw among everyday experiences and responsibilities, and
become a country gentleman. The range of his duties has now
been narrowed to that of looking after his property, doing his
duty as justice of the peace and quorum—it is to be hoped after
the originally equitable fashion of Mr Justice Clement[3] rather than
in the 'countenancing' ways of Mr Justice Shallow—attending
to musters and surveys of arms, perhaps occasionally riding up to
Westminster as a parliament man. His years do not permit of
his taking much share in the sports of younger country gentlemen
—among which hawking holds the first place, hare-hunting or, in
some places, stag-hunting coming next; but he can lend his
countenance to the various country feasts which, from Shrove
Tuesday to Martinmas or Christmas even in protestant England
still dot the working year.

Although the contrast between court and country which has
served us as a text is rhetorically overstated, yet there can be no
doubt that the increasing sense of the more intense, and more
diversified, ways of life and thought now characteristic of the court

[1] Harrison repeats Ascham's lament over the dangers of the seductions of Italy.
Coryate, to whose travels there are many allusions in later Elizabethan dramatists (*e.g.* Fletcher's *Queen of Corinth*, act IV, sc. I, and Shirley, *The Ball*, act II,
sc. 1), is an admirable example of a traveller conscientiously intent upon seeing and
describing everything.

[2] So, the scene of the first version of *Every Man in his Humour* is laid at Florence.

[3] See *Every Man in his Humour.*

and of the capital in or near which was its ordinary residence, as well as of the classes of society finding in that court and capital the natural centres of their wider interests and more ambitious projects, had contributed largely to the gradual change in the social conditions of Elizabethan England. As yet it had by no means lost its insular character; it was still completely isolated from the rest of Europe so far as its language was concerned, together with its literature, of which the continent knew nothing—unless it were through the violently coloured glass of the performances of English comedians. At home, the people was gradually losing the character of a mainly agricultural community, of which the several classes, though not differing very much in their standard of tastes, amusements and, to some extent, even of daily toil, were broadly marked off from one another by traditional usage, and in which society still largely rested on a patriarchal basis. Necessarily, it was an informal line, and one to be effaced with very great rapidity by the revolving years which divided what remained of the old nobility from the new that had sprung up by their side or taken their place. The demarcation between nobility and gentry, which, in England (where the contention between the armed nobility and the commons had come to an end with the conflict between the two races), had long since ceased to be definite, now retained little social significance. More striking was what has been justly recognised as one of the distinctive phenomena of this age—the growth of closer relations between the nobility and gentry, on the one hand, and the wealthier class of burgesses, the merchants, on the other. As a matter of course, this tendency to the removal of traditional distinctions was deplored by contemporary observers, anxious to escape the stigma of a tacit assent to the inevitable processes of social evolution. In this case, the change was hastened partly by intermarriage, partly by the custom according to which younger sons of noble or gentle families frequently took to trade, when they did not prefer to enter the service of their elder brothers[1]. It was further advanced by the fact that it was becoming not unusual for

---

[1] That mercantile venture of one sort or another thus often meant something very like an opportunity of social emancipation for younger sons seems clear from a comparison of such statements as that in *The English Courtier*, p. 66, according to which even gentlemen of good descent were found toiling as farm labourers (cf. Thomas Heywood's *English Traveller*), and the assertion of the author of *The Serving-man's Comfort* (1598) (*query* Gervase Markham?), that 'he knew at this day, Gentlemen younger brothers that weares the elder brothers Blew coate and Badge, attending him with as reverend regard and dutifull obedience, as if he were their Prince or Soveraign.'

gentlemen landowners to seek to make industrial and commercial profits out of their estates (instead of valuing them, as in the old warlike days, for the number of retainers furnished forth by them), 'turning farmers and graziers for money[1],' and, like other farmers and graziers, making the soil do something besides sustain themselves and their families[2]. Class interests and habits thus met halfway, so that the upper and the upper middle class, as we might call them in our ugly terminology, tended to amalgamate, and a practical stratification of society was introduced, destined to a long-enduring existence in English life. And there was also set up that form of social pride which an acrimonious moralist like Stubbes could denounce as a capital instance of the vice which he regarded as the 'verie efficient cause of all evills.' Everyone, he says, vaunts himself, 'crying with open mouth, I am a Gentleman, I am worshipful, I am Honourable, I am noble, and I can not tell what : my father was this, my father was that ; I am come of this house, and I am come of that[3].' It need hardly be said that a powerful impulse was added to this widespread desire to claim the distinction of gentility by the practice introduced under James I of the sale of peerages and baronetcies—the latter an honour specially invented for the purpose[4]. The general movement of the well-to-do classes of society towards equalisation on the basis of exclusiveness manifested itself, among other ways, in the wearing by many persons not belonging to the nobility of the sumptuous apparel which had hitherto been held appropriate to that class only. In the Elizabethan age, though merchants still dressed with fit gravity, their young wives were said to show more extravagance in the adornment of their persons than did ladies of the court[5]. So far, however, as landowners in a large part of the country were

---

[1] Harrison, p. 243.

[2] See the instructive section on Elizabethan commercialism by Prothero, R. E., in Traill, H. D., *Social England*, vol. III, pp. 352 ff. The break-up of the old agricultural system is there explained, and the effects of the process of enclosure, of legal chicane worked in the spirit of Sir Giles Overreach and of the growth of the wool trade up to the middle of Elizabeth's reign, when arable farming once more became profitable, are succinctly traced.

[3] *The Anatomie of Abuses* (Part I) (New Shakspere Society's Publ., 1876), p. 29.

[4] Cf. Sheavyn, Phoebe, *The Literary Profession in the Elizabethan Age*, p. 2. The tendency noted in the text continued even when political and religious reasons were beginning once more to deepen class distinctions. Cf. a passage in Shirley's *Gamester* (1634), act I, sc. 1:

> 'We... cits, as you call us,
> Though we hate gentlemen ourselves, yet are
> Ambitious to make all our children gentlemen.'

[5] Harrison, pp. 172—3.

concerned, the infusion of the new element must have overthrown many cherished traditions of life and manners, and, while bringing the country into closer contact with court and town, have contributed to substitute, for the easy-going and quiet conditions of the past, a *régime* in which 'lawyers, monopolists and usurers' became founders of some of the county families of the future[1].

The general increase of commercial and industrial activity had led to a rise of prices, which, as a matter of course, benefited the money-making part of the community, though not the whole of it in the same degree. Primarily, this rise was to the advantage of the great merchants of London and of the other chief ports of the country, and persons engaged in large farming operations, such as landlords of the old style had shrunk from undertaking. Smaller tradesmen, and the middle classes in general, to some extent profited by the change—chiefly by obtaining more comfortable conditions of life. Not so the labourers, whose wages long continued stationary, while the cost of necessaries advanced. This rise of prices, although partly due to the influx of silver from 'old Philip's treasury[2],' may, no doubt, be dated from the time when protective restrictions were applied to the importation of foreign goods[3], and was advanced by the buying-up processes of the 'bodgers' and other tricks and frauds of the corn market[4]. The price of corn rose wildly, and, no doubt, it was more than once thought that 'there will soon be no wheat- or rye-bread for the poor[5].' A serving-man is cited, about 1598, as declaring that, in his lifetime, ordinary articles of wear have trebled in price, 'and yet my wages not more then my great grandfathers, [he] supplying the same place and office I doe[6].'

Usury—a remedial process in times of dearth which rapidly accommodates itself to the needs of any and every class—had become a crying evil of the age which Greene and Lodge ser-

---

[1] See the section 'The Landlord' in Hall, Hubert, *Society in the Elizabethan Age* (3rd ed. 1901).

[2] *Doctor Faustus*, sc. i.

[3] Harrison, who recalled with something like regret the times 'when strange bottoms were suffered to come in' (p. 131), was an imperialist as well as a free-trader, and 'could hardly believe' that corn exported from England served to relieve the enemies as well as the friends of church and state (*ibid*. p. 297). As to exportation, that of sheep was strictly prohibited, while, as a matter of course, that of wool was open. See Symes, J. E., *ap*. Traill, *u.s.* vol. iii, where a summary is given of the Elizabethan regulation of trade, industry and labour.

[4] Harrison, pp. 297—301.

[5] *Ibid*. p. 153.

[6] *The Serving-man's Comfort*.

monised in *A Looking Glasse for London and England*[1], and established itself as one of the ordinary themes of the satire of English comedy[2]. Of old, loans had usually been made without interest being demanded, and any demand of this sort had been illegal; but, after the principle of the illegality of interest had been abrogated by parliament in 1545, Elizabeth's government had proved unable to revive it. About the middle of her reign, ten per cent. was the legal rate; but twelve per cent. was quite common. Under James I, the ordinary rate sank to eight per cent.[3]

Though the general condition of the labouring classes does not appear to have changed very much for the worse during the reign of Elizabeth, it was, on the other hand, not materially raised from the low point to which it had sunk by the sixth decade of the century. In some parts of the country, the poor were so much at the mercy of the rich that small houses seem to have been almost swept off the face of the ground; and a general decay of towns set in, of which, however, the statistics, as is frequently the case in the matter of depopulation, hardly admit of being either accepted or rejected[4]. Yet, in defiance of such phenomena, mercantile enterprise swept forward on its course, made possible, in the first instance, by the wise initial policy of the queen's government in establishing coinage on a sound basis, and continuously expanded, thanks to the farsighted intelligence of those who watched over both the emancipation and the development of English trade. Crown and city cooperated, with a notable concurrence of insight, in this policy, which, during a considerable part of the queen's reign, was under the guidance of Thomas Gresham, as great a minister (though without a portfolio) as has at any time taken charge of the commercial interests of a modern state[5]. Largely under the influence,

[1] See, especially, the scene in which the usurer's poor client Alcon is on the point of losing both 'cow' and 'gown' unless he resorts to corruption, and the tirade of Oseas:
> When hateful usury,
> Is counted husbandry, etc.

[2] Among the usurers of Elizabethan comedy, there were several who, like Sordido in *Every Man out of His Humour*, 'never pray'd but for a lean dearth, and ever wept in a fat harvest.'

[3] Cf. Symes, *u.s.*, and see Harrison, p. 272.

[4] They are given in Harrison, pp. 257—8.

[5] Hubert Hall, who has chosen 'the great master of exchange, the useful agent of the Crown, the financial adviser of ministers, the oracle of the city, the merchant prince, patron and benefactor,' as the type of 'The Merchant' in *Society of the Elizabethan Age*, pp. 58 ff., has, while maintaining the proportion necessary in the treatment of such a theme, shown how unscrupulously Sir Thomas Gresham also took charge of his own interests. Heywood, in *Part I of If you know not me*, etc., appends to the imposing figure of the great merchant a good deal of what may probably be set down as idle fiction about his family troubles.

or through the personal agency, of this 'merchant royall[1],' English trade had been freed from subjection to that of the Hanseatic league, and to that of the great Flemish towns ; colonial enterprise on a comprehensive scale was encouraged, and great merchant companies were established, which came, it was said, to absorb the whole English trade except that with France[2]. At the same time, the home trade and the home industries on which that trade depended were actively advanced—especially those which, like the crafts of the clothier, the tanner and the worsted-maker, might be trusted to bring money into the country[3]. Companies of craftsmen under the authority of the crown took the place of the old municipal guilds; attempts at a better technical education (not for the first time) were set afoot ; and a select immigration of skilled foreign workmen in special branches of production was encouraged. English trade abroad, so far as possible, was protected, and a vigorous banking system—the sovereign instrument for the facilitation of commercial and industrial activity at home and abroad—was called into life. Thus, while English merchants became familiar visitors in distant lands, the goods, domestic or imported, with which the English market abounded were countless in their mere names—'all men's ware[4].'

The point which we have reached in this fragmentary survey seems to allow of a brief digression concerning one of the causes of that engrossing love of wealth in which many observers recognised one of the most notable signs of the times. Among these observers were the comic dramatists, and those of them—Ben Jonson above all—who wrote with a didactic purpose recognised in this master passion one of the most dangerous, as from an ethical point of view it was one of the most degrading, of the tendencies of the age. Yet, even the love of wealth for its own sake has aspects less ignoble than those which belong to the pursuit of it for the sake of a luxurious way of living unknown to earlier generations or less affluent neighbours. In his whole

---

[1] As a technical term, this designation seems to have superseded that of merchant venturer. See the passage from *Tell-Trothes New-Yeares Gift*, ed. Furnivall, F. J., Publ. of New Shaksp. Soc., ser. vi, No. 4, cited by Vatke, T., *Culturbilder aus Alt-England*, p. 201. Antonio, in *The Merchant of Venice*, is more than once called a 'royal merchant.'

[2] Cf. Symes, *u.s.* p. 370.

[3] See the interesting series of dialogues by William Stafford, *A Briefe Conceipt of English Policy* (1683), p. 71.

[4] So early as 1563, the great variety of the articles of English trade and manufacture is illustrated by *A Book in English Metre of the rich merchant-man called Dives Pragmaticus* (rptd in Huth's *Fugitive Tracts*, 1875), an enumerative effort of extraordinary virtuosity.

conception of luxury, as well as in the names which he bears, Sir Epicure Mammon[1] is the consummate type of the man whose existence is given up to this worship of the unspiritual.

The two favourite kinds of luxury in Elizabethan and Jacobean England, needless to say, were those associated with diet and with dress respectively. Already in queen Mary's day, her Spanish visitors were astonished by the excellent table usually kept by Englishmen, as much as by the inferiority of the houses in which they were content to dwell. The building of English houses seems to have struck foreign observers as more or less unsubstantial; but, though the sometimes fantastic and sometimes slight style of house architecture in vogue may have been partly due to the influence of Italian example, even magnates of the land had ceased to care much for residing in castles. For the houses of the gentry, brick and stone were coming into use in the place of timber, although most English dwelling houses were still of the latter material. One of the most attractive features in English houses was to be found in the rich hangings usual in the houses of the nobility, and the less costly tapestry in those of the gentry, and even of farmers[2]. Noticeable, too, was the store of plate, kept, in proportionate quantities, of course, in both upper and middle class houses, and even in the cupboards of many artisans. On the other hand, a sufficient number of chimneys was still wanting to many houses, where logs were piled up in the hall[3] —stoves of course were not ordinarily used—and though the general quality of household furniture was imposing, bedding was still sparse in many houses, and a day bed or 'couch' a quite exceptional indulgence[4].

The greatest charm of an English house, its garden, might almost be described as an Elizabethan addition to English domestic life: previously to this period, private horticulture had chiefly directed itself to the production of kitchen vegetables and medicinal herbs. Flowers were now coming to be much prized, and the love of them and care for them displayed by several Elizabethan dramatists, and, pre-eminently, by Shakespeare, was,

---

[1] In *The Alchemist*.

[2] *Paul Hentzner's Travels*, p. 64. Of course, the 'arras' plays a part, both tragic and comic, in the Elizabethan drama corresponding to that which it must have played in real life; cf. *Hamlet* and *King John*, and both parts of *Henry IV*.

[3] Cf. *Love's Labour's Lost*, act v.

[4] Cf. Beaumont and Fletcher, *Rule a Wife And have a Wife*, act III, sc. I. The last two illustrations are borrowed from Vatke, T., *u.s.*, where a large number of others are to be found.

no doubt, fostered by a desire to gratify a widespread popular taste[1].

Even from the few facts given above, it will appear how simply, even in these days of material advance, Englishmen were still lodged, and how small a part was played, in their daily life, by its household gear, as, on the stage (which represented that life), by its 'properties.' On the other hand, even the rector of Radwinter, whom we may safely conclude to have been temperate in habit as well as in disposition, and who calls special attention to the fact that excess in eating and drinking is considered out of place in the best society, avers that 'our bodies doo crave a little more ample nourishment, than the inhabitants of the hotter regions are accustomed withall,' and that 'it is no marvell therefore that our tables are oftentimes more plentifullie garnished than those of other nations[2].' Stubbes's assertion[3] that, 'whereas in his father's day, one or two dishes of good wholesome meat were thought sufficient for a man of worship to dine withal,' nowadays it had become necessary to have the table 'covered from one end to the other, as thick as one dish can stand by the other,' seems to point in the direction of unnecessary display rather than of gluttony. Harrison notes[4] that the ordinary expenditure on food and drink had diminished, and that the custom which has been succinctly described as 'eating and drinking between meals'—'breakefasts in the forenoone, beverages, or nuntions after dinner'—had fallen into disuse. But, of course, there was a great deal of gross feeding and feasting in all spheres of life, and illustrations of the habit are not far to seek in our comic dramatists[5]. That excess in drink was not uncommon in Elizabethan England, is, to be sure, a fact of which evidence enough and to spare could be adduced from contemporary drama; but the impression conveyed by what we learn on the subject, from this and other sources, is that in no section of English society was intemperance, at this time, the flagrant vice which it afterwards became, except in that 'fringe' of tipplers, among

---

[1] See, especially, of course, friar Laurence's soliloquy in *Romeo and Juliet*, act II, sc. 3. As to early English herbals, see *ante*, vol. IV, pp. 394—5, and cf. *ibid*. p. 542 (bibl.) for a list of these and of works on gardening. Bacon's essay *Of Gardens* was, no doubt, in part suggested by the interest taken in the gardens of Gray's inn by the benchers and other members.

[2] Harrison, p. 142.   [3] *Anatomie*, pp. 102—3.   [4] p. 162.

[5] See, for instance, the beginning of the sheriff's dinner to which 'the gentle craft' is summoned by 'the Pancake bell,' in Dekker's *Shomakers Holiday*, and the elaborate description of a more elaborate city feast in Massinger's *City-Madam*, act II, sc. 1.

whom 'ancients' and other officers and soldiers without pay or record were prominent, and of whom, in Falstaff's crew, Shakespeare has drawn perennial types. Heavy drinking was not customary at ordinary repasts; indeed, much talking at meals was avoided by those who studied good tone, and the well known custom of encouraging guests to 'call a cup' when they chose was introduced in order to avoid a continuous supply of liquor to any one person at table. On the other hand, there was much drinking at the 'ale-houses,' which, for this purpose, took the place of the old-established taverns, and increased in number so largely as to make their licences a profitable source of general income ; and, doubtless, there was not a little drunkenness in the streets, notwithstanding the five shilling fine[1]. It would take us too far to enquire how far the change of taste noticeable in this period from light French to Spanish and other sweet and heavy wines increased the tendency to intemperance ; Harrison, who reckons that, besides homegrown, there are 56 sorts of light wines and 30 of strong, insinuates that the stronger they are the more they are desired[2]. There is every reason for concluding that, in the days of James I, the intemperate habits in vogue at court spread into other classes of society, and that the drinking houses of this period deserved the description given of them by Barnabe Rich[3].

Long after its introduction, the use of tobacco was regarded as a fashionable, rather than a popular, indulgence, but its consumption must have increased with extraordinary speed, if Barnabe Rich had been correctly informed 'that there be 7000 shops in and about London, that doth vent tobacco.' Shakespeare never mentions this article of Elizabethan luxury[4].

In the Elizabethan and early Stewart ages, an excessive care

---

[1] See Vatke's note (*u.s.* p. 170) on a well known passage in *Much Ado about Nothing*, act III, sc. 3.

[2] pp. 149 ff. He also mentions, besides march and home-brewed beer, metheglin and 'a kind of swish swash' called mead. He does not mention 'oburni' (a spiced drink) or 'hum' (ale and spirits). See *The Divell is an Asse*, act I, sc. 1. For a fairly complete account of the favourite drinks of the Elizabethan age, cf. Sandys, W., introduction to *Festive Songs, principally of the sixteenth and seventeenth centuries* (Percy Soc. Publ., 1848, vol. XXIII), where see especially as to the aristocratic beverage sack. As to the change of taste in wines, and the *bonus* on heavy sorts which encouraged it, see Hall, H., *u.s.* chap. VI ('The Host'), where there is much information on the whole subject.

[3] Cf. *The Honestie of this Age*, etc. (Percy Soc. Publ., 1844, vol. XI), pp. 18—19.

[4] Cf. the well known passage as to the scientific training of 'tobacconists' in *Every Man out of His Humour*, act III, sc. I. As to the date of the introduction of tobacco, see Mary Bateson, *ap.* Traill, H. D., vol. III, pp. 571—2, where Shakespeare's silence on the subject of the herb and its use is noted.

for dress was at least as marked a characteristic of large sections of English society as a fondness for the pleasures of the table. Neither sumptuary laws nor moral injunctions proved effectual preventives, though it may be asserted that, among social failings, the love of fine dress, on the whole, was that which puritans visited with their sternest censure. Andrew Boorde (who was by no means a puritan), a generation earlier, had dwelt on the fickleness exhibited by Englishmen in connection with this particular foible, and the mutability of the extravagance continued to remain one of its most constant features. 'Falconbridge, the young baron of England,' we remember[1], 'bought his doublet in Italy, his round hose in France, his bonnet in Germany.' But Spain and France were long the rival schools of apparel for young Englishmen of fashion, though, of the pair, notwithstanding the strong predilection for things Spanish which long prevailed at the court of James I, the French model, on the whole, maintained its ascendancy. In accordance with the general tendency, noticed above, of luxurious habits of life to efface class distinctions, censure of all this extravagance is found accompanied by regret that 'it is difficult to know who is a gentleman and who is not from his dress[2].' As a matter of course, it was inevitable that, in the matter of dress, the extravagance of men should be far outdone by that of the other sex, more especially in the way of those artificial supplements to the attractions of nature, which left women, in the severe words of Stubbes, 'the smallest part of themselves[3].' While many effeminate men aped the devices of women's toilets, women, quite as often in search of notoriety as for purposes of disguise, wore doublet and hose ; and the confusion of the external attributes of the sexes to which exception was taken as a practice of the theatre thus, in this instance also, reflected, at least in some measure, a social licence of the age. In the matter of dress in general, the mimic life followed, while, perhaps, as in earlier and later times, it now and then suggested, the extravagances of the society which the theatre at once served and imitated. The sumptuousness of actors' costumes, both on and off the stage, is illustrated by direct evidence as well as by many well known passages and anecdotes —among the former, by Gosson's assertion that 'the verye hyrelings

---

[1] *The Merchant of Venice*, act i, sc. 2.

[2] Stubbes's *Anatomie*, p. 29. There follows an elaborate description of the apparel which the moralist censures. Further details will be found in the introduction to Vatke, T., *u.s.*

[3] *Ibid.* p. 75. Cf. the passage in *Cynthia's Revels*, act v, *ad fin.*, satirising the 'pargetting, painting, sticking, glazing and renewing old rivelled faces.'

of some of our plaiers, which stand at reversion of vis by the weeke, jet under gentlemens noses in sutes of silke[1].'

Thus, the increase of luxury and the desire of securing as large a share of it as money could buy must be reckoned among the chief causes of the *auri sacra fames* which contributed to the unrest of the Elizabethan age, and which, in the next age, remained a strong motive of private, and, too often, of public, action.

In queen Elizabeth's time the military and naval professions can hardly be said to have played any part in the social history of the country. No standing army was kept up for foreign warfare; when a force was required for that purpose, it was collected partly by feudal obligation or impressment, and partly by the enlistment of volunteers[2]—the last-named, for political reasons, a very convenient form for collecting a body of troops. It is true that, already under James I, such forces were often not disbanded immediately on their return home. Meanwhile, the defensive force of the land, in principle, and (at all events till the reign of Charles I) in fact, was a county militia, called under arms by means of commissions of array, officered by country gentlemen and under the command of lords lieutenant—though the name 'militia' was only coming into use at the time when the civil war broke out on the question of the command of the body so called. The composition of the force, the numbers of which looked magnificent on paper[3], depended largely on the high constables of the hundreds and the petty constables of the parishes, who seem to have taken good care to draft into it all the disreputable elements of which they were fain to get rid[4], as well as the unemployed 'Shadows' and 'Mouldies' of their generation[5]. Recruits were supplied with arms—armour proper was falling out of use, and, by the close of the century, the bow had been entirely superseded by the musket. Munition was kept in readiness under some sort of inspection in every town and considerable village; for there were no garrisons existing except in a few coast towns. The navy was

---

[1] *The School of Abuse*, p. 29. In *Part II of The Returne from Pernassus*, act v, sc. 1, Studioso complains of the 'glaring satten sutes' in which actors rode through the gazing streets.

[2] Maitland, F. W., *The Constitutional History of England*, pp. 278—9.

[3] According to Harrison, the number of able-bodied men on the roll in 1574 and 1575 was 1,172,674, though one-third of this total were not called out.

[4] See 'The Maner of chosing Souldiers in England' cited from Barnabe Rich's *A Right Exelent and pleasaunt Dialogue, between Mercury and an English Souldier, etc.* (1574), in P. Cunningham's ed. of the same writer's *Honestie of the Age*, p. 48.

[5] *Part II of Henry IV*, act iii, sc. 2.

made up of a growing number of ships of war, besides merchant vessels (including ships chartered by the various trading companies) and fishing boats. Harrison reckons[1], with pride, that queen Elizabeth could have afloat as many as from 9,000 to 10,000 seamen ; and a census held for the purpose a few years before the coming of the Armada reckoned more than 16,000 persons in England (exclusive of Wales) in some sort accustomed to the sea[2]. The wonderful year itself proved a great deal more than that England had the winds and the waves for allies—it also proved that her ships were much superior to those of her arch-foe in both manning and gunnery. Though shipbuilding was much improved in the later years of the century, when the queen built about one ship a year, much needed reforms in what had now become a regular profession did not begin till 1618. Thus, in the Elizabethan age proper, the military, and, here and there, the naval types which dramatists, in this period, were fond of presenting were largely of an exceptional sort—men in whom a mixture of volunteer or privateer and patriot lends itself to picturesque treatment[3]. Besides these, there must have been in real life many swaggerers and pretenders, of the Pistol and Bobadill sort, who on the stage furnished variations of the time-honoured classical or Italian types[4]; and there was, especially as a legacy of the struggle in the Low Countries, a constant influx of discharged soldiers, quite as often objects of satire as of sympathy, because of the counterfeits who were largely mixed up with them and who were one of the pests of the age[5]. No doubt, too, Harrison's observation was correct[6], that soldiers who had seen service in the field could not easily be prevailed upon to resume the habit of ordinary daily labour, and thus became a disturbing element in the population. For the rest, in London and elsewhere, order was kept by watchmen with their brown bills—a familiar type of

---

[1] p. 291.

[2] See the section by Oman, C. W. E., on 'The Art of War,' *ap.* Traill, *u.s.* vol. III, where will be found much valuable information concerning the navy under Elizabeth.

[3] *E.g.* Young Forest in Thomas Heywood's *Fortune by Land and Sea*, lord Momford, in Day and Chettle's *Blind Beggar of Bednal Green*, etc., etc.

[4] Jonson, who had himself seen service, preserved a sincere respect for 'true soldiers.' (Cf. *Epigram* cviii.)

[5] Of these, who 'generally represented themselves as wounded in the Low Countries when fighting against Spinola, with Essex at Cadiz, or Drake in St Domingo,' see a graphic account in G. W. Thornbury's amusing *Shakespeare's England* (1856), vol. I, pp. 279—80.

[6] p. 231.

Elizabethan comedy[1]. The general security of the country, no doubt, was greater than of old; but it was still necessary for serving-men to be armed when going out at night time, and highway robberies were not uncommon, especially about Christmas time[2].

More surprising, perhaps, than the smallness of the share belonging to army and navy in the life of the Elizabethan age is the relative depression of the position held about this time—certainly so far as the evidence of the contemporary drama goes—by the clergy. As is well known, the recovery of that body, including part of the episcopate, from the disrepute into which they had sunk in the earlier part of the reign, was gradual and, for a long time, uncertain. A considerable proportion of the episcopate remained for many years in a position of degrading dependence or absolute insignificance alike unworthy of their order, while of the parsonages a large number were not filled up at all, or, in more ways than one, most unsuitably[3]. As the reign wore on, and the prudent exertions of the sorely tried archbishop Parker and others gradually bore fruit, an increasing activity and devotion to their duties manifested themselves on the part of the bishops; and an advance was also visible in the case of the inferior or parish clergy, alike in parochial zeal and in scholarly attainments. Knowledge of Latin was again becoming universal, and that of Hebrew and Greek was growing common, among clergymen. The recovery in question, which was quite distinct from the puritan movement, though each, in its way, helped to leaven the lump of academical, as well as of national, life, led, indeed, only very slowly and very partially to the awakening, in high ecclesiastical places or in quiet country parsonages, of higher and deeper conceptions of religion. Yet this tardiness of progress was by no means wholly due to the decline of the political and social position of the church, and to

---

[1] See among the various counterparts to Dogberry and Verges, those in Samuel Rowley's *When you see me*, etc., in Marston's *Insatiate Countesse*, in Beaumont and Fletcher's *Coxcombe*, and, above all, Blurt and his attendant Stubber in Middleton's *Blurt Master-Constable*.

[2] Harrison, p. 284. Hall, Hubert, *u.s.* p. 74, gives a number of cases of armed violence which ended fatally; but they only occasionally come under the above category.

[3] For a highly coloured picture of this condition of things, see Hall, H., *u.s.* in his chapter 'The Churchman.' Harrison's account of the condition of things in his own day conveys the impression of being written with both knowledge and judgment; though not puritan in spirit, he is, on the whole, favourable to moderate reform. He is, however, very acutely sensible of the hardships of various kinds to which his cloth was subject, and fully alive to the perennial experience that the 'common sort' are always ready to cast reproaches on the clergy. In high places, few were quite fair to their griefs, although Burghley was an exception.

the many alterations in its formularies. It was also due to the changes which had for some time been at work in

> Englands two eyes, Englands two Nurceries,
> Englands two nests, Englands two holy mounts,
> I meane, Englands two Universities [1].

To all appearance, in the middle of queen Elizabeth's reign, Oxford and Cambridge were in a flourishing condition ; their joint attendance of students was reckoned at 3000, and, according to modern notions, it may seem a healthy sign that, in far larger proportions than in earlier times, the sons of the nobility and gentry were resorting to these places of learning in common with a poorer class of young men or boys. As a matter of fact, however, more especially at Cambridge, which, for the better part of two generations, had taken the lead in the intellectual life of the country, learning, after having, as elsewhere, become largely absorbed in theology, was, in the latter half of the century, exposed to a new danger. The sons of the gentry, whose importance in the general social system of the country and in its government was, as has been seen, steadily rising, now frequented the universities for the purpose of acquiring what may be called 'general culture' rather than theological or other professed learning. In a word, a new conception of the work of the national universities was forming itself which, in more ways than one, was to become of great importance for the future of the nation as well as for that of the universities. On the one hand, the risk was being run that deeper study and research would be elbowed out of existence by endeavours to gratify the wish for a higher education which should suit a young gentleman desirous of making his mark in some recognised public or professional capacity, and which should not take up too much of his time [2]. And this risk was materially increased by the introduction into the colleges of the universities and into the schools which were their feeders of the system of jobbery which was one of the bad features of the age : both school and college elections were packed or otherwise influenced in favour of the well-to-do against the poor, and, more especially, the best prizes of the university, fellowships, were awarded in obedience to mandates obtained by fair means or other at

---

[1] *Tell-Trothes Message and his Pens Complaint* (1600). New Shaksp. Soc. Publ., 1876.

[2] See, on this head, a very striking passage in William Stafford's *Dialogues*, cited above, pp. 20—21.

court[1], or as the result of other corrupt methods. This endeavour to appropriate the universities and their endowments for the advantage of particular sections of society had many unsatisfactory consequences—among them an increase of riotous living at college[2], in deference to gentlemanlike tastes. Against this was to be set the fact that a very considerable proportion of the classes whose sons now frequented the universities was tinged with such general culture as was to be found there, while many of these young men acquired something of a real love of learning—and a few something of learning itself—into the bargain. The later Elizabethan and Jacobean dramatists take little or no notice of these results— the academical enthusiasm fostered by the 'university wits' died out with them, and the usual playhouse type of the university student was now the feebler variety of undergraduate, whose chief occupation was to spend his father's money[3]. At the same time, the public interest benefited directly by the encouragement given by the queen's government, desirous of attracting nobility and gentry into the service of the state, to the study of law at the universities, scholarships being instituted for the support of favoured students of this subject. The class of students whom these changes hit hard were the poorer youths, especially those who intended to devote themselves to the study of theology, with a view to ordination, and on the training of whom the universities, for some time previously, had concentrated their activity. Complaints are constant that, in the bestowal of livings, the same system of corruption prevailed, in favour of the dependents of nobility and gentry, or of those who had gained the goodwill of patrons by illicit means[4].

In general, there can be no doubt that the intellectual condition of Cambridge, in the later years of the century, was

---

[1]   Letters of commendations—
        Why, 'tis reported that they are grown stale
        When places fall i' th' University.
                    Webster, *The Devils Law-case*, act i, sc. 5.

[2] So Greene 'consumed the flower of his youth' at Cambridge 'amongst wags as lewd' as himself. The habit of drinking to excess long remained a reproach to the universities; readers of Clarendon's *Life* will remember how its prevalence at Oxford, about 1625, afterwards led him to rejoice that his father had soon removed him from residence there.

[3] So, for instance, Credulous Oldcraft in Fletcher's *Wit At severall Weapons*.

[4] A very unattractive account of the methods by which advancement can be best secured in universities and colleges, as well as in other walks of life, showing how the system endured and progressed, is given in *Tom of all Trades, or the Plaine Path-Way to Professions* (1631). The reader will, of course, compare the graphic picture of these things in *Part II of The Returne from Pernassus*.

superior to that of the sister university, **and** reflects itself as such in our literature. Puritanism, after being repressed at Cambridge, largely through the influence of Whitgift, held its ground at Oxford under the patronage of Leicester as chancellor[1], and, in the later part of the period under survey, recovered much of its ground in Cambridge also. To the reaction against Calvinism at Cambridge in the later part of the reign of James I, and at Oxford under Laud, a mere reference must suffice. It is curious to notice the impression of a foreign observer like Paul Hentzner that the puritan form of faith or religion was distinct from that of the church as by law established; in his account of the universities, he expresses his astonishment that puritans (whom he describes as 'entirely abhorring all difference of rank among churchmen') 'do not live separate, but mix with those of the church of England in the colleges[2].' Such was not the position taken up by those consistent adversaries of puritanism, the English dramatists of the Elizabethan and subsequent ages. It has been well pointed out by Creizenach[3] that, of course with exceptions, it was not so much the doctrine of the puritans as their conduct of life and treatment of its outward forms which dramatists visited with their contempt and ridicule. The satire which puritanism provoked from them was that which has always directed itself against the assertion, actual or supposed, by any class, profession or association of men or women, of a claim to an exceptional degree of moral excellence or virtue, and against the hypocrisy which this assertion seems to involve. This was a sort of pretension or 'humour' which robust commonsense, coupled with keen insight into character, such as signalised Jonson[4], would be certain to expose to ridicule and censure, quite apart from any religious party feeling. Protestant sentiment proper was hardly a marked characteristic of the Elizabethan or Jacobean drama, except when it formed an integral part of anti-Spanish or anti-Jesuit patriotism, and thus directed itself, as a matter of course, against a representative of the Marian reaction like Gardiner or an agent of Spanish policy like Gondomar[5]. In a general way, however, it was natural that this political protestantism should grow weaker in the Stewart days, when the court was no longer

---

[1] Cf. Mullinger, J. Bass, *History of the University of Cambridge*, vol. II, p. 283. To this standard work, the reader must be referred for a complete treatment of the subject.

[2] *Travels in England*, English transl. by Horace Walpole (1797), p. 41.

[3] Vol. IV, part I, pp. 123—4.

[4] See *The Alchemist, Bartholomew Fayre*, etc. The drift of the ridicule in Middleton's *Famelie of Love* is equally unspecific.

[5] See Heywood's *Part I of If you know not me*, etc., and Middleton's *A Game at Chesse*.

responsive to this kind of popular sentiment. In a few dramatists, such as Massinger and Shirley, personal reasons contributed to favour Roman Catholic ideas and views; but it cannot be said that these received from them anything beyond platonic goodwill. It may, perhaps, be added that the popular feeling which prevailed in England against Jews cannot be set down as more than the continued unthinking and undiscriminating acceptance of a popular prejudice of ancient standing; for Jews in London, during the whole of this period, were only few in number and very little known, and neither Shakespeare nor Marlowe is likely to have made the acquaintance of any Jews abroad[1].

Except in the fields, now narrowing rather than expanding, of purely academical scholarship and religious education, London had more than ever become the centre of the life of the community. Here, alone, politics, society and intellectual pursuits and diversions of all kinds were at the full height of activity; and here was the great market for the supply of the luxuries, as well as of the necessaries, of existence. The influx of inhabitants into London and its suburbs was very notable. The overgrowth of the population beyond the walls was, indeed, arrested by drastic provisions, dating from 1580; but the total of the metropolitan population increased with extraordinary rapidity, and, in the century after the accession of Elizabeth, probably, at least quintupled—and this notwithstanding the ravages of the plague, which, at times, decimated—and even decimated twice over—the number of inhabitants. But it was not numbers only which gave to London its supremacy. The pulse of life beat more rapidly here than elsewhere; character and talent—individuality, in short—here had the best chance of asserting itself. This was largely due, as has been seen, to the court and, in the same connection, to the great houses of the nobility built along the pleasant Strand, with the river, London's great highway, running by the side of fields and gardens on the way to Westminster. It was due, in the second place, to the city as the centre and representative of the mercantile and industrial life of the nation, with Cheapside, and Goldsmiths' row on its southern frontage, displaying the magnificence of that life to an admiring

---

[1] Cf. Koeppel, E., 'Konfessionelle Strömungen in d. dramat. Dichtung d. Zeitalters des beiden ersten Stuart Könige,' in *Shakespeare Jahrbuch*, vol. XL, pp. XVI ff., where the victorious Jewish money-lender in R. Wilson's *Three Ladies of London* is contrasted with Barabas, Shylock and the villainous Jewish figures in Daborne's *A Christian turned Turke*, Day and William Rowley's *Travailes of The three English Brothers*, and Fletcher's *Custome of the Countrey*. As to the attempt to identify Shylock with an actual personage, cf. *ante*, chap. VIII.

world. But it was also due to the various colleges of law and physic, as well as to cathedral and abbey, and the great schools[1].

Among the professions which had their proper seat in London, none, perhaps, in the Elizabethan age and that which followed, played a more important part in the social system of the country than the profession of the law. There has assuredly been no period of English history in which the relations between law and politics have been more intimate than the age of Bacon and Coke; and the study of the history of even a single inn of court, such as Gray's inn, would show how far back in the later Tudor period this important connection extends. But, apart from this, though Harrison was of opinion that an excess of lawyers, like one of merchants, was a clog in the commonwealth —'all the money in the land' he says 'goes to the lawyers[2]'— it was quite inevitable that two characteristics of the age—the frequent change of ownership in landed property and the frequent establishment of new trading concerns—should be accompanied by a large increase of legal practice. This practice was of a kind which did not necessarily bring its reward in a great harvest of fees to the London barrister, for there was much more self-help in that age than has been held admissible in later days either in law or in medicine; and, with regard to the former at all events, every man was expected to know some law, so that many of our dramatists—with Shakespeare at their head—were, more or less,

---

[1] Nothing can be said here of other favourite centres of intellectual and social intercourse, among which the taverns—to be distinguished carefully from lesser and more evanescent places of entertainment—did duty for the clubs of later London life. T. Heywood gives a short list of them in one of the songs inserted in *The Rape of Lucrece*, in another of which the cries of London are reproduced. By 1633, the number of these taverns was reckoned at 211. Cf. Sandys, W., *Festive Songs*, etc., *u.s.* (introduction), and see Vatke, T., 'Wirthshäuser und Wirthshausleben' in *Culturbilder aus Alt-England*. As to 'ordinaries' (the fashionable *tables d'hôte* of the day), see the amusing tract *The Meeting of Gallants at an Ordinarie, or The Walkes in Powles*, 1604 (Percy Soc. Publ., 1845, vol. v). To the main walk of the great gothic church of St Paul's, a club open to all—even to those who came only to dine with duke Humphrey —there are frequent allusions in our dramatists. (Bobadill was a 'Paul's man,' and Falstaff 'bought Bardolph in Paul's.' See, also, L. Barry's *Ram-Alley*, act IV, sc. 1, and Mayne's *City-Match*, act III, sc. 3.) These and other features of London life are described in numerous works of easy access; for a graphic picture of Elizabethan London, drawn with the author's usual felicity of touch, the reader may be referred to the section 'Le Pays Anglais' in vol. II of Jusserand's *Histoire Littéraire du Peuple Anglais*. *Creizenach*, vol. IV, part I, p. 486, goes so far as to assert that, with the exception of university and school plays, not a single dramatic work of consequence saw the light of day anywhere else than in London town.

[2] p. 204.

familiar with its terms and processes[1]. It was with landed property that litigation, so far as lawyers were called in, seriously concerned itself; and it was through the management, direct or indirect, of country estates, and through speculation as well as litigation respecting them, that fortunes were made and, as already noticed, county families were founded by Elizabethan lawyers[2]. If we glance at the other end of the professional ladder, it will appear that at no time before or since has a legal training been so clearly recognised as the necessary complement of the school and university education of a man called upon to play a part in public life. The inns of court were one of the great social as well as educational institutions of the Elizabethan and early Stewart period; and within their walls, in their halls and gardens, in their libraries and chambers, was pre-eminently fostered that spirit of devoted loyalty towards the crown, as well as that traditional enthusiasm for literary and other intellectual interests, which in other periods of our national life have been habitually associated with the universities[3]. The occasional 'brawls' in the streets by gentlemen of the inns of court, like those of their democratic antipodes, the city 'prentices, were demonstrations of self-reliance as well as of youthful spirits. To the Elizabethan regular drama, whose beginnings the inns of court had nurtured, and to some of whose masterpieces they had extended a cordial welcome, as well as to the lesser growths of the masque and cognate devices, these societies stood in relations of enduring intimacy[4].

[1] Cf. Sturge, L. J., 'Webster and the Law: a Parallel,' in *Shakespeare Jahrbuch*, vol. XXII (1906); where it is pointed out that Webster, like Shakespeare, displays a very extensive and, generally speaking, accurate knowledge both of the theory and practice of the law, and the construction of the plot of *The Dutchesse of Malfy* is cited as a striking instance of the extent of Webster's legal knowledge. The writer cites the observation of Sidney Lee, in his *Great Englishmen of the Sixteenth Century*, that Ben Jonson and Spenser, Massinger and Webster, employed law terms with no less frequency and facility than Shakespeare, though none of them was engaged in the legal profession. It would, perhaps, be fanciful to ascribe the predilection for trial scenes, which the Elizabethan bequeathed to the later English drama, to anything more than a sure instinct for dramatic effect.

[2] See, on this head, the section 'The Lawyer'—perhaps the most instructive of all the sections in Hubert Hall's *Society in the Elizabethan Age*.

[3] In the 'letter from England,' to her three daughters, Cambridge, Oxford, Innes of Court, appended to *Polimanteia* (Cambridge, 1595), while the inns of court are acquitted of disrespect towards the universities, and of having, 'received some of their children and ... made them wanton, the Inns are admonished not to regard their training as sufficient without that of their elder sisters.'

[4] In his *English Dramatic Literature*, vol. III, p. 223, note 7, the present writer has cited a passage from 'A Player' in Earle's *Microcosmographie* (1628), which suggests a very natural secondary reason for the interest taken in the acting drama by members of the inns of court : 'Your Inns of Court men were undone but for [the player]; hee

The physician's profession, about this time, was being disentangled, on the one hand, from that of the clergyman, with which of old it had been frequently combined, and, on the other, from the trade of the apothecary—a purveyor of many things besides drugs, who was more comfortably and fashionably housed in London[1] than was his fellow at Mantua—and from that of the barber, who united to his main functions those of dentist and yet others, announced by his long pole, painted red[2]. The pretensions of both physicians and surgeons to a knowledge of which they fell far short were still a subject of severe censure[3]; but little or nothing was said in or outside the profession against what was still the chief impediment to the progress of medical science—its intimate association with astrology[4]. The physician took every care to preserve the dignity which lay at the root of much of his power, attiring himself in the furred gown and velvet cap of his doctor's degree[5], and riding about the streets, like his predecessor in the Middle Ages, with long foot-cloths hanging down by the side of his horse or mule. The education of physicians was carried on much like that of lawyers, with care and comfort, and seems, at least sometimes, to have been deemed a suitable stage in the complete training of a gentleman[6]. The scientific and practical value of the medical training of the day is a theme beyond the purpose of this sketch. Medical treatment, in many respects, was oldfashioned in no flattering sense of the term; in the case of new diseases, it was savage; in the case of mental disease, barbarous—'a dark house and a whip[7].'

It is unnecessary to make a more than passing reference here to another profession, which in the Elizabethan age already existed, although it might be said to have only recently come into

is their chiefe Guest and imployment, and the sole businesse that makes them Afternoones men.'

[1] See *The Merry Wives*, act III, sc. 3: 'these lisping hawthorn-buds that...smell like Bucklersbury in simple time.'

[2] On this subject, see Vatke, T., *u.s.* p. 172. A dentist-barber appears in Lyly's *Midas*.

[3] So, in the pious Joseph Halle's *The Chyrurgens Book*.

[4] An honest, though futile, attempt to distinguish between true and false, valuable and 'frustrate,' astrology is made in *Polimanteia*, a curious tract printed at Cambridge in 1595.

[5] Cf. *The Alchemist*, act I, sc. 1, where Subtle takes care to appear in this costume.

[6] Paul Hentzner (*u.s.* p. 31) asserts that in the fifteen colleges within and without the city of London 'members of the young nobility, gentry and others, are educated, and chiefly in the study of physic; for very few apply themselves to that of the law; they are allowed a very good table, and silver cups to drink out of.'

[7] *As You Like It*, act III, sc. 2, *ad fin.*

existence. The general conditions which affected the publication of books, and, with it, the exercise of the profession of author, have been discussed in a previous volume[1] and more will be said in a later chapter as to the special conditions of the writing of plays[2]. The number of playwrights who, at the same time, were stage actors, probably, was by no means so large as has sometimes been assumed; Miss Sheavyn reckons that, to our knowledge, not more than nine combined the 'equality' of actor with authorship[3]. Thus, there was no reason why 'gentlemen and scholars' should extend to dramatic or other authors as such the scorn which, at different times, they were wont to manifest for the profession of the actor, despised by them as, traditionally, a menial or envied as the well paid and gorgeously apparelled favourite of the public. Yet the professional author—the man, that is, who sought to live by his pen, or, at least, to make it contribute appreciably to his means of earning a livelihood, had no easy life of it in the Elizabethan age. Patrons were rare who gave sums of money—especially large sums such as that which Southampton is held to have bestowed on Shakespeare—or provided hospitality on a large scale, such as Jonson enjoyed from lord d'Aubigny; though there may have been other cases of quasi-hereditary support, such as that granted by the Herberts to Massinger, or of spontaneous generosity like that extended to Greene by a successful player. Fewer still were those to whom, as to Munday and Jonson, the goodwill of city or crown secured an official salary by the side of their literary earnings. The universities reserved none of their emoluments for the 'university wits,' whose flattering dedications were more profitably addressed to the goodwill of individual magnates. The laborious gains of proof correcting and the like hardly came into account, as they had done in the earlier days of the renascence, when such accomplishments were still confined to a small number of scholars. It was more tempting to take to the writing of pamphlets, even if these often really only hovered on the outskirts of literature[4],

---

[1] See *ante*, vol. IV, chap. XVIII ('The Book-trade, 1557—1625').

[2] See *post*, vol. VI, chap. X ('The Elizabethan Theatre').

[3] The names given by her are Field, Greene, Heywood (Thomas), Jonson, Peele, Munday, Rowley (William), Shakespeare and Wilson (Robert). The order is alphabetical; but a comparison of the names will show that Miss Sheavyn is right in her conclusion that 'it seems to have become in time less usual to unite the two professions, though Marlowe and Kyd, of the earlier writers, probably never acted.' See Sheavyn, Phoebe, *The Literary Profession in the Elizabethan Age* (p. 93)—a valuable piece of work, of which free use has been made in the text.

[4] Cf. *ante*, vol. IV, chap. XVI, and bibl. There is no reason, in the Elizabethan

if not to descend into other depths and enter upon one or more
of the harassing employments of the news factor, the prophetic
almanac maker, the ballad and jig writer, or the craftsman who
composed lascivious verse to suit the taste of his public.

It has been shown above[1] that, though the charter of the
Stationers' company was confirmed in the first year of Elizabeth's
reign, and the licensing and censorship of books was instituted
by the injunctions issued in that year, the actual operation of this
censorship did not begin till near the middle of the last decade
but one of the sixteenth century—an epoch of intense public
anxiety. In 1586, when the agitation largely due to Jesuit
missions and their actual or supposed results was at its height
and the so-called 'discovery' of the Babyngton conspiracy was
calling forth wild alarm, the Star chamber issued the decree
which confined printing, with the exception of the two universities, to the liberties of the city of London, and subjected all
books and pamphlets before publication to the licence of the
archbishop of Canterbury and the bishop of London. Those
licensing regulations were enforced by the court of High Commission (though the actual process of licensing, in part, was handed
over to particular expert authorities—as, in the case of plays,
to the master of the revels), and the activity of the court was
easily set in motion wherever the interests or susceptibilities of
church or state seemed to call for its interference. The drama,
of course, most frequently and most readily laid itself open to
official suspicion. Thus, on the single occasion of the imminence
of trouble on the part of Essex and his supporters, the authors of
at least two plays, *Philotas* and *Sejanus*, were in some danger,
and the performance of a third (*Richard II*) led to further
official enquiry[2]. As in the days of the early Roman empire, a
class of informers rose into being, called, in Elizabethan parlance,
'moralisers' or 'state decipherers,' whose business it was to discover and denounce passages, situations and even single words

---

age for distinguishing translators from the general body of authors, among whom
their position was one of honour and distinction. Cf. *ante*, vol. IV, chap. I.

[1] *Ante*, vol. IV, pp. 381—2.

[2] 'Application,' says the dedication of *Volpone*, 'is now given a trade with many,
and there are that profess to have a key for the decyphering of everything.'
Miss Sheavyn (p. 67) has drawn up a list of writers who suffered from the interference
of authorities moved by information of the above or of other sorts; it comprises
the names of Cartwright, Chapman, Daniel, Dekker, Drayton, Fletcher, Heywood,
Holinshed, Jonson, Kyd, Lodge, Marlowe, Marston, Middleton, Munday, Nashe,
Rowlands, Selden, Shakespeare, Smith, Stowe, Stubbes and Wither. Of course, the

which seemed to betray a dangerous meaning. The spirit of Jacobean government did not fail to carry further a system congenial to its mode of working. Such, in this age, were a few among the troubles of authors—troubles in which dramatists had more than their share.

The attention bestowed in this period upon the fine arts should not be overlooked, though it cannot be discussed here. The cultivation of music, indeed, was one of the most attractive features of Shakespeare's age and seems to have been common to both sexes[1]. The subject of Elizabethan and Jacobean architecture has been already touched upon, but cannot here be pursued further. Painting, with the exception of miniature painting, was mainly left in foreign hands. The external conditions of the drama proper were such that it could owe little or nothing to architect, sculptor or painter; the achievements of Inigo Jones belong to the history of the masque[2].

At the lower end of the social scale, in the Elizabethan age, a very marked division is observable between those who, more or less, were moving upward and those whose doom it seemed to lag behind. The smaller tradesmen and manufacturers of the towns, though they could not, like the great city merchants, have any claim to be of the councils of the sovereign or of those who carried on the government, still found themselves occasionally chosen to represent in parliament the interests of the communities in which they lived, though, in the new boroughs established under the influence of the crown, that influence was powerful in securing the election of persons belonging to the gentry on whom it could directly depend. In other ways, too, the industrial element was asserting its right to the social advantages within its reach; probably, such a case as that of Gabriel Harvey's father, the ropemaker of Saffron Walden, who sent not less than four sons to the neighbouring university, was not a very unusual one in the social

whirligig of time brought its revenges on both sides; and, finally, the Star chamber, which, in 1634, had ordered the burning of Prynne's *Histrio-Mastix*, and inflicted what shame it could inflict upon the author of that work, was, seven years later, swept away with the High Commission court, and several other tyrannical tribunals.

[1] As to Elizabethan music, and its association with the drama, see chap. VI of vol. IV of this work, cf. also Schelling's chapter, *u.s.* 'When Music and sweet Poetry agree.' As to the favourite composers of the period between 1589 and 1600, see *Lyrical Poems selected from musical publications, 1589—1600*, ed. Collier, J. P., Percy Soc. Publ. (1844), vol. XIII. See, also, the note of Rockstro, W., on 'The Sixth English School,' *ap.* Traill, H. D., *u.s.* vol. III, p. 309.

[2] 'Painting and carpentry are the soul of mask' is Ben Jonson's sneer in his *Expostulation with Inigo Jones.*

history of the times[1]. Many yeomen, too, although their class was supposed to be marked by a definite limit of income, and although it was customary to address them and their wives as 'goodman' or 'goodwife' instead of 'master' or 'mistress,' were, by their cleverness and industry, constantly raising themselves on the social ladder—'buying up poor gentlemen's land, educating their sons for professions and learning them how to become gentlemen.' 'These were they,' adds Harrison[2], in picturesque remembrance of the days of Henry V, 'that in times past made all France afraid.' An admirable dramatic type, dated still further back, of the stalwart yeomen of whom many an example must have remained in Elizabethan England, is George-a-Greene, the pinner of Wakefield, in the play named after him[3]. Hobs the tanner, in Heywood's *Edward IV*, may serve as a companion picture of the honest handicraftsman, imperturbable alike in his good sense and in his good humour[4].

Neither traders nor yeomen were to be confounded with the labouring class proper, still a part of the population which Harrison, as well as Shakespeare and his fellow dramatists, regarded as proper to be ruled, not to rule others. It has been seen that their condition during the Elizabethan age and the ensuing period cannot be described as one of advance, although the social misery which had resulted from the break-up of the old agrarian system and the widespread substitution of pasture for tillage abated with the practical recovery of arable farming. The labouring classes, generally, remained in a condition of depression, or not far removed from it. Yet they were not altogether ignored in the working of the machinery of church and state, labouring men being occasionally summoned on juries or even chosen to hold office as churchwardens. But, though it would not be impossible to cite exceptions in which human sympathy or humorous insight assert their rights, men and women of this class were usually counted only by heads, and, as individuals, they failed to interest the dramatists, who were content to use them as an obscure background or colourless substratum. It is not just to illustrate the contempt of the Elizabethan drama for the masses either by satirical pictures of mobs and popular rebellions, or by particular phrases

---

[1] Marlowe's father was a shoe-maker; but this, perhaps, is hardly a case in point.

[2] p. 133.

[3] Another, which seems to have attained to great popularity, was that of old Tom Strowd in Day's *Blind Beggar of Bednal Green*.

[4] Dekker's *Shomakers Holiday* is a genial glorification of the craft, founded on one of the stories in Thomas Deloney's *Gentle Craft* (the second title of the play).

'in character' with the personages employing them[1]. But the want of sympathy towards the inarticulate classes with which the dramatists, as a body, are chargeable, must indisputably be regarded as a limitation of the range of their art, which they only accepted to their own disadvantage[2].

Wholly distinct from labouring men proper were the serving-men, whose large numbers in the Elizabethan age are the subject of frequent comment, and who were a legacy of medieval times and conditions. Harrison[3] dwells on the 'swarmes of idle serving-men, who are an evil to everyone[4],' and observes that, while many of them brought their young masters to grief by their wastefulness, not a few of them fell into bad ways themselves, and ended as highway robbers. It was easier to insist, in the interests of society in general, that the numbers of these hangers-on should be lessened, when not only was service continually passed on from generation to generation, but many sons of yeomen and husbandmen entered into the condition of serving-men, in order to escape the obligation of military service, and, generally, to secure easier and more comfortable conditions of life. On the part of the gentry, the custom of keeping up a large show of servants was by no means confined to the wealthy, and the author of that interesting tract *The Serving-man's Comfort*[5] draws a humorous picture of the needy Sir Daniel Debet, pacing the middle walk at St Paul's, with six or seven tall hungry fellows in attendance.

We pass to a yet different stratum of the population. It is well known how the most important of the poor laws of Elizabeth[6],

---

[1] The queen, *e.g.*, in *Richard II*, act II, sc. 3, addresses the gardener as 'thou little better thing than earth' (Vatke, *u.s.* p. 221).

[2] Harrison, p. 151, gives a kindly picture of the friendliness and geniality of the lower classes of his age, which is justly commended by Furnivall. Sympathetic touches of the same kind are not frequent in the plays of Shakespeare and his fellow dramatists, though, in the phrase of the old shepherd in *The Winter's Tale*, they contain plenty of 'homely foolery.'

[3] p. 135.

[4] Combining the turbulence of those in *Romeo and Juliet* with the roguery of those in *Coriolanus*. But these do not exhaust Shakespeare's gallery of servants, good, bad and indifferent.

[5] *A Health to the Gentlemanly profession of Servingmen or the Serving-man's Comfort* (1598). In Hazlitt's *Inedited Tracts*. Serving-men, though some varieties of them did not escape the satire, may be said to have largely attracted the goodwill of Elizabethan playwrights, including Shakespeare, who, according to a tradition said to have been current at Stratford, himself performed the part of Adam in *As You Like It*.

[6] Of these and Elizabethan pauperism there is a masterly account by Hewins, W. A. S., *ap.* Traill, H. D., *u.s.* vol. III.

passed near the close of her reign (in 1601) and revived in the first year of James I, made provision for its poor compulsory upon every parish. The pressure of pauperism was felt throughout the whole of this period, and already at an early stage of the queen's reign the principle of the 'old Poor Law' had been affirmed by legislation, and it had become customary to hold weekly collections in each parish for the poor who had not demonstrably fallen into indigence by their own fault. But the evil continued, and was not diminished by the provisions against vagabonds, among whom, against the wish of the house of lords, common players and minstrels had been included in the act of 1572. In describing the great increase of poverty in the land, Harrison[1] indignantly repudiates the proposed remedy of stopping the growth of the population by turning arable into pasture land—a process by which English rural prosperity had been impaired in a past too recent to be forgotten. The control of the spread of poverty and desolation attempted by the Elizabethan poor laws proved, on the whole, a failure; and things went on from bad to worse. Hundreds of hamlets were desolated[2], and the number of small occupiers steadily dwindled, till they were almost completely extinguished by the legislation of the reign of Charles II. From this all-important side of the social life of the country, the drama, as might be supposed, averts its eyes. On the other hand, the more or less vocal or picturesque phase of poverty which may be described as beggardom, with the nearly allied developments of vagabondage and roguery, forms one of the most glaring phenomena of the age; its griefs and self-advertisement crying aloud for notice. Harrison, who denounces idle beggars of all sorts as 'thieves and caterpillars of the commonwealth,' reckons their total number in England at ten thousand, and, at the same time, dates the beginning of their trade as falling not yet fully sixty years back—which seems to point to the dissolution of the monasteries, though, as a matter of fact, Henry VIII's act as to beggars and vagabonds was passed as early as 1531. Our guide then proceeds to comment on twenty-three kinds of vagabonds, and to discuss the various methods of punishment applied to them and to the army of 'roges and idle persons' in general, including, as aforesaid, 'plaiers' and 'minstrells[3].' But there can be no necessity in this place for more than touching on a topic

---

[1] pp. 212 ff.　　　　[2] Hall, H., *Society in the Elizabethan Age*, p. 105.
[3] Bk II, chaps. x—xi.

which has always had a fascination of its own for literary observers and enquirers, and which supplied abundant material to English comic dramatists, from the authors of *Bartholomew Fayre* and *The Beggars Bush* to their pupil or imitator, the author of *A Joviall Crew*[1].

And, since the transition from the subject of vagabondage to that of crime is at all times cruelly facile, a word may be added as to an aspect of the age which cannot be neglected by the student of its physiognomy, more particularly as it is recognisable in its reflection in contemporary English drama. It was by no means unreasonable for a contemporary such as Harrison to disclaim what, to the eyes of Elizabethan England, might have seemed abnormal either in the character of the crimes which were frequently committed or of the punishments which they entailed. An examination of the themes of the English domestic tragedies which in the last decade of the sixteenth century, or thereabouts, harrowed the feelings of London audiences, bears out the statement that 'horrible, merciles and wilfull murders,' such as are 'not sildome seene on the continent,' were comparatively rare in contemporary England; the hankering after such sensations belongs to a rather later time, when 'revenge' plays had passed into a more advanced stage, and Tourneur and Webster were fain to satisfy the appetite of their audiences for exotic horrors. Again, in the Elizabethan age, it is not difficult to notice, in the administration of penal justice, indications of a tendency to avoid an excess of brutal cruelty; various signally inhuman forms of execution or of bodily suffering or degradation added to execution were modified or fell out of use. Still, for a number of crimes regarded as specially heinous, there were special punishments calculated to excite the sensibilities or deepen the awe of spectators[2]. Poisoners and heretics were burnt to death; and witches were liable to suffer the same punishment in lieu of death by hanging, the method of execution applied to felons and all other ordinary criminals. It will be remembered that but few persons suffered death on the charge of witchcraft under Elizabeth, and that it was only under the more rigorous act passed immediately after the accession of James (1604) that the fury of persecution found full opportunities for raging.

[1] As to the literature of rogues and vagabonds, cf. *ante*, vol. IV, chap. XVI, and *ibid.* bibl. p. 529.

[2] Torture seems to have been regarded as a practice to which resort should not be had in ordinary cases; but it was not altogether out of use.

There cannot, of course, be any sort of pretence that rational views on the subject of witchcraft and magic obtained in the reign of Elizabeth, or that the queen herself (who consulted Dee about Alençon's condition) was more enlightened on this head than other English men or women.   Of the dramatists, it may be roughly stated that in not a single one of them can be found any suggestion of a disbelief in the thing itself, even where a fraudulent use of it is exposed or derided[1].   On offenders against religious law and social morality, a variety of formal penalties—in part symbolic, in part simply degrading—were inflicted, which alike suggest a desire on the part of the state or society to 'improve' the opportunities afforded it ; even before the ascendancy of puritanism, there were always practical moralists clamouring for a severer system of retribution.   Yet, at the same time, a great laxity is observable in enforcing the penalties denounced by the law upon proved wantonness of life ; and it is impossible to escape the impression that there existed a general *consensus*, from which even the clergy only slowly came to express clear dissent, that some allowance should be made to laymen in the matter of the sins they were 'inclined to.'   The whole significance of the licence of the Elizabethan and Jacobean drama, which, in some respects, reflected the licence of the age, cannot be fully understood, unless this fact be borne in mind.

The darker side of the social condition of England in the Elizabethan age should not be overlooked by those who dwell upon the high aspirations and great achievements which have cast an enduring halo round it in the eyes of national historians and their readers.   Nothing can be said here as to the defects—only too palpable, but not by any means to be construed as evidence of mere *incuria*—in the provision made for the protection of the

---

[1] The whole question of the treatment in the Elizabethan age of the superstition of witchcraft has been left aside as too wide for discussion here.   For an account of the origin of this superstition see *ante*, vol. III, chap. V ; and cf. the note on the Witch-controversy, with a bibliography of it, in vol. IV, pp. 534—5 (bibliography to chap. XVI). The present writer has given a summary of the subject, illustrated by references to those Elizabethan and Jacobean dramas which reflect the sentiments of the age in reference to it, in his introduction to Marlowe's *Dr Faustus* (4th ed.), pp. xlix—lii. As to Dee, see *The Private Diary of Dr John Dee*, ed. Halliwell[-Phillipps], J. O., Camden Soc. Publ., 1842.   Though it was abroad that Dee's associate Kelly came to grief, alchemists ran some risk in England.   In *The Alchemist*, act IV, sc. 1, Dol Common warns Sir Epicure Mammon that he

<blockquote>
may come to end
The remnant of his days in a loth'd prison
</blockquote>

for merely speaking of the philosopher's stone.

public health against the dangers to which it was exposed, more especially in London, from the incursions of the plague, and, in a lesser degree, from those of other diseases[1]. If, however, we confine ourselves to the moral sphere, the impression left by an open-eyed survey of the ordinary relations and conditions of life in this age is one of a dominating violence and turbulence ; and this impression is confirmed by a study of the drama of which those relations and conditions largely make up the material. At the same time, this passionate unrest, and the impetus with which, in the midst of it, the age pressed on to the performance of its great tasks, explain, in some measure, how they were accomplished. The high spirit—often high in death as it had been in life—which the renascence and reformation ages had infused into their men and women, of all classes and beliefs, no doubt imparted something of recklessness to martyrdom as well as of ruthlessness in the infliction of suffering. But the final cause of this high spirit was the belief in things worth living for and worth dying for—a belief which lies at the root of mighty actions, and without which no nation has ever been great, and no dramatic hero heroic.

It is impossible to close even this scanty notice of some of the social characteristics of the Elizabethan age without a more special reference to its women. For, in the history of western civilisation (not to venture on applying the remark still more widely), it is generally the women whose code of manners and of morals determines the standard of these in any given period of national life. No doubt, the women of the Elizabethan and Jacobean age, as they appear before us in contemporary drama, are, primarily, the creatures of the imagination of the dramatists ; yet it would be idle to ignore the twofold fact, that the presentment of the women of this period on the stage largely reproduces actual types, and that the way in which dramatists looked upon women, their position in life, and their relations to men, was the way of the world, and the way of the age. Queen Elizabeth was not the only highly educated Englishwoman of her family or times ; but, though the type, of which the continental renascence produced many illustrious examples, is never wanting in the society of the Tudor and Stewart times, it is comparatively rare and can hardly be said to be a frequent characteristic of their women. The fashions of intellectual, and mainly literary, refinement which passed over court and society, from that of Euphuism to that of

---

[1] Concerning this subject, as affecting the history of the drama and stage, see *post*, chaps. x and xiv of vol. vi.

Platonic love, were fashions only, to be followed for a season and then discarded. Far more striking as a distinctive feature is the virility which many women of the age shared with the great queen— the high courage, the readiness for action, the indomitable spirit which no persecution can abate and which the fear of death itself cannot quench. This quality of fortitude the women of the age shared with the men, as Portia shared it with Brutus, and to this they bore testimony with the same readiness on many occasions and in many places besides the scaffold and the stake. The German traveller Paul Hentzner, describing England as a sort of woman's paradise, says of Englishwomen that 'they are as it were men[1]'; and, just as we hear that ladies were willing to undergo with their husbands the toils and exertions of country life (as they afterwards came to join in its sports), so there was a noble distinctiveness in the readiness of Elizabethan women to take their part in the duties and the responsibilities of life at large, and to defy cavil and criticism in the consciousness of their own strength and steadfastness. There is not, as has been suggested, an element of mannishness in the Venetian Portia, or a touch of the virago in Beatrice : they are women born to play their part in life and society, and to stand forth amongst its leaders. But here, also, we are in the presence of exceptional personalities, though the conception remains constant in the English drama, as it did in English life, to the days of the civil war and beyond.

As to the women of everyday life, there can be no reason for doubting a close correspondence between many of their characteristic features in life and on the stage. Their emptiness and shallowness, due, in part at least, to a defective education which cared only for imparting a few superficial accomplishments, their inordinate love of dress and all manner of finery, their hankering for open admiration and search for it in the open fashion of earlier times, sitting at their doors during the greater part of the day[2], or, from the closing years of the reign onwards, under shelter of the masks which had become the fashion at public places—all these, and a hundred more, are follies and levities in which observation and satire have found constant materials for comment and censure. The looseness and licence of the age form a feature of its life and character well enough known to students, and were by no means, as is sometimes supposed, derived altogether, or perhaps even mainly, from the example of court or town. But a comparison, from this point of view, between different periods,

---

[1] Cited by Marcks, E., u.s. p. 94.   [2] Stubbes's *Anatomie of Abuses*, p. 87.

whether or not adjacent to each other, is a hazardous process, and, in any case, is remote from the purpose of the present chapter. The dramatic poets discussed in the present volume and in its successor, at times, preferred to reproduce in their plays what they found in the scene of life around them ; at times, they were fain to dwell on those aspects of society and its experiences which seemed most likely to serve as occasions for exciting the emotions of pity or of horror.   The Elizabethan and Jacobean drama would have been unable, even if it had been willing, to detach itself altogether from the conditions of things in which it necessarily found much of its material, and to which it could not but, in many ways, assimilate the remainder.   Neither, again, were its reproductions of manners always correct, nor were the 'problems' of its actions always those with which the experience of the age was familiar.   But, as a whole, and though it only gradually developed, and in some respects varied, the methods and processes by which it worked, this drama remained true to its purposes as an art ; and, in the sphere where its creative power was most signally asserted—in the invention and delineation of character—its range was un-surpassed.   In many respects, the conditions of the age might have seemed unfavourable to the production of the most beautiful, as they are the most enduring, examples of female excellence. Yet the legend of good women which a historic record of Shakespeare's age might unfold would not be a nameless tale. And, together with the sunniest and sweetest, the very noblest of all feminine types—that of sovereign purity and that of self-sacrificing love—will not be sought for in vain in the Elizabethan and Jacobean drama ; and he would err who should look for them only on the Shakespearean heights.

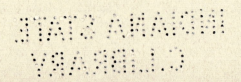